Elizabeth Young was born in ... Scotland. She was educated i... American Literature and pub... ...dely as a critic and arts journalist. She was co-author of the book *Shopping In Space: Essays on American 'Blank Generation' Fiction*. She lived both in West London and her native Scottish Highlands until her death in spring 2001.

Pandora's Handbag

Adventures in the book world

Elizabeth Young

Library of Congress Catalog Card Number: 00–109880

A complete catalogue record for this book can be
obtained from the British Library on request

First published in 2001 by Serpent's Tail,
4 Blackstock Mews, London N4 2BT

website: www.serpentstail.com

Printed in Great Britain by Mackays of Chatham plc

10 9 8 7 6 5 4 3 2 1

For Peter, forever

Contents

2 Writing columns

3 In the bag

4 UK Literature

5 Short monographs

Introduction by Will Self

Like all the best ones, the title of this collection of writings by the late Elizabeth Young perfectly describes its content. As you will recall, the statue of Pandora was made by Vulcan at Jupiter's request. The golden golem, with her gift box of horrors, was aimed at Prometheus, who had stolen the forbidden, flammable knowledge of the gods. But Prometheus smelt a rat and it was his brother, Epimetheus, who ended up marrying the sexy cyborg and opening her box, whereupon out flew all the evils that the flesh is heir to and which have continued to afflict the world ever since. The last thing that flew from Pandora's box was hope.

Elizabeth Young, whom I had the privilege to know for the last eight years of her life, was a woman who, while no doubt created by God or man, possessed the hardened alloy of someone who had very much smelted herself and been forged in the white heat of extreme experience. One of the writers whose work is reviewed in this volume, and with whom Liz had a great affinity, was Jane Bowles. I don't think Liz would altogether castigate me for quoting her remarks about Bowles and applying them to herself: '[her] creative work embodies her life and her personality in that her highly developed sense of the ridiculous, the juxtaposition of the trivial and the profound in her conversation, and her startling non-sequiturs all informed [it] and were much remarked upon in her social life . . . She was both imperious and childlike.'

Like Bowles, Liz was a compulsive reader and an instinctive writer, whose interest in the bizarre, the peripheral, the mordant and the obscure, belied a perfectly rigorous analytical mind. And like Bowles, Liz, who wrote in all the principal genres: fiction, memoir, essay, feature article, column and critical review, never found words easily. She was akin to some reclusive opiomane in a Wilkie Collins novel, the sound of her own fingertips tapping on word processor keys was chiefly an exquisite torture.

It is a wonder, therefore, that shortly before her death she managed to complete the compilation, re-editing and autobiographical glossing of the pieces contained in this, her posthumous *Pandora's Handbag*. If you pop its clasp, I guarantee that you will cower and bleat as a great many of the ills – serial murder, drug addiction, mutant viruses, banality, prurience – that have afflicted the western world over the past three decades, come flying out from its capacious interior. It would be too Pollyanna-ish to be true to say that the last thing to emerge is Liz's own Hope for the Future.

On the contrary, as a devotee of the transformative power of the imagination, it was Liz's great sadness to have presided, as a critic, over an era during which she saw the primacy of pure literary creativity being effectively traduced on all sides by commercialism, by the deadening of affect, by crude literalism, by psychobabble dressed up as poetry and autobiographical tittle-tattle gussied up as profound revelation. It is with profound disgust that she relates in these pages an anecdote about an American woman writer, who on being told by Liz that she kept an exhaustive diary, 'urged me to change names and publish immediately.'

And be damned. For, in place of any such optimism, at the very bottom of Liz's handbag, her varnished fingernails, like the talons of a literate raptor, scrabbled through drifts of lint and wads of congealed tissues, only to come up with the bitter, fluff-wreathed, mislaid pill, that in the absence of there being sufficiently imaginative new books for her to read, 'I'll just have to try and write them myself. Damn.' It is a tragedy for us all that she wasn't able to do this.

I wonder who the hell will read this book? And I wonder whether it will sell? On the face of it, *Pandora's Handbag* is not a surefire hit for any publisher, being the collected writings of a critic and journalist who, while not obscure, was by no means well known. Moreover, these are the collected writings of someone who is no longer in a position to undertake the increasingly gruelling business of promoting serious thought, proper insight and the kind of extended attention span required to digest important books. In an era effortlessly dominated by trivial whimsy and a sense of cultural history as radically foreshortened as the bonnet of a bubble car, where are the readers who are prepared to take on a text that can be read in so many different, countervailing ways? It is to the profound credit of Peter Ayrton at Serpent's Tail, who served Liz faithfully as her publisher, editor and all-round encourager when she published (together with Graham Caveney) her first book, *Shopping in Space* (1992), a collection of critical essays on contemporary American fiction, that he has stuck with this project.

Writing introductions – which must, perforce, be more definitive than the texts that they preview – is always a difficult task. But writing this one has proved particularly hard. I had read many of Liz's pieces before – and now I read them again. Then reread them and took notes, then took more notes, until my copy of the typeset MS began to resemble some strange piece of raffia work, so replete was it with Post-it notes indicating where the goods lay. Reading this book is an opportunity, for anyone who has been a spectator of the last few decades (as opposed to merely living), to mount a myriad of aesthetic and critical trigonometric points and from these to join Liz in the act of surveying the territory.

So, if you are out there in the counterpane land of the serious reader, like Liz herself, with a book permanently propped on your blanketed knee, I urge you not to lose faith. More than this, I want you to take the volume you are holding as an article of that faith which Liz so lucidly espoused. The best of writing presents intimacy as a given tautology; it is aimed at precisely the right kind of person, the person who will feel and understand just this writing. Liz was, in this respect, the best of writers. She was also a writer who believed in the secret communion of readers and texts; that the text, like some vastly superior analog precursor of the internet chat room, provided a neutral arena within which individuals of all ages, genders, races, classes and sexual inclinations could meet and freely mingle. Again and again in her literary criticism she confronts us with this idealised zone, that yet for her – and any other committed reader – is nonetheless profoundly real.

The analogy above is important, because Liz wasn't only a reader and writer, she was also a kind of bibliophile. A former bookseller herself (she managed the fiction section of Compendium Bookstore in Camden Town in the early eighties), she liked the weight, the feel and sheer heft of a book. The flat she occupied with Peter Mannheim, her husband of twenty years, was a testimony to this kind of bibliophilia. The upended box file in which the two of them lived, read and socialised, wasn't so much a book-lined room as a room-lined book. There was promiscuity in Liz's love of books that is adequately reflected in this collection and, just as she reviled the narrow sensibility that will feign to adore 'literary' fiction but deride the genres, so she eschewed the sort of trainspotting mentality that leads ineluctably to leather elbow patches, plastic dust jackets and the Royal Society. 'Books . . . ,' as she says herself, 'need to be warmed by flesh and blood if they are to respond.'

No, it's a living respect for books and writers that Liz exemplified and it's this reverence that comes across most clearly in these pieces. These are not simply old book reviews and occasional fillers, what Liz herself talked down as 'miles and miles of ingenious bubble wrap', they are elements of a palimpsest which she was rubbing away at over a decade or so and which, given the right inclination and the benefit of hindsight, she might well have turned into the most incisive critical study of contemporary fiction. Put simply, Liz was the great avant-garde literary critic the British had, but never really knew existed. How bloody typical.

Like Liz, I've never quite understood those who weren't drawn to the profession by visions akin to that of the young William Burroughs, who thought writers '. . . were rich and famous. They lounged around in Singapore and Rangoon smoking opium in yellow pongee suits.' Like Liz, I've always conceived of writing fiction in particular as requiring what Flannery O'Connor (one of Liz's favourite authors) termed 'a certain grain of stupidity'. Liz thought that this 'quality of having to stare, of not getting the point at once', had been drubbed out of her by a formal education in literary criticism, but I'm not so sure. While Liz's criticism exhibits a close familiarity with structuralism, deconstruction and more traditional Leavisite modes of critical theory, there's a sense in which her writing about other writers conforms to what she herself says about the relationship between literary fiction and criticism. This is worth quoting at some length: 'Literary fiction seems to have evolved entwined like ivy in tandem with literary criticism, so it is no longer possible to tell which one is the parasite. Literary fiction tends very often towards the self-referential, the paradoxical and the autobiographical. Informed by the tenets of theory it plays with narrative and narrator, with life and fiction. There is a sense that the unrestrained play of imagination and the telling of stories is somewhat vulgar.'

Liz, wrongly, held herself of no account as a fiction writer because she felt she did not possess this 'unrestrained play of imagination'. But in truth, the few stories she did write manifested a fully evolved ludic sensibility. No, I think her unwillingness to commit herself to the business of writing fiction was a function of her bondage to the thankless task of trying to survey the undulating swamp of contemporary letters, while irradiated by the harsh light of the canonical empyrean. Again and again in this collection you can feel the sheer effort of will and the terse annoyance, as Liz shifts her critical theodolite to another mound, only to feel the terra firma shiver beneath her feet. In place of the parasitic convolvulus of literary fiction and critical theory, Liz seeded these pages with her own organic symbiosis, between her autobiography and her aspirations, her passions and her proclivities. What transforms *Pandora's Handbag* from an orthodox collection of pieces, into something altogether less ephemeral and more absorbing, are Liz's later interpolations, which mix the stock of hindsight with the broth of understanding, to thoroughly thicken the whole soup.

Liz's spirited and principled defence of Bret Easton Ellis's *American Psycho* was one of the few critical acts to gain her much notoriety in the stagnant little pond of English letters, but while the lineaments of that defence may have a certain familiarity, less expected is the consistency with which she persisted in defending the work of other writers, similarly ethically excoriated by established opinion, but far less well known. Liz was the pre-eminent supporter of A. M. Holmes's novel about a paedophile, *The End of Alice*, and she could also claim to have been one of the critics who brought the minatory, shopping mall malevolence of Dennis Cooper's work to the British reading public. Liz had a particular interest in true crime writing as well as fictionalised representations of evil. Her own, personal style could be described as 'proto-Goth'. She was wearing black nail polish and festooning herself with fetishes and amulets long before such practices had crystallised into any definable youth movement. But what's most compelling about Liz's absorption into the dark side, the dark arts, the penumbra of darkness in general, is that she understood her own motivation to be – as it undoubtedly was – highly moral.

Once again, it's worth quoting her own remarks about Jane Bowles: 'She felt shamed and condemned. The qualities that most defined her – her dreaminess, her creativity – had been judged and found wanting. Her own fierce and personal sense of morality with its unending emphasis on a very individual idea of sin and salvation would never allow her to be at peace with herself. Thereafter, her imagination, which was her very essence, comprised both sin and salvation.' Surely, it was the same with Liz; if you attempted to unpick the relationship between the critical sensibility that not only appreciated, but positively enjoined, that the rights of the imagination be absolute and the personal sensitivity that utterly recoiled from cruelty in all its manifold forms, you would've been hard put to discover which had been the parasite, before both had expired.

Liz herself accounted for her intense awareness of good and evil, of sin and salvation, as a product of her Calvinist upbringing. Her parents were Free Presbyterians, as she styled it 'even more puritan and joyless than other Presbyterians'. There was this and there was a childhood that encompassed all the possible forms of abuse: social, sexual, psychological, and that shaded, imperceptibly, into an adult life marked by mental health problems and eventually reclusiveness. But it would be wrong for people who didn't know Liz to mark her down as some eccentric malcontent, the Pandora's bag lady of Ladbroke Grove. While an enthusiastic avatar of the avant-garde that was, she was too shrewd to be altogether absorbed into Bohemia for its own sake. She resided there – she did not take up citizenship. Indeed, an expatriate by birth (her early years were spent in West Africa), Liz's character was that of the permanent, internal exile. As it transpired, she had the few heady years of the London punk scene of the late 1970s, in which to feel more or less completely at home, but I feel sure that her own particular brand of principled, intellectual nihilism would have taken root in far less fertile soils.

Inasmuch as Liz defended the writers she saw as unable to help themselves making bold, transgressing statements using the spray gun imaginations they'd been given, so she championed as well a swathe of women writers whom she identified as the most eloquent advocates of lives that were never any the less for being ordinary. Flannery O'Connor, Jean Rhys, Alice Munro, Jean Stafford are among them; and what Liz says about Munro's writing can bear testament to this very different aspect of her promiscuous love of literature: 'No one else has traced with such terrifying accuracy the way in which these emotions and impulses (shame, humiliation, mortification, embarrassment) work within us. And indeed how their ripples, like ink in milk, stain our sexual lives, our friendships and relationships.' This was the intense shyness within Liz that was able to appreciate directly, through the intimate anonymity of fiction, the very quiddity of those other lives. She loathed – and could not 'do' – gossip.

Yet another string in her polyphonic harpsichord of literary criticism was Liz's intense feeling for and championing of contemporary Scottish fiction. In the last years of her life she and Peter bought a small flat in a village on the shores of the Kyles of Bute, the ancestral landscape of the Young family and it is here too that Liz is now buried. She never claimed to be Scottisher-than-thou, but rather connected with young Scottish writers in just the way that she connected with every literature she admired: intensely, personally, privately. It's a testament to her acuity as a reader and critic that she was the first literary journalist to secure an interview with the then wholly unknown Irvine Welsh; it's a testament to her bloody-mindedness that she was able to get it printed, much against the bandwagon-chasing mentality of metropolitan editors. Liz also adored the novels of Alan Warner and Alasdair Gray and her pieces on these writers deserve a careful reading.

But *Pandora's Handbag* is far more than the summation of a literary critic who took books seriously, no matter that this in itself is a rare contemporary phenomenon. Any remotely perceptive reader cannot fail to notice, throughout the text, numerous references to drug addiction and to the malaises – both psychic and physical – associated with it. These seep, like a maculate seam, through her observations on other things, until – to paraphrase Liz above – like ink in milk, they stain the totality. The pieces on methadone, on state drug policy in Britain, on the revolting American gulag, on the lives of Anna Kavan and Herbert Huncke, and finally on Hepatitis C, the virus that finally killed Liz at the premature age of fifty, all contain not only meticulously researched facts, but also shrewdly assayed and painfully felt rage at a peculiarly modern form of state-sponsored cruelty.

It would be impolitic, presumptuous and quite contrary to Liz's own spirit (she had a well defined dread of 'twitching away the decent drapery' as De Quincey puts it) for me to trespass into her psyche any more than I have already done, so I shall leave it to the readers of *Pandora's Handbag* to examine the facts of the text itself and cultivate their own rage. I don't quite know how to leave this introduction, but since quitting it is saying goodbye to a friend it seems better to end with a personal anecdote. A hot summer's day in North East London in 1996. I'd driven Liz, together with my children and my then girlfriend, Victoria Hull, up to a barbecue at the house of Suzanne Moore, the journalist. Liz had, that day, given me a plastic doll about six inches high, a pouting, blonde, sex dolly, with heavy eyelashes that opened and shut over impossibly big, blue eyes. The doll – which I still have, and who I dubbed 'Serena' – sat with her legs drawn up to the side, wearing a semi transparent peignoir, which kept slipping down her bulging breasts. I was very taken by Serena and kept showing her off to all and sundry, something that enraged Victoria.

Deborah Orr, who was the following year to become my wife, turned up at Suzanne's and observed the tensions surrounding the doll with dour cynicism. Eventually Suzanne said to her, flummoxed by the bad vibes surrounding Serena: 'Have you got any idea what's going on?' Deborah thought for a while and replied: 'Liz has given Will a doll and Victoria's jealous.'

Liz sat in the harsh sunlight, black clad as ever, blinking and smiling slyly. She was a ready wit and a fine conversationalist herself, but I wonder, did she appreciate then, as I have increasingly come to over the intervening years, what a particular kind of genius it takes to feed someone the line 'Liz has given Will a doll and Victoria's jealous.'

London, June 2001

'Mr Earbrass allows himself to be taken to a literary dinner in a private dining room of Le Trottoir Imbécile . . . The talk deals with disappointing sales, inadequate publicity, worse than inadequate royalties, idiotic or criminal reviews, others' declining talent, and the unspeakable horror of the literary life.'

The Unstrung Harp, Edward Gorey

Introduction: How people become writers, although they shouldn't

It seems inconceivable to me that a critic would enthusiastically compile a volume of their old book reviews and then expect anyone to want to read it. Just *one* lonely book review, however well-executed, does not usually give rise to tidings of great joy even amongst literary enthusiasts. Personally I have a fondness for the form and can read any amount of reviews and criticism but, being a sort of literary dustbin, I'll read anything. Slowly, painfully, I have become aware that – incomprehensibly – most people do not feel the same way. Why should they? (Because they would experience the sublime, ineffable ecstasies of bibliophilia, but again that is just my opinion and, as I am frequently reminded, it is a minority one.)

In compiling this book I seemed to have two options. I could download my entire cobwebby litcrit hard disk in haphazard fashion and zing it over to the publisher in a Jiffy Bag. (The Quick Method.) Or I could try and structure it all into something more coherent. (The Long, Slow Method.) Fortunately I discovered that I had written a lot of non-fiction that was not just about books, so I have been able to vary the nature of the inclusions.

Obviously nothing is going to turn this into a starkly honest but oddly heartwarming book about soccer, bulimia, marital strife, incest or the murder of close friends (and especially not all at the same time). However, after litcrit, my specialisation is bizarrerie (the word is in the *Oxford*), so when I have restored all the cuts made by unfeeling editors, perhaps the final product might divert those at stool in the manner of such compilations.

What this actually seems to have turned into is a book not only about writing but about being a writer. What does an ordinary full-time writer do, how did they start doing it, why do they do it anyway? Why don't they stop and give us all a break from book-shops like multi-storey car parks which insist on selling you caffé latte, Moschino stationery and thumbnail-sized platitudinous bookettes?

Close textual study will have shown that this heading is actu-ally a whopping platitude along the lines of if you want to be a writer, don't – at least not if you can do anything else at all. Writers often say things like this to aspirants and manage to sound simultaneously sweetly helpless and deeply smug. 'Oh, I'm com-pletely unemployable. Wouldn't be a writer otherwise . . .' It is usually not quite true. Even *I* managed to be an adequate academic and a passable bookseller. But having that sort of job means that you have to get up and go out to work nearly every day.

What's more, if you are a girl it means dealing constantly with an Everest of grooming products, all the way from mousse, gel, shampoo, conditioner, follicle thickener at the top, through tweezers, dryers, earrings, undercoat, overcoat, gloss, blush, lip-brush, scent, body lotion, SPF, bronzer, shiner, toner, cleanser, astringent, razors, infected nipple-rings, hand-cream, deodorant, powders, baby-wipes, essential oils, cucumber masks, friction gloves, bath milks, suds and shower goo, all the way down to pep-permint foot balm and scented toenail polish – and this is the shorter version. Also, let's not even dwell on hairdresssers, Clarins' salons, gyms, pools, opticians, cosmetic and other den-tistry, therapists, consultants, tests, doctors, chiropodists and the most time-consuming activity of all, clothes.

Please don't misunderstand me. I have nothing against any of this. In my teens and twenties I just loved it – partly because the choice of products was less insanely dizzying, partly because there was a much less hectoring, bullying, conformist tone imploring one to apply unguents, partly because there was still a chance of accidently achieving some originality and partly because the end result was pleasing to myself and passing strangers. So I streaked my hair and stepped out to the workplace.

During my thirties, as I anticipated, my family's marked hermit gene began to wake up and stretch. My paternal relatives have always had an extremely strong tendency to withdraw. They take up their beds and walk into their libraries and are rarely seen again. They live off fried egg and banana sandwiches with a lot of pepper on them. All these impulses surfaced with great ferocity in my psyche. (Right down to the pepper – the laziness gene I can understand but a *pepper* gene?) All I wanted to do was stay in bed forever and read and drink tea and smoke cigarettes and one or two other recreational substances. Unfortunately nobody pays you for reading books. If they did, I'd be a squillionaire. So I had to shovel aside all the kittens, ashtrays, mags and mugs and install a wooden drawing-board and a laptop in the duvet and start to write.

I did get a desk too, eventually.

Many people endure the uniformly horrible experience of being a child by reading maniacally. At least they used to. The classic neo-Victorian Unhappy Childhood that I knew (Calvinism, farming-out of infants, remote parents behaving like crazy free-wheeling gods, no showing of emotion, public school, abuse, the whole predictable sob story) seems to be on the wane. Children have (I think but am not sure) a somewhat happier time now. I do hope so. At the very least they have Wave Machines and Bouncy Castles and those wonderful glass rooms full of squashy, coloured balls. And they have psychology and Childlines and parents who don't seem at all nervous about being human and fallible, so perhaps that is why there are fewer bibliophiles. But there are always some alienated, sensitive young things who feel frustrated and privately rather special and often they like books and think that they'd really really like to be a writer. They imagine it to be, as William Burroughs did when he was an adolescent, thus: 'Writers were rich and famous. They lounged around Singapore and Rangoon smoking opium in yellow pongee suits. They sniffed cocaine in Mayfair and penetrated forbidden swamps with a faithful native boy. They lived in the native quarter of some exotic city, languidly caressing a pet gazelle.' That's exactly what I believed too.

Like many others, I loved reading and writing equally through-out childhood and adolescence. My first novel was called *The Hackles Rise*. It was about a cocktail party. My first novella (which owed a profound, quite unmistakable debt to *The Fall of The House Of Usher*) was called *The Haunting of The House of Henderlost* and won some big newspaper prize. And it's been downhill ever since . . . I wrote poems and novels and memoirs and letters and plays and diaries but I won't weary you with any more specifics. Then I went to university, and had to think continually of those that were truly great and completely lost confidence, not that I had a lot to start with. I will deal more specifically with the writer and acad-eme later. Suffice it to say that university helped me to think more clearly but stopped me writing anything apart from non-fiction. As Flannery O'Connor wrote in *The Nature and Aim of Fiction*: 'there's a certain grain of stupidity that the writer of fiction can hardly do without'. They removed my grain (well, an entire haystack) of stupidity. O'Connor, incidentally does not mean ignorance – she means an unworldliness, an innocence, a con-templative quality, or as she herself puts it: ' . . . the quality of having to stare, of not getting the point at once'. Instead I learned to analyse and organise and annotate and research. In the end it all proved to have been quite useful when I had to write for money because very, very few British writers can make a living out of fiction, and almost never out of literary – as opposed to popular – fiction.

It is a common myth that there are different sorts of writers in the UK – novelists, poets, journalists, dramatists, critics. There may be some purists, particularly in areas like political journalism, but most writers here do a bit of everything. They have to. Writing is incredibly badly paid. The money bears no conceivable rela-tionship to the labour involved. So writers do novels and stories and reviews and arts journalism and scripts and introductions to books and essays and columns and travel pieces and they teach creative writing – and I am talking about seriously successful writ-ers here, big fish, as well as all the competitive plankton splashing in their wake.

It is EXTREMELY DIFFICULT to earn anywhere near an ordinary, professional annual wage by full-time, freelance writing in Britain. In fact, unless you are an academic, or under contract to a newspaper, or get lucky with a surprise bestseller, or produce regular books for a firm fan base as do the likes of Beryl Bainbridge or Ruth Rendell, I'd say it was almost impossible.

Anyway, let us suppose that for reasons of genetics, egomania, lust for power, love of language or whatever, you are absolutely determined to see your name in print, preferably all over the place. How do you achieve this? The best and simplest way is to have some talent, loads of ambition, a private income, an Oxbridge degree, a mildly conformist nature, appealing youthful features and parents who are themselves very famous media personalities, preferably writers or journalists. This method is more or less infallible.

Otherwise, lacking some or all of the above, the best thing to do at first is to move to London. Even fiercely regional authors tend to have served their time there. It is not absolutely essential, but it does make things a lot easier if you are unpublished and unknown. Later, of course, if you're successful you can live anywhere, although people often don't. (*Private Eye* once mocked Bruce Chatwin as 'An insatiable nomad, he lives in Notting Hill like everybody else.')

Writers are in the same catch-22 as aspiring actors, differing only in the detail: no-one wants to commission you to write unless you have already been published.

I understand that previously would-be serious journalists spent their postgrad years on some provincial daily, reporting on the local fêtes worse than death and canal-jumping competitions until they had solved the murder of a sweet-shop owner or something and swept into what used to be Fleet Street on a tide of true grit. Personally, I have never met anyone who has done anything like this. But then, I know nothing whatsoever about Real Journalism – only about Arts Journalism, which is the miles of ingenious bubble-wrap that is constantly needed to fill up the space between advertisements in newspapers and magazines.

So you move to London if you can – and I know this is no longer an easy thing to do – and then you either sign on and write (if they give you a moment between questionnaires, motivational interviews and hideous pep talks about rising through Sainsbury's), or you try for a vaguely arty job – lecturing, book-selling, museums, BBC, sub-editing, publishing, office work for a literary magazine or a newspaper books section. I'll have to concentrate on the strategies of literary journalism here but, if you want to write about fashion, or opera or art, you obviously try and get some work – any work – on the appropriate circuit. I've certainly known people who've started out selling advertising space for the NME or doing secretarial work on a broadsheet who have ended up writing successfully for the paper.

The first big hazard is that such jobs, however awful, are hugely, cruelly in demand. It is ironic really – all these fey, arty people, quivering with tension at the thought of trying to solicit work when you actually need the nervous system of a clam to survive the vagaries of life as a writer. This is why it is better to be ambitious rather than talented, socially skilled rather than hyper-aesthetic, acceptable rather than weird. You will suffer less and you'll do better, certainly as a journalist. And of course it is not fair, nothing is. I don't think talent will necessarily out. It often needs help and encouragement; at first, anyway.

I am trying to suggest a strategy for aspirant authors in response to those who have sent me enquiring letters (usually accompanied by an immense manuscript about sadomasochism in space or growing up gay in Basildon).

Everything I've outlined so far has avoided the issues of class and gender. Obviously these are potent but most certainly not insurmountable. Education being undemocratic in this country means that, by and large, the literary and media worlds exude a steady beam of absolute middle-classness which accounts for the predictable quality of much of the product. This is the remnant of literature having been, at one time, a Gentleman's Profession. Young aesthetes down from Oxbridge would pay a sort of dowry to work for free in publishing. Hence the dire wages that still prevail and the resultant difficulty of making a decent living as a writer without either some independent means or a very supportive and safely employed partner, both being, once again, the spoils of privilege.

But despite the educational inequalities, I tend to think you will manage if you read enough books. As Mr Burroughs has observed: 'I have never known a writer who was not at one time an avid reader.' I believe it was T. S. Eliot who said that, if a writer has a pretentious literary style, it is generally because he has not read enough books. My own secondary education was hideously expensive and largely useless. I learned to walk with a book on my head and to open a garden party, although no-one has ever asked me to do either. Odd, that.

It would almost have been more useful the other way round.

I used to teach creative writing (most notably in a Northern prison where amongst my students was one of the Hosein brothers reputed to have fed poor Mrs Mackay to the pigs on their farm). I used to try and impress on classes that the only way to be good at anything, in this case writing, was to be completely obsessed by it. You have to think about books and language and phrases and authors all the time – it has to be quite impossible for you to be truly interested in anything else at all. As a nun is a bride of Christ, so you are indissolubly wedded to words because you just can't be any different. That is what you are like. Obsessed. Fanatical. You wake up trying to remember who said 'Some people say that life is the thing but I prefer reading' and go to sleep murmuring the last paragraph of *Wuthering Heights* or *The Great Gatsby*.

Pretension comes with the territory, I'm afraid. And ideally, when you are not reading you should be writing, although one does tend to put it off and read *Vanity Fair* instead, and of course life and love get in the way, particularly when you are young and want to go out all the time. But books and their contents must preoccupy you. I suspect this sort of monomania applies to all the arts, if you are going to be even adequately professional, but I might be wrong. At university I thought everybody reading Eng Lit would be similarly compulsive but not one single person was. Just one or two of the staff. Some of my creative writing students were pretty obsessive (this bookish quality has nothing to do with age, educational attainments or class) and they duly got published, although they could never make a living from it.

Anyway, you get to London (if you can), you are obsessed with your subject and you want to get published. You will observe on sale, in independent bookstores, newsagents, record shops and so on a vast range of publications – literary mags, 'zines, glossy porn, publications on every conceivable subject. Editors need writers, although you sometimes wouldn't think so. Unless you have a stellar career as an undergraduate journalist behind you and the clippings and awards to prove it, there is little point in cold-calling or cold-writing editors, however sublime your ideas and prose. They are busy and do not want to risk a commission on someone who might not know how to do it properly in terms of presentation, housestyle and meeting the deadline. Some publications, though, are much more likely than others to take a gamble on unknown writers: music magazines, listings magazines, bubblegum pop and poster teen mags, literary magazines and specialist ones – say, film, or computers, political, anarchic, eco-angst-animal-rights sheets and local newspapers. Whatever. Try modestly. Through friends and your arty McJob and its attendant festivities, you should eventually find someone who will let you write a short book review. Most publications have a books page. Don't expect to get paid, necessarily. It depends on the publication. If the editor likes your review, they will give you another and another. You will probably have a particular subject specialisation in books that you can emphasise, and if you get on well with the editor on the phone, you can diffidently suggest titles suitable for review. Later on editors may take you to lunch and all that, but in the initial stages they emerge only once a year at a Christmas party – and look nothing at all like what you expected from the phone.

Then the editor leaves. The new one always dumps you to prove that they're abrim with original ideas and better contributors, so one then seems to spend years and years photocopying. Send out your clippings, find a new editor, go to book launches and eventually, if you are any good, they will start ringing you up themselves. For the first few years, always, always meet the deadline. Eventually you'll write for posher publications, branch out into non-literary features, get paid a little bit more and then probably think 'Sod this for a life', jack it in and take a nice, undemanding editorial post. What you should really do at this point, now that you are no longer completely invisible, just almost-invisible, is start writing books, fast, and get an agent.

But there are no absolutes here at all. Some people write the novel first. Some people, like myself, may want to be writers but feel inept and, having resigned themselves to life as a serial reader, become a writer by accident. I moved to London from Yorkshire one Saturday, on impulse, in a van that was going down to a demonstration. I foisted myself upon a noble friend in her teeny Whitechapel squat and started working in the fiction section of Compendium Bookshop, in Camden Town. Eventually the books editor on a London listings magazine asked me to try reviewing for him, which I did. Some years later, when I left, got married and started going into withdrawal-from-life mode, I was able to carry on writing as I had to earn some money. I reassured myself that Colette used to write in bed. Much later I was diagnosed with a slow but terminal liver disease (see page 233) which at least saved face when it came to *sous* duvet.

That is all the advice I can think of right now. I can't go into all that gunk about presentation, double-spacing, not writing on both sides of the paper at once and consulting the current *Writers' and Artists' Year Book* or *The Writer's Handbook*. Get one of these useful volumes and read the relevant bits.

When I started reviewing books, an old literary lag pointed out to me that reviewing was fine at first. It is much easier to write cruel criticism in an entertaining fashion than it is to praise good work. But in time, he said, I would probably meet a lot of authors at literary gatherings – launches, lunches, readings, awards, parties (when I could still rouse myself to communality) – and, because I would meet these people in civilised, social surroundings, they would seem pleasant and affable. I might even get to be proper friends with some of them and really care about them. In either case it would become harder and harder to review their books in a detached manner and, in many cases, ultimately impossible. He was right. One point – having been sternly trained by journalism and even more sternly by universities never to use the word 'I' in serious, critical prose (for some reason it is seen as vulgar and amateurish), it has taken me a long time to start doing so and even now I employ the word with some embarrassment, despite being as egocentric as any other writer. My early literary journalism eschewed the word completely and later I spent ages writing 'one' instead and sounding incredibly po-faced. Finally, when I proceeded to the sort of non-literary journalism that actually demands first-person ranting, it was a great relief. It had slowly become clear in any case, that even the most apparently sober and detached criticism is really all about its author, so why pretend?

Autobiography still makes me nervous though, but naturally I can only summon personal experience and opinion in these matters of literary career and critical tastes. However much purists despise the anecdotal, I can see no alternative here. So please indulge me or skip straight to a section you prefer.

My final *pensée* for the time being is a vexatious one. I used to assume, as I suppose most people do, that what I read in newspapers and magazines was exactly as it had emerged from the author's iMac. This is not so. Every piece is edited and invariably cut. When first faced with a hack 'n' slice job that bore minimal relation to what I had actually written, I was mildly distressed. Fortunately, yet another Grub Street adviser was at hand to tell me firmly that an 800-word book review was hardly deathless prose to be cherished and that really almost anything could usually be cut from a piece and still leave something printable. *Tant pis.* So I clobbered my nascent, unworthy vanity and stopped fretting thereafter, unless it was a particularly savage distortion of my work by some inebriated sub-editor. Out of all the articles in this book, I believe only two were printed exactly as they had been written.

But I still harbour a spark of resentment so I have restored nearly all the cuts that were made in these pieces, unless they were sufficiently intelligent as to have actually improved the article. And in any case I've lost some of the published versions by now, so I only have my original copy. Of course I understand about shortage of space and pressure and all that but so often editors cut from the bottom up, losing one's conclusion, and they cut the introductory paragraph as being extraneous and then, worst of all and seemingly particular to literary journalism, they cut out the jokes. I think literary journalism should be as funny and entertaining as possible, because otherwise who would want to read it? Not many do anyway. Shortage of space is always given as the reason for cuts, although there are in fact numberless reasons for someone wishing to cluster-bomb your critical edifice.

This is not to say that there cannot be a fruitful exchange of ideas and decisions about any piece with your editor. This is how it should be and sometimes is. No-one minds changes they have agreed to. In literary journalism I have worked for a number of great editors who have understood implicitly that even a book review is, in its tiny, pathetic way, a work of art with all the construction, rhythm and thought that this involves and that, if you remove an integral part of that structure, the whole will collapse. I am more than grateful to such understanding books editors who have included Boyd Tonkin, Jason Cowley, Deborah Orr, James Wood, Blake Morrison, Jenny Turner and Richard Gott.

Still, it is better to write books. You have a lot more autonomy.

Anyway, overall I do not recommend being a writer. There are too many already. On the matter of creative writing classes, Flannery O'Connor observed 'Everywhere I go I am asked if I think universities stifle writers. I don't think they stifle enough of them. The kind of writing that can be taught is the kind you have to teach people not to read . . .'

Trying to write serious fiction is agonising. Colette summed it all up when she said 'It is wonderful having written.' It is.

Even nowadays, without people creating and writing things down there would be no culture, learning or entertainment (no Treasure Island at Disneyland, no soaps, no movies, no philosophy or great novels, nothing). Nevertheless, writers are usually impoverished and often treated like shit. Everyone (especially your bank) assumes that you do not have a Proper Job and are always available. You really do have to be compulsive to want to do it all the time.

I still think I would rather read (if it paid), but there seem to be very few new books published nowadays that I can get interested in.

So I guess I'll just have to try and write them myself. Damn.

1

America and literature

The hunter gets captured by the game

When I went away to boarding school at the age of eleven, my Uncle Archibald gave me three books which he felt would help me cope. They were *The Man with the Golden Arm* by Nelson Algren, *On the Road* by Jack Kerouac and Allen Ginsberg's *Howl*. They were very useful; I decided that when I grew up, I would be not just a writer but a beatnik junkie writer.

I was lucky to read them at all before they were confiscated. I kept two of them up the classroom chimney and the slimmest (*Howl*) inside other textbooks but it was no use. By this time, my uncle was an ageing Glaswegian misanthrope whose fine library was a solid testament to the classics of English literature – there were complete, much-annotated sets of Hardy and Scott and Dickens, H. G. Wells, Wodehouse, Saki, Firbank, Conan Doyle, Orwell and so on and on. He had always plied me with books, especially those forbidden by my stoutly Calvinist parents. However, when he gave me these three American classics, he insisted that it was important that I read them carefully and observe their style – he even marked some descriptions of jazz playing in *On the Road*. Uncle Archie had no literary pretensions – he just read what he enjoyed. But if, by the mid-sixties, he could see perfectly clearly that the post-war decades were to be domi-nated by American literary achievements, why did it take so long to filter through to everyone else? Ten, or even fifteen years later, British critics and literati were still looking blank at the mention of Black Mountain College. It really was terrible. Our notorious national conviction that *the English*, the English are Best at Every-thing, including literature, has proven incredibly hard to shift.

I didn't want to go to university because I didn't understand what it was. I had spent all my life reading novels and they never explain what a university does, they assume you know. I wanted to go to art school because the art students in our small, provincial city looked cooler than anyone else. My parents managed to convey (God knows how, as they were not speaking to me at the time) that, while I was very good at reading books with my fingers in my ears, I was much less good at painting pictures. So they made me send in a university application form.

However, despite gaining as anticipated three grade As and a C at A level, not a single university would accept me. This was because the confidential headmistress's report which accompanied the initial applications was apparently so violently insulting that nowhere would even consider me. I never saw it but it must have been bad, because the next year when I re-applied with a different testimonial I was accepted immediately by every single institution I'd chosen. Perhaps it was just as well I was so vague about the world. Had I realised that in addition to rendering my adolescent years wretched, that awful woman had then tried to ruin my entire future life, I might have inflicted murderous injury upon her, immediately fulfilling some of her dire predictions for me. Actually I would have done everyone a favour by dropping a netball packed with gunpowder on her head. She was a dreadful headmistress, narrow, sadistic and hypocritical, who tormented children in ways that now would defy belief. She couldn't tell the difference between a gifted child and a day-old doughnut anyway.

That particular appellation was foisted upon me very early, although I don't mention it solely to show off. (It is more of a curse than a benison anyway. Research shows that so-called 'gifted children' who receive no appropriate nurture almost never fulfil their potential.) The vast majority, maddened by boredom, swiftly drop out or become delinquent. A surprising number seem to end up working in motorway service cafeterias. My own parents declined offers from a couple of special schools. They wanted me to grow up completely normal . . .

Admittedly, my secondary school headmistress was an extreme case, but she does provide clues to something that puzzled me for a long time. Eventually I was forced to conclude that many adults feel an intense dislike towards clever children. I don't mean the sort of inconsequential, patronising, mild antipathy that any adult can feel towards a particular child but the real thing – a full-blown, mature, adult detestation. Children, however clever, have not yet learned to disguise, to dissimulate and be disingenuous in the cause of appearing less bright and thus sparing the feelings of others. They tend to show off their knowledge, to be bumptious, enthusiastic and smart-arsed until they run into this wall of adult disapprobation (excepting always those kindly angels of English teachers, at least one of whom is sent to lighten the schoolday hell of all neurotic young outsiders). In retrospect, a recognition of this distaste has cleared up some personal imponderables and makes a certain amount of cultural and historical sense – England retains its tradition of treating serious intellectual effort with levity and disrespect – which is, I now realise, not *always* a bad thing. Also, during the immediate post-war decades the average adult did not possess even a modicum (and that is usually enough) of ability when it came to insight or self-analysis. The whole country was emotionally stunted on a vast scale in that there was none but the most sparse and inadequate vocabulary for the expression of feelings in everyday life. These factors, together with the faint intimation of a storm on the horizon that children did not appear to be growing up to respectfully emulate their parents, might have conspired to make many adults feel even more threatened and unforgiving towards articulate children than they would have done anyway.

Finally I was aimed at university. Unsurprisingly, I wanted to go on doing what I had been doing for years, reading American literature. So I was surprised to find that, as far as Oxbridge was concerned, it did not exist. Their English Literature courses stopped around 1854. At that time I think there were only three universities in the UK where one could study any American literature at all within the context of an Eng Lit degree course. So I ignored a rather grudging offer from the dreaming spires – actually it was from the other one, the one that had the spying dreamers instead. Cambridge's offer was unenthusiastic, I think, because they realised that I was worse than unstable. And, unfortunately, my teenage personality paralleled that of Simon in Shena Mackay's lovely story 'Pink Cigarettes': 'Simon, for whom the word *decadence* was rivalled in beauty only by *fin de siècle* . . .' It was no fun being an ur-Goth.

In fact I was in no fit state to be let out alone. Since the age of twelve when I was in the third form I had suffered from that most hideous and unwanted of illnesses, clinical depression. So awful is it that I just cannot dwell on it. I always tried to repress it – it is not the sort of thing you want to burden your friends with. I could pass exams and go to parties and function within very narrow limits but eventually crack-up time would arrive, complete with melodrama and bureaucracy and the NHS. Even at the best of times, everything and everybody puzzled me. I was lost; I didn't have the first idea how the world worked. On a quotidian level, things like shopping, cooking, laundry, nourishment, transport were a mystery to me. Unfortunately my upbringing had been sufficiently privileged to allow me the luxury of not noticing things. I don't like to confess just how inept and out of touch I was. I'd never noticed, for example, kettles or towels. I'd never boiled water. I didn't dry myself after swimming and bathing. Shamefully I must admit that other people (paid and unpaid) did a lot of these and similar things for me. I suppose it was learned helplessness. I didn't even notice when my third NHS psychiatrist raped me; I truly believed it was necesary for him to enlarge my vagina with a variety of instruments, warm and cool. I feel now that it is indefensible to be like that and yet at the same time I know, if I was back there again, I couldn't have coped in any other way. If I let everything try and rush in, I was overwhelmed to the point of catatonia. Some years later, when I took acid, I found it affected things very little; they were always like that for me anyway (and I was given a huge dose by mistake). So in pitiful defence I can only say that I was ill, physically, although I didn't know it then and most certainly mentally ill according to my NHS archives.

At the time there was much discussion among the intelligentsia, in the wake of R. D. Laing, as to whether mental illness existed or not. It seems that it does and I can tell you that it is absolutely hellish. Unfortunately mental illness didn't exist in Scotland then (for cultural rather than revolutionary reasons). So, as I drifted around, causing a lot of trouble, my parents suggested that I went to work, for free, in a geriatric hospital in Edinburgh. So I did. (I was floaty as sea-kelp and hopelessly suggestible – if I'd been ordered to join a coven or murder Jimmy Savile, I'd probably have done it.) My parents, in sending me to the geriatric hospital, were applying the only known cure for 'nerves' in Scotland at the time, known as Counting Your Blessings. Doubtless they hoped that I would come to value my own youth and privilege, engage in useful activity to take my mind off myself and mature suddenly into someone deeply happy, compassionate, practical and hard-working. All these are excellent aims but they worked no better than they would have had I been riddled with buboes and the same cure applied. I became even more depressed and developed a lifelong phobia about excrement.

Those who rely on books for all their knowledge of life are likely to be as imbecilic as I was then. This does not contradict my earlier assertion about the importance of reading and obsession if one wants to be a writer. It is, as it usually is, a question of balance. If you read, as I did, desperately, compulsively, for escapism alone, your actions are pathological. And you end up knowing a great deal about books but absolutely nothing about anything else. This is not obsession, but insanity. Contrary to popular myth it seems that an artist needs to be far more sane than normal if they are to attain the mental order necessary to creation.

But then, being saner than others makes one peculiar too.

Finally, to everyone's relief, I went to university where I was very happy reading Old and Middle English as well as French and US fiction. So happy (in my work that is; my personal life looked like a Jackson Pollock) that I stayed on to do research. And if I'd had any sense I'd have stayed there forever.

BUT . . .

The west is the best?

In honour of my late Uncle Archie and his part in introducing me to US literature, let us start with the Beat Generation. My uncle's gift assisted my willing degeneracy – for books can deprave and corrupt. They are so powerful they can do anything:– *enlighten or defile.*

In addition, let the following strike a mild blow against the interview form. The media interview is one of the most pointless human exchanges ever devised. (Unless, of course, the interviewer is especially skilled, obsessed and so on.) The interviewee doesn't really want to talk to you but they have a book to promote. You will not get to know them, or learn anything about them.

In real life people tend to confide in me – and naturally I always offered to turn off the tape-recorder if the interviewee wished it. But few were likely to trust a journalist not to remember and print the stuff anyway, although I never did. So I was probably a very bad interviewer, in editorial terms. This interview with Herbert Huncke was one of those rare interviews where some degree of rapport was established. I can't really say we became friends but I did see him again and maintained a sporadic contact. Anyway, I'd always wanted to go to Bruges because of that amazing dyke horror film Daughters of Darkness.

And I got a great T-shirt with 'Guilty of Everything' on it.

Later I wrote the Guardian *obituary for Huncke but it does not add to what is said here. RIP.*

Guilty of everything:
Interview with Herbert Huncke

The Guardian, 20 October 1994

'Herbert Huncke . . .?' repeated my friend, tapping her cigarette, 'I know! He's the real William Burroughs!' It was as good a description as any. Burroughs, the Harvard-educated wandering WASP took a tiptoe on the wild side and ended up addicted to morphine. Huncke has been slogging up and down that same boulevard of broken dreams all his life, drifting past its ramshackle rows of doss-houses, brothels, crack dens, endless heartbreak motels and grim, towering penitentiaries.

The Beat Generation were intensely autobiographical writers; they drew their artistic prey from the same small circle of friends, lovers and acquaintances. The central trio, Ginsberg, Kerouac and Burroughs, were all alienated college boys who wanted to get down and dirty with the natural born outlaws of uptight forties America. And so they dragged home their pariah curios, the weirdest examples of human wreckage they could find on their nervous forays into the underworld. As one of the few girls around, Joyce Johnson, wrote later: 'There was surely some hidden, rock-bottom truth in that treacherous all-night world of pushers and addicts, thieves and whores, that you couldn't get at by reading Dostoevsky or Céline – it had to be experienced directly.' So Ginsberg and Kerouac produced bisexual Denver wild child and car thief Neal Cassady as well as the precocious street-smart poet Gregory Corso. And Burroughs met Herbert Huncke. Huncke the junkie, con-man, charmer, petty criminal, ex-rentboy and graduate of Dannemora and Sing Sing Prisons. They all stayed for that long strange ride into an international bohemian future that they would influence beyond all belief.

Huncke, with his erratic charisma, outrageously colourful stories and amoral originality was the perfect muse. He appears as Herman in Burroughs' *Junkie* (1958), as Elmo Hassel in Kerouac's *On the Road* (1957), Junkey in *The Town and the City* (1950), Huck in *Visions of Cody* (1960) and *Book of Dreams* (1961) and as Ancke in John Clellon Holmes' *Go* (1952). In Ginsberg's *Howl* (1956) Huncke 'walked all night with [his] shoes full of blood on the /snowbank docks waiting for a door in the East River to/ open to a room full of steamheat and opium'.

Huncke, dealer, addict, homosexual, recidivist, has not only survived, but thrived. His fifth book is due to be published. He has been undertaking a successful reading tour of Europe where, as one of the few surviving central Beat Generation figures, he is revered by every half-literate post-punk cool cat. He is now due in London to give three readings.

Neptune Music/Press, managed from Amsterdam and Bruges by an indomitable American, Suzanne Hines, is re-issuing two of his earlier autobiographical books, *The Evening Sun Turned Crimson* (1980) and *Guilty of Everything* (1990). They will publish his new work *Adventures and Strange Experiences* in the spring.

Simultaneously this month Neptune are releasing a spoken word CD 'From Dream To Dream' which has Huncke reading from all three books. Surrealistically they are also releasing a CD single, a club and radio mix of 'Guilty Of Everything' with Huncke intoning the title behind a hypnotic dance beat provided by Intransive Care.

Accordingly, I went to meet Huncke in Bruges where he was working on these projects. Bruges is a neat, sweet and orderly town, Huncke a living testament to chaos and chemicals. This guy had virtually defined hardline, heavy-duty, lifelong hipsterdom – I'd read the books. But he was in his eighties now. How could he still be involved in all this . . . *activity*? A dance record for Chrissakes . . .

I needn't have worried. Mr Huncke had more stamina than any of the young acolytes drifting in and out. Huncke has used heroin since his early teens and is an excellent advertisement for the restorative properties of opiates. A Beat associate once famously wrote: 'Huncke was a beautiful kid when he first came to New York. The trouble is, he lost his looks.' But, in one of the best memoirs of Huncke ever written – part of *Sheeper* (1967) by Burrough's first publisher, Irving Rosenthal, he observes 'He must have been a secret wise old man when he was fifteen and his skin glowed like his eyes – those eternally adolescent eyes that every-one remembers as blue, although they are hazel.' It's true. Age suits him. He is quite unlike any average blanked-out geriatric. He is small, fine-boned, a little wizened and twisted, feral-looking with very high cheekbones. His eyes are as riveting as Rosenthal recalls, maliciously bright and sparkly. He sits on a divan, chainsmoking Marlboros. The shutters are wide open; the heat wave has worn us out. The evening sun turned crimson and was replaced by a huge werewolf moon.

Huncke, now on a methadone programme ('You can't score on the streets at my age' – although he was last bust for a street buy in his sixties), seems to feel the cold, as junkies do. He wears two T-shirts, neatly laundered. Given the chance he is something of a dandy. His hair is still – somehow – black. The veins on his lower arms and hands stand out, blue and knotted. They have served him well. He speaks teasingly, insistently in a gravelly voice. His wit is very dry, acerbic. He likes to wind people up. Despite the awful, sudden death of his close friend Louis Cartwright – stabbed a month ago on Second Street – Huncke is open, pre-pared to talk about anything. He must have seen so much. Death, tragedy, madness, breakdown.

Huncke has written of feeling nervous when he first met Burroughs and the other Beats – 'They were all so very, very intel-lectual.' He says now: 'In the beginning you don't *know* people. And they were such a tightly bound group, all university people. I was the outsider, so it's only logical that I would feel somewhat intimidated.'

Had he wanted to write to try and be like them? After all Neal Cassady also attempted an autobiography and produced *The First Third*. Huncke considers.

'I've maybe always wanted to be a writer but I just kept that to myself. I still don't have a hell of a lot of confidence as far as writing is concerned. For me to say that I'm a writer takes an awful lot. I think there are certain things one must do to show respect for the craft. It wouldn't have hurt me to have at least made the effort to learn to spell which I *cannot do* – No! – Not at all, not worth a shit!' He laughs, coughs.

All Huncke's writing is directly autobiographical and has the beauty of naif or primitive art. Its style is slightly reminiscent of Kerouac, punctuated by dashes as if he were speaking aloud. It is devastatingly honest, and direct. It is also very tender and loving in a surprisingly idealistic way. Huncke appears to have none of the psychic armour of ordinary people. In his writing he reveals everything, however poorly it reflects on him. He says poignantly, 'Everything I've written is true. I try not to tell any lies, I swear.' Hmm.

Born in 1915, Huncke was brought up in Chicago and drifted towards sex, drugs and liquor very young. Why?

'How do I know? – Just a sense of feeling at a loss as to how to get along. I soon discovered that everything I did was contrary to the rules and regulations – everything I felt, everything I thought. – I was always being accused. My father was a great one for saying I'd never learn the value of a dollar. I could never *please* anyone and it seemed that everything I did was wrong. I'd rebel against commands – so it finally got to where I needed to lie or dodge things altogether so of course this created a lot of havoc. It didn't lead to a pleasant home life at all. My father and mother were young and excitable people without too much knowledge of the undercurrents of sex and what it could do. People were not all hip in that period – they were just beginning to learn. I just tried to escape it as easily as possible. I just walked out one morning and said "Fuck this shit, I'm going to California."'

From the age of twelve onwards Huncke drifted all over America from New Orleans, to Memphis, to LA. 'I'd frequent places where I could run into people pretty much like myself. Do you know where Pirate's Alley is, for example?'

'In New Orleans. Where Lafitte hung out?'

'Yeah. Well, I wasn't exactly inconspicuous (general laughter) – and I was *most* agreeable about meeting people of all kinds . . .'

He settled in New York in 1939, hustling constantly for drugs and money. Sexologist Professor Kinsey paid him ten dollars to describe his experiences as a male prostitute for the famous Kinsey Report of 1948. It is fascinating to hear Huncke talk of pre-sixties bohemian culture.

'The widespread use of drugs was just beginning. There was already an established population of drug-users but they were of a different calibre then. They weren't usually connected with the arts. They weren't Thomas De Quincey types. They were just knockaround people, prostitutes, pimps – the Chinese were still using opium. New York was honeycombed with all kinds of places around Chinatown. A lot of people in show business and Hollywood were interested in drugs. I ran into a woman in her mid-twenties – I was about seventeen – she was a stripper, she claimed to be Turkish. She wasn't pretty – but what a wild woman!! You know, hennaed hair – she told me she used to have an orgasm when she went out onstage. She'd load herself to the eyebrows on cocaine and do these wild numbers, grinds. So that was my introduction to the burlesque world. I wasn't into cocaine too much then, any I got was medical – pharmaceutical. This nurse I'd run into – she'd bring in these little packages, *cubes* of pure white cocaine, and shave it off. It was the real rock. Oh boy!' (A collective sigh goes up.)

One of the most endearing aspects of Huncke's books is his total lack of ambition, snobbery or greed. Also his interest in the women who had dropped out of straight society at that time is in marked contrast to the other Beat writers. Kerouac was racked on the Madonna–whore complex and produced literary archetypes like Tristessa or Mardou. Ginsberg showed little interest apart from in his mother and Burroughs was often frankly misogynistic. But Huncke writes movingly about all the women he knew – 'I loved all of them in a funny way,' he says, and in particular Burroughs' wife Joan Vollmer – 'one of the most charming and intelligent women I've ever met.'

Huncke is ecstatic at receiving attention and respect from younger admirers and writers. 'I'm just *so* pleased by it. God, I just GLOW. Kids are so fascinating especially these students and I feel so honoured – well, when they say nice things to me! I get more from younger people than I do from my own peers.'

Huncke is a brilliant talker. He has known everyone – and all the gossip. Drugs remain the constant in his life. He says he used opiates because of 'the peace and harmony I felt the first time I turned on. At long last I was at peace with everything. Once one has the experience of opiates one never forgets it. You may never do it again but you'll be fighting it for the rest of your life. It changes the metabolism. I don't use much speed anymore. I wouldn't mind if it came back on the scene. I'd like to try it again, see if it's working. I like hard rock cocaine. Now speedballs (heroin and cocaine) – they're the best. But drugs are not what they were. The quality's not so good. And they're so *expensive* . . .' (General agreement. This conversation carries on for a long time.)

'Do you have any regrets?'

'None that I can think of right now. I would like to have avoided a lot of the headaches but I wouldn't have changed the hunting ground!'

Huncke had a notorious reputation for pushing the envelope of friendship. Old friends describe him as slippery. He has had to steal all along to support his habit. But when I was persuaded, effortlessly, to part with my aeroplane Valium, I felt pleased to have met and been conned by a legendary master.

Literary outlaw: *The Life and Times of William Burroughs* by Ted Morgan

(Bodley Head)
City Limits, 1998

Most serious readers have the sense to grow out of the Beat Generation authors, with the possible exception of William Burroughs' work. These days the only book on the subject I truly love is Joyce

Johnson's Minor Characters *(Washington Square Press, 1990). In the course of this memoir of her affair with Jack Kerouac and her friendships with the other Beat illuminati, Johnson neatly skewers minor Beat writer, John Clellon Holmes, author of* Go *and of the judgement 'The social organization which is most true of itself to the artist is the boy gang.' Oh yeah? Still, that was in 1954. But in 1977, in a preface to a new edition of* Go, *although Holmes matches each male character in his* roman-à-clef *to its original, he says of the girl characters that they were 'a type rather than an individual'. Johnson comments, both acidly and sadly, 'He can't quite remember them [the girls] – they were mere anonymous passengers on the big Greyhound bus of experience. Lacking centers, how could they burn with the fever that infected his young men? What they did, I guess, was fill up the seats.'*

It is extremely difficult, now, to convey how utterly NOTHING one was, as a girl, in the years before seventies feminism.

Be grateful. Be very grateful that you live now, not then.

Junkie, killer, gun-freak, Swiftian satirist – who is he really, the ghostly man in the soft grey Homburg hat who looks out gravely from a thousand jumbled photographs over the last forty years? Here he is in the Medina of Tangier smoking a hookah with his Spanish boyfriend and here, standing nervously in a Moroccan garden with Allen Ginsberg, Gregory Corso and Paul Bowles in that far-off psychedelic summer of 1961. Here again, huddled in a London flat with a Piccadilly hustler, and here, peering into the Colombian jungle in search of the mysterious hallucinogenic, *yage.* And here, finally, being inducted into the American Academy and Institute of Arts and Letters, now and forever to be enshrined in American literature along with Saul Bellow, Norman Mailer and Arthur Miller. This must be the longest, strangest trip ever, through all the counter-cultural galaxies of the post-war world. Sex, drugs, violence, fragmentation, mysticism, mayhem, the Wandering WASP, the beatnik remittance man has seen and done it all. William Burroughs has remained the still point of the turning world for generation after generation of deviants, punks, poseurs, lunatics, junkies and every scramble-brained, wild-eyed arty, avant-garde fanatic who ever set out to change the world with a syringe and a sheaf of unpublished rantings.

So, hold onto your hats, Ted Morgan is going to show us the guy who blazed the trail. Burroughs was the middle-class St Louis intellectual loner who fell in with Jack Kerouac and Allen Ginsberg in New York, forming the nucleus of the Beat Generation writers. The archetypal rebel, Burroughs drifts into crime and drugs and develops a dogged heroin addiction. He is gay but fathers a son and later accidentally shoots his wife. The ultimate anarchic cv slams on; busted flat in Texas and Mexico, exile in Tangier, Paris and London. The writing of *Naked Lunch*, the violent, scatological classic which uses addiction as a metaphor for control in consumer society. The book's obscenity trial which effectively ended literary censorship in America. Misogyny, conspiracies, Scientology, literary experimentation, love affairs. The tragic disintegration and death of his son. The punk years when Burroughs receives waves of youthful celebrities bearing drugs in his windowless NY flat; an ageing queen and his courtiers. The last great trilogy, *Cities of the Red Night*. Respectability, honours, riches, fame. And finally, the elderly sage, alone with his cats and guns in Kansas.

Morgan is extremely illuminating on the contradictory aspects of Burroughs' character and on the spiritual impulses behind his writing. As an introduction it couldn't be better. But for those he calls the 'Unconditional Burroughsians' who know the myth by heart, it is an odd book. Morgan transposes large chunks of Burroughs' writings and sections from other memoirs straight into the text, without acknowledgement, as if they were his, Morgan's, words. And ultimately the most fanatic fan must wonder – was it worth it, after all? Burroughs, as a writer, is a genius. He has survived, and romanticised a tragic trajectory. 'My life is an evil river,' he moans, alluringly. How many lesser, faltering comets have burnt out helplessly in his wake?

Jane Bowles: Gnawing at the bone of our lives

Foreword to Jane Bowles' *Plain Pleasures*
Penguin 21st Classics, 2000

Jane and Paul Bowles were not really Beat Generation writers. They were polite, mannerly, self-conscious, conventionally unconventional. It was Jane who when asked by Allen Ginsberg if she believed in God said 'I'm certainly not going to discuss it on the telephone.' Her fiction is quite remarkable and it is very sad that her lifelong writer's block allowed her to produce so little. They might as well go in here.

Although Jane Bowles was able to complete relatively little creative work during her lifetime, her prose has received an extraordinary amount of attention and near-veneration from the most discerning of her peers. Poet John Ashbery, in his review of *The Collected Works*, described Jane Bowles as 'one of the finest modern writers of fiction, in any language'. Carson McCullers wrote to Jane saying, 'your curious, slanted and witty style has always given me boundless delight'. To Truman Capote she was 'a genius'. Gore Vidal in a characteristically waspish essay conceded her 'superb talent'. William Burroughs in a short piece on prose style quotes approvingly from the first story in *Plain Pleasures* – '"In his youth he had considered raising alligators in Florida. But there was no security in the alligators." Janey Bowles – who else?'

Who else indeed? Any sentence written by Bowles tends to be instantly recognisable. Her words are fey, puzzling, bizarre, original – all adjectives that were applied to Jane herself. A friend, academic Wendell Wilcox, opined that 'no-one but Jane could have written a line of them' (the stories) but still considered that 'the really exotic element was Jane herself'. Jane Bowles' magnificent reputation rests on one novel, one play and the six stories collected here in *Plain Pleasures*.

In coming to appreciate this small body of work it is essential that the reader have some emotional sympathy with the kind of pain that the act of writing produced in her. She found writing difficult to the point of torment. 'Every word is like chiseling in granite,' she wrote. Although her work was rarely directly autobiographical she did produce a very brief summary of her life which began 'I started to "write" when I was about fifteen and was obliged to do composition in school. I always thought it the most loathsome of all activities and still do.' Yet she always felt driven to write and said to friends, 'I must write but I can't write.' To her husband, Paul Bowles, she explained, 'It is not laziness . . . there is such a thing as failure of the will which is agony for the person who suffers from it.' One of her doctors concurred: 'It wasn't a matter of laziness in her that she didn't work. There was a basic instability.'

Reading the stories in this volume it is possible to sense the immense effort that went into their creation, even without knowing that the author wrote very slowly and laboriously. This basic tension permeates the prose and is the foundation of all the other conflicts that her fiction describes – the conflict between sin and salvation, between the imaginary and the real, between men and women, between mothers and daughters. Jane Bowles' creative work embodies her life and personality in that her highly developed sense of the ridiculous, the juxtaposition of the trivial and the profound in her conversation and her startling non-sequiturs all informed her fiction and were much remarked-upon in her social life. Such idiosyncracies were seen as charming, amusing facets of her most unusual and eccentric character. She was both imperious and childlike or, as Paul Bowles put it, 'a combination of enormous egotism and deep modesty'. Jane herself could make no distinction between her life and her work. The one predicated the other.

Psychiatric theory alone seems limited and almost reductive in trying to account for a personality as complex, contradictory and tortured as that of Jane Bowles. She was born Jane Auer on 2 February 1917 in New York and was the sole child of a comfortably middle-class, non-practising Jewish couple, Sidney and

Claire Auer. Jane rarely seemed overtly conscious of her Jewish heritage and indeed was always to avoid political issues of any sort during her life.

Her family moved to a Long Island suburb when Jane was small. She suffered tuberculosis of the knee as a child which left her with a permanent limp. From the outset Jane was wilful, hyper-sensitive and highly imaginative. One childhood friend recalled: 'She looked like an elf with large luminous eyes and a ski-jump nose. Her imagination was so magical that I was swept up into it with her . . . She was very mystifying and mercurial . . . I never understood the origin of her anger. She was moody . . . a moodiness that bordered on depression.'

Her mother was apprehensive rather than imaginative and doted on Jane in a somewhat suffocating way, calling her 'my million dollar baby'. However, it was her father, by all acounts a gentle man, who seems to have unwittingly inflicted some terrible psychic wound on Jane. There are few clues as to its nature. In 1954, in another brief autobiographical note she wrote, 'Nothing has changed. My father predicted everything when he said I would procrastinate until I died . . . it was terribly painful to know this as a child. Now that I am nearly forty and in North Africa it is still painful . . .' In 1967, when Jane had become deeply depressed, her mother wrote to her, 'Darling, there is nothing wrong with you. Your own father would have told you to "stop dramatizing your troubles." '

Her procrastination and the terrible powers of her own imagination were the dominant themes of Jane's life. Her father's sudden death when she was away at camp aged thirteen left her forever stranded without any hope of resolving the judgements he had made about her. She felt shamed and condemned. The qualities that most defined her – her dreaminess, her creativity – had been judged and found wanting. Her own fierce and personal sense of morality with its unending emphasis on a very individual idea of sin and salvation would never allow her to be at peace with herself. Thereafter, her imagination, which was her very essence, comprised both sin and salvation. Her imagination was sinful in the eyes of the outer world, the world of the father, and simultaneously spiritually essential to her: 'I must write but I can't write.'

After her father's death Jane gradually developed an entire

range of terrors and phobias. She was scared of fire, water, mountains, elevators, dogs, sharks and more. One friend, Oliver Smith, commented, 'Her life was in terror but disguised terror . . . she had a great self-destructiveness and at the same time an enormous will to live.' Additionally she started to find any decision, however trivial, almost impossible. Again and again friends have remarked on her brooding over the most microscopic details or, in the words of Tennessee Williams, her 'extreme kind of excited indecision'. Paul Bowles said 'Every choice (for Jane) was a moral judgement and monumental, even fatal. And that was even if the choice was between string beans and peas.'

Sadly, Jane's self-mockery and sophisticated sense of the absurd suggested to many people that her fears and agonies were exaggerated and affected, a form of play-acting that seemed very piquant and charming when she was young and flirtatious. Her terrors were actually hideously real and were eventually to mutate into clinical depression and agonising mental illness.

In 1938, in Manhattan, Jane married Paul Bowles, then a young composer. Although she initally perceived him as 'my enemy' she quickly became very devoted and dependent. As a conventional marriage it was short-lived – both partners reverted to their individual homosexual inclinations – but otherwise their union was to endure until Jane's death. Paul Bowles too had been badly hurt by a father, although in his case his father had been deliberately cruel and abusive. Paul had endless patience and respect for Jane's idiosyncracies and was captivated by 'her wonderful elliptical way of seeing things'. They were extremely close and played private games together – in one of these Paul was a man-shaped parrot called Bupple Hergesheimar. Paul also encouraged Jane to write and most of her fiction was written during the early part of their marriage when they travelled widely in South and Central America. When in New York they were friends with the bohemian group of the time including W.H. Auden and E.E. Cummings. Jane in particular was very sociable, partied, drank and fervently pursued her labyrinthine love affairs. She sometimes referred to herself as 'Crippie, the kike dyke'.

In 1947 Paul Bowles moved to Morocco and started work on the series of nihilistic novels that were to make him famous, the first being *The Sheltering Sky*. Jane followed in 1948 and thereafter they were both based in Tangier. Although Jane's novel *Two Serious Ladies* had been published to almost universal mystification in 1943 and she was still to finish her play *In the Summer House*, she was nonetheless nearing the end of her creative life. She made copious notes towards two further novels, *Going to Massachusetts* and *Out In the World*, but was unable to complete them. Much later she wrote of Tangier 'In the twenty years that I have lived here I have written only two short stories, and nothing else. It's good for Paul but not for me.'

It has been suggested that Paul Bowles' increasing success as a novelist and cultural icon discouraged and blocked Jane. This seems unlikely. Her mental balance was always so precarious and the psychic space available wherein she could function and create was always so limited that it seemed inevitable that her demons would ultimately force her to a standstill. The polarities of emotion and anxiety that pulled at her were so extreme that the task of balancing and unifying them in fiction became increasingly difficult and finally impossible. Jane's chief focus, both in her life and in her fiction, was her fascination with the hidden lives of apparently ordinary middle-aged women. She was sexually attracted to such women and pursued a number of lengthy affairs, although her sexual life was probably more restrained than has been rumoured. It is difficult now to appreciate how very idiosyncratic was Jane's intense interest in middle-aged or elderly women in the context of her time. Over the past three decades the attitude to women in Western society has changed so dramatically that it is almost impossible to convey the dismissive atmosphere of those earlier decades. Up until the 1970s women were discounted and despised. They were, *en masse*, classed with children in terms of capability but, unlike children, were the butt of virtually every joke in the comedian's repertoire. They were considered trite, gossipy, vain, slow and useless. Older women were hags, battle-axes, mothers-in-law, spinsters. Women were visible in the real world, the world of men, only while they were sexually desirable. Afterwards they vanished completely, buried alive by the creepy combination of contempt, disgust and sentimentality with which they were regarded.

One example from Jane's own life illustrates these attitudes. When she became seriously ill in middle age, a neurologist in

England reproved her thus – 'You are not coping, my dear Mrs Bowles. Go back to your pots and pans and try to cope.' The tone of patronising condescension is coupled with an implicit assumption that no woman of middle years could be of any interest or be doing anything important. Such assumptions were deeply entrenched in the fifties and ran, like a coda of all despair, underneath all relations between men and women.

The strength of her feelings towards such women often struck others as odd. Paul Bowles commented: 'She always cultivated the most eccentric characters.' After moving to Tangier Jane fell in love with Cherifa, a Moroccan peasant woman who worked in the local grain market. Cherifa was a lesbian and thought to be a witch. Jane employed her, supported her, adored her, feared her and remained permanently involved with her. Truman Capote was to write, 'The late Mrs Bowles lived in an infinitesimal Casbah house . . . with her Moorish lover Cherifa, a rough old peasant woman . . . an abrasive personality only a genius as witty and dedicated to extreme oddity as Mrs Bowles could have abided.'

One of the stories here, 'Everything Is Nice', documents with great economy and precision Jane's early attempts to become friends with Cherifa and her circle. She was naturally drawn towards the hidden, hermetic world of the Muslim women and the leisurely pace of their lives with its grave emphasis on ritual, detail and nuance.

'Everything is Nice' was originally published in 1951 as a non-fiction article on Morocco in *Mademoiselle*, entitled 'East Side: North Africa'. Paul Bowles made minor changes and resuscitated the piece as fiction in the sixties. In story form it reveals all the comic frustration and helpless confusion suffered by anyone who has tried to bridge the great gulfs between different nationalities and languages. Jane's tone is wry and faintly mocking although not without an undercurrent of real desperation which veers suddenly into an admission of psychic tragedy at the end. Throughout the text the protagonist Jeanie is helplessly aware of the distance between herself and the Moroccan women. Everything is displaced. Her intelligence and sophistication have become quite useless: '"I shall see you tomorrow, if Allah wills it." "When?" "Four o'clock." It was obvious that she (Zodelia) had chosen the first figure that had come into her head.' So extreme and ludicrous is Jeanie's isolation during this visit to three Moroccan women that it seems to function as a parodic, exaggerated version of the general alienation from others that the author seemed to feel in her earlier life. In this story she maintains a remarkable balance between opposing forces – Jeanie's sense of 'apartness' and her hunger for intimacy, her playfulness and her pain. During her lifetime Jane Bowles' published work was usually greeted with bafflement. Reviwers called it 'pointlessly morbid . . . useless . . . neurotic'. They said that it 'provokes revulsion and fear' and that 'all the important characters were . . . mentally deranged'. Even though Paul Bowles helped her complete her major story, 'Camp Cataract', he himself found it 'strange and mysterious' and said 'I don't understand it.'

The stories herein are certainly disturbing. They seem to have been carved out on the far edge of sanity by someone who finds human life and social intercourse to be farcical, grotesque and puzzling, someone who has the greatest difficulty maintaining control over their perception of the world. Dualities abound and at times artifice predominates as if the characters were dolls pushed around by a child At other times the tremendous force of feeling in the dialogue renders the protagonists almost too painfully 'real' and human. Jane Bowles' style is both mannered and artless and her use of language particularly noticeable. The title of the story 'Plain Pleasures' could refer to the prose as much as to anything else; it is a very clear prose, stark and unadorned. It is prose stripped down to the bone of meaning and as such it is impossible to evade or hide from its force. Yet, despite its clarity, the prose retains a guarded and elliptical quality. In 'Plain Pleasures' it is necessary to infer that Mrs Perry has been raped in the night by the proprietor of the restaurant. Any hint of this in the text is so subtle as to be virtually subliminal and yet the narrative flow and evolving meaning are so strong that the reader is forced to realise what has occurred.

In terms of content the stories focus largely upon the tension between opposing dualities alongside the paradoxes and contradictions inherent in human behaviour. Similarly, the prose delivers the most surprising juxtapositions and veers abruptly from the banal to the profound. Such transpositions discourage any final sense of static, stable meaning. Just as, in Millicent Dillon's words, 'the prose slips and glides in unexpected associations' so too does the meaning twist. There can be no stable resolution, only a multiplicity of oppositional points of view. Jane Bowles appeared to have an intuitive understanding of ideas propounded later by Jacques Derrida and deconstruction theory, these being that 'meaning' is inherently unstable and the use of language involves 'slippage' away from fixity. Language cannot access inner meaning nor locate 'essence'. Concepts such as 'knowledge' or 'truth' are permanently elusive. Similarly her focus on binary oppositions anticipates structuralist investigations of sign systems.

On a conscious level she would make use of symbolism – the defunct power-station adjacent to Mrs Perry's house in 'Plain Pleasures' is a good example. A friend commented, 'Jane broke down the world into tiny little things that she was obsessive about – symbols, finally.'

'A Guatemalan Idyll' is more overtly sexual than most of the other work. Jane maintained that 'sex is in the mind' and demonstrates this clearly in the story. Mrs Ramirez is lavishly sexual and quickly seduces an American travelling salesman in a Guatemalan hotel. The ensuing experience is dramatically different for each one of them; there is no possibilty of communication or union. The traveller is consciously repelled by her easy sensuality – 'We are like two gorillas', and yet 'he felt . . . as though he had somehow slipped from the real world into the other world, the world he had always inhabited as a little boy'.

A recurring theme in Jane's work is tension between mothers and daughters: Mrs Ramirez is struggling with her two daughters, sulky Consuelo and strange, perverse Lilina, of whom the traveller thought: 'She was a person who could fall over and over again into the same pile of broken glass and scream just as loudly the last time as the first.'

Jane had observed to Paul Bowles: 'Men are all on the outside, not interesting. Women are profound and mysterious – and obscene.' The story 'A Day in the Open' and the short puppet play included here, 'A Quarrelling Pair', pursue these ideas about women. In the story Julie and Inez, both prostitutes, are lovers but a picnic with a client reveals how fragile is their communion.

The play is based on Jane and an older woman, Helvetia Perkins, with whom Jane was much in love during her twenties.

Puppets Harriet and Rhoda are two sisters in their fifties. Harriet is indulgent but highly critical of Rhoda's high-strung nature and games – 'You love to pretend that everything is a riddle.' They fail to connect with each other too. Each one sings a separate, highly ambiguous song on the stage and this serves to emphasise the distance between them.

The controversial 'Camp Cataract' also concerns sisters. It is a story about fear and the terrible powers of the imagination. The title alone is ominous – Jane was on holiday at camp when her father died and the name of this fictional camp evokes loss of vision, blindness. Harriet, oppressed by her two sisters, has manipulated her doctor into advising her to go alone to the camp. At home, her sister Sadie is terrified. Fear of Harriet leaving forever was her 'strongest emotion'. Secretly she decides to visit Harriet – 'to her secrecy was the real absolution from guilt'. Both sisters are actually terrified of the same thing – participation in the outside world, the 'real' world. Harriet rationalises and distorts her fear, convincing herself that she dreads becoming a vagrant, a bum and descending to promiscuity. Sadie, 'an obsessive', is more direct. 'Sadie certainly yearned to live in the grown-up world' but 'she did not understand it properly'. Sadie travels to Camp Cataract. Harriet is unwelcoming but acknowledges their bond: 'Everything that goes on between us goes on undercover.' Nothing is as it seems at the camp. With difficulty Sadie persuades Harriet to meet her alone and talk. 'Let's you and me go out in the world,' Sadie proposes, but seeing Harriet's eyes near to her, 'the pupils pointed with a hatred,' Sadie 'knew then that this agony she was suffering was the dreaded voyage into the world'. Although even this supremely important moment proves illusory this does not invalidate Sadie's 'voyage' and its tragic aftermath.

This highly autobiographical story contains Jane's own fears – fear of madness, fear of her own imagination, fear of the outside world. Similarly her last story, 'A Stick of Green Candy', is also very personal. Sad and final, it concerns the death of her imagination. Mary, a young girl, likes to play in the clay pit where she commands a troop of imaginary soldiers: 'She could feel the men's hearts bursting with love for her.' Her father forbids her to play there and directs her to the park where all the other children play: 'They provide you with swings, see-saws and chin-bars.'

Repulsed by this, Mary returns to the pit where she meets a boy, Franklin, follows him home and realises that, inconsequentially, she has developed powerful feelings of love for him. But afterwards she is unable to find again 'the dark gulf' of imagination and cannot reanimate her soldiers. Thus Jane returns to the idea of her father and his devastating judgements, concluding that these in tandem with her emotional susceptibility to the world have wrecked her creativity.

In 1957, aged forty, Jane had a stroke which resulted in slight paralysis, partial blindness and some difficulty with speaking. One neurologist said 'if you were to best devise how to undermine the mind of a writer you couldn't think of a more effective means than this'.

Tangier gossip held that Cherifa had poisoned Jane, although her biographer thinks this unlikely, stressing that Jane was genetically predisposed to vascular illness and drank heavily while mixing medication. From then, until her death in 1978, Jane's life was a nightmare of neurological and psychiatric symptoms. She suffered increasingly from depression and deemed her life to have been 'a tragedy'. Without the diversions of youth, her terrors and phobias – which no longer seemed entertaining to others – overpowered her. Writing had always been dreadfully difficult but maturity and wider experience of people must have led her to despair of being able to represent a more complex vision in a medium as inherently unstable as language.

Jane Bowles' fiction was obviously written by someone who felt a powerful sense of unreality in life. Her attempts to combat this meant that in her work she was, as she put it, 'sucking at the bone (of my life)'. She experienced her fear of the world as a personal failure which induced guilt and shame. Her imagination seemed to stand between herself and the world, barring her from true participation. She once wrote: 'By suffering I mean living.' Considering how near she lived to depression, inertia and deadlock it is surprising that she managed to write at all, let alone to create work that has endured. Her own personality was extreme but, in that we all suffer and are afraid, we see our terrors reflected in Jane Bowles's work, mercifully coupled with a highly comic sense of the absurd which constitutes a sort of salvation.

Diamanda Galas at the Shepherd's Bush Empire

The Observer, 6 November 1994

Actually, nearly all my favourite writers are women – Jean Stafford, Flannery O'Connor, Alice Munro, Jean Rhys, Shena Mackay, Jane Gardam, Barbara Trapido and so on. I admire Diamanda Galas' arrogance in calling her book The Shit of God *(well, DOES He? I suppose not), but still really prefer her as a singer.*

It is Hallowe'en and all the werewolves of London are out tonight. The tribes are here, the lost, the damned, the beautiful, the bizarre, united as celebrants in the psychic assault course that is a concert by cult diva Diamanda Galas.

Galas trails a fearsome reputation behind her, like some newly-slaughtered animal. Famed in America as an avant-garde performer, poet, singer and musical terrorist, her recorded works include 'The Litanies of Satan' and 'Saint of the Pit'. Famously, during the eighties she concentrated on recording and performing her elegiac 'Plague Mass' – an anguished, excoriating requiem for the victims of AIDS.

Galas' voice is legendary. Classically trained, she can span over three octaves. Now, in what initially seems an improbable collaboration, she has recorded a new album. *The Sporting Life* with John Paul Jones, ex-Led Zeppelin bassist.

Jones has admired Galas since he heard her *Wild Women with Steak Knives* in 1982. Respected now as composer and producer, Jones has eclectic tastes, having worked recently with REM, The Butthole Surfers, Brian Eno and Raging Slab.

'Sporting life' is old American pimp slang for the street hustle of tricks, johns and whores. Galas' work has continually focused upon the brutal realities of dominance and submission that underlie our blood-flecked sexual arena. She is a Sadeian woman with all de Sade's bleak views of human nature. She is also Luciferian in the original sense of light-bringer, one who defies orthodoxy and authority. Denounced for blasphemy, she continues as a warrior, an obsessive. She developed her 'technique' she says, to 'ride the outer limits of the soul'. Her furious, terrifying performances weave together dementia, schizophrenia, stigma and pain, whilst straining for cathartic release. Her concerts have evolved into ritualistic, shamanic exorcisms. At the Empire her natural audience awaited.

It was a restless crowd, a club mix of proto-punks and hairdos from hell. Endangered species had endured; the multi-coloured Mohawk, tranvestite Goths with floor-length magenta dreadlocks. There were stilettos and sequins and mussed-up *kinderwhores* with Cleopatra eyes. There were the shaven and tattoed alongside the clean-flowing hair of the old air-guitar Led Zep freaks. There were the bondage beauties, fetishists and slaves. Peroxide dominatrixes were tight-lacing red silk bustiers in the flooded lavatories. There were chains and leather caps and full rubber bondage masks with their eerie facial zips and wet, red holes where the drinks went down. A man in a vampire cloak and hessian bondage hood with eight-inch steel spikes protruding from his necklet had space priority at the bar.

Galas was late. Finally – blue stage lights, teasing electronic whispers. And then the lady started, one note, one word that went on and on, sliding up and down the scale, longer than seemed believable. 'I . . .' she sang, interminably, impossibly, ear-piercingly loud and the silver spot went on and she's standing there, imperious, the self-styled 'she-wolf' in a tiny, skintight, crotch-skimming black slip, and the bass crashes in.

Well, you had to be there. Galas, Jones and Attractions drummer Pete Thomas went through the album but hearing Galas sing these 'homicidal love songs' live shifted it into the primordial dimension of the Furies. Jones contributed impeccable bass and lap steel guitar. Thomas's drumming managed to contain and control the need, shock, rage and emotional holocaust that poured out of Galas in a confrontational flood.

It is an awesome, incredible voice. She squeaks and gibbers and wails and sings *glossolalia* scat, shaking spasmodically like some voodoo adept. Suddenly she swoops right down to a batrachian croak, squatting in front of the audience, her witchy shock of black hair obscuring her face. Hollow-eyed, pearl-pale, she pounds her piano frenziedly or stalks the stage with the predatory authority of a dominatrix gone completely mad.

Highlights were 'Do You Take this Man?' – 'Husband, with this Knife/I do You Hold . . .' – and a heartbreaking rendition of the classic deep-soul ballad 'Dark End of the Street'. Jones and Thomas had contributed to many of the lyrics but Galas' own 'Baby's Insane' with its deranged, bluesy, country edge was particularly memorable.

The entire performance was so potent and visceral – indeed so shamanistic – that it generated involuntary physical reactions amongst the audience; one's bowels started to loosen, the gorge rose suddenly, unconsciously.

It all ended quite suddenly, like a clap of thunder as they finished 'Hex'. One encore and the bright lights came up, sending midnight's children tumbling out, back to the dark end of the street. Diamada Galas' performance was more than a triumph. She was overwhelming, unforgettable. People looked at each other with round, puzzled eyes, raised eyebrows. How DID she do it?

Alice Munro: *Open Secrets*

(Chatto & Windus)
The Guardian, 11 October 1994

Although there are many, many writers I like, some of them rather tepidly, there are a few, a very few that I WORSHIP. One of these writers is Alice Munro; Flannery O'Connor and Jean Stafford are two others. By 'worship' I mean that I can read them again and again and always learn something new. By comparison with Munro, fellow Canadians Carol Shields and Margaret Atwood are mere hod-carriers of the alphabet. Munro's Selected Stories *published not long after* Open Secrets *is probably the best general introduction to her impeccable prose.*

Books don't last long nowadays. My old Alice Munro books are all held together with gaffer tape and Pritt. Someone who appears to write with such effortless fluidity needs to be read and re-read. Her first book to be be published here, *The Beggar Maid* (1980), was shortlisted for the Booker. It has become commonplace nowadays to praise Munro immoderately and marvel at her abilities. Some samples: 'A writer of extraordinary richness and texture'; 'brilliance and depth . . . almost Proustian in its sure-ness'; 'These are sparely written, richly resonant pieces'; 'shining clarity'; 'honest and lovely'. On and on they go, a swelling critical consensus that proclaims her excellence. But what does it all mean? There is something almost complacent in these rich, gen-erous, conventional assurances of her superiority. They seem to contain an undertone that whispers '*Such* a fine writer. A person of any discernment will perceive this. If not – (shrug) – go back to your game shows.'

One of Munro's many talents is that she makes no such dis-tinctions. Any life, however humble, narrow and provincial, is potentially of interest to her. She writes in *Open Secrets* of lives 'long and complicated and strange and dull'. Munro's writing itself does not produce some sort of non-specific radiance. As with most distinctive writers there is a territory, a locale that she has made her own. This is rural Ontario. Much of her best work is set in the 1930s, 40s and 50s, a time that now seems so distant it is 'as if an entirely different lighting had been used'. For example, 'In those days it seemed to be the thing for women's bodies to swell and ripen to a good size twenty if they were getting anything out of life at all . . . girded into shapes whose firm curves and proud slopes had nothing to do with sex, everything to do with rights and power', she wrote in *The Moons of Jupiter*.

Another of Munro's virtues is her very acute sense of the vio-lence of the post-war social revolution, the sixties monster whose tentacles went on quivering and twitching in rural pockets of the west for decades. In *Friend Of My Youth* she says 'It seemed that all sorts of marriages begun in the fifties without misgivings . . . blew up in the early seventies, with a lot of spectacular – and, it seems now, unnecessary, extravagant – complications.' Munro can set a story in 1852 or 1992 with equal facility but in *Open Secrets* she dwells largely on the decorous decades in Canadian rural history that she has made so memorably her own. 'Nobody has a good word to say nowadays for such narrowness and proud caution and threadbare decency. I don't myself . . .' she wrote earlier but she is drawn repeatedly, wonderingly, to a time when values and conventions were accepted innocently and without irony.

Munro writes about people. Naturally the territory is limitless – love, death, disease, insanity, friendship, age, chance, change. But in common with other compelling, timeless authors she has certain central themes running through her work. The most persistent of these is her exploration of shame. Shame, humiliation, mortification, embarrassment. Aligned to these are self-deception, pride, craven impulses, slyness, hypocrisy, malice, the strategies of deceit. No-one else has traced with such terrifying accuracy the way in which these emotions and impulses work within us. And indeed how their ripples, like ink in milk, stain our sexual lives, our friendships and relationships. She focuses tightly on what we choose to reveal to others, what we would prefer to conceal and the inadvertent chasms between the two that leave us psychically naked.

In *The Beggar Maid*, the heroine, Rose, detects in her father 'some objection to Flo's rhetoric, some embarrassment and reluctance'. With Rose herself, 'all her need for flaunting, her high hopes for herself, her gaudy ambition, were not hidden from him'. Rose's stepmother Flo also despises Rose's inclinations: 'It was love she sickened at. It was the enslavement, the self-abasement, the self-deception.' Rose approaches sex fearfully: 'It was pitiful, infantile, this itching and shoving and squeezing. Spongy tissues, inflamed membranes, tormented nerve-ends, shameful smells; humiliation' and 'She was terrified that they would not manage it, that there was a great humiliation in store, a great exposure of their poor deceits and stratagems.' Class, too, can be part of this shame. Rose is from the small-town background that is Munro's speciality. Meeting someone similar, Rose thinks she perceives only 'the weariness, suppleness, deviousness, meanness, common to a class'.

Munro continues all these themes in later books. In the story, 'The Progress of Love', the narrator writes of her mother: 'It seemed as if she knew something about me that was worse, far worse, than ordinary lies and tricks and meanness; it was a really sickening shame.' One story, 'The Turkey Season', is a study of shame – amongst other things. Munro is far too subtle to over-emphasise this dark artery that tendrils through the body of her work. But it continues, her agonising ability to look into our most tender, secret and vulnerable parts and to dissect them without judgement. Now, in her new book of stories, it is still there. A teenage girl wonders whether 'there was a sense of contempt being held in check' as she tries to understand a possible boyfriend. She knows too that 'You cannot let your parents any-where near your real humiliations.'

Open Secrets is Munro's strongest, most powerful collection to date, certainly the best since the incomparable *The Progress Of Love*. She concentrates on two very small Ontario towns, Carstairs and Walley, ranging from the early days of the first settlers up to the present. She has tightened her grip on language. She could always reproduce the nuances and insinuations of small-town conversation in dialogue. Here is a mother talking of a local homosexual: 'Then she said, "Poor Poppy. There were always those that were out to get him. He was very smart, in his way. Some people can't survive in a place like this. It's not permitted. No." '

Now this rhythm and its unspoken 'fog of platitudes and pieties' is incorporated directly into her text. 'A man came along and fell in love with Dorrie Beck. At least, he wanted to marry her. It was true. "If her brother was alive, she would never have needed to get married," Millicent said. What did she mean? Not some-thing shameful.'

All Munro's glorious, unpretentious talents are brought together in these beautifully crafted stories. She never underesti-mates people. Long ago she wrote 'I no longer believe that peo-ple's secrets are defined and communicable, or their feelings full-blown and easy to recognize.' She abides by this commitment to unpatronising complexity and ambiguity. Emotionally, as a writer, she has perfect pitch. The title story is so clever, so subtle, so *terrible* – the unsolved disappearance of a teenager from Carstairs in 1965 – that one's understanding of it, one's realisa-tion of the murderer's identity goes off suddenly like a depth-charge in the mind, hours later. Can that really be what she meant? One re-reads it. She did. Yes.

Bret Easton Ellis: *American Psycho*

(Picador)
City Limits, 1991

We are in Trouble Town now. I reviewed Bret Easton Ellis' notorious novel on its first publication in 1991 when the entire western world seemed to be fussing and fighting about Ellis' allegedly repellent, misogynistic and cannibalistic meisterwerk. *However, as I reviewed it for* City Limits, *a small London-based listings magazine, now defunct, naturally no-one took any notice at all of what I said. That didn't bother me so much as the ongoing misapprehensions about the book. I don't think many people, even the critics, actually read the book and if they did it was certainly in a cursory fashion. The delusion that the novel's protagonist Patrick Bateman is a fully paid-up multiple murderer and devourer of human brains has sunk deep into the popular mind.*

In fact, Bateman is a wholly unreliable narrator and for every murder he claims to commit there is a viable alternative scenario. The mass misreading of American Psycho *preyed on my mind so much that I have been banging on about it for nearly a decade and even devoted a lengthy book chapter to a full deconstruction of the novel.*

Bret Easton Ellis indicated, through third parties, that he did not find my criticism unacceptable, so I must have been roughly on the right track. I had the opportunity to meet him a couple of times but bottled out. I really admire (most of) his work.

If ever literary critics were needed to swoop in like Caped Crusaders and calm the populace with textual exposition it is now with *American Psycho* finally quivering on the stands. But who will listen? Fussing and fighting are far more fun. Ellis is not, judging from his interviews, about to help – and why should he? He has written an extremely careful and coherent book.

From the first line 'ABANDON HOPE ALL YE WHO ENTER HERE', to the last, 'THIS IS NOT AN EXIT', Ellis defiantly defines his territory. We are in hell. 'Guys – my life is a living hell,' our protagonist Patrick Bateman moans to his fellow NY yuppies but they never hear. They just chitter on – *GQ* and sorbets, foreclosure, ricotta cheesecake, Armani, Ferragamo, Larizzi – an icy blizzard of brand-names and snobbery, greed and trivia. The books acts like a stun-gun; a marathon tickertape of materialist monotony and status frenzy. Ellis is describing a society in the process of pulling itself apart like one of sculptor Jean Tinguely's self-destructing machines. He is defining a sensory overload that affects us all. Bateman's agonised cry in the video store, 'There are just too many fucking movies to choose from', is a universal. MTV, Hitachi, gravlax, aerobics, AIDS, CDs, PLAX, television that gives equal weight to homeless schizophrenics and coke bimbos – our affect is bludgeoned, flattened and finally obliterated. Form and content have rarely been so totally integrated.

So Bateman, terminally yupped-out, yelps along with the rest of his Wall Street pack, running on empty from gym to club to restaurant. The evil of banality. *In partibus infidelium*: these people are ignorant, fanatical, pitiable. Ellis surveys them with a savagely witty, puritanical eye. Patrick is disintegrating; repetitions and slip-ups begin to occur in his ghastly, obsessive monologue. He also claims to kill people, arbitrarily, sadistically. However, on at least three quite specific occasions, we are forced to question his version of events. This raises interesting textual issues. Whether or not the murders actually occurred, the effect on the reader is the same. Patrick describes murder like everything else in blank tortuous detail, reflecting a society incapable of meaningful distinctions and consequently grotesquely needful of hyper-stimulation . . .

Posters from *Les Misérables* litter the town, forcing the contrast between Hugo's spirited starvelings and Ellis' *misérables*, stuffed with esoteric foods but so spiritually bereft that they lack the means to apprehend their condition. Like Scott Fitzgerald, Ellis takes a risk in trying to capture the spirit of a decade. Will the book endure? Brand-names date before the ink is dry but this very fact underscores Ellis' hellish vision of the unappeasable hungers that drive us and our ever more extreme, tormenting desires, designed never to be sated.

Paradoxically, the very act of portraying the emotional

affectlessness that permeates the book indicates vast, outraged affect. In literary terms the book is outstanding as a portrait, an indictment of the anorexic soul of the eighties. It demands that we attempt moral redefinition.

Bret Easton Ellis: *The Informers*

(Picador)
The Guardian, 18 October 1994

Did you know that Los Angeles is full of vampires? Nowadays, Ellis suggests, they might have a customised coffin with 'FM radio, tape cassette, digital alarm clock, Perry Ellis sheets, phone, small color TV with built-in VCR and cable (MTV, HBO)'. Is the notion of vampires in Hollywood an original one? No. Is it a tacky idea? Yes. Is it meant to be funny? Only up to a point.

Reading Bret Easton Ellis' new novel the words from an old Velvet Underground song keep wandering through my mind. 'Here we go again/Acting hard again . . .' And here we go again, back in Ellis' favourite moral abyss, the heaven-into-hell that is contemporary California and was the setting for his first novel *Less than Zero*. This time there are fewer teenagers around, some of the characters have kids themselves but they are all still the same non-people, blonde, bland, tan, rich, jaded and stupefied on downers. In each chapter a different voice – male or female – drones on nihilistically about their Nembutal, their shrinks, their hair colour, or the dead rats in their swimming pools. *Plus ça change* . . .

This is White Zombie country. 'You were never there,' says one character, 'you were never alive.' 'What was I then?' he asks. 'You were just . . . not dead.' These are the walking dead, the hollow men, those without souls. Ellis signals this conspicuously by quoting from T. S. Eliot and by having some of his blanked-out cast watch Romero's classic zombie films, *Night of the Living Dead* and *Dawn of the Dead*. Further similarities to *Less than Zero* are heavily underscored. The same sign 'Disappear Here' looms over

Sunset Boulevard. This novel also moves gradually away from the totally trite and superficial deeper and deeper into gothic horror until finally Beverley Hills is alive with the sounds of paedophile butt-fucking, bodily mutilation and the ripping of arteries as the cool neighbourhood vampires join in a feeding frenzy.

Suppose you were a young writer appalled at the materialism and moral nullity of Californian culture and you wrote a small classic called *Less than Zero*. The rot is nationwide and you extend these concerns to the East Coast in a subsequent book. Then you write your masterpiece, *American Psycho*, an agonised shriek set in eighties New York, a book that spells out in giant neon letters the inescapable fact that we have substituted fashion for ethics, lifestyles for lives; that our twenty centuries of stony sleep have brought us no greater wisdom than that money is everything. What do you do next?

The Informers is an intensely oppressive and listless book. At the same time it gives the impression of being a sort of security blanket. It traces known and undemanding territory. These sensations are not contradictory. They suggest a profound authorial depression.

Even at their weakest Ellis's books have the ability to capture modern reality with the ferocity of a collector driving a pin through a social butterfly: 'Danny is on my bed and depressed because Ricky was picked up by a break-dancer at the Odyssey on the night of the Duran Duran lookalike contest. And murdered.' In addition there are always moments of acute poignancy and insight. A rock star is aware of 'a boredom so monumental it humbles'. A female newsreader is tentatively flattered when a gang of post-punks ask for her autograph, although it is wincingly clear that they are mocking the very concept of autographs. And one chapter 'Letters From LA' is a beautifully balanced, carefully judged précis of all Ellis' themes in the book; a girl student from Ellis' fictitious Eastern college, Camden, goes to stay in LA. Eventually she decides not to return. The letters chart her moral deterioration and decay. At the beginning she is writing 'Dear Shaun . . . I keep feeling that people are becoming less human and more animalistic. They seem to think less and feel less so that everything is operating on a very primitive level.' Within a few months it is 'Dear Shaun . . . no one has seen Carlos for weeks.

Last I heard he was in Vegas, though someone else told me that they found both of his arms in a bag off La Brea. He was going to write the screenplay for me. My grandmother . . . said it was commercial.' This is the Ellis who wrote so hauntingly in *Less than Zero* of 'parents who were so hungry and unfulfilled that they ate their own children'.

This book is a profoundly sad, empty rerun of *Less than Zero*, without hope, without progression and demeaned by its desperate splatter effects. Less than less than zero. It redefines Ellis' central dilemma – how to portray the trite and morally worthless without merely mirroring it and driving the reader to head-banging despair. It is uncertain whether Ellis actually lacks the ability to portray character and has merely turned this to his advantage for the purpose of portraying people as interchangeable clones. But over the long term, clones and zombies lack a certain something as literary companions. Ellis often gives the impression of being appalled, saddened, judgmental but very rarely does he exhibit empathy. As an author he is a closed system. His talent has proved itself both narrow and deep – rather like a coffin. And now, as in Poe's *The Premature Burial*, he may knock and knock but whether this talent can be released to thrive is anyone's guess.

On *Glamorama* by Bret Easton Ellis

The Guardian, 16 January 1999

Glamorama was barely out of the Jiffy bag before it became apparent that the first section of the novel was a sort of idiot's guide to *American Psycho*. HarperCollins intend to republish Ellis', previous novel, the infamous *American Psycho* in an expensive, deluxe edition. It is unsurprising that Ellis should wish to clarify what he was actually doing in that book. Rarely, if ever, has a serious novel been so totally misread, misunderstood and vilified on its initial publication.

It is unfortunate that Ellis has been linked again to his brat pack writing peer Jay McInerney recently. Although both *Glamorama* and McInerney's novel *Model Behavior* are concerned with models and fashion, the two authors are wholly unalike. McInerney espouses a fairly traditional, linear narrative structure. Ellis deconstructs narrative. McInerney is interested in personality, Ellis in the dissolution of personality. McInerney relies on the reader's conventional suspension of disbelief in presenting his characters, their psychology and their relationships. Character is a meaningless construct in Ellis' work. Although both authors are obsessed with style and *Zeitgeist*, McInerney provides a non-judgmental social commentary whereas Ellis is a diehard moralist.

In short, Ellis's focus is the primacy of text and the nature of fiction itself. He operates within a clear literary context – that of the American postmodern novel, complete with all the irony, paradox, lack of closure and refusal to mirror 'reality' that this implies, together with a constant examination of the way in which fiction itself is constructed.

All this was completely lost on the original UK critics of *American Psycho* who insisted upon reading it as though it were a work of realism or naturalism. The longest section of *Glamorama* is a mini-*American Psycho* without the murders, thus forcing the dimmest of readers to forgo self-righteous outrage and concentrate. Both novels are written in prose that superficially apes the most trivial, glossy, celebrity-spotting magazine style – the sort of endless supercharged ad-speak that is usually skimmed through. Paradoxically this style mag style demands very close reading in both novels.

Glamorama both mimics and deviates from its predecessor in ways that bear examination. For anyone still unfamiliar with *American Psycho*, it was a bitter, witty satire on eighties New York and the hysterical pursuit of money, status and designer commodities that characterised the decade. The book's narrator, Everyuppie Patrick Bateman, is so awesomely unreliable that the fact that anyone took him seriously stands as a monumental tribute to careless reading. Even very briefly – early on, Patrick claims to have seen Bigfoot interviewed on television, also a piece of cereal which sat in a very small chair throughout the interview. By the end he's laughing at nothing and flossing his teeth constantly, sleeping underneath his futon, his ATM is speaking to him and he notices that 'a park bench followed me for six blocks last Monday evening'. The novel is replete with inconsistencies, ambiguities and discrepancies. Patrick's account of events invariably conflicts with what others say. Patrick also claims to murder thirty-three people during the book, describing these atrocities in excruciating detail. This makes him an impossibility – someone who is both a serial sex-killer and a mass murderer, who democratically kills across all lines of race, class, sex and gender.

(The point being that, whether Patrick 'really' kills anyone or is fantasising, the effect on the reader, fictionally, is exactly the same in descriptive terms.) There is always a rational alternative to his most outlandish claims. At one point Patrick allegedly rages through Manhattan, killing a busker, a cab-driver and some cops. He flees to his office chased by a helicopter, a SWAT team, police-cars, ambulances and armed men. Shortly afterwards he is back in bed, quite normally, with a girlfriend. And this is the novel an eminent UK critic called 'a work of Zola-esque naturalism' . . .

Ultimately Patrick fragments into different voices and disintegrates – he is no more than a sign, a cipher and is reconsigned to the start of the book, the whole being structured as a circle of hell.

Ellis said that his real interest in *American Psycho* was 'in the language, the structure and the details'. The same undoubtedly goes for *Glamorama*, in many ways a very similar text. Again Ellis provides a vignette of wealthy Manhattan life – but it is now the nineties so the minutely described designer clothing has changed (now Jil Sander, Hilfiger, Prada), as has interior decor. AIDS is considered *passé*, girls wear dresses 'the color of crayons', carry straw bags and wear lipstick with names like 'Frostbite, Asphyxia, Bruise'. They drink Diet Melonberry Snapple, hazelnut decaff iced latte. They light citrus-scented votive candles, smoke heroin and chat about 'the new Siberian-Eskimo supermodel . . . "aggressive" hairdos . . . tattooing babies . . . Klonopin and Xanax . . . stalking, Japanese magazines . . . technobeat, moonscapes, Semtex, nirvana, alien abductions . . . people who've signed suicide notes with smiley faces . . . Nokia cell phones, Nars lip gloss, portable digital recorders.'

Our narrator is 'model slash actor' Victor Ward, fashionable 'It Boy of the Moment' who 'gets written about . . . for doing nothing'. Victor is elusive. His name is assumed. His age oscillates between twenty-seven and twenty-eight. He is not really certain of his sexual orientation despite his affair with supermodel Chloe.

He can't recall any of the girls he's had affairs with. This is the world of the instant celebrity, the photo opportunity, the rent-a-name, where actors and models and directors and artists and rock stars and DJs and make-up people and designers and photographers are all preening and pushing and panicking in the revolving lottery of cool – as one of them notes, describing the status cycle: 'Nobody, up-and-comer, star, has-been. Not necessarily in that order.' The world of Tara and Kate and Liam and Quentin and Naomi and Johnny Depp and Diandra Douglas and . . .

At the start of the novel Victor is preparing for a club opening and his alphabetised guest-list induces intense stress. In *American Psycho* there are too many things. Here, there are too many people. Both are commodities with built-in obsolescence. When Patrick Bateman goes crazy in the video shop and screams 'There are too many fucking movies to choose from', he defines the sensory overload that afflicts us all. This non-stop blizzard of infotainment and semi-demi-famous names is the empty heart of Victor's world.

Victor's narrative, like Patrick Bateman's before him, contains numberless discrepancies and inconsistencies, but this time they are positively bellowed out and emphasised so heavily that not even the dimmest reader could miss them. Victor denies being at the Calvin Klein show, at the Alfari show, or in Miami, or at the party for Jarvis Cocker despite the captioned photographs and the recollections of others. He says he didn't send Chloe the flowers that turn up. In Indochine, Victor claims to see a girlfriend at a table 'where she's on her Nokia 232 cell phone to Nan Kempner and eating cake with Peter Gabriel, David LaChapelle, Janeane Garofalo and David Koresh, all of them discussing . . . the new monkey virus.'

This accentuation of Victor's derangement means that, unlike Patrick Bateman, he emerges not so much a subtly unreliable narrator as a complete moron. After being accused of harbouring murderous misogynist fantasies, post-*American Psycho*, Ellis has taken care to distance himself very considerably from Victor. Victor's intellect is micro-lite anyway – he's never heard of Susan Sontag. He doesn't know what 'eviscerate' means; Notting Hill is 'Nothing Hill' (or is that just a joke?!) – although he allegedly attended Camden College, this being but one of many references to Ellis' previous books. Victor's conversation seems like brain-damaged bricolage: he speaks in tag-lines, pop lyrics – 'What's new, pussy-cat?' – fragments from movies and adverts. But, inevitably, even these wisps of language reward scrutiny. Victor's catch-phrase 'What's the story, morning glory?' is central. What *is* the story?

The text is carefully divided into six ever-shortening sections, each one set in a different city. A 'plot' is grafted on to Victor's New York life and he is sent to London to find an ex-girlfriend/actress who has vanished. At this point Victor starts presenting events as if he were in a movie, referring distractedly to scripts and directors. From thenceforth it is impossible to trace what is film – if anything – and what is Victor's 'life'. This plot device links again, in bold, Victor's inability to differentiate between fact and fantasy. And ultimately, in terms of literary theory, the issue is redundant, because this is a novel anyway. An ensuing fiasco of bombs, terrorism, torture-murder and snuff movies culminates with a sanguinary aeroplane explosion, after which Victor, rather like Patrick Bateman after his climactic murder spree and SWAT chase, is suddenly restored to his normal name-dropping life as at the start of the book.

Victor's immaturity and other thematic references recall Ellis' debut novel *Less than Zero*. Such elements, plus the amplified literary devices of *American Psycho*, do not quite cohere. His themes remain the same – the affectlessness and boredom of the privileged, the consumer carnival, the role of 'truth' and 'lies' in fiction. But his (very understandable) contempt for his readers and critics and the resulting attempt to underline his purpose often push Victor into apparent imbecility. This obscures much of the delicacy, intelligence and wit that still characterises Ellis's work. No-one has a better eye for the telling detail or stylistic clue, as is clear in the classic *American Psycho* which will eventually achieve the recognition it deserves. Meanwhile, the fashion field as in *Glamorama* is already so parodic that it resists satire, although this could have been a great novel about the proliferation of semi-celebrity. At times it is.

Dead Elvis: A chronicle of a cultural obsession by Greil Marcus

(Viking)
New Statesman, 28 June 1992

I have already felt sufficiently restless to include some non-fiction pieces so I think it would be salutary to proceed and vary the tone even further.

As they age, rock critics – who are usually intellectuals manqué *anyway – start to feel a bit . . . diffident, hanging around grizzled and balding at the back of the mosh pit. They then tend to either get out and write different things if they've got any sense, or become junkies, or more ominously, get too big for their cowboy boots and start to believe that their analyses of rock music are extremely significant, profound and perceptive, true cultural artefacts to be valued. US rock critics seem particularly vulnerable to this sense of humour leakage and I'm afraid the man Charles Shaar Murray calls 'The Holy Greil' must stand accused.*

Still, he can be readable. Elvis may have left the building but he is still God so no-one is going to go far wrong writing about him.

'Elvis paid ten million dollars to a California genetics institute to have himself cloned. The year after his death the clone escaped and is now on the loose, somewhere in Los Angeles.' 'When Elvis Presley, in the song "Jailhouse Rock" sang "If you can't find a partner grab a wooden chair" he freed a whole generation of young people to love furniture.' An ordinary day's reading can easily turn up two such – averagely weird, jokey – references to Presley so how much more can Greil Marcus do in a book devoted to all the posthumous ephemera of the Presley cargo cult? *Dead Elvis* is a hurricane of 'songs, art works, books, movies, dreams' whirling around the ever-mutating icon at the centre: it's a cow-licked country kid with bruised eyes and an orgasmic judder, it's a fat freak encrusted with rhinestones, sweating drug soup under the spotlights, it's the Twentieth Century Boy, it's a rotting corpse, it's the Second Coming and (listen to the loss) it's a voice like toffee, like manna, like heartbreak.

Here is some of what Marcus turns up in his book-shaped collage. Elvis was a Voodoo Sex Zombie. Elvis killed Laura Palmer. An Elvis statue was found on Mars. Elvis was a half-caste. You can see 'Elvis: The autopsy' on bootleg video. Elvis was a supernatural being. Elvis was just a big, dumb hillbilly. There is a radio show called 'Breakfast with Elvis'; every morning listeners call in with appropriate menus (Moon Pies with crushed Alka-Seltzer. Chow down, Elvis!) Elvis is 'channeled' almost every day at the Berkeley Psychic Centre. Elvis is Moby Dick. There are many shrines to Elvis. Elvis unconsciously expressed the raw sexual power of the pantheistic *loa* gods from Haitian voodoo ('Hear that Long Snake Moan'). Many people have necrophilic fantasies about Elvis. After his death Elvis's body was minced down and turned into Presleyburgers at $1000 each. The hamburger is very important in Presley hagiography. Elvis-think goes like this: hamburgers are quintessentially American. So was Elvis. Elvis loved hamburgers. Elvis was Jesus. The burger is round, like the Host. The hamburger epitomises the many in the one and the one in the many – just like Elvis, just like the Holy Ghost. Elvis is a burger. America is Saved!

And so it all goes on – sightings, in-fightings, emanations, visions, dementia, art. The skeins of Elvis-hood are everywhere. We are all haunted by Elvis. 'He walks our hills in a long black veil,' mourns Marcus, lyrically. This is, as Marcus points out, a book of many voices. There is only the author's succinct commentary for narration. Marcus claims that beneath all these myriad manifestations of Elvis in our culture is 'bedrock, obsession, delight, fear'. He is interested in the way all this functions, finally . . . beyond irony. People really care. They want to know – did Elvis go to Heaven or to Hell? Was it Graceland or disgraceland? What rough beast was born in Tupelo in 1935? There is real mystery here, real emotion. Blasphemy has become unavoidable. 'He went walking on the water/with his pills' goes one tribute. Elvis was wholly mediatised, intimately, uniquely accessible to billions and yet he remains tormentingly elusive. How can one apprehend this 'anarchy of possibilities' through a culture Elvis himself created?

Marcus is aware that in collating all this bizarrerie he is documenting a 'great common art project', something which by its very nature is indicative of that democratisation of artistic process that Marcus admired in punk.

In juxtaposing academia, fiction, faction and fandom Marcus shows how Elvis moves – in mysterious ways – within the universal unconscious. He succeeds in revealing more about Elvis and on a more profound level than might ever have seemed possible, considering the mountains of schlock associated with the King. Elvis has left the building – but the joint keeps right on jumping.

Venom

Anyway, back to literature – inevitably – and time for some vitriol. Despite all the good things feminism has achieved it has also produced some horribly twee female authors, predominantly North American. They are the Pollyannas of political correctness and I hate them.

Their 'Inner Child' indeed. I'm still trying to find my Inner Adult.

Here are three such of the worst offenders. I am somewhat bewildered by their inane popularity. When it comes to easy readability (and it often does with me) I still prefer bright, prickly Cosmo *girls like Jacqueline Susann, Jeannie Sakol, Judith Rossner et al.*

Turtle Moon by Alice Hoffman
The Guardian, 6 August 1992

Thirteen divorced women live in the apartments at 27, Long Boat Street in the steamy little Florida town of Verity. They have washed up there on tides of emotional turmoil and now lie out by the pool, drinking Diet Dr Pepper and fretting about child support. One of their number is Lucy, a beautiful depressive, her hair tinted green from the chlorine. Her son Keith is a twelve-year-old delinquent, invariably referred to as 'the meanest boy in Verity'. One day a neighbour is murdered. Keith is both witness and suspect. He panics, scoops up the victim's baby and runs for the swamps. He is tracked by the police dog-handler, saturnine Julian Cash. Lucy decides to clear her son's name and the scene is set for rapture and ruin.

Verity is such a lush, throbbing place that it might be the nation's G-spot. Hoffman's lubricious prose pumps up the volume on the heat and languor: the air, scented with lemons and seaweed is 'thick as soup', turquoise and jade parakeets scream amongst the gumbo-limbo trees, over-ripe figs drop constantly, wind-chimes tinkle 'like stars falling' and baby alligators swoon in the sun.

At her best Hoffman has something of Truman Capote's ability to evoke the doom and decay of the South but her style lacks any of the perverse depths and intricacies of Southern Gothic. What she delivers instead, underneath the adjectival incontinence, is a set of romantic conventions, adroitly updated into New Age schlock. Some of these are: divorce wrecks children's lives. Mysterious ugly-attractive men are irresistible. Mother love is all-powerful. Telling lies is wrong. Bad boys respond to tough love. And so on in a relentlessly heartwarming excess of cutesy sentiment. Hoffman describes how in May the turtles of the town would migrate, mistaking the glow of the street-lamps for the light of the moon. In naming the novel for this misapprehension Hoffman evidently wishes to illuminate some aspect of truth and illusion in Verity: nevertheless, what is produced is never more than truism.

Hoffman's imagery can be ravishingly pretty but, overall, the writing veers feverishly between a torrid lyricism and sketchy Hollywood plot conventions. She is at times both patronising and corny in the most winsome filmic manner. Cold-hearted Julian the dog-handler sure knows how to deal with Keith, 'the meanest boy in Verity', when he catches him. 'I've got your number,' he says and 'Have a goddamned cigarette' and other manly stuff. Julian *understands*. He was once a hurting, hostile little boy himself. And gee, Keith is all heart really. He loves animals and babies. We reach a most conventional climax – a knife at Keith's throat and rescue by a fierce dog he has somehow tamed, a very noble beast.

This is TV soft soap for people who prefer books. Unfortunately it is not just trash but sensitive and intelligent trash designed for those who feel themselves to be a bit poetic and deep but would probably have little love for the horrors and conflicts of most contemporary literature. *Turtle Moon* is both sophisticated and safe. It is also peopled by remarkably decorous characters: Lucy is 'completely shocked' by public mention of a blow job. These are inconsequential characters, self-serving moralists already more than half-way towards their Hollywood consummation: aching mother, wayward son, tough but sensitive cop. Anguish, suspense and a picturesque backdrop of Spanish moss.

When reaching for the ineffable, Hoffman employs a suburban magic realism which has local ghosts hanging around the Donut Shop. In writing about sex, she deftly combines tenderness and sensuality. Altogether, her interweaving of the passionate and the precious creates what is women's magazine writing of a very high order – and that is not to imply any more contempt for women writers and readers than is already inherent in the existence of the genre. Hoffman creates an illusion of high seriousness which manipulates the readers as if they themselves were turtles by lamplight.

Hoffman has never flinched from contentious issues in her books and it is a pity that her undoubted talent is undercut by the simpering, predictable attitudes of her work. She effortlessly achieves the sort of awesome tweeness that can afflict certain bright, imaginative American women writers. It is a style that speaks of privilege, self-absorption, high-school success and self-conscious artistry. The work of Ellen Gilchrist, although more subtle, is not dissimilar.

Turtle Moon is a novel that will shamelessly tell you the star sign of one of its characters. It is a novel for those who dot their i's with flowers, who communicate by greeting-card, who believe in past lives, speak in bumper-sticker slogans and cherish their inner child. It is far closer to *The Prince of Tides* than to any real tides in the affairs of men. Or women.

Pigs in Heaven by Barbara Kingsolver

(Faber & Faber)
The Guardian, 23 November 1993

Barbara Kingsolver writes feel-good fables for the politically correct. She does so with great charm and pathos and perhaps it takes a heart of stone not to join her army of adoring fans. The novel that made her famous and to which *Pigs In Heaven* is a sequel was *The Bean Trees*, published in 1990.

The Bean Trees told the story of plucky, gritty Taylor Greer who leaves her home in rural Kentucky in order to avoid becoming pregnant like all her contemporaries. A few miles down the road she is handed a baby in a car park and selflessly discards her resolutions. The child turns out to be a three-year-old Native American who has been physically and sexually abused. This allows Taylor to fight injustice in a number of topical ways. She calls the baby Turtle and eventually, acting like a postmodern Pollyanna all down the line, Taylor contrives an illegal adoption. Even this slight naughtiness is muted. Taylor helps to rescue a couple of Guatemalan political refugees along the way, and in gratitude, they agree to pose as Turtle's natural parents. It is all indescribably cute and wholesome.

Pigs In Heaven opens three years later when Turtle is six. Taylor has acquired an improbably loving and wonderful boyfriend called Jax. The book kicks off when Turtle (already Doing Good like her mom) rescues a retarded man who has fallen off the Hoover Dam. Subsequently, when Taylor and Turtle appear on television, they are observed by a steely young Native American lawyer, Annawake Fourkiller. She notes that Turtle, like herself, is Cherokee and knows that her adoption must have been illegal. Under the Indian Child Welfare Act, tribes now have the final say over custody of their children. Fourkiller contacts Taylor, insisting that Turtle needs her Cherokee heritage. Terrified, Taylor grabs the child and flees to Seattle, where they struggle with urban poverty and Taylor does things like drive a bus for blind people and go on dates with physically-challenged men.

For once, Kingsolver has raised a serious and significant point – the issue of whether children from other races should be adopted by white parents and risk losing their cultural background. However, rather than confronting this matter in any depth, Kingsolver chooses to resolve it with a preposterous combination of coincidence and sentiment. Taylor's mother, Alice Greer, goes off to see a cousin who married into the Cherokee Nation and lives in the same community as Fourkiller. Alice meets and eventually agrees to marry a very suitable Indian widower, Cash Stillwater, who turns out to be . . . none other than Turtle's grandfather! Thus, although Cash is awarded guardianship of Turtle, he and Taylor will have joint custody and Turtle will end up spending so many months a year with someone she already knows as her grandmother. Taylor meanwhile has nobly caved in, asserting that love is not enough and that Turtle needs her relatives – even though, just for good measure, the Greers have discovered a full-blooded Indian ancestor and are allowed to enrol as Cherokees themselves. At this point one expects all the characters to burst into a rousing chorus of 'Life is just a great big melting pot'. To render the whole scenario even more saccharine, Taylor decides to marry Jax who has been sighing romantically back in Arizona and saying things like 'Can you believe God made a woman like that?' Frankly, no.

Kingsolver makes some mild attempts at realism – allowing Jax to sleep with another woman and suggesting that there might be a spot of poverty amongst the Cherokees. These are temporary. Much of the book is devoted to pious accounts of the Trail of Tears and Alice's idyllic experiences of stomp dances, hog fries and Indian wisdom. Life amongst the Cherokees is impossibly utopian – Alice is startled by 'adolescent boys being polite' and 'demonstrating love'. Much is made of the Indian love of children and the virtues of the hugely extended family. Naturally it wasn't a Cherokee that abused Turtle but a nasty white boyfriend of Cash's daughter.

This is a fairy tale. A beautiful mother and child are menaced by a big ole monster who turns out to have a heart of gold. Everyone gets married and lives happily ever after. Well, as Hemingway cynically said: 'Isn't it pretty to think so?'

Kingsolver has considerable abilities as a writer – she is vivid, animated and amusing – but her reliance on sophisticated schlock and easy answers cannot hope to bear the weight of the very real tragedies of Native American history nor convey the complexities of contemporary Native American identity. Fiction of this sort encodes a certain set of stock, bromidic attitudes regarding race and sex and encourages automatic responses. As such, it belongs to idealistic feminist therapy rather than to literature which is supposed to illuminate human behaviour. The persistent emphasis on worthy conduct is not even helpful in feminist terms. The male characters are relatively slight and the onus for high-minded moral action lies firmly with the women which, after all, is where it's always been.

The Magician's Assistant by Ann Patchett

(Fourth Estate)
Commissioned by *The Guardian*, 1998, unpublished

It is difficult to warm to a novel in which the main characters are called Parsifal and Sabine. As it turns out, there is not enough rough magic in the book for it to be irritating. Reading it is more akin to being force-fed artificial sweetener.

Sabine is a fabulously beautiful, rich, forty-something whose husband Parsifal has just died suddenly. Magician by profession, gay by nature, he had been much loved. Mourning their long, chaste relationship and her job as his assistant, Sabine is shocked to find that Parsifal was not, as she believed, an orphan. In fact, he was one Guy Fetters from Alliance, Nebraska, where his mother, two sisters and two nephews still dwell.

In search of Parsifal's past, Sabine leaves her beloved Los Angeles. She leaves her mansion of 'creamy stucco swirled like frosting', her turquoise pool, her improbably doting parents and her sad memories of Parsifal's lover, now dead of AIDS, and she heads for doleful Nebraska. There she discovers the pitiful, dark secrets of Parsifal's youth and, acting as a sort of kindly fairy godmother, transforms the fortunes of the forlorn Fetters family. In doing so she naturally finds herself, finds happiness and potentially sex, and is metaphorically promoted from magician's assistant to magician.

The theme of the novel is, inevitably, magic. 'Parsifal did not believe in magic. Everything was a trick.' There is that sort of magic – art – which is essentially hard work. Then there is the other sort: real magic, that is, real American magic – empowerment, dreams, forgiveness, reconciliation. The final insights of the book are stunningly trite (and probably true): 'Everyone has their problems'; 'Magic can seem like love' and so on. To be fair, the depressing cauldron of domestic abuse in Nebraska provokes some slightly grittier writing although a Happy Ending hovers ominously over it all. But most of the characters are so vapid and vacuous that it is impossible to suspend disbelief and care much about them. That the most memorable of them is a huge, Flemish rabbit (like the ones in 'Teletubbies'), retired from the magic act, proves the point.

Nevertheless, this is a nice, too nice book, bland and frothy as a competent restaurant soufflé and just about as slow. It is even affecting at times but not without pretension. Stylistically, it is an unhappy union of literary self-consciousness and narrative realism. There is some vague, uncertain sub-textual reference to Wagner. Although much less cloying than Alice Hoffman, and much less arid than Anne Tyler – both of whom Patchett has been compared to – it will probably appeal greatly to fans of these bafflingly popular writers. This is the kind of novel that keeps the world turning, that keeps publishers in business but is ultimately as mild, insipid and forgettable as, well – a soufflé, a daiquiri. It is a particularly feminine and American genre and should really have a name – Literature Lite, or Reduced Romance.

What's the story? – Edward Gorey

The Guardian, 18 December 1995

I would like to include something that documented a real coup. Edward Gorey had long been one of my favourite artist/illustrators and I had managed to collect almost all his published work. He has never had any sort of wide recognition and acclaim – not that he has sought it – and by the time this piece was written I, along with many others, assumed he was dead.

Unfortunately, Billy Chainsaw and Simon Henwood went their different ways and the magazine Purr *ceased to exist after this interview so I have deleted a little about projects that were never realised. Otherwise I've left it alone as information about Gorey, both his work and personality, is very hard to come by.*

Incidentally, any titles left at the start of articles are mine. Editors always delete these immediately as they like to choose their own.

Silently, seemingly overnight, the small sedge-green hardcover volume has seeped into the bookshops. Entitled *The Beastly Baby*, its pen-and-ink cover – a bloated, maddened infant brandishing a knife – suggested that it should not be nestling into the children's section. It was attributed to 'Ogdred Weary' and dedidated to one 'Ydora Wedge' – names guaranteed to alert the real creator's myriad admirers. Both are anagrams of Edward Gorey, a legendary Sphinx with the Quink, a fabled idiosyncratic icon and bizarre genius. Amongst author-illustrators, critics rate him more highly than Edward Lear or Aubrey Beardsley. Gorey – writer, illustrator, artist, set designer, stylist, bibliophile and balletomane – has inspired legions who, including devotee Tim Burton, have stumbled upon one of his many exquisitely designed and illustrated book-length narratives: *The Gilded Bat* perhaps, *The Fatal Lozenge* or *The Curious Sofa*. He has illustrated countless other books, from *Little Red Riding Hood* to Beckett and T.S. Eliot. He has self-published, been published by major and minor US and UK publishing houses, by small presses, in limited editions; a lethal legacy guaranteed to induce the vapours amongst future executors. And yet, until now – particularly in Britain – Gorey remains as enigmatic as J. D. Salinger. Many of his fevered fans believe that he was English and is now dead.

Until now there has been but one photograph published and few interviews granted. His resurrection now, here in Britain, is a spectacular publishing feat, testament to the determination of a young multimedia company, Purr Ltd. Originally a stylish, glossy magazine, *Purr* first appeared in 1993. Founded by Cathi Unsworth, cartoonist Dix, ex-illustrator Simon Henwood and Billy Chainsaw, long-term PA to Siouxsie and the Banshees, it was intended, in Henwood's words 'to combine illustration, journalism, fiction, bring in music, film and comix – to cross-fertilise so you really couldn't tell the difference between one thing and the other.' Somewhat similar to US book/'zine *Re/Search* in its contents and cults, *Purr* has been successful. Its – unpaid – contributors have included Iggy Pop, Harry Crews, Hubert Selby, Richard Hell, Henry Rollins, Derek Raymond, Lydia Lunch, sleaze snapper Richard Kern and comix star Ted McKeever. Purr have now expanded into book publishing and an art gallery.

I spoke to Billy Chainsaw, a biker giant with waist-length hair like black spun silk, arms adorned with ominous fetish jewellery, and Henwood, a pale aesthete with a shaggy white Warhol cut.

Henwood had managed to meet, photograph and interview long-term hero Edward Gorey for *Purr 4*. Gorey agreed that Purr might reprint his first ever book *The Beastly Baby* (originally published in 1956). This will be followed by a reprint of his classic morbid alphabet *The Gashlycrumb Tinies* ('M is for Maud who was swept out to sea, N is for Neville who died of ennui . . .'). Gorey participated in *The Beastly Baby* reprint, lettering the spine and contents. 'We're working book by book', says Simon. 'He's also hoping to do some new stuff for us. He actually offered us something for the magazine which we're going to develop as a book project.' All this is a feat comparable to enticing Michael Jackson down The Good Mixer pub for long, intimate chats with the regulars.

Gorey's narratives are deceptively simple. Any close study reveals vast erudition, endless wordplay, sophistication and wit. He can flash from Firbank to Heliogabalus. His books are simultaneously light, charming, deeply disturbing and macabre. Many tales are set in Gorey's version of Edwardian England. Dim, grim mansions ('The people at the grey hotel/Are either aged or unwell') harbour mysterious flocks of men in fur coats and handlebar moustaches and twittering, neurasthenic women. Wan children – Embley, Yewbert, Drusilla – suffer grisly fates. Odd creatures move in. 'The Doubtful Guest' is a furry, snouty, determined thing which lies in tureens and hide all the towels from the bath: 'It would carry off objects of which it grew fond/And protect them by dropping them into the pond.' Other inexplicable things occur. In 'Les Passementeries Horribles' the adults are menaced by elaborate and sadistic curtain trimmings. (Just like home.)

Gorey is from Boston. He appears briefly in Alison Lurie's 1975 memoir of V. R. Lang and the Boston Poets' Theatre in the 1950s. 'The Doubtful Interview' which prefaces the book *Gorey's Posters* is delightful, eccentric and reveals almost nothing. ('I write about everyday life.')

Simon Henwood had an introduction to Gorey through a NY agent. Henwood sent him some work and Gorey asked him over to visit. 'It's incredibly difficult to correspond with him as he only opens his mail every six months or so. There are stories of fantastically rare books that have been stacked outside his house for months.'

Henwood continues: 'He left New York in 1983 after having lived there for some twenty years. He was obsessed with a celebrated dancer from the NY Ballet – to the point where he almost never missed a single NY Ballet show in twenty years. He was social then. He was going out all the time. He is one of the biggest authorities on ballet as well as on Japanese literature – and on *The Golden Girls* and *Star Trek*! When this dancer died it signalled the end of an era for him. He's been in Cape Cod ever since. He occasionally used to go down to the Gotham Book Mart. Once or twice a year they have a show of his work and he signed books but he doesn't even do that now.'

Were you apprehensive meeting him – was it like going to Gormenghast?

'It was fucking amazing for me. I was totally apprehensive. His body of work alone is daunting enough and I'd heard about his vast literary knowledge. I had to get a "pond-hopper" – a small three-to-four seater propeller plane to Hyannisport. I could see him from the air, the airport is so small. We went to his house. I met his cats. He has six. Jane is the most friendly – the one in the photos. It's hard to really get at the roots of his ideas because he's into so much. He'll zoom from silent films to Oriental literature and then he'll flip to something like *Priscilla, Queen of the Desert*. He finds quality in endless things. His biggest influences were silent films and Jane Austen. He loves English literature. He is scared to come to England in case he never wants to leave.'

Billy Chainsaw ponders the disparity between Gorey's vision and the bleak Edgware road outside. 'He admits to finding crowds of people tiring,' continues Henwood. 'He prefers one-to-one situations, being slightly deaf. He loves company. He's very INTERESTED. *Purr* has weird comix, nude photographs – I was terrified – but he was completely into it. Living in the Cape on his own, he's sucking in as much writing and film and theatre as he can. He's involved in amateur dramatics again. He has a lot of friends there.'

Is he very private, functioning on a cultural, rather than a personal level?

'I'd say totally. I had a lot of preconceptions about what he was going to be like and I wasn't disappointed. It was one of those rare occasions where – superficially – he was exactly as I imagined –

the huge, rambling house, piles of books on the floor, cats running around. He makes toys. Beautiful toys. He gave me one – The Figbash. It looks like a pterodactyl without wings but with very long arms and legs, like an ape. It's an acrobat. Very strange. It's almost like a beanbag but it feels as if it's a sleeping animal. He makes the toys from all different types of fabric while he's watching TV. He's always busy.'

There have been numerous attempts to 'market' Gorey. Disney approached but Gorey would not go to Hollywood. 'He's a simple man, he won't leave his cats.' There was the famous 1977 production of *Dracula* with Terence Stamp in London when Gorey's original sets were imported. Simon explains, 'He's got a very pessimistic nature. He doesn't believe anything will happen. Many people have tried to promote him but he's not that interested. He's very modest. He's always surprised by people's interest. The book that had the most reaction was *The Loathsome Couple* (Gorey's version of The Moors Murders in which Harold Snedleigh and Mona Gritch meet at a Self-Help Institute Lecture against decimalisation. Harold has a constant cold and is impotent. They lure a little girl named Eepie Carpetrod to a "remote and undesirable villa". After killing her they eat turnip sandwiches and artificial grape soda. They end in the asylum where Mona spends decades licking the walls. It is totally chilling and seems to be set in the twenties). 'People sent it back to bookstores disgusted. Very often, because of his small book format, his work gets misconstrued as children's books . . . This is a serious author who occasionally appeals to children.'

Simon and Chainsaw's attitude is generous. They are hoping for an 'opportunity to put Gorey on the map in this country. He's a myth.'

As Chainsaw says, 'You cannot make a distinction between the writing and the pictures. They're simple, they're funny, they're dark and they stay with you.' You have to hunt down the Tribbit, the Ulp and the Veazey 'which makes a creaking noise and has no dignity or poise' and see for yourself. Most fall in love, forever.

Dennis Cooper: *Closer*

The Guardian, 1 October 1994

For many years I admired Dennis Cooper's fiction almost unreservedly. I admired his ability to take the most extreme and transgressive of subjects and render them inescapable in prose of extraordinary grace and beauty. I came to regard Dennis personally with feelings of affectionate friendship. Change and distance have now eroded regular contact, although my amity persists. Although I tend to distrust writers (including myself) for many excellent reasons, Dennis' diffidence, humility and straightforwardness were very appealing.

Gradually, though, I realised that we were very different. My initial interest had been sparked by his work whose macabre and morbid qualities were bound to appeal to me – although these qualities are rarely aligned with really good writing. But the components of our interest in transgressive art were very disparate. Dennis' focus was primarily on sex and his individual sexual fantasies, whereas my attraction to morbidity had little to do with sex and more to do with inchoate psychological issues. Dennis being a gay man and moreover a man particularly involved in fantasy, meant that I could not really be involved in the core issues of his life, either spiritually or in person.

When his most recent novel **Guide** was published, I was surprised when I found it less interesting to read than the earlier books (not that it was any worse). I think I had just got exhausted by then and didn't want to read any more fantasies about the evisceration of teenage boys, however beautifully they were written. This had nothing to do with Dennis' abilities as a writer. I lacked the ability to connect with the books on a permanent emotional and sexual level and so, inevitably, they would have run out on me sometime. For an author to remain perpetually fascinating, their content has to intertwine permanently with many aspects of one's psychic being. Few authors can succeed in touching you deeply with every single word they write – normally it is a book here and a book there to which one is devoted.

The fact that I still love Dennis' earlier novels so much is its own testament to his talents.

'I've always hated adults and still do,' he says, passionately. Dennis Cooper is a fortyish, very successful, highly respected professional writer, a workaholic. An adult. He is also a desperate, wrecked, clumsy teenage boy. This dichotomy, this fissure runs right through his work. There has always been this split between the cold, watchful eye of the cultured, intellectual writer and the tortured emotional intensity of someone whose psyche is an adolescent furnace of desire, fantasy, adoration and need.

Cooper has worked long and hard for the sort of fame and credibility that no amount of hype could ever buy. He is admired by some of America's foremost writers. 'Dennis Cooper is reciting Aeschylus with a mouthful of bubblegum,' raves Edmund White. William Burroughs gasps, 'Dennis Cooper, God help him, is a born writer.' He has been repeatedly compared to such 'ghoulish geniuses' as Jean Genet, Flannery O'Connor or Georges Bataille. But stylistically Cooper remains absolutely contemporary, emanating a post-punk anger and chaos that oscillates between sadistic fantasy and the blank, numbed inarticulacy of the alienated teen.

His prose remains resolutely Californian, perpetually tuned into MTV, indie bands, music magazines and trash film. It suggests the Marquis de Sade stalking through Mcdonald's, Genet and Céline sharing a Slurpee together at Disneyland or Baudelaire stage-diving in some thrash metal dive. Cooper sends his admirers over the top.

Although he has been writing professionally since his teens, Cooper's fame – and notoriety – rest on a series of novels and stories published in the nineties. These books – *Closer*, *Wrong*, *Frisk*, *Jerk* – with their combination of elegant prose and violently perverse content brought him huge local fame in Los Angeles plus a surrounding circle of reverential younger writers who think that he is the coolest man on earth. Simultaneously he has attained avant-garde cult status throughout the west. His fiction attempts to unravel a nightmarishly complex knot of predatory homosexual desire, murderous fantasy and perversion – shot through with shards of tenderness, vision and a fragmented, potent humanity.

Glossed with the sophistication of the aesthete and the torment of the intellectual facing a moral bombsite of sexual psychoses, it spins the critic down endless corridors of deconstruction and analysis. The books all revolve around an archetypal figure, Cooper's muse – the beautiful, blurry, narcotised and blunted teenage boy. The original was a boy Cooper knew at school – 'He was just a little kid and he adored me and he was really really fucked up on drugs . . . this kid was really blank and I gave him all this love and he sort of became warmer.'

This boy's successors have often been drawn from life, from relationships both sexual and celibate. Unfortunately these books were often misread; whilst tracing the most hellish zones of desire and pondering the profundity of the corporeal, they also dissect the fantasy urge 'to kill someone cute during sex'. Cooper says, 'It's taken people a while to figure me out. My work is very easy to read and very easy to misinterpret.'

Cooper has suffered attacks from literal-minded gay activists. Some members of Queer Nation issued a death threat against him. Cooper sounds both wry and desperate when he says, 'People think I'm a person who's going to like KILL people. They read my books and they think I'm a monster. In a way I wish I'd never written those books – they've gotten me in so much trouble. I mean, I'm anything BUT a monster. I'm like this . . . Dad figure!' He continues: 'I'm much more famous than I am read. I'm famous for this gay thing, transgressive sex, for being experimental and being wild and being into punk.' He sounds disgusted.

It is only now with the publication of his new and most mature novel *Try* that Cooper's serious intentions and ethical concerns have become accessible to a wider audience. Although he has always written about the great, classic concerns of literature – love and death, fear, tragedy, vision and faith – even now, despite the excellent reception accorded *Try* in America, he has difficulties. 'I was going to get a lot of major stuff in *Newsweek* and *The New Yorker* but they didn't happen because the material was too weird. I'm not in the official group of "new writers". I'm still marginal. I'm happy there.'

Before ever meeting Cooper I had expected some frail, super-aesthete, with high cheekbones and discreet, expensive, rather sinister jewellery. I was so wrong. Cooper is a tall, shambling, lanky man, his skin extraordinarily pale for a Californian. He has floppy, once-fair hair now bleached and aged to dishwater blonde and silver streaks. His eyes are improbably blue, his expression anxious and preoccupied. He is courteous, moody. Initially his conversation follows an attenuated Beavis and Butthead model – 'That's cool'; 'Awesome'; the all-purpose, dismissive 'Whatever . . .' and in moments of real excitement 'That's pretty intense . . .' In time he invariably becomes loquacious, relaxed, amusing. Sartorially, Cooper is indifferent to the point of grunge. Whether in the Malibu sands or the London snows it is rare to see him in anything other than blue cotton trousers, plain grey sweatshirt and flip-flops. His car, an old Toyota, begs you to finger-write 'Dust Me' on it and clanks along the freeway as the pastel convertibles whisk past. Until recently he worked on a typewriter missing the letter T. His apartment in Los Feliz, LA is small, spectacularly unkempt. In short he has all the disregard for material possessions of someone who has never known want.

Artists drawn to morbidity and horror are constantly asked *why*, as if expected to justify it. Of course, its attraction is that it is unjustifiable. It is indefensible. It is horrible, depraved and corrupt. It is wrong, otherwise one wouldn't be interested. To evoke evil with conviction, one must have a powerfully developed sense of its opposite – just as for the religious, there is no Devil without a God. However, for those inclined to psychiatric theory, Cooper's childhood provides partial answers.

Born in 1953 to a prosperous family in Pasadena, California, he says: 'I had a really bad homelife, right? My mother was an alcoholic and I was very abused – in a very complicated fucked-up way. She was just really a mess – threatening to kill us and threatening to kill herself. We'd be, like, watching TV and she'd come in with a handful of sleeping pills and threaten to take them or go to the top of the stairs and beg us to push her down and she'd be in the car with us and just drive full speed at a wall and we'd have to grab the *wheel* . . . She was really nuts.' He speaks in a rush. 'I'm sure that's part of why I was really fucked up – just feeling, like, that helplessness. With her, I kept saying "I didn't do anything wrong." I *hadn't* done anything wrong. I wasn't a bad kid. It was confusing to me that nothing I could do or say would ever save me. It was this constant alcoholic psychic abuse. Maybe that's why I'm interested in these kids. They're totally innocent. They're passive because they're frightened. They just drift and that's the way they get through the world. Inside they're so sad and scared and lonely. I think that's the way I ended up being to try and protect myself. My mother tried to have sex with me once – but I don't feel like it's any big deal. It's such a weird thing to have happened. The incident I remember as the most horrible was – I didn't want to get a haircut or something and I locked myself in my bathroom and my father came and kicked down the door and chased me with his belt and I ran to my mother in the doorway and grabbed her and started crying, saying "Help me, save me, help – help" and my mother didn't, she turned me around while my father whipped me in the face with his belt. That was like a really big thing – I remember thinking "I have nowhere to turn."

At age thirteen Cooper was sent to a private school where he was heavily influenced by punk music – 'It was a clarion call' – and encouraged to write.

'I was always very creative but writing ended up being the focus. I guess I could express myself more complexly in that way than in any other form. I learned from punk. I wanted a very complicated tone that seemed very flat and simplistic. I wrote this book – an imitation of de Sade's *120 Days of Sodom*. I took all the cutest guys in high school that I wanted to sleep with and cast them in it and just killed them off! I burnt it. At school the teachers really liked my work and I published this little book called *Terror of Earrings* in 1973.'

'*Terror of Earrings*?'

'Uh – yeah.' He laughs.

Cooper was encouraged by an older LA poet. 'I really don't like him now and he was always expecting me to sleep with him but he helped me get *Idols* published.' *Idols*, a book of poetry, was published by Seahorse Press in 1979.

Throughout this period Cooper developed his serial obsession with his muse type – the younger, troubled unhappy boy who turned to him for care and nurturance. 'These are very rich people to me. I am *fascinated*. In a way it's like recognising myself. It's someone very smart and very fucked-up who's developed this very strange sense of the world that's very centred but it's also hidden away because they're so afraid of the world. Usually they're younger 'cos there's a part of me that wants to take care of them. In my books they generally don't find these people to care for them. I guess that's really the most terrifying thing for me that someone like that would never find anyone to care for them. They make it very difficult for people to love them. They're very circuitous and they do these weird things and you have to really break it down to get close to them. All these archetypes I've used in my books have been like that.'

'Suppose someone had taken care of you?'

'Writing saved me. That's all.'

Thus Cooper developed from being a beautiful, abused, sexually exploited boy himself into a man who now prefers celibate relationships with his current friend/muse for fear of exploiting them in his turn. He's been down the whole road. 'You see my books – when sex happens it's almost always exploitative.' He often comments that perhaps one can show real love best by not having sex, by not demanding anything. 'I always get in these intense relationships with guys who're looking for a father figure and with me it's a safe place. Then to have sex in there? That's when everything goes insane.' It is his fictional adults who appear repulsive, corrupt and morally barren – serial killers, fetishists, perverts, abusers, although Cooper is too subtle a writer to create teenagers that are any less complex in their different ways.

I ask about his focus on death and murder. 'It's been really hard to pinpoint. I always go back to when I read de Sade when I was fifteen – but I must have recognised something there that was already in myself. The thing people always misunderstand about my books – and it's complicated by it being the first thing they see – is that I'm the person who wants to kill boys and *I'm not*. I've had fantasies about that and always have but I've had fantasies like that because they terrify me. That stuff is interesting to me because I feel such INTENSE HORROR at kids being taken. The *120 Days of Sodom* was powerful for me because I felt such terrible agony about these kids yet I understood the impulses. I also find them erotic. I *do* understand why it's so attractive. Partially because the *horror* of it is very sexy or something.'

All the diverse strands of Cooper's tortuous self have been brought together in the new novel *Try* – the adult sexual aesthete, the damaged fantasist, the tender, loving carer who perceives all too well the unhappy adolescence he has never deserted and finally the visionary.

Try is the story of Ziggy McCauley who was adopted as 'a hyperactive hard-to-place two-year-old' by two gay gays, Bruce and Roger. Roger left LA for New York when Ziggy was still a baby. Ziggy grew up with the filthy-tempered Bruce who beat him constantly and started sodomising him at age eight. The novel opens when Ziggy is about eighteen – nervous, jumpy and very screwed up. When not at school, he edits *I Apologize – A Magazine For the Sexually Abused* and frets constantly about his best friend Calhoun who is becoming increasingly strung out on heroin. Both Ziggy and Calhoun have girlfriends but Ziggy adores Calhoun to whom he looks for warmth and nurturance. 'And love, however fucked up, is the beginning of what Calhoun needs these days.' Calhoun seems to return this love but is too smacked out to contribute much, so the question of sex does not arise. The book charts several important days in Ziggy's life. Ex-Dad Roger, now a rock journalist, has decided he is in love with Ziggy and is coming to LA to have sex with him. Roger writes to Ziggy, 'Teenaged boys are my weakness, particularly the slim, depressed, cute, intelligent, haunted ones who feel askew in some way from their peers. My interest seems to reinforce these boys' secret if fragile belief in themselves.' Ziggy also spends time with his Uncle Ken, Bruce's brother, a paedophile and maker of kiddy porn videos. Ken is fucking and filming a pitifully camp, doomed little twelve-year-old boy. Ken's friends are into super hardcore porn – paedophilia, sadomasochism, necrophilia. Cooper says: 'They're totally interested in the body and what's inside it. That's always going to be interesting to me.'

In Ziggy's world the adults have complete power over his body and yet he has the spark and spirit to try to understand himself, to try to help Calhoun. This is a love story, a story of emotional and spiritual redemption. 'It's like this sublime thing,' says Cooper.

Try is the most visceral, emotionally wrenching book I have read since Hubert Selby's *The Room* (1972). It is overwhelmingly powerful, compressed and intense. Cooper is the first author to capture the lives and emotions of contemporary teenagers with artistic authenticity. No-one else has come close to expressing the essence of these benumbed, too-knowing adolescents. It seems incredible that a book which straightforwardly explores one of our most familiar topics – child abuse – should prove so rough, so raw, so chilling that, as Cooper says, it is still 'too weird' for people and keeps him 'marginal'. William Burroughs spoke of the 'courage' required to be a writer and describes it as 'the courage of the inner exploration, the cosmonaut of inner space. The writer cannot pull back from what he finds because it shocks or upsets him, or because he fears the disapproval of the reader.' This is Cooper's courage, the ability to trace the extreme boundaries of human behaviour and follow them unflinchingly into lust, torture and death. To Cooper, the body itself is text; it is a 'problem' to be 'read'. He speaks repeatedly of reading the body like 'Braille' or of 'scholars' of the ass. Ziggy's ass is described as 'garrulous', recalling Shakespeare's 'nether voice'. It is as if the mouth speaks rational, ordered language and the anus the true language of the body. Roger's erotic focus is the buttocks. Their very structure suggests Cooper's dichotomy, the split between adult and teenager. He penetrates the body of his text so obsessively it is as if, like J. M. Barrie, he believes life to be effectively over when boyhood ends.

Try also makes clear the ways in which an author's emotional life can be transmuted into art. Cooper agrees that, while Ziggy is partly based on someone he knew, he himself was also the model. Roger is another aspect of Cooper. 'That's a voice I've used before and I wanted to turn it to candy and gentrify it to death,' he says. 'I wanted to kill that voice off.' For Cooper, it is 'like I'm mining this stuff that's really a psychosis for me'.

It is a psychosis that is no longer likely to destroy him. He has been in therapy for a year. 'It's helped me to be sane. I was going to kill myself or something.' He continues his generous support of younger writers. He's making extra money writing for *Spin* music magazine, interviewing Courtney Love and other current idols. And he's writing a new book 'partially about psychedelics and rave culture'. The teenager is still there.

All Cooper's writing leans towards the sublime, towards rapture; what Roland Barthes called *jouissance*. In this visionary sense he is very close to the work of Flannery O'Connor and her grotesque, stunted characters. O'Connor described the preacher in *Wise Blood* trying (and failing) 'to get rid of the ragged figure who moves from tree to tree in the back of his mind'. For O'Connor, that figure was specifically Christ. For Cooper, the ragged figure who moves in the back of his mind is a wounded, damaged boy.

It may seem like a long way from Holden Caulfield to Ziggy McCauley, but the two characters are both individuals and archetypes. Ziggy may seem extreme but his numbed, needy soul belongs to us all. He is our child. He is the moonchild that the adults of our time – a generation singularly steeped in self-indulgence and sexual obsession – have collectively, unconsciously created. And, as Charlie Manson said, society gets the children it deserves.

Robert Mapplethorpe: A biography by Patricia Morriswroe

New Statesman, 15 September 1999

I don't think there is anything I can usefully add to this following piece.

'When you are in an art setting you want to appear sophisticated and broad-minded . . . It's like the emperor's new clothes. You have to prove that you're unflappable.' So spoke a curator on first looking at Mapplethorpe's more extreme photographs and seeing a man pushing his finger into his own urethra, another man drinking urine like a sacrament, Mapplethorpe himself with a whip handle up his open rectum and a close-up of a razor-slashed penis streaked with blood and semen.

Morriswroe's authorised biography of Robert Mapplethorpe – who died of AIDS in 1989 – is a powerful, painful book which makes very clear what an exceptionally notorious and influential figure he was. Although it was much praised in America, some Mapplethorpe associates have found the book distressing – not on the usual count of sexual frankness as Mapplethorpe himself celebrated his perverse sadomasochistic urges in his art – but because Morriswoe raises a much more significant and contemporary point. She questions whether Mapplethorpe would have received any attention, let alone adulation, without the very pronounced degree of publicity and relentless promotion that characterised his career. 'Certainly no photographer of recent years – perhaps no photographer ever – has been so ruthlessly hyped, so skilfully merchandised' wrote *The Times* shortly before his death. Another curator endorses this: 'It doesn't take a genius to figure out that Robert wasn't a genius. It's all about marketing and building up a myth.' By emphasising such comments, Morriswroe slowly and inevitably executes a portrait of a deeply unappealing man: 'His greed was coupled with social pretension and a hunger for publicity.' He was just 'a street kid who figures he can make lots of money by packaging his slick portraits and S & M photographs as art'. And so on.

Was Mapplethorpe merely a sharp art hustler short on talent? Born in 1946 he was one of a large, Catholic, middle-class family, living in a spectacularly dull New York suburb. The young Mapplethrope is an engaging, sympathetic character, the traditional sensitive, artistic boy struggling against a very conformist, conventional and disapproving father. This had the traditional result: Mapplethorpe became increasingly morbid, eccentric and decadent whilst simultaneously struggling for his father's acceptance.

Mapplethorpe's life did not really begin until he met the equally frustrated, ambitious Patti Smith in 1967 and the book documents their love affair, lifelong friendship and the twists and turns of Smith's career. Heavily interdependent, intertwined like vampires, they assaulted New York avant-garde culture, networking furiously – what they called 'making connections'. Their instincts were ahead of the times – Smith with her starved, sexually ambiguous 'Gothic crow' look and Mapplethorpe, a combination of street-tough and angel decked in his fetish necklaces of skulls, bones, feathers and dice. However, their artistic gifts lay in their personalities rather than in specific skills. Such artistic all-rounders – attractive, sporadically brilliant – usually succumb to drugs, dire relationships, or mere ageing, but they were unusually tenacious. Mapplethorpe snared a heavyweight art

world figure, Samuel Wagstaff, middle-aged, still gorgeous, a curator, collector and millionaire who was looking for 'a boy to spoil'.
Thus, having tried all the visual arts, Mapplethorpe ended up as
a photographer by default. It was the least hassle, he found, when
someone gave him a Polaroid camera. He could concentrate on
what most interested him – himself and his sexlife. He never
developed a film in his life. Wagstaff, who had just started a huge
photography collection, promoted him furiously. Mapplethorpe's
first dealer Holly Solomon commented: 'I would never have
touched Robert without Sam. And there were others . . . who felt
the same way.'

Mapplethorpe certainly possessed an exquisite, highly refined
aesthetic sense; that is, he had very good taste – an instinctive
understanding of line, form, light, shape and pattern. By now
wholly homosexual, Mapplethorpe immersed himself in the
sleaziest aspects of the seventies sexual supermarket. Wagstaff
stood by indulgently and bought him a loft to play in, which
Mapplethorpe furnished with religious and satanic iconography
and a black leather bedspread.

As so often happens with notable artists, Mapplethorpe's tim-
ing was impeccable. He was documenting the great wave of
homosexual hedonism that marked the period and doing so at a
time when a gay aesthetic was increasingly adopted by the cultural
mainstream via icons like Andy Warhol, Bette Midler and the
camp cocaine fripperies of Studio 54. Additionally, photography
was finally gaining acceptance as a serious, collectable art form
and Mapplethorpe's creativity paved the way for contemporary
luminaries like Cindy Sherman, Barbara Kruger, William Wegman
and particularly, Joel-Peter Witkin who has managed to trump
every Mapplethorpe excess.

Mapplethorpe had a sophisticated understanding of self-
promotion. Initially he exhibited his inoffensive, more saleable
work – society portraits and flowers – uptown, and the leather-
hooded bondage boys in a downtown gallery, the two styles uniting in the rapidly growing myth of his personality. His pictures –
beautifully and expensively framed – were presented as complete
works of art. Fussing over frames, Mapplethorpe commented jok-
ingly but revealingly that he was no more than 'a fag decorator'.

When a curator accused Wagstaff of exercising undue influence over Mapplethorpe's rocketing fame, Wagstaff snapped 'You naive bastard! How do you think anything gets done in the world if not by power and influence?' – a fair comment, although again and again Morriswroe implicitly damns Mapplethorpe by highlighting less generous opinions at the start of chapters. 'Robert will do anything for his career'; 'Without the support of Sam and that whole homosexual sadomasochistic universe, no-one would ever have heard of him'; 'Image was everything to him'; 'Love was impossible with him because the only people he wanted in his life were rich people, famous people and people he could have sex with.'

The emperor's new clothes? Mapplethorpe's pictures are more than that. Chilly and voyeuristic certainly but possessed of that stunning aesthetic sense and frequently subtle ambiguities, as in the portrait cover to Patti Smith's album, *Horses*. Both he and Smith were wracked by binary oppositions – Smith pulled between her 'aggressive' masculine aspect and submissive feminine one, and Mapplethorpe, more basically, between good and evil. However, as everything Mapplethorpe photographed essentially concerned himself and his own sexuality, his art remained emotionally static, even immature. There is little trace of any progress towards wisdom or compassion.

Morriswroe tries to balance the portrait of Mapplethorpe as an exploitative, coprophiliac voyeur who urged his subjects to 'Do it for Satan' by including more positive testimony. Some found him humble, sweet and shy. 'Everybody loved Robert in a weird way,' said regular subject and bodybuilder Lisa Lyon. 'People were totally fascinated by him as a person,' commented a dealer, and an assistant described him as 'One of the most tortured, tormented individuals I've ever met.'

Obviously complex characters – even none-too-bright, non-verbal ones like Mapplethorpe – have many different, contradictory facets. In that his art was so autobiographical it is significant to note that, as it gained in aesthetic strength, Mapplethorpe's personal development becomes increasingly chilling. Satiated and jaded with the most extreme of sexual perversions he turned to black men. As a size queen he succumbed to myth and found all their proportions to be nearer his ideal of beauty. However, his anti-Semitic views were compounded by his treatment of these new subjects and sex partners. He spoke of always being able to 'catch a nigger with coke'. The most disturbing parts of the book describe his relationship with a young, black country boy, a Navy deserter called Miltom Moore. Moore, befuddled by unaccustomed drugs, suffered greatly under the stress, heat, lights and covert racism of Mapplethorpe's high society life. He became emotionally incapacitated and violent, commenting 'I think he saw me like a monkey in a zoo.' Mapplethorpe's attempts to love and shelter him reveal gross insensitivity. Moore's successor's judgement that 'Frankly his [Mapplethorpe's] lifestyle was gross and I had my own reputation to think of' is horribly poignant and revealing of the huge disparity between this rich, white artist and his deprived, unemployed, homosexual black partners desperately trying to retain some self-esteem. Lisa Lyon said: 'Robert's relationships with blacks were all terribly sexual but he didn't actually like them. He constantly called them "niggers" and said they were stupid.'

When diagnosed with AIDS, Mapplethorpe – quite unfairly – blamed his black partners and continued his sex life, calling them 'human garbage'. Morriswroe doubts that he practised safe sex. Bullying fathers and fragile, damaged children are all too common but nothing can excuse such bitter, violently selfish, murderous behaviour.

Mapplethorpe himself died, wreathed in worldly glory after hugely successful exhibitions in London and New York.

Overall, there is slightly less emphasis on Mapplethorpe's art than one would like – no mention, for example, of the profound influence of Kenneth Anger. Although the book is well researched and covers the posthumous obscenity trials over his work it reads mainly, compulsively, like high-class gossip. But Mapplethorpe's life *was* high-class gossip – 'His social life was more interesting to him than taking pictures,' says one source.

Mapplethorpe was well aware that his art lay in the transgression of taboos. But sex and drugs are no longer taboos in the society Mapplethrope inhabited. Our understanding of taboo-breaking is measured by our reaction to his private racism – there he was really transgressing a contemporary societal taboo – and if that shocks and revolts us it also explains the increasing number of artists and intellectuals at present on the far fringes of the avant-garde who are prepared to confront political correctness and publicly espouse a sub-fascist, neo-Nietzschean aesthetic. If, as Derek Jarman says, Mapplethorpe's story is the story of Faust, then there are those who will take it further into versions of hell that will never end.

Interview with T. Coraghessan Boyle

The Guardian, 1995

I know that I was disparaging about media interviews at the beginning of this book and have consequently restricted my reproduction of them here. It is a cliché, unfortunately frequently verified, that the better the writer the less they have to say. It's true – they tend to say things like 'Read the book' or 'It's all in the poetry' and then shut up. Impressive, profound even, but somewhat lacking in the wit and repartee so necessary at the average literary launch or similar jolly-up. (There are exceptions, thank God.) But generally it is the semi-creative persons, the hacks, hangers-on, journalists, ad-folk and similar urban detritus who are the really brilliant conversationalists. Apparently it was always thus. Biographies over the centuries frequently attest to the superlative conversational creativity of some minor author or eccentric, except no-one can ever remember what was said as everyone was too drunk. Whether quaffing mead from rough-hewn earthenware or Oddbins' worst from plastic beakers, it has always been the same. 'God! (or Egad!) Sir Roger de Coverley was on form last night! Laugh – we nearly peed on the tapestries! All the horses bolted, we were roaring so much!! Sarcastic bugger, but clever, y'know – he was talking about whats-his-name – yes, that little pissant – fucked if I can remember a word – pissed as a foetal newt I was – but great craic, great, I'll never forget that night etc. etc.'

A pity but there it is. Produce a tape-recorder and I bet even Oscar Wilde would have sounded like Andy Warhol.

Going by the photographs I had always envisaged Tom Coraghessan Boyle as being a rather piratical, menacing San Bernadino biker type with a lifetime of heavy shit somehow slotted in alongside literature. Boyle has heard it all before: 'People romanticise me as someone burning the candle at both ends, doing drugs all night long. It may have been true at one time – I'm no angel – but all that is now suppressed in the interests of creating good work. Recently my life has been very conventional because increasingly all that matters to me is my work.'

The somewhat cool outlaw image has probably helped, however. In America he is an extremely well-known and very successful writer, having published five novels and four short story collections. But over here even the literati still go 'Corra – who?' until reminded of *The Road To Wellville* and Alan J. Pakula's eponymous film. His situation is analogous to that of Don DeLillo who published endless excellent novels in the US before breaking through here with *White Noise* and *Libra*.

At his best Coraghessan Boyle is a lavishly talented satirist, combining overwhelming vivacity with an imagination so violently crazed that the effect is akin to being picked up and shaken furiously in the jaws of a huge hound. His latest novel is *The Tortilla Curtain*, published by Bloomsbury, and Boyle hopes that doing book tours here might help amass a dedicated following as it has done in France and Germany. Boyle's 'readings' are high-octane performance art. 'I am a showman and a ham. I used to front a rock band. I love to get before a crowd. You have to blow them away. You give them a great show and just stun them and they might think "W..e..ll, perhaps literature ain't so bad; maybe I could read a book instead of watching TV."'

Boyle describes his own – originally Irish – background as being 'working class. My father was a janitor raised in an orphanage . . . My mother, unlike him, graduated from high school. That's as far as their education went. They were both alcoholics. But they instilled in me that education was the way to go and that I was the equal of anyone and could accomplish anything I wanted.' Boyle attended New York State University where he discovered fiction and some of his main enthusiasms and influences – Flannery O'Connor, Robert Coover, Ionesco, Genet, Becket, Absurdist theatre. He progressed to the University of Iowa's Writers' Workshop and graduated in 1977 with a doctorate in the nineteenth-century British novel. For all his black humour and bohemian aura, Boyle's own narrative comprises a standard, tasteful version of the American dream – from poor kid to intellectual celebrity awash in dollar bills. Much of his recent fiction, notably *The Tortilla Curtain*, deals precisely with the tensions and dissensions of rich, white, liberal California, a Valhalla he now inhabits himself; a classic, traditional go-getting success story whose contradictions often seem to puzzle and frustrate him. For example, he is adamant that he would NEVER write for Hollywood, obviously on principle.

So, despite the goatee and wildly expressive hair, Boyle is not only a highly prolific novelist and short story writer but also a workaholic professor of Creative Writing at the University of Southern California. 'My students miss me and they need me and they're begging for me to return. I never take off more than a semester because of my students. My agent doesn't want me to teach any more as it costs us money but I'm very dedicated to it although I'd make much more just writing. *Much, much more.* But I'm helping to create a very strong cadre of readers and writers. They can't all be great writers but afterwards they might go off and work as editors, in publicity, as professors, or on magazines. Or as degenerates begging on the sidewalk 'cos writing doesn't pay! But you're converting young people to books and literature.'

Boyle's messianic zeal on the supreme importance of literature comes across with all the force and conviction of a fundamentalist preacher. I suggest that it sounds like a personal crusade to persuade people that literary fiction can be great to read and really cool and not just nerdish. 'You take the words out of my mouth. You see, I have all the credentials. I have the Ph.D, I'm a professor, I've written the books, I've won the prizes, I don't have to prove anything. I can be exactly what I want to be – very relaxed, very casual and what I love to do is take literature from this plane where it can only be interpreted by professors, i.e. it's not for the mass of people. I insist that it is. GOOD WRITING IS FOR EVERYONE WHO CAN READ.' This defensive note regarding his achievements peppers his conversation, a sliver of personal uncertainty – possibly a ghostly emanation from a life of having to prove himself. He happily admits to being 'an egomanic' and despite his deadpan humour and freewheeling conversation there are hints of a formidable and intransigent character who must make some enemies.

Encouragingly, I mention that I'd certainly rather read a book than have sex or do drugs. 'REALLY? I'd prefer to do all three simultaneously. When I was young we passed books around like kids do with CDs nowadays. What I object to in the US is this culture of the new – the culture of the electronic media. There is no alternative. People don't know about reading. They snort cocaine with a TV changer in their hand and channel surf, a new image every five seconds. In contrast, writing and reading take effort. You have to close yourself off and release yourself and let the unconscious mind take over. You need to be used to that. You need to have time and space for it. Many people in this frenzy of contemporary life, their frenzy to acquire things – they need to get used to the idea that reading is cool, it's hip, it's important.'

Every year Boyle spends several months in a cabin in the Sierras and reads. 'Reading allows you to be absorbed in a work of art and to recreate it in your own voice. It is a totally unique entertainment because of the amount you put into it yourself – you interpret according to what you know and what you've read and what you've experienced.' (We politely acknowledge post-structuralism at this point but do not dwell on it.)

Boyle's work is notoriously hard to describe as he is so committed to experimenting with different styles. The books are linked by their fierce satire, irreverent black humour and tendency to catch readers off guard 'to make them laugh uneasily' by confounding their expectations of tragedy and comedy. *Water Music* and *The Road To Wellville* share a 'real' protagonist. The former tells of the eighteenth-century Scottish explorer Mungo Park who died in his second attempt to chart the River Niger while Dr Kellogg, all too real and burstingly healthy, stars in the latter.

Water Music is perhaps Boyle's magnum opus. Partly a parody-pastiche of both the nineteenth century and the historical novel, it deals simultaneously (as does all his work) with urgent contemporary issues, in this case imperialism. 'It's a way of taking history and revising it and seeing how it applies to our lives today.' It is a richly ornate, baroque book detailing the squalor of eighteenth-century London in detail so intense as to suggest time travel. Despite extensive research Boyle has never been to Africa. Those who have, myself included, have been confounded by the extensive sequences set there. Boyle's imagination in full untrammelled flow pours itself into the book like some psychic Victoria Falls and conjures the elusive essence of the Congo – albeit in an historical sense.

Boyle's reverence for the powers of the imagination, 'a kind of voodoo', is profound. 'The gift of writing comes to me in the form of a dream; the ability to inhabit other people, alien cultures. My job is to seduce and convince you that this is a reality.' Boyle continues: 'Now Dr Kellogg, he was similar to Mungo Park – noble, had some wonderful ideas, was ahead of his time. But for my purposes Mungo becomes a numb-headed symbol of imperialism and Dr Kellogg becomes a martinet, a dictator of health.' Both characters have an alter ego, an anarchic figure who opposes the controlling worlds of Park and Kellogg, and it is with these outsiders that Boyle claims to identify. Even a brief meeting with Boyle suggests that he epitomises aspects of Park and Kellogg too – certainly the vision, the self-discipline and, one suspects, more.

The Tortilla Curtain is very different; troubling, humane, it focuses on the plight of illegal immigrants in LA and the confusion of liberal whites who feel threatened and overrun. 'I wrote it to sort out my feelings. I was very disturbed with what was happening in LA with regard to illegal immigration which I oppose but as it turns out I am MUCH MORE opposed to the demonisation of a class of person, making them faceless, almost inhuman. People say I'm hard on my white liberal characters but they're the ones like me who need to be reminded about certain things and who do have a voice. We should not ignore the guy selling the oranges on the street as if he were a lamp-post. We're all human, all our aspirations are the same.'

What really enrages him however is the fact that 'some of the politically correct politburo' in America have said: 'How dare I presume to write in the voice of a Mexican?' A miasma of gloomy psychic policing creeps in with the dusk. 'No-one can tell me what my material should be.' He rants on, quite justifiably. 'There are plenty of PC people willing to proscribe certain topics for authors. I stand in absolute opposition to that.' (Me too.) 'An artist is obligated to inhabit anybody and write from any point of view.' Boyle rages on – 'How can anyone in a free society presume to tell me what to write?! It is also absolutely, pathetically stupid. Not being Mexican, I'm not allowed to write about Mexicans. Only

Mexicans can write about Mexicans and presumably only Mexicans should read it in their language. Not being a woman I can't inhabit a woman, not being a dog I can't write from a dog's point of view. It's patently absurd. I have no obligations to anyone. If I wanted to use all my gifts to write extravagantly beautiful novels in praise of Hitler, then it is my right and my prerogative. I would never say "Fiction must be this or this." It undercuts what art is – a personal expression. Some PC people can't even see that it is a sympathetic portrait of the Mexican couple in the book. They take satire straight. If they read *A Modest Proposal* they would accuse Swift of wanting to murder children. THEY JUST DON'T GET IT!!' Boyle's furious tirade vaporises the PC thought police.

Boyle's view of the future varies. Sometimes he thinks that 'Nature will seek us out', that all those viruses and bacteria will find an opportunity in this 'seething sea of fat, bloated, interesting bodies'. At other times he hopes the novel will win out and survive the academy and media. And so, still talking, still jet-lagged and worrying about its effect on his pineal gland, he leaves for the movies.

The End of Alice by A. M. Homes

(Anchor)
The Independent, 1 November 1997

When I started reviewing books and they kept turning up in the post, completely free, of course I thought I had gone to heaven. This exultation did not last. I found that if I reviewed a book, however much I'd liked it, I lost it, in the sense that I could not re-read it or think of it again with pleasure and interest. Books I had read before I read them again for review were OK but otherwise I found that, if I wanted to feel close to a book I'd reviewed, I had to find some way of reclaiming it, of moving it out of the real world back into my own world. Otherwise, when I tried to re-read something I'd reviewed I was haunted by the notes I'd made, the conclusions I had come to and so on. I couldn't surrender to it properly. The link with the outside world somehow aborted poetry, mystery, magic. Reclaiming a book took some effort – it had to be re-read in such a way as to silence echoes of my work on it and see that it was, page by page, returned to me and realigned with my interior, imaginative world. It was such a bother, this reclaiming a book for my own library, that I didn't do it very often. I had to feel quite strongly about a book to recapture it. Once retrieved, it was fine; I could then read it any number of times.

One of the novels I did care about sufficiently to bother repossessing was the controversial A. M. Homes novel The End Of Alice, reviewed below. When this was finally published in the UK, it set off a major literary commotion because it was a novel about a paedophile. W. H. Smith refused to stock it and there were cries for it to be withdrawn. Jim Harding, Chief Executive of the NSPCC, writing in The Evening Standard called it 'the most vile and perverted novel I have ever read'. Besides myself I think only Will Self in The New Statesman gave it a serious, positive review but I might be wrong about that as I didn't see them all.

After my review was published, Private Eye anonymous reviewer 'Bookworm' attacked me quite comprehensively. 'Bookworm' hadn't read my piece very closely so I had to write to Private Eye who printed my letter with its corrections.

After the review below I have included some of 'Bookworm's' comments plus my own letter in reply. I haven't done this to try and score points (I don't see how it could, really) but because my letter explains more concisely than I could here my attitudes towards trangressive writing in general. It took me a long time to understand that fiction and real life were very different things, but once I did, I still felt books were a Good Thing, healing and beautiful and knowledgeable, whereas real life was often cruel and distressing. I don't think that there is anything that should not be written about; censorship merely imports the deceit, hypocrisy and ignorance of real life into the world of the imagination which is the only place in which we can, and should, be free.

If I believed that a literary novel about a paedophile led just one extra person to hurt a child, my opinions would be different but I don't. I think people are much less simple, much more strange and arbitrary than that. The book that has been cited most often and has been most intrumental in driving abusers and murderers is The Bible. (And don't forget the serial-killers' favourite The Catcher in the Rye).

I had a strict Calvinist upbringing and I think that The Bible
*has caused a lot of suffering but would I ban it? No. Is it regularly
vilified amidst demands that it be withdrawn? I don't think so. So, if
we are not going to ban something that has quite unequivocally caused
suffering to children, why moan about literary works of the
imagination which have a positive duty to undermine stereotypes and
explore demonisation which no-one has ever cited as a force that drove
them to hurt anyone? (And which hardly anyone reads anyway.)*

A. M. Homes' novel *The End Of Alice* was misinterpreted and
excoriated by the moral majority on its original, highly controver-
sial American publication. Like Bret Easton Ellis before her, the
author was practically imprisoned for having written *fiction* . . .
Homes is a thirty-five-year-old teacher of creative writing at
Columbia University in New York. Her previous books – the novels *In the Country Of Mothers* and *Jack*, the short story collection
The Safety of Objects – have attracted praise and awards. No longer.
Michiko Kakutani, the influential lead reviewer on *The New York
Times*, has called her new work 'revolting trash'. '*The End Of Alice*
made me sick,' added Elizabeth Wurtzel.

Anyone who doesn't understand this novel knows little of
human nature. It is certainly the best novel I have read this year –
and not because it is sick or deviant but because it is the most *literary* of books.

From the epigraph, taken naturally from Lewis Carrol – 'A
stopped clock is right twice a day' – to the heartbreakingly
poignant death-rattle of the final sentence, we are seduced into a
horrific hall of mirrors where we catch grotesque, lightning
glimpses of ourselves and the book's varied protagonists. They
include a dead giant, an insane, incestuous mother who smears
her small son's lips with her menstrual blood for lipstick, a gang
of suburban teens, and far away and long ago a nymphet chasing
butterflies in the sun. Alice.

Chappy, our paedophile narrator, orphan of the above giant
and crazy mother, is spending his twenty-third summer in gaol,
having received a life sentence for the abominable crimes he
committed against that twelve-year-old Alice. He is the stopped
clock. He literally has a looking-glass in his head – splinters from
an accident.

The prisoner starts receiving mail from a college girl aged nineteen, on vacation in suburbia. ('*Scars*dale', as Chappy writes it). She has, and again Chappy translates, an 'oddly acquired taste for the freshest of flesh': she lusts after the insouciant crudity, the unselfconsious purity of a local twelve-year-old, Matthew.

Chappy is hooked. Although she is far too old for his tastes (like John Ruskin he detests pubic hair), he is drawn excitedly into her desire, pursuit and seduction of prey, even though he claims that his own 'fang of flesh' prefers 'pussies not pricks'. In fact he takes over and we read little of her actual letters, written 'in the stinted, stilted language of youth'. She is one of the 'overly under-educated'. Pruriently, voyeuristically, he refashions her fantasies and invites us 'Herr Reader' to share them.

When she finally writes 'And then we did it', his always barely-suppressed rage roars out 'I cannot forgive her the imbecilic nature of her communication.'

And, because to Chappy, lust is indistinguishable from memory he starts to tumble helplessly down his own rabbit hole, away from the charged, homosexual tension of gaol and back to his deadly encounter with Alice herself.

The book is stitched so tightly that it would take another to unpick, or deconstruct it. It is Homes's mastery of form that allows her to depict Chappy's mental disintegration, his spiralling confusion of memory and desire as he starts to accept 'after a life-time of abstinence' the illicit drugs from the Sicko Wing's in-cell dealer. And always we are brushed with the softest wings of inter-textuality, suggesting Lewis Carroll's *Alice* which was begun on Chappy's recurrently important day, the fourth of July. More important is Nabokov, and Chappy's fictional predecessor, Humbert Humbert of *Lolita*.

As in *Lolita* there is the constant dialogue with the reader who is being 'teased' and unwillingly made complicit. Also Chappy, like Humbert, is pathetic, sympathetic, funny and clever. A. M. Homes has said of her elusive narrator: 'I think he's deeply crazy. Smart – but not as smart as he thinks he is. He has a certain moral center.' This is where she dives deep.

Through Lolita, Humbert surveyed the crass, gum-chewing commercialisation of fifties America. So Chappy, through his young correspondent, gazes at and judges the nineties suburbs.

Trangression, rape, corruption and *ennui* lurk behind the sunlit piles of consumer 'toys' in a slack, soulless vista familiar from Homes's previous books. And Chappy sours on his young correspondent: 'God, they are so annoying when they believe they can think for themselves.' Her 'silly summer's delight', her Matthew, is merely 'a rite of passage' before she sails away (to Europe) into adult womanhood. She is not to be compared with him, a 'true connoisseur'. Chappy damns the emptiness and sterility of America, as did Nabokov before him: 'The decay is everywhere . . .' To Chappy these teenagers 'were fucking because . . . it was free . . . because there was nothing else to do, because it was easy . . . Everything had gone loose and lazy, they'd lost their grip.' Chappy then loses his and is swept after a much more old-fashioned child, wholly unlike the glazed and sugar-doped Matthew: Alice herself, delightful, lethal, 'the devil'.

Thus, delicately, Homes presents a panorama of paedophilia in its cultural and historical context, the different facets flashing by – the dumbing-down of our civilisation (Chappy is white trash compared to Humbert), the changing images and expectations of childhood, our deeply savoured repulsion towards its abusers, the gross dichotomy in our attitudes towards woman and boy, man and little girl. And then the infinitely subtle, sadomasochistic nature of such encounters – the zigzag of power and seduction from one to the other and the tragic misreading of signals on both sides that can constitute paedophilia.

Chappy, like Humbert, is something more devious than an unreliable narrator. It takes a very close reading indeed to differentiate between fact and fantasy in his memories, between truth and the self-serving pleadings of a murderous paedophile. That we can still see Chappy as a victim even throughout the utter agony of what happened to Alice is a tribute to Homes's genius here.

They meet by the waterside – like Poe and his lost Annabel Lee, Humbert and his first nymphet. Alice at twelve is bewitching, feral, precocious, with poetry written on the soles of all her shoes including Plath's 'Out of the ash I rise with my red hair/And I eat men like air.' 'She was the one,' Chappy writes, 'one in a million', recalling his wretchedness, his moral struggles with his nature and his inevitable capitulation as his memories re-animate that long-ago summer of poisonous bliss.

Again we hear the whispers from *Lolita* when Alice initiates sex with Chappy. Like Lolita she has had previous experience (almost certainly abuse) but is not quite prepared for the full, adult reality: 'it was she . . . who took me' with an 'apparent, if addled understanding of adult desire'.

The final hundred pages are a miracle of controlled cohesion when the present (Chappy's appearance before the parole board) and the past (his time with Alice) combine seamlessly in his drugged mind. A symmetry of the senses has seldom been better evoked.

Despite a few moments of wobbly judgement, somewhat stagey stylishness and a love of alliteration, this is everything fiction should be – wrenching, deeply disturbing and emotive. Shame on British publishers who rejected it (such as HarperCollins). And congratulations to Anchor's Jon Saddler who argues that 'people don't have to read it, just as they don't have to see "Sensation"'. Homes seems to acknowledge Nabokov, rightly, as *il miglior fabbro*, implicitly including her own work in the process of general cultural deterioration. 'Is being explicit the same as being pornographic?' she has asked.

Read. Re-read.

The 'A', by the way, stands for 'Amy'.

'Literary Review' by 'Bookworm', *Private Eye* No 937, 14 November 1997

. . . Nadir was reached in a risible piece in *The Independent* by Elizabeth Young (mild-looking Ms Young gets famously excited by fashionable novels about sex and violence and all the literary editors phone her up when one comes out) 'defending' A. M. Homes from her detractors, hailing the power of her 'art' and suggesting that the explicit is not necessarily pornographic.

Which is true, I suppose. But there is a word for all this – Elizabeth Young's maunderings and the novel that inspired them – and that word is *callow* . . . There are people writing about pain who scarcely seem to realise that pain hurts and somehow imagine that calling what emerges 'art' will miraculously absolve them from the traditional responsibilities of the artist . . . The final letdown, of course, is that it's not even a very good novel and the fault – equally inevitably – lies in the aroma of splayed limbs and bodily fluids that Ms Young so ecstatically commends . . . as we know there are no more good and bad characters in fiction; there are only interesting subjects for study. Well, I want the good to triumph and the bad to be damned . . .

So do I actually but not necessarily in fiction.

Letters to the Editor, *Private Eye* No 938, 28 November 1997

Sir,

Your Bookworm has made a number of assumptions about me from my review of *The End of Alice* which I would like to correct. Firstly, the Books Editor of *The Independent* did not ask me to review A. M. Homes' novel. I approached him on the subject.

Nowhere in the review do I use the word 'art' nor do I 'ecstatically commend . . . splayed limbs and bodily fluids'. Instead I refer to 'abominable crimes' and 'utter agony'. I do not find violence, fictional or otherwise, to be exciting or erotic.

Nor do I indiscriminately defend any and all transgressive writings. I endorsed *American Psycho*, a novel in which all the killings are delusions, but have frequently declined the opportunity to comment on far more sensational books – David Britton's *Lord Horror*, for example, or Peter Sotos' *Tool* – novels so indefensible that they did not merit any discussion.

I have no difficulty in differentiating between good and evil or between fact and fantasy. Having experienced sexual abuse and other setbacks in childhood I am extremely aware of the vast gap between real life and fiction. My attitude towards convicted murderers and molesters is not liberal.

Books themselves have not caused me pain but helped me to understand it. Thus I will continue to oppose any censorship of the imagination. Certainly I am drawn to the Gothic but this is surely a matter for my NHS psychiatrist, not some ignorant amateur who feels entitled to castigate me as morally incontinent on the basis of a piece that was concerned solely with textual analysis.

Yours etc.

Books have never hurt me. People have.
    Anyway, so it goes in the war-torn literary trenches where we risk all in the noble cause of text with only proof copies for cover and

punctuation for ammunition. Who would true valour see, let him come hither; goodness, it's a hard life . . .!

Interview with Pamela Des Barres: For the good times

Commissioned by *The Observer*, 1996; unpublished

I am going to end this American section on a slightly curious note because the interview below with Very Famous Groupie, Pamela Des Barres, was never published. The editors acknowledged that there was nothing wrong with it as an interview but, by the time I'd written it, their agenda had changed and it no longer suited their purposes.

What happened was this: I was familiar with all Des Barres' books and we had acquaintances in common although I had never met her, so I seemed a logical choice as an interviewer. But by the time I made my deadline and handed in the rather gentle and sympathetic interview printed below, the very nice and able journalist Suzanne Moore had had a much harsher interview printed in Another Broadsheet, in which she excoriated Des Barres for having been a groupie. After that the Observer *got nervous, doubtless feeling that my interview was much too wimpish and uncontroversial so they never ran it. I didn't mind (except for Pamela's sake because Suzanne's attitude set the tone for all other coverage and because I only got a 'kill' fee – that is a mere half of my agreed payment!). Suzanne Moore expressed a perfectly valid point of view in her condemnation of Des Barres' life.*

Anyways as they say in North American fiction, although I could understand Suzanne's attitude towards Des Barres, I did not altogether share it and I cite the reasons here, not to make a big deal out of some transitory journalism, but because they involve issues that recur in this book.

Although I am younger than Des Barres, I am still closer in age to her than I am to Suzanne Moore and thus I have extremely vivid recollections (albeit from about knee height) of a decade I detested as soon as I became conscious of having landed in it. 'The fifties' – the very words make me want to spit – especially now when you get

*shrinks like Oliver James insisting that it was bliss back then and
everyone was as happy as Ovalteenies on E. They were not.*

*If my infantile loathing seems improbable, it must be recalled that
the fifties, in terms of attitudes, cultural mores, class structure et al
carried on at least until 1975 in the provinces and Scotland.*

*During the early part of my life, at the times when I was in
Britain, I found it a hateful place. My analyses were not very
sophisticated but there were a number of things I found it impossible to
avoid noticing. Women were treated with derision. Nearly every joke I
read or heard told by adults turned on the stupidity and inadequacy
of women. Naturally I first observed this in my own home life. My
father had preserved, perfectly fossilised, the world view of a Victorian
paterfamilias, all the way to the concept of the angel in the house. So
my mother had to be worshipped (in theory) but scorned and
disregarded (in practice). Women did not have brains. Instead they
performed what my father called 'kitchen witchcraft'. Women seemed to
be on a par with children, comprising a separate, dependent, foolish
world of 'womenandchildren' quite separate from the real, manly
world: they were there to be teased, mocked, condescended to, insulted,
bullied, dismissed and never, ever taken seriously for a moment.*

*Lots of people living now were born too late to see anything of this
virtually universal state of affairs. Many, many others seem truly to
have forgotten just how absolutely bloody awful things used to be.*

*Other things common to the culture then were the all-pervasive,
creepy, grovelling hegemony of the class structure. This was very
strongly allied to an emphasis on the outward trappings of
respectability and convention. In essence this led to a quiet fascism of
the soul – which allowed men – and some women – whose demeanour
seemed correct and decorous to abuse their status and torture all the
vulnerable ones whom no-one was ever going to believe – children,
patients, women, foreigners. To give one very crude example: dentists
did not inject anaesthetics at the time and I remember one who
definitely got off witnessing girl children in pain. I didn't know then
why he kept vanishing and returning with his hands stinking
disgustingly of sweet soap but I do now.*

*This, I hope, is not just some lengthy digression. I am trying to
make clear how it is that someone born just a few years after me
would miss seeing anything of life in Britain at that very specific time
– that post-war period when the old imperial order was just hanging*

on and when life here was at its nadir; static, stale, publicly over-civilised to the point of an all-embracing hypocrisy that could conceal every form of private corruption and abuse. I believe there is less child abuse nowadays – it is not as easy as it used to be. There are certainly fewer murders of children in the UK than there were then.

Americans growing up in the Eisenhower years faced a slightly different but equally restricting menu of wholesomeness and conformity, mired deep in the extreme conventions of racism and sexism. A girl who missed seeing something of that period could never really imagine, I don't think, just how bad it had been for women then, immediately before things changed for ever.

Think of those old Pathé newsreels – the standard received pronunciation, the enforced jollity, the hint of domination and enforcement, the sneering undercurrent of contempt. Everything was like that.

Other reasons to be fearful in the fifties: the middle-class enclave which enclosed me was mind-numbingly boring. No adult ever said anything of interest – and certainly not to a younger person. No-one ever spoke about what they were feeling or thinking. Nothing could be revealed. I was once reprimanded during a meal for saying how pretty the rain looked sliding down the window. Children were literally supposed to be seen (not too much) and not heard. It was all manners and formality. These things are fine but not to the utter exclusion of anything else at all. No wonder I wanted to grow up and be a bohemian. Obviously I'm not saying people didn't love their children or whatever, just that there was no way to show it, or say it. In my home there was no vocabulary for so many things – bodily functions, parts of the body, personal feelings of any kind. Not that I endorse the culture of public display that has replaced it, the endless emotional exhibitionism and loud self-obsession – but there has to be something in between.

For me, the true symbol of the fifties is that vile, serial necrophile John Reginald Halliday Christie, murdering women in his squalid W11 flat, propping up the garden fence with a femur and ensuring that his upstairs neighbour, Timothy Evans, went to the gallows for two of Christie's murders. Evans was a classic member of the vulnerable majority of those times; he was young, Welsh, a petty criminal and borderline-retarded – ripe for the corrupt ways and coercive powers of our noble British bobbies. Testifying against Evans,

Christie won the heart of the court when he claimed to have been gassed in the war (untrue) and to have worked as a Special Police Constable (true). One barrister noted: 'Christie bore the stamp of respectability and truthfulness.' Christie was hanged in 1953.

This really was the worst aspect of life in the fifties and early sixties – the opportunity enjoyed by adults, shielded by a thin veneer of apparent respectability, for indulging in unlimited sadism and brutality, knowing there would be no comeback. It is only now that the truth is starting to emerge about practices in institutions during the period. No-one would have listened back then – particularly to a child. By the time I was adult I had known various institutions – children's home, boarding school, hospitals of various sorts, remand home – and there is nothing, absolutely NOTHING, however evil that I would not believe could have happened in any of those places at that time. I was reading recently about the abuses perpetrated by nuns on girls in Dublin children's homes of the period and contemporary commentators seemed appalled by the most minor, everyday horrors, such as children being forced to eat their vomited-up meals. Without wanting to sound like a competitor in the 'Hey, I suffered' Sicko Olympics, it is true that in one of my schools if you couldn't keep down the food that you were forced to ingest, you ate the vomit.

Essentially, my point is that if, as a girl, you lived in that sort of society and were not nurtured by super-humans, it was virtually impossible to grow up with a sense of self-worth or self-respect. Even Pamela Des Barres, who grew up in a conventionally ordinary, happy family, mentions in her first book how inadequate she felt, how nothing. I think that that entire generation of girls who grew up in the fifties and sixties tended to feel a huge amount of guilt and confusion. After all, you were brought up in one culture, brought up to consider yourself essentially useless, brought up programmed to please and then you were spat out into a world that was moving (thank God) dizzyingly fast towards a totally different culture – one in which you could, for example, please men and receive peer group approval by having sex, in direct contradiction to one's upbringing.

Religion plus a demented hypocrisy about the Royal Family also swam about in Britain during the fifties. My parents were Free Presbyterians, a Highland breakaway, Calvinist sect, even more punitive and joyless than other Presbyterians. However, I was born in Africa and for the first decade of my life we moved between our home village in Scotland, London and Africa. The people who looked after me in Africa, Tomas and Adamoo, may have been nominally Christian but they still depended on the jujuman (the witchdoctor, if you must) when he visited the village. I was too young to sort out any syncretism, but the juju guy was very spectacular and inadvertently Tomas and Adamoo taught me about their own, original animist religion (which was imported to America and the Caribbean as voodoo). Every night the drums would play, picked up by one village after another and my father would always say, 'There's the evening paper doing the rounds.' Now I wouldn't mention the following theory – it sounds too fanciful – except that it has already been propounded by an American writer/scholar Michael Ventura (in the essay 'Hear That Long Snake Moan'). I didn't hear those drums again until a bit later when I started playing US R'n'B records and listening to Radio Luxembourg where they sometimes played old, early Elvis or Jerry Lee Lewis. Then I recognised that insistent beat. It was as if the source music, primevally irresistible, had returned to reclaim the dead lands. And I am not talking about sex, but about life.

Soon afterwards, magicians were everywhere, like Pied Pipers, and all the kids in the west for reasons they couldn't understand were being lured away.

Seeing old clips of Mick Jagger now with his not-very-long hair and V-neck Marks and Sparks jersey, it seems inconceivable that he could have caused the sort of choleric outrage that he did. Now, he looks like someone making a sort of postmodern retro style statement – but he wasn't. It wasn't ironic, it was real. And if you had any spirit at all, you did want to get close to the music. When the Stones were playing an early gig in my provincial town, I slipped out of boarding school one Sunday and went round to their hotel. Unfortunately they didn't lasciviously rip off my school uniform in the Lounge Bar. They sent me down to the station to buy their Sunday papers which, I was disappointed to note, were all broadsheets.

Later I went to a lot of gigs and hung around backstage and had several affairs with musicians so I guess I was a sort of groupie. But I was nothing like as dedicated and determined as Pamela Des Barres because I quickly found out that rock musicians were the most boring people in the world. They didn't want to talk about books. They didn't usually want to talk at all and when they did it was about music, or about themselves, or even worse, both together. The only persons around with a smidgen of intelligence seemed to be the journalists and record company personnel, which is probably why I eventually married a manager, although he's an IT consultant now, like everyone else.

If I'd been born a few years later, like Suzanne Moore, I'd probably have shared her attitude towards Pamela Des Barres and felt that her life had been a demeaning one. But if I'd been born a few years later, my parents wouldn't have had any authority at all and they wouldn't have been able to force me to go to university and I'd have run away and hit the streets much earlier. So at least I was spared some of my vast adolescent stupidity. My home was just too strict. You couldn't smoke, or swear or anything. I don't see that sort of home now, so mixed credit where mixed credit is due.

But I think if one had actually lived through the years before the revival of feminism in about 1975 and, as a teenage girl, been made to feel totally useless, powerless and brainless, with only one thing to offer if you were lucky enough to be pretty, one might be a little less censorious of someone like Pamela.

Also Pamela had had to fight her way out of the (still-extant) rigid, hidebound caste system of the American high school at a time when none of her peers supported her interests. (They didn't support mine much either, at school. They didn't have a lot of spirit at first.)

So the music came back and everything changed and many other equally valid socio-cultural theories were propounded – increased prosperity and leisure, easy, infallible contraception, the creation of the teen demographic – they all played a part, I suppose, and eventually almost everybody got a chance to play, however briefly, at the kind of bohemian hedonism that had previously been restricted to the very rich and privileged.

I was prepared to treat Pamela with respect – partly because I admired her for having turned her teenage diary into a book (something I'd always meant to do but had been too lazy). Moreover, that first book I'm with the Band was good – honest and engaging without revealing stuff that would hurt people or evoking too much of the squalor underlying Pamela's romantic dreams.

Also I felt I had at least some understanding of the forces that had propelled her and the courage involved initially in defying the intense stranglehold of US suburban convention and trying to formulate a new way of life, with nothing but immature experiences and inchoate *longings to draw on when facing issues that had never previously confronted women at all – an accelerating breakdown of the social order which left women without certainties or guidelines in their lives. Individual attempts to cope, to thrive and triumph may seem tacky and demeaning in retrospect. We have all become sophisticated now.*

Certainly we did not become friends-for-life, although I took to Pamela enough to let her drag me to something I'd normally have paid money to avoid, namely the musical Jesus Christ Superstar. *I liked her even though I thought some of her ideas, particularly about Mary Magdalene, were completely barmy. Pamela has never claimed to be a major-league brain-box, and indeed is almost professionally lightweight, but I thought she was sweet and easy, relaxing company, although I just couldn't understand her continued penchant for rock guys now that she's all growed up.*

I couldn't integrate any heavy-duty politico-feminist cerebral issues with Pamela's persona at all, even though she considers herself a feminist and has written about the next generation of rock chicks 'I . . . believed I had paved the way for these infant upstarts and I thought they should show me some kind of respect, or at least recognition for my ground-breaking, strip-walking efforts. Needless to say, they didn't show me jack shit.'

To me, Pamela seemed almost innocent, quintessentially someone who was made for pleasure, someone who was meant to make life more enjoyable and entertaining for others, and not necessarily in a sexual way. She was like flowers, or a ribbon or sweeties or a cute cuddly toy – she was for giggles and gossip and fun and brightening the place up. Castigating her seemed as pointless as dumping on the Teletubbies. But then I'm not very good at assessing people outside of books; I'm broadminded to the point of inanity so that you can hear the wind whistling through the cracks in my head and I am very reluctant to judge individuals, publicly at least, as I have minimal faith in my perceptions.

I am not quite sure why I've written all this around what was essentially an inconsequential and transient interview. I think it is because there are millions of people out there who are much older than me, so they must remember how things were and yet they just seem to accept the present and never comment (other than in inappropriate and specious nostalgia-mode) on the past and on just how overwhelmingly, how dramatically and how quickly *everything has changed.*

Perhaps they have really, truly forgotten. Perhaps they don't keep a diary like I do. But I really cannot understand it. And this means that nobody younger knows what a nightmare they escaped, either. I just had to put it down. The interview was only a jumping-off point for issues that bother me daily.

I guess for most people it is usually always easier to moan about the present than to celebrate one's good fortune in escaping the past.

'How does it feel to be the world's most famous groupie? That's the question I have the hardest time with. It's a real negative word, "groupie". I use it 'cos it sells books.' Pamela Des Barres' comment encapsulates her odd combination of vulnerability and shrewdness. Ever since her memoir *I'm with the Band* (1987) became a bestseller in America she has had to cope with considerable abuse. Pamela's real story has nothing to do with the stereotype of masochistic, status-crazed degradation. As she says, 'I never had any one-night stands. I was living a normal life for girls at that time only it was in the music scene and the guys I fell in love with sometimes lived over the sea. But the feelings were the same as those between any lovers. I never slept with someone just 'cos of who they were. Couldn't do that. Still can't.'

Pamela is now forty-eight, a writer and journalist. She is a tiny, delicate California girl with blazing red chilli pepper hair, a heart-stopping smile and a way of calling everyone 'doll'. She's all grown-up now – her third book *Rock Bottom: Dark Moments in Music Babylon* – is published this week and yet she is still dogged by that first memoir and those long ago party years.

Pamela Miller was a nice middle-class Valley girl zapped into tortuous teen lust and longing by the Beatles and Rolling Stones in the early sixties. She was at high school with a spacey long-hair called Victor Haydon (later the Mascara Snake) who was cousin to one Don Van Vliet aka Captain Beefheart. 'They were a very big influence,' she says. 'All of a sudden I could know these amazing people. Captain Beefheart was about as hip as it gets when I met him and if I could hang out with him, why not with Mick Jagger? I wasn't content just to listen to the music. I realised there was something going on, right there in my own sphere, so I thought I should take advantage of this . . .'

Transported by their music Pamela got to know more LA

musicians – The Byrds, Buffalo Springfield – and teamed up with several other eccentrically alienated girls. Known as the GTOs (Girls Together Outrageously/Overtly/Orgasmically etc.), Frank Zappa formed them into a group and soon they they were making an album with Rod Stewart squawking on background vocals.

The GTOs pioneered a style of thrift store finery that helped define the era – ancient silk dresses and patchwork, rags of lace and beadwork, sequinned see-through chiffon, floppy hats, artificial flowers, ruched romper suits, stilettos and Carmen Miranda strappy platforms. They were a traffic-stopping entourage and soon became notorious. Miss Pamela, Miss Mercy, Miss Cynderella, Miss Lucy and all. 'Our main aim was to turn people's heads, to shock them,' says Pamela now. Few of those old friends are left today – the others have been lost to AIDS, drugs and cancer. Pamela is grateful for not having had 'an addictive personality. I *enjoyed* getting stoned. I was taking coke and I craved it a lot but when I decided to stop it was easy.'

Pamela also lived with Frank and Gail Zappa, acting as babysitter to their oldest children, Dweezil and Moon Unit. 'All the English musicians wanted to meet Zappa and they'd keep my number and call me up . . .'

During this period Pamela – admittedly starstruck – had romances with a number of luminaries including Mick Jagger, Jimmy Page, Keith Moon, Noel Redding, Waylon Jennings, Don Johnson and other actors. It would have been odder in that environment if she hadn't. Jim Morrison lived next door at one point and she introduced herself by just walking in and doing a back bend on the carpet.

She didn't set out to be a groupie. 'For the most part these interviewers ask me (she mimics a lascivicious hiss) "How d'ya get backstage?" But that's where I *lived*. That was my *life*. These were my *friends*.' She concedes that as the seventies progressed, the groupie scene did become increasingly squalid and mindlessly competitive. 'This girl Connie admits to sleeping with thirty-two guys in one night – everyone's roadie, everyone's driver – and she's *proud* of that.' Robert Plant has commented: 'It's a shame to see these young chicks bungle their lives away in a hurry – to rush to compete with what was in the good old days, the good-time relationships we had with the GTOs . . .'

Having spent some time in a very minor way in the same arena, I ask if she didn't find musicians boring and silent. 'I always thought they were having deep and profound thoughts – but that wasn't the case! I was so damned young and so insecure that I just thought they were way deeper and more amazing than me and I had nothing important to say.'

Pamela was unusual in being aware at the time that she was involved with scenes and characters that were to have a lasting cultural significance. So she wrote it all down. 'I *knew* it was important. I just *knew*. Something inside me said "You're living an amazing life." I was documenting things as they were going on. I kept my diary up to date in the back seat of limousines and clubs – I carried it around with me! I was in the middle of this incredible, tumultuous eye of the hurricane – I sat in rooms with Page and Plant while they wrote songs and asked my opinion. I was at Altamont with The Stones – and with all of them in the room afterwards – things like that. There was just so much going on. Everything was being done for the first time. When people started playing music in the sixties it was innovatory. Everything was new. Everything is retro now.'

I'm with the Band is a sweet, poignant book which embodies all the confusion of sexual longing and self-doubt that teen angels felt around rock music. 'I was really honest about what I was like. I was baring my soul, my heart, my feelings. I didn't keep that much back. I was as candid as I possibly could be without hurting people. I didn't think about hurting myself either. I really walked a fine line. No-one was mad at me except Jimmy Page. He didn't appreciate the bit about him crawling across the floor to get the bag of drugs.'

The whole world knew about that stuff!

'Yeah, I know!' She laughs and continues, 'Those guys treated me as I expected to be treated. I was very subservient to them at the time. I always felt that they were more wonderful than I was. I was a very young girl. I was still watching my Mom cater to my Dad. I was trapped between the fifties and sixties eras. I didn't have enough self-confidence to feel totally equal. These guys were inspiring me – in such a huge, vast way. Even so I gave away too much probably.' She wrote: 'I still looked up to and felt lesser than an awful lot of people . . . I waded through those feelings of

complete and utter inadequacy . . . and slowly my fraudulent com-
posure started breathing by itself.' Pamela agrees now: 'I put that
feeling on paper for girls.' She regrets missing the Beat era, 'I
would have been right there at Kerouac's feet.' Her memoirs link
her with the pioneering, naturally feminist women of that time
who wrote accounts of their times with the boy-gangs – Joyce
Johnson, Diane Di Prima, Hettie Jones.

'Overall,' says Des Barres, 'writing about my sexuality as a
woman – I really took shit for that.'

I reject the US – at last

When I first started going to the US (and I didn't actually
get there for ages), I thought it was the Promised Land. As the
plane came down you could see all these thousands of tiny, bright
blue squares and I realised they were suburban swimming pools.
A swimming pool is the only material thing (apart from clothes
and cosmetics) that I have ever really longed for.

I thought the United States was beautiful. Even the awful,
nothing bits were interesting to me and the literary places virtually
orgasmic. So I just couldn't understand why my US friends – even
those in New York and San Francisco – complained constantly
about what hell it was to be a writer or an artist in North America.
It is true that I never liked the cloying, dualistic wholesomeness
that was spread all over the media, nor its underlying simple-
mindedness. But it wasn't until the end of the twentieth century
that I understood and internalised the unhappiness of my friends
and came to find America as maddening as they did.

At first it was the most obvious things – the endless rows over
art and censorship; the pitiable confession culture; the rise and
rise of that awful happy-clappy fundamentalism with its denial of
Darwin, its rallies for 'born-again virgins' (duh?) and its explicit
support for Southern homophobia and racism.

Many of their feminist writers drove me crazy (Mary Daly,
Andrea Dworkin – and, yes, I know that she is supposed to be,
and probably is, a nice, sweet person). The extreme political

correctness was dreadful, even though I could see that in a country so big one had to deal in broad strokes to get *anything* across
– but surely anti-smokers didn't need to scatter gunpowder in LA
ashtrays so that smokers got their fingers blown off? A wizard
wheeze, no? Oh and all the anti-abortion nonsense and high-
school anti-intellect peer pressure which drove kids to shoot their
classmates. The endless self-righteousness, the whole everyone-is-
a-victim crap and, yes, even the lack of nuance and satire.

Much worse, however, was my growing awareness of the US
Gulags. Having learnt absolutely nothing from their prohibition of
alcohol and the organised crime it spawned, the US has continued
to try and enforce an unenforceable, death-dealing war against
drugs, and moreover has strong-armed their political allies,
including Britain, to support this ludicrous policy which has completely crippled and corrupted America itself. Heroin has been
banned, even for medical use, since the twenties. Cancer patients
can just scream themselves to death on the much-less-effective
morphine. Anyway, it's not just that, it's the more recent developments. The US has TWO MILLION people in prison – twenty-
five per cent of the whole world's prison population. It has more
citizens in gaol than any country in history. Half a million of these
are non-violent drug offenders. Of those in federal, rather than
state prisons, sixty per cent are drug offenders with no history of
violence. In New York one in three black youths is either in custody or on parole. This is LUDICROUS. This is INSANE.

There is more, and worse. California's 'Three Strikes' has
ended up imprisoning people for life, convicted for their use of
cannabis. Federally, it is just as bad. Bob Gomez, who helps fellow convicts with legal problems in Arizona, says: 'A few years
ago, Congress devised some harsh new sentences for drug offenders. Those terms were drafted with the thought in mind that
offenders could be paroled in one-third or do the entire sentence
in two-thirds of the total amount. When the new non-parolable
sentences were approved, they simply grafted the big numbers on
to the new sentencing code. No politician had the temerity to
jump up and say: "Hey, We're giving these guys too much time." '

Since 1987 federal sentences have been non-parolable. The
maximum good time that can be earned is fifty-four days a year,
meaning that someone with a twenty-year sentence will serve

about seventeen years if they are a model prisoner. And who is, in such circumstances?

Patrick Grady, forty-two, was repeatedly decorated – and wounded – in Vietnam. On his first felony charge of conspiracy to possess and sell cocaine he was sentenced to thirty-six years. He will have to serve at least thirty-one of them. He has a wife and four-year-old daughter. His wife will be seventy when he gets out. He says, 'How is it that I get thirty-six years in prison for selling cocaine when people who rape a woman, bash her head in with a rusty pipe and leave her for dead only get ten years? Am I supposed to be four times more evil than them?'

Danny Martin (who as 'Red Hog' was eventually able to contribute to the Sunday edition of the *San Francisco Chronicle*) is appalled at this situation. He writes: 'Those I see in here who are weighed down by the years are not gun-slinging stereotypes; they are real, hurting people, and they have families outside whose lives, like their own, are devastated.'

A former college professor from the Bay Area gets life without parole for seven kilos of cocaine. A Sacramento man receives twenty-seven years for conspiring to manufacture methamphetamine. Aminah Muhammad's husband is doing twenty-three years just for being in a house where drugs were found. Martin says, 'Twenty or thirty years is a Mount Everest of time and very few can climb it.'

He was also appalled by the US Supreme Court's decision in 1990 to give prison officers sweeping powers to force convicts to take psychotropic drugs – 'that make them total zombies' – against their will. He also notes ironically the growing length of the voluntary chemical pill line daily at the prison hospital where desperately unhappy men take major 'chemical straitjackets' such as Haldol (Halperidol) and Prolixin. Martin notes 'men who are spending decades incarcerated for their illegal drug activities are now doped up by government doctors to help them bear the agony of their sentences'.

Then there is the huge growth in the private prison sectors which now run over a hundred facilities in twenty-seven states, holding over 100,000 inmates. US prisons are notoriously brutal, but there is no-one to oversee how people are treated in private facilities. The cost of building prisons has averaged $7 billion a year for the past decade. The prison industry is the country's biggest employer after General Motors. And prisoners – especially in the private sector – work. They make everything from jeans to handbags. (Levi Jeans certainly had a contract with a private prison although I am not certain that this is still the case.) Anyway worker convicts are paid slave wages. They *are* slaves. The prisons are full of 'new immigrants, the poor and people of colour'. This state of affairs describes a prison-industrial complex. These are GULAGS.

American goods – and certainly those that are made in prisons – should be boycotted as much as possible until non-violent offenders are treated in a humane manner and the reported one in seven innocent people executed are also taken seriously. The situation is even worse for women prisoners who, as in Britain, are given much harsher sentences for minor offences than their male counterparts. Unfortunately, Amnesty International does not regard those in prison on drugs charges as being political prisoners – even though the legislation that put them there is highly political.

I keep thinking of the all-Sicilian Genna clan who helped to make Chicago into a blood-streaked Murder Central in the twenties. Sponsored by Capone, they paid the police $200,000 yearly to look the other way. They were the chief suppliers of liquor to the Chicago dives. The liquor was abominable. They were such hopeless distillers that their liquor actually possessed a poisonous residue (like street drugs today). Someone who purchased a 'bad' Genna bottle would wind up blind, paralysed or dead. A big family, they were known as the 'Terrible Gennas'. I have a picture of them all having lunch. They look pleased. And very prosperous.

The final thing that turned me against the US (and I know this is irrational) was the death of Kathy Acker. I did not get to know her well until her last years in Britain, after she was ill and had had a double mastectomy. Like many talented people, she could be a bit of a monster (if you paid her too much attention, you were crowding her, if you didn't, you were neglecting her and so on). But she was beautiful and brave and ferociously clever and wholly devoted to art and literature. Again, as in the case of many intellectuals, she was emotionally infantile. (That's why psychiatrists –

among others – don't like intellectuals. Everything psychiatric takes much, much longer.)

Kathy drove her friends crazy when she denied still having cancer, completely rejected the NHS and replaced it with a battery of alternative healers. She would phone her psychic in San Francisco every day and this person would somehow *sense* her condition down the international lines. Oh yes? I'd go, 'It's supposed to be *complementary* medicine, you know' and she'd get cross, for a bit.

She was always so healthy and disciplined and gym-crazy that it seemed really cruel that she was ill. She had done all the right things. I wished I had known her in my twenties as I would have found her very sexy. She was very intuitive about people and very sharp about rooting out the bits of personality they kept under wraps or didn't even have until Kathy released them. She would egg me on, trying to get me to do or say things which I felt uneasy about. I don't mean standard wrongdoing. Kathy was far too subtle for anything so obvious. She realised very quickly that I was pretty much antithetical to gossip and saw it a a form of lying or betrayal, so she would push and push me until I laughed and at least made a show of giving in. And then she'd point out the contradictions. No wonder she was fascinated by sadomasochism.

Kathy Acker's early contributions to literature were truly revolutionary and ground-breaking. Books like *The Adult Life of Toulouse-Lautrec*, *The Childlike Life of the Black Tarantula* and *Great Expectations*, published in small press editions, should really be collected and re-issued. She was absolutely wonderful to talk to. She was a real artist and a true bibliophile. I loved her and I miss her.

2

Writing columns

Too serious – not serious enough

What I really like to do most of all is to write columns. I *have* written columns but they have mainly been books columns – I did one for *Spin Magazine* and for five years I wrote one for a glossy magazine, but I am certainly not going to impose any of those on you. What I actually like to write is the regular, non-specific personal column where you get to inflict your opinions, however demented, on patient readers and are actually encouraged to rant on about your current obsessions. However, I'm rarely asked to do this – usually only when the regular is sick or propagating and needs a stand-in.

I suspect that there are several reasons why editors don't think of someone like myself when it comes to commissioning columns. Firstly, I am supposed to be a literary journalist. Oddly, this seems to give editors the impression that I am deeply preoccupied with serious thoughts rather than being deeply preoccupied with the glimpse of a pair of multi-coloured Robert Clergerie shoes or cogitating seriously as to whether op-art nail-extensions with tiny silver bells through the end of each nail would actually conceal my nail-biting or just be too awful. And, even if such lightsome things were on my mind, they assume I would not be longing to tell the world about them.

Secondly, and moreover, editors probably consider levity and friable entertainment to be beyond my powers – as I have mentioned, frolics, jests and blithe spirits are invariably excised from literary journalism, presumably in order to convey high seriousness as far as the eye can see in every direction. (Any regular book reviewer will confirm this – although everything is changing now; see the Epilogue.)

I also suspect that editors do not think that I am representative of their readership and that the good punters would be puzzled by my peregrinations and therefore generally unresponsive. Now, even though I am obviously no Bridget Jones or Dulcie Domum, this may still be paranoia on my part. When I do publish some-thing personal-ish, lots of people write to me! However, such exclusion-zoning has been going on most of my life. For example, I love answering questionnaires, but when I approach people with clipboards in the street, begging to be allowed to contribute to their research, they repulse me! They say they want a majority viewpoint! Verily, such data-compilers have fled from my front door, even as I have begged pitifully like Blanche Dubois, that they stay and ask me questions.

Throughout my adolescence in a provincial city, I would go into shops and ask for quite simple, ordinary things – black under-wear, silver paint, purple lipstick, scented writing paper – only to be told, day after day, in tones of intolerable smugness, 'There's no demand.' Obviously there was – *me*. (One of the local emporia – Thomas Cook's – were so discomposed by my fashion sense that they refused to let me into their horrid little office at all, let alone export me elsewhere.) But the point is, they were all Wrong. We know now that there is a demand for *everything*, however *outré*; things I would have killed for back then – sequinned hairbands, skull-shaped candles, chocolate dildos, a wind-up action toy of a man buggering a sheep (safe sex by the way), violently coloured Smeg fridges – you can get anything you can think of now *some-where* (so much so it's taken all the fun of the chase out of shop-ping) – so you see I wasn't unrepresentative, merely a bit *previous*. (I've been longing to use that expression for years and never had a chance.)

Now that that I have outgrown, in every sense, my youthful fashion victimhood, I feel that I exude normality of the precise sort required for penning a column: long-married, self-employed, tax-paying, failed home decorator *and* I have a terminal disease! I even live in Notting Hill! Surely I am awash with worldly wisdom? What more do they want?

Also, as a bonus point, readers can feel superior to me. I have really bad taste outside of books (and many would dispute my dis-cernment there as well). Whenever I can afford to buy some art or music, everybody goes 'eww' and won't let me play and display. I especially like glittery things and toys. (And I don't mean in an ironic or kitsch sense, although I like a bit of that too.) As men-tioned, I badly need to locate my inner adult.

Last week, for my niece's birthday, I sent her: one deep-pink handbag embroidered with silk rosebuds, one teddy bear in a white lace tutu and tiara clutching a bunch of flowers with sparklets on, one pair of knee-high leggings made of what looked like very long, silky, combed grey yak fur but obviously wasn't, one transparent cushion full of suffocated pink and blue mini teddy bears, one huge pink perspex ring which lit up and flashed if you pressed a button. My niece was ecstatic; she is nine. I LOVED everything except the tutu teddy – I'm not big on bears, except my own ancient one, Lazy Teddy. I went back later though and got myself a bubble watch with what appears to be an opium pipe inside. So you see, anyone could despise my taste. I won't even mention my home decor Horrors.

I've probably got it all arse-backwards though. Readers may not seek *schadenfreude* but prefer to graze in easy envy on the words of perfect stylists living in industrial spaces, with a ship's hull for a dining table, scattered driftwood, obtrusive radiators and shiny chandeliers made out of twisty, recycled Spam cans.

So I will never be able to tell the world about the fish that swim all through the flat at night, the poltergeist I invoked by mistake who won't leave and has just moved the medicine box into the Hoover bag, my first trip to the USA to eat grits (yuk) and see if everything was like it is in the books (it wasn't), my improbable love of dinghy sailing, the successes and failures of the voodoo altar, the long-ago partner I made work right through the *Kama Sutra* with me and the results, the time I believed I was a bat for weeks, my unhelpful attitude towards twelve-step stuff, my profound and considered opinions on issues of the day, the way my library moves itself around at night – oh, sorry, no books.

If I think I hear a susurration of relief arising at being spared all this, it would have to be my deluded grandiosity.

After all, who cares really?

Anyway, I'd rather have a books column than no column.

Rough trade kitty

The Big Issue, 4 August 1997

Some years ago we saw a cinema listing in a northern provincial paper. The film showing was Apocalypse Now: The Director's Cat. *How I wished I could have seen it.*

I received more letters and comments about the column below than I have about almost anything else I have ever published. It concerns the death of our much-loved eighteen-year-old cat. Although it was more than a couple of years ago now, I still haven't been able to confront the ashes. They are hidden away somewhere. Pathetic, isn't it?

Our kitty was born at Rough Trade Records. He was the smallest, least-musical, much-bullied member of a large litter. He was a weird colour – an astonishing pure beige without a hint of ginger; like one of Jean Muir's posh silk dresses.

Returning to collect him, we were determined to avoid separation trauma and came armed with cuddly toys and soothing velvet wraps. All unnecessary – he couldn't get out of there quick enough. Greeting me possessively he rushed us away, seemingly unfazed by the Night, the Big, Wide World and the Small, Crap Car. Head tucked beneath my chin he gazed out ecstatically at the tower blocks of West London. He purred deafeningly. He did everything but squeak 'The Hallelujah Chorus'. We bore him into a King's Cross council maisonette on a silken palliasse and made obeisance unto him. And things went on like that.

Cat-owners are often thought to be loveless, frustrated wimps with horrible taste, their calendars and diaries all encrusted with bug-eyed kitschy kittens. Or else they are dysfunctional bores, droning endlessly about their astonishingly gifted, unique, psychic, supra-intelligent moggie.

Our little wisp turned out to be astonishingly gifted, unique, psychic and in short the most remarkable cat ever. The first night home I was sitting crying on a mattress and he mountaineered right up me on his tiny needly claws and licked all the tears away. He then ate a huge supper, fitted himself neatly into the Kleenex box on our bed and went to sleep.

From thenceforth he always wanted to kip in a Kleenex box, but alas, soon he overflowed the sides. So he had to sleep on us.

He loved cheese. He was frightened of grass and his own sneezes. And thunder – he thought I controlled the weather.

OK, none of this seems especially miraculous. In many ways he was the average house-cat – an awesomely, self-willed tyrannical despot, eerily reminiscent of Caligula and Machiavelli.

Like a bad restaurant we had Frenchified his name. He was Chat or Chat-chat. Perhaps this accounted for his terrifyingly expensive tastes. He demanded an ensuite bathroom; his litter tray was the size of a jacuzzi. He disdained tinned catfood unless it was called something like Gourmet Rip-Off. Thwarted by our budget he would suck plastic bags loudly for hours in revenge. He didn't see why he should eat off the floor and would join us on the pine bench at meals. A dilemma! Surely it was specie-ist to exclude him?

He liked to sleep in the wash basin in summer so we were always plunging our hands deep into a bowl of hot, cross fur in the dark.

Insanely loyal, Chat would barely acknowledge other people who could never understand what we saw in him. 'Cold . . . distant . . . sarcastic,' they muttered. But once he'd seen them off, he would revert to his all-singing, all-dancing combination of psychic torturer and adoring love bunny. He wanted to talk – he was very opinionated – and he wanted to be entertained. Constantly. He wanted to be brushed (he was a closet long-hair), he wanted to do balletic leaps, he wanted to play Fetch! and and Climbing Round the Room Without Touching the Floor. He wanted us to pretend to fall over and squash him. He wanted to be worn round our necks like a fox-fur. He wanted to butt our foreheads in a cat-kiss.

Castration didn't stop him pursuing an active, apparently satisfactory sex life with our best shirts and jerseys. Jealously, at the first signs of connubial activity, he would tunnel up the bed until his head emerged triumphantly between us. It was not sexy. He wanted us to croon his favourite songs – Bob Marley's 'A Hungry

Cat is An Angry Cat' and later on, Baby Bird's 'You're Gorgeous'. He hated us to go out. He boycotted holidays – tucking himself deep in the luggage to come with us. When I found myself phoning him every day from Florida we decided this was ridiculous – he was spoilt. We stopped going on holiday.

I always tried not to be anthropomorphic. I reminded myself that if our sizes were reversed he would treat us with the offhand sadism he accorded to moths. It was no good. He had weaselled his way into the centre of our hearts and lives.

When you spend nearly eighteen years in close contact with another living being, they can communicate anything to you, no matter how subtle. He'd wait for my return from the shops: 'About time too! Could you turn off the rain, please? Did you bring my Treat? Oh no, the piece of cod that passeth understanding . . . Ok, Ok, I did vaguely lick the butter. Oh and my tail sort of brushed over that stuff you left out on a mirror – Oops, no need to be like that. It was an Accident. And could you tighten up my collar a bit? Kiss kiss. Actually I've got a slight ache in my left hind leg. Massage it! Now!'

Veterinary medicine became increasingly sophisticated during Chat's lifetime and his incipient kidney problems were kept at bay by low-protein American catfood. It was not until last year that his health really failed.

We nursed him for a year. It was exhausting, manic and often tragic. Pills, for example. The books say nonchalantly, 'Ease open the cat's mouth and pop the pill on the back of the tongue.' Yeah! They never mention the Sudden Spit-Back or The Slow Dissolve and Drool. He eventually took them – with butterscotch Fromage Frais.

Chat dreaded incontinence and I vowed that he would suffer neither that nor pain. Ironically, I could do far more to protect my cat than my father who died during this period with all the indignity and agony we reserve for humans. Chat became so frail he could fit in the Kleenex box again.

Cats know when it's time to go and finally he was tired and hid himself away to die in the umbrellas. But he couldn't die, because of all the medicine. So he selected the one window without a balcony beneath and jumped out when I turned away for a second. He wanted me to notice – he knew he might need help. When I saw my darling four floors down on the concrete I nearly went berserk with anguish. We rushed down with a stepladder and checked that he could be moved. I wrapped him up gently and he nuzzled beneath my chin. He wasn't badly injured although his poor nose was bleeding.

The vet had been due that week anyway. Chat had made his wishes quite clear and trusted us to sort it out. The vet put him to sleep. He died bravely and affectionately. I cried and cried. I see him everywhere – a little blond ghost. I hear him calling.

The passion flower failure

The Big Issue, 16 March 1998

Columns are usually self-explanatory, although sometimes the editor nominates a subject for you to write about. This was the case in these following columns from The Big Issue. *Becky Gardiner was* The Big Issue*'s editor at the time and I am grateful to her for letting me write about a wide variety of topics.*

In the first piece (below), they wanted to know how I lost my virginity, although my scrupulously truthful account was not received with cries of joy. I had to add some sexual advice for today's teenagers (!) and the piece was edited in a knockabout fashion (not by Becky) that made some of it incomprehensible: for example, the words 'pipe cleaner' were substituted for 'pipe dottle' on the assumption (I suppose) that modern youth would not be familiar with a pipe dottle. Well, they should be. It is in novels. It is a bit of metal with a flat bottom and a sharp point embedded therein. It is for reaming, tamping and I assume . . . dottling pipes. A pipe cleaner, by comparison, is very bendy and could not be used to extract anything *from* any *orifice.*

They also wanted a column about nannies who harm their charges. I vivaciously over-researched the this topic and as far as I recall the piece was too long to print.

Anyway, here they are, as they were.

Losing one's virginity is always a problem. Still, I would be interested to know if anyone else has ever made such a complete, well . . . cock-up of it as I managed to do.

My first attempt went like this: my friends and I at boarding school had decided that we would try extra hard to get de-virginated during the Xmas holidays so that we would have something interesting to talk about during the long and hellishly dreary Spring Term. We had practised for ages with Tampax and candles and even I think once, some vegetables, but my friend Dede got a candle stuck up her and she panicked and I had to get it down with my uncle's pipe dottle.

Anyway, every day after the routine misery of Xmas I got a bus from my parents' house in the country into the nearest town and looked for someone to oblige me.

One rainy afternoon I ran into Dave in Smith's downstairs record department, listening to new releases on the earphones. He was a Yorkshire boy, a drop-out and traveller who sometimes came up to our school in the evenings to sell speed at the back door that led into the orchard. He had spiky, choppy blonde hair and wire-rim glasses. He was nice, although a bit moody because of all the speed he took. He told me he had taken a bedsit in town for the winter, so we went there.

His room overlooked the railway. On the far side of the tracks you could see the local lunatic asylum. It was a horrible room, tiny, with sticky lino on the floor. There was nothing in it except some trays of dirty cat-litter (very full) and an iron bed with a mattress, a cushion and a thin, grey blanket on it. Also on the floor was a big saucepan containing a lot of God-knows-what, because whatever it was was covered in thick green and grey mould. I didn't like to comment in case Dave was cultivating something important, like yoghurt. I asked him to draw the curtains as it was still raining outside and the view was really depressing.

We took our clothes off and lay down. I shut my eyes. After a bit I thought Dave whispered to me, 'Don't worry, I've got some French lettuce,' so I sat up and screamed. I had never heard the old-fashioned term for condoms, 'French letters'. I thought he meant he was going to wrap some disgusting herbal remedy round his prick and put it in me. Dave asked me how old I was and, when I said 'thirteen', he threw me out. I got the bus home.

The next term I was going out on weekend afternoons with a boy called Sam from our all-male brother school across town. Sam was in the Sixth Form and very good-looking, although his personality was boring. He had hair the colour of cinnamon and beautiful long legs. He wore sunglasses in winter. We were allowed to go for walks with the boys, but not to sit down. The staff went around town by car and bicycle to check that we didn't disobey this very strict rule. Well, one afternoon Sam and I actually did sit down. We were sheltering from the rain on a wooden bench in an outside alcove of an old, locked-up church. I sat on Sam's knee. He pushed up my uniform blouse and jersey, and my skirt, and started to twiddle around. Just then an old man – a tramp, I think – came round the corner. He had long, white hair and was wearing a greyish-looking plastic mac, no trousers and shoes without laces which were full of water and made a sloshing sound. I watched as the old man took off his plastic mac. He was naked underneath, all goose-pimply. His genitals were maroon-coloured and seemed shrivelled. I was shocked – it was very cold. Then the old man began to eat his plastic mac, tearing at it with his teeth, chewing and gobbling so I ran away.

By the Summer Term I was going out with another boy, called Mark. He was the drummer in the boys' school rock band. One Saturday we bicycled out to the country and lay down on the grass. We were not allowed sexy *agent provocateur*-type undies but we were allowed to wear long-johns so I had on bright scarlet woollen ones with white lace round the legs. They were a bit hot but I thought they might be erotic, with any luck. I hadn't even got them off before something sharp pinged on my thigh. It hurt. I could hear laughter far away and then a hail of pellets were thudding into the trees and grass around us. We were right next to the army shooting range at Catterick. The army cadets, full of vile, youthful high spirits, were firing at us. I suppose I made a good target.

After this I went off sex for while – well, until the next time.

When I finally did lose my virginity, afterwards I went into the bathroom and took a huge overdose of pills. That was really because the student involved had decided to do the job thoroughly and buggered me too.

This is, unfortunately, all true.

We don't want to think about it

The Big Issue, 1997

Nobody can ever understand it. But it keeps happening, again and again. And each time there is a great flurry of confusion and theory and psychology and legalities and still, at the centre of it all, there is an act that puzzles everyone. As soon as one name is forgotten by the media, another one takes its place.

In 1991, twenty-year-old Swiss nanny, Olivia Riner, apparently poured fuel around the carry-cot of her three-month-old charge, Kirsty Fischer, and burnt the child to death. This was in Westchester County, USA. Although Riner was officially acquitted of the crime, later evidence made it almost inconceivable that she could have been innocent.

Over the last year it has been impossible to avoid the name of Louise Woodward, another nanny tried in the US for a very similar crime, in this case the murder of toddler, Matthew Eappen. Woodward is British and just as the Swiss authorities and populace vigorously defended Olivia Riner, as if the very suggestion of such a terrible crime was a slur on the entire country, so too Louise Woodward became a national heroine in Britain. The tabloids whipped up patriotic outrage and the whole sad story became an international issue, to the point where the trial was rendered farcical.

And now, during the past fortnight, yet another live-in nanny has appeared in court, charged with shaking Caroline Jongen, a six-month-old baby, so hard that the child has suffered severe and possibly even fatal brain damage. The nanny, Louise Sullivan, is Australian. It seems obvious that such cases are, tragically, going to continue. It is also obvious that no-one has the remotest handle on what is going on. During each trial the biggest problem has been the apparent lack of motive. The usual motives for murder – love, hate, money, revenge – are lacking. We are not talking about deprivation. These nannies were not ill-treated. They were hired by well-to-do, working couples usually via some apparently reputable agency. They had good references (although Riner's were later found to have been forged); they were installed in comfortable surroundings. They are bright girls, all of whom professed to love babies.

All such cases inevitably attract immense concern. Not only do they heighten our awareness of the very contemporary issue of working mothers and the paucity of childcare facilities but they also stir a much deeper, primal taboo – the abhorrence we feel towards women who have intentionally harmed defenceless children. So deeply entrenched is this feeling of revulsion and mystification that a society, or a nation, will invariably choose to deny that such an act could have occurred. We just do not want to believe that sweet, young girls can carry out vicious, murderous attacks on babies. Denial is an infinitely more comfortable option than any attempt to get at the truth.

These cases in which nannies harm children are presented to us as if each one were an unprecedented aberration, wholly baffling. Yet such attacks are very far from being unprecedented. Long ago, right at the start of this century, one doctor was so troubled by accounts of young girls harming infants in their care that he devoted a great deal of research to it.

Karl Jaspers, who died in 1969, is known to us as a leading existential philosopher. However, as a young man he wrote an unusual dissertation for his medical doctorate at the University of Heidelberg in 1907. Its subject was a well-known eighteenth- and nineteenth-century phenomenon – young European girls sent away from home to be employed as live-in nursemaids who, seemingly inexplicably, set fires and attacked or murdered the infants in their care. Such cases were numerous and they had much in common. The girls were almost all of apparently good character – indeed, there was a very marked contrast between their apparent docility and innocent appearance and the heinous crimes they committed.

At the time of Jaspers' thesis, forensic psychology had barely begun. Additionally, Jaspers' findings were swiftly overtaken by technology and, gradually, the practice of hiring immature adolescents to look after small children died out. This sort of indentured labour (which is what it is) did not appear again until late in the twentieth century when it became common practice for both husband and wife to have full-time jobs. By then, of course, Jaspers' doctorate was long forgotten.

Jaspers was studying girls who found themselves in a situation that has once again become very common. Unsophisticated girls, with extremely limited experience of the world, go off to a completely alien environment, severed from all the emotional bonds of family and friends. They are left wholly unsupervised with no company save that of a baby or children. Some of them do not speak the language of their new country.

Jaspers theorised that this situation was potentially cataclysmic for a certain type of rigid, dutiful or merely immature personality. None of the girls he studied had a criminal past. Indeed, they were all perceived to be kind and trustworthy. Most were very conscientious and behaved affectionately towards their infant charges. Yet, they murdered these babies – they burnt them, they choked them, they poisoned them, they drowned them. When presented with the proof of their actions, they all took refuge in the same sort of flat, childlike, affectless denial of the crime.

Jaspers' underlying theory was that all these girls were linked by suffering from a peculiarly intense form of homesickness – what we would call culture shock. These girls, he posited, were absolutely unable to deal with their changed circumstances and their only solution was one of infantile logic – to remove the barrier to their freedom, that is, the child or children. They could not think beyond that. It was as if they had all stepped into some strange, psychotic parallel universe – although they appeared to be acting normally, in reality they were sleepwalking inexorably towards an act of insanity which they did not really understand themselves.

These crimes occurred spontaneously all over the old Austro-Hungarian Empire, throughout Middle Europe. The girls were completely unaware of one another. Each felt entirely alone and seemed almost to be exhibiting some terrible personal primal impulse. Boredom, homesickness, confusion, alienation – it was as if the awesome violence of their actions afforded the girls some desperately needed emotional release from circumstances that they could not live with and yet could find no logical explanation for why they must leave.

These cases were so common that other doctors had struggled

to understand them. In 1795 a researcher noted that most arson attempts were made by young girls sent straight into servitude from their parents' homes. Doctors wondered whether there were strange forces within adolescent girls that drove them to commit evil acts. They could find no motives – no jealousy or hatred – just the stark horror of the acts themselves. Oddly enough for a punitive era, such cases were treated with a certain amount of leniency as if it were generally understood that these girls had become temporarily deranged.

Jaspers' case histories are harrowing. He called his thesis *Heimweh und Verbrechen* (Homesickness and Crime). Once our contemporary understanding of culture shock is also included, we can see how very strong the parallels are with the cases of today's nannies. Olivia Riner is a classic example: she was helplessly homesick, on an almost unconscious level. A book on the Riner case unearthed Jaspers' theory, but it seems to have been forgotten again. Unfortunately – because it provides an indispensable psychological, historical and cultural model for the current study of such cases.

Jaspers concluded that, just as a young plant will die if uprooted into alien soil with the loss of all its nutrients and supports, so some young people cannot adjust to sudden, complete change. He felt that these girls' attacks were an all-or-nothing, desperate attempt to hang on to their sanity.

Olivia Riner returned to Zurich as a heroine to be greeted by journalists, supporters, flowers, applause and rejoicing. Louise Woodward too became a celebrity.

No-one is suggesting that all these cases are identical. There can be accidents, there can be a plethora of forces at play. But there is enough in Jaspers' theory to give considerable pause for thought.

Jaspers found one constant characteristic amongst the girls he studied. In their behaviour and appearance, they were all quite childlike. Most appeared to be intelligent and mentally healthy but their emotional development was very immature and had failed to keep pace with their reasoning processes. And if you look at pictures of Riner and Woodward – well, they could be sisters.

With thanks to Joyce Egginton's Circle Of Fire, *Avon Books, New York, 1994*

A kind of reading

The Guardian, 18 March 1993

This piece is really more about adolescence than about books, although I can understand that some readers might dispute that. Anyway, I have left it, mainly because it seemed to appeal to Guardian readers who wrote me lots of nice letters about it. Thank you all, if rather belatedly.

The book cover looks like *Their Satanic Majesties' Request* or *Disraeli Gears* or a Fillmore West poster. There are amoebic globules, rainbows and bubbles. The title is spelt out in the bodies of topless nymphs: LOVE LOVE LOVE it says. This is a volume of poetry published in 1967, a period piece of arrant bandwagon-jumping by Corgi Books. Until very recently, it seemed like a forgotten relic. However, for front-line readers like myself who spent the sixties locked in provincial boarding schools, such publications evoked at the time the faraway glamour of seismic social change: a world of photographers and crimpers, moptops, poets and fools, incense and candles, velvet cloaks and jewels. Out there was *Oz* and *IT* and CND and Dylan at the Albert Hall and we were too young – doo wah! Nevertheless, despite the restrictions of pocket money and school censorship (most of our books had to live up a chimney) it was possible, even in isolation, to follow a less strident but in the long run more telling revolution: the one that occurred in writing, in publishing and in bookselling.

British publishing was extraordinarily adventurous at that time. Penguin's inspired editor, Tony Godwin, was our main supplier. Penguin bought us *The Catcher in the Rye* and the interminable adventures of J. D. Salinger's Glass family but they also published James Leo Herlihy's equally momentous tale of adolescent disillusion *All Fall Down* (1962). Pan published Jack Kerouac, Corgi published Nelson Algren's great trilogy, *The Man with the Golden Arm*, *A Walk on the Wild Side* and *Never Come*

Morning and Mayflower Paperbacks even published Barbara Probst Solomon's *The Beat Of Life* (1966), an aching story of abortion and betrayal amongst the hipsters of the Lower East Side. British readers looked to the US for guides to the New World and Truman Capote, James Baldwin, Carson McCullers, Tennessee Williams, Hunter S. Thompson and the Beat writers were all available in paperback. In 1965 Grove Press produced *The Olympia Reader*, excerpts from books published by Maurice Girodias' Paris-based Olympia Press. It contained, amongst other pieces, work by Henry Miller, Lawrence Durrell, Beckett, Genet, William Burroughs, Raymond Queneau, Georges Bataille and Gregory Corso. Most of these writers soon became available in Britain. Calder & Boyars, Peter Owen and Jonathan Cape were enthusiastically responsive to American and European writing. Burroughs was published by Jonathan Cape and Calder & Boyars before appearing in Panther Paperback. Genet was also available in Panther Paperbacks, as was one of the first British gay novels *Winger's Landfall* by Stuart Launder (1966). Calder & Boyars published Georges Bataille, Alex Trocchi and in 1966 Hubert Selby's *Last Exit to Brooklyn*. Tom Maschler and Ed Victor at Cape smashed the tweedy pipe-puffingly respectable image of literary editors and Victor became one of the founders of the underground paper *Ink*. In paperback Sonny Mehta founded Paladin in 1969 which swiftly published Jeff Nuttall's *Bomb Culture*, Nik Cohn's *Awopbopaloobopalopbamboom* and Richard Neville's *Playpower*. In the early seventies Caroline Lascelles established the very influential Picador imprint.

Despite the massive influence from abroad, there was plenty of new British writing. My friend and I wanted to be writers which meant we wanted to be poets, who were glamorous at that time, which really meant we wanted poet boyfriends who would serenade us as sad-eyed ladies of Harrogate. Primed by Penguin's excellent *Modern Poets* and *Modern European Poets* series, we heard all about the 'Wholly Communion' poetry event at the Albert Hall in 1965. Allen Ginsberg played Tibetan fingerbells, Adrien Mitchell read 'Tell Me Lies about Vietnam' and poets of all nations performed Kurt Schwitters' Sneezing Song! The Liverpool Poets – Adrian Henri, Roger McGough and Brian Patten – were rushed out in Penguin and accorded the status of pop stars. We had been unable to respond to the Larkin-led 'Movement' poets – the name alone grossed us out. Who wanted to read about civil servants and cycle clips when the new poets were writing about sex? Ultimately, the real legacy of the British beatnik poets lay less in their work than in their receptivity, the links they forged with US poets like Ginsberg and Louis Zukofsky, with Black Mountain College and the New York poets, links which enabled Ed Dorn to come and teach in England and which encouraged Tom Pickard to open the Morden Tower Bookshop in Newcastle. Pickard also reminded us that we had our very own world-class poet – Basil Bunting – right there in Northumberland and the Morden Tower championed other local writers such as Barry MacSweeney.

In fiction the Angry Young Men swiftly seemed parochial and dated, although we still read the books. They were all available in Penguin. Alan Sillitoe's *The Loneliness of the Long Distance Runner* and David Storey's *This Sporting Life* were a bit too testosterone-driven. John Wain's *Room at the Top* was more poignant – there were plenty of Joe Lamptons around town. Keith Waterhouse's *Billy Liar* was an acceptable alternative to incomprehensible stories of American adolescence and Stan Barstow's *A Kind Of Loving* in which the hero is vividly sick on his mother-in-law's carpet seemed particularly daring. Lawrence Durrell's *Alexandria Quartet* was available in Faber paperbacks and led to embarrassing outbreaks of teenagers trying to act like Justine. However, Durrell's first and superior work, *The Black Book,* which so coruscatingly describes 'the little death . . . the English death' remained marooned in Olympia Press.

Most influential of all was Colin MacInnes' *Absolute Beginners* which not only attempted to deal with the emergent youth culture but also provided a noble cause in its descriptions of the Notting Hill riots. By this time we felt hugely welcoming towards any gaol-bird, junkie, card-sharp, black person or anti-war demonstrator who might chance past the dormitory, but none did.

The most significant change was in women's writing. At the beginning of the decade we were reading Daphne Du Maurier, Anya Seton and Margaret Mitchell. Gradually, a less romantic tone crept in. From the US came books by Grace Metalious,

Jacqueline Susann, Elaine Dundy and Sylvia Plath, along with Mary McCarthy's very sexually instructive *The Group*. At home there were the various visions of Brigid Brophy, Muriel Spark, Edna O'Brien and Nell Dunn. The catalyst was Lynne Reid Banks' wrenching *The L-Shaped Room* (1960). Margaret Drabble – who had recently vacated our school – published *five* novels during the decade, all of which charted the transition from provincial gaucherie to a more sophisticated if slightly tame and academic world.

Most important was Shena Mackay's *Dust Falls on Eugene Schlumberger/Toddler on the Run* (1964) which actually described bohemian girls, running away from school, living rough and generally going to the bad, bringing it all back home to us that everything similar we had read was about men. The work of all these writers paved the way for the publication of Germaine Greer's *The Female Eunuch* in 1971.

The final brick in the wall of literary change came with the opening of Compendium Bookshop in Camden Town in 1968. It arose out of the ashes of Tony Godwin's Better Books and Miles' Indica Bookshop. Bibliophile troubles were at an end; any publication, however obscure or obscene, could now be procured. Compendium, the Shakespeare & Company of North London, celebrates its twenty-fifth birthday this year, having provided the model for countless independent bookshops in the interim. Its relaxed agenda is now duplicated in corporate form by Waterstone's. By the end of the decade the literary scene had changed out of all recognition – comics, import books, small publishers, poetry magazines and fanzines were flourishing. At the time, unlike now, a certain amount of reading was obligatory for a fully paid-up party animal. And we left school and headed for *la vie bohème*, absurdly confident that British paperback publishing had left us fully forewarned and forearmed.

I'm against Nature, me . . .

The Sunday Times, 24 April 1994

The following column was written in response to one of those requests to write about your all-time favourite book. It is hopeless trying to choose ONE favourite book. I have lots. So all you can do is pick one of them at random and try to entertain.

The girl from The Incredible String Band smashed my bottle of Balmain against a drystone wall. 'Perfume, ugh!' she said, 'It's just not natural' and went inside, probably to put the electric kettle on. It wasn't easy being a provincial decadent in the late sixties. There was a marked lack of ancient grimoires and incunabula in the north-east. During school holidays I sulked around, trying to match my Cocktail Sobranie cigarettes to my outfit and clutching copies of Baudelaire and Burroughs. Just another tortured teen. The local hippies baked bread so ferociously healthy it chewed back. Compost heap living was obviously hell, especially for the women, which is why they all took the pill surreptitiously – it was about the least natural thing a professional Earth Mother could do.

Still, at least I had my books which I devoutly believed would deprave and corrupt me. Finding a paperback translation of J. K. Huysmans' *Against Nature* (1884) in a Scottish post office seemed to confirm my dark fate. This was it, the Unholy Grail, the book Arthur Symons had called 'the breviary of the Decadence'. This novel had corrupted Dorian Gray and caused Oscar Wilde to write 'It was the strangest book that he had ever read. It seemed to him that in exquisite raiment and to the delicate sound of flutes, the sins of the world were passing in dumb show before him.'

My haphazard reading had not really taught me that less than a century before there had been a veritable army of red-eyed Symbolists and Decadents, cross-eyed on absinthe and narcotics, who had craved weird and complex sensations and longed to extend the boundaries of human experience. They had attempted every excess, every possible perversion, every blasphemy and eccentricity. They were obsessed with death, crime, necrophilia, demons, chimera, artifice and the ecstasies of sexual pleasure and pain. They kept snakes, frogs or lobsters as pets. Their interior decor leaned heavily towards Orientalism, hookahs, intoxicating vapours, skulls with moonstone eyes and bizarre bibelots long before such extremes made their sixties revival.

Against Nature gave me a crash course in the original European Decadence of the 1890s, and considering that Huysmans was living at that disordered time, it did so with impeccable taste and foresight. It extolled the art of Gustave Moreau, Odilon Redon, Felicien Rops and the poetry of Paul Valéry, Stephane Mallarmé and other forerunners of Modernism including Baudelaire, whose giant, syphilitic shadow looms over every page.

Des Esseintes, the novel's hero, was the first fictional dandy and Huysmans drew on several real-life prototypes. The most prominent was the Comte de Montesquiou, a languid sybarite. Huysmans shamelessly appropriated Montesquiou's extravagances including his gilded tortoise which Des Esseintes further burdens with impossibly obscure gems until the wretched chelonian dies.

Joris-Karl Huysmans himself was no satanic majesty but a minor civil servant and prolific writer previously associated with Zola's school of Realism or Naturalism who now resolved to 'extend the scope of the novel'.

The fictional Des Esseintes was an enfeebled, decayed, aristocratic hypochondriac free to sample the 'unnatural love affairs, perverse pleasures' of *fin-de-siècle* Paris. Splenetic and disgusted, he decides to isolate himself amongst his priceless *objets d'art*. First, however, he gives his famous black banquet, a funeral feast for his late virility. The garden is strewn with charcoal, the ornamental pond filled with ink and the unhappy guests satiate themselves upon rye bread, olives, caviar, chocolate creams, mulberries and cherries, washed down with kvass, porter and stout. When I tried to emulate this with my more prosaic but much cheaper Mashed Potatoes in Mourning, I found they didn't sell black food colouring ('There's no call for it, Miss').

Huysmans conducts us ponderously through every tiny detail of Des Esseintes' new house. We meet the replica ship's cabin, the blasphemous parody of an anchorite's cell, the 'mouth-organ' that can formulate any alcoholic concoction, the carnivorous plants that gulp raw meat and perversely appear artificial; we see it all down to the last watered-silk book binding flecked with gold. Thoughts and memories enliven this inventory. Des Esseintes advocates feeding by enema to defeat the vile, natural, gustatory digestive process . . .

Reading it again, so much later, it hardly seems like the Michelin Guide to malignancy and sin it once appeared. The orange leather and indigo decor, the mechanical fish entangled in artificial seaweed resemble an old set for *Eurotrash*. To a mind bludgeoned by animatronics and virtual reality, it now appears mild.

However perverse Huysmans' subject matter, he never deserted the naturalist creed of conscientious documentation. He was the trainspotter of Decadence. He had little imagination but great style. He filched, borrowed and stole from the most obscure sources. Self-obsessed, he could be original only about his endless spiritual crises which he projected upon his characters. And yet, eccentric, unique *Against Nature* endures. Ironically so, because Des Esseintes was no decadent but an aesthete, a bibliophile, a scholar. With the democratisation of pleasure, it is Decadence – the old tired trappings of novelty, perversion, drugs and sado-masochism that have triumphed – all the obvious stuff that Des Esseintes fled, his anguish and alienation presaging future fiction.

Against Nature is also the first part of Huysmans' great spiritual odyssey. Under the influence of two satanic clerics, the Abbé Boullan who advocated bestiality and Father Louis Van Haecke who had crosses tattooed on the soles of his feet to profane the crucifixion, Huysmans wrote *Down There* (1891) a paint-by-numbers account of a Black Mass. He then rejoined the Church and wrote about that.

As for me, I tried to create a *paradis artificiel* in my university room. The (real) altar candles set the curtains alight and this being an ultra-modern, plastic, cellular structure, the bright, white study-bedroom walls just melted away completely.

It could have been me!

The Big Issue, 1997

And this one is about the time I tried to murder someone.
Deliberately.

When ex-model, Tracie Andrews, was finally found guilty last
month, of killing her lover, Lee Harvey, *The Sun* described her as
giving 'a defiant flick of her long hair as she was taken to the cells
below'. Of course her blonde fringe couldn't just have got into her
eyes – she had to exhibit the insolent, hardened traits of a convicted murderess. So run our prejudices. And very inaccurate they
are too.

Tracie appears to have been guilty of an instantly recognisable
offence – the crime of passion or *crime passionnel*, as it is known
under the Napoleonic Code still governing laws in France. This
concept does not exist in Britain. There is no definition for the
hot-blooded, violent, usually murderous attack carried out in a
frenzied eruption of raging endorphins and pheromones, love and
lust, hatred and jealousy. The offender has usually been driven
temporarily insane by their partner; they feel they cannot live with
or without this person and give vent to their confusion, hysteria
and frustration in a desperate, retaliatory assault.

While Monsieur and Mademoiselle regularly drench their
smouldering affairs with the potent petrol of passion and explode
into inflammable melodrama, Mr and Mrs Crazy Paving UK are
considered to have no such sultry impulses. But most of us have
been there, which is why many countries proffer a certain sympathy. (What *would* our courts have done with Othello had he
reached them? Straight to Broadmoor and that ultimate hell-on-
earth, Sociology A Level, I suppose.)

Murder here must proceed in an orderly, methodical manner
with straightforward motivation – greed, revenge, self-defence,
witness obliteration or the random paraphilias of sexual slaughter.

British law's disregard for the ambiguities of human behaviour has always caused considerable problems – notably in the hanging of Ruth Ellis for the classic *crime passionnel* shooting of her impossible lover, David Blakely. By then, in 1955, the execution of women was very rare. (Electric chair occupant, Donald 'Pee-Wee' Gaskins, once remarked 'I never heard of no women libbers demanding their equal rights when it comes to capital punishment' . . .)

UK crimes of passion seem to lack a certain flash and filigree – they often have a seamy quality, redolent of hot tea, dirty gin bottles and grubby lino. Ex-society 'It Girl', Elvira Barney, was a bedraggled piss-artist by 1932 when she was acquitted out of sympathy for her distraught, lovestruck state, although she had very definitely fatally shot her toyboy, Scott Stephen. (Class wins out – Ruth Ellis was a divorced mum and club hostess.) Yvonne Chevallier was acquitted in France, in 1951, after killing her husband, an adulterous government minister. But more recently, in very similar circumstances, Jean Harris received life in the US for shooting her diet-doc lover, Herman Tarnower. All three women claimed their guns went off by accident.

Such thwarted love and psychic torment still induce arbitrary verdicts and unease, despite the crocodile tears shed for Ruth Ellis. Ironically so, because any one of us could react similarly during a totally screwed-up relationship. There has been little sympathy extended to Tracie Andrews although, as in divorce or spousal abuse, it can take two to twirl the torture tango. Aged twenty-eight, in a society that cringes from demise, it is quite possible that Andrews has had no contact with, or possibility of understanding, the utter horror and finality of death. She doesn't seem to have even been a morbid sort of temptress (unless you count shagging to 'Bat out of Hell', which seems more a lapse of taste than of sanity).

I, too, at the same age as Andrews, tried to kill my boyfriend. It was not an especially abusive physical relationship – we were both culpable; we bared our fangs, chopped, kicked and screamed. (I bit his leg, he broke my rib sort of thing.) But I had been an exceptionally ghoulish child, obsessed with graveyards, owls, wolves and horror stories. I had two, rather sinister imaginary companions, right up to university. One, Melchior, was skeletally thin, with long, lank black hair, green eyes, adze-like cheekbones and sharp silver fingernails. He came wrapped in a black sable cloak, intoning blasphemous Latin and poisoning the odour of sanctity. I don't think he was a very good influence. Even less so was his cohort, a piece of rough called The Masque Wouse, a dwarf with an ever-changing face like a blob of paint. (His name comes from a painting by James Ensor.)

Gothically-inclined kids like myself enter a long flirtation with Death in their teens. They have dirty aubergine silk sheets, they droop around in black lace and leather with black-dyed hair and Cleopatra eyes beneath their shades. Gorged on the decadent output of authors like Baudelaire, Bataille and Burroughs, they live at night, by candlelight, listening to music for suicide and encrusted with the impedimenta of death – fetishes and bones and gris-gris, animal skulls with blazing gemstone eyes. They try voodoo, they try *anything*. Oddly enough, they will inevitably select unstable partners! They risk their lives in every possible way and not just by having terrible taste. And then one day, Death gets tired of it all and he whips round and roars foully into their faces, 'LOOK at me when I talk to you, you little shit!!' And they grow up.

This is what happened when I was driven to attempt a crime of passion. It was the mental agony that did it – the days of wine and neuroses, the uncertainty, the jealousy, the verbal taunts, the apparent lack of feeling from my lover. Of course I was in love with him – that's what made it all so unbearable.

I had a French policeman's baton, rubber, spring loaded with steel. While the Loved One was cleaning the bath (and generally being objectionable), I drew the baton from my jeans, ready to bop him on the head. He would tumble senseless into the bath and drown beneath the running shower and then I would explain dolorously how, cross-eyed on drugs, he must have stumbled over the edge and knocked himself out. Fortunately, he sensed my crazed presence drawing closer and, exhibiting lightning reflexes not usually associated with heavy-duty chemical devotion, snatched away my weapon. Noting his displeasure I shot out a window, still wearing only jeans and he chased me tempestuously across the North London rooftops.

This particular story, unlike that of Tracie Andrews, has a happy ending. We both found saner partners and we are now the best of friends. After we had parted and the essential insanity of *crime passionnel* faded, I realised how lucky I was in having been prevented from causing myself and many others the most terrible grief and regret. But as someone who up till that point – and since – has refused to kill even clothes moths or cat fleas, I knew I had had a tiny glimpse of the real face of Death and it was far, far more monstrous than anything I had ever imagined.

For all we know, Tracie Andrews may feel similarly. Certainly, those who kill in the course of a volcanic relationship are very unlikely to do so again. So perhaps the avoidance of words like 'Evil Tracie' and a modicum of leniency and compassion might be in order.

In *Cold Comfort Farm* Stella Gibbons describes the English as outwardly stolid but 'blazing with poetry in their secret souls'. Blazing with poetry and passion in your secret soul will get you nowhere at the Old Bailey.

The agony of losing your looks (by Ligeia Winter)

The Independent on Sunday, 2 February 1997

Editors have sometimes complained to me that they could never get any woman to write about being, or having been, beautiful. Rashly, I agreed to try. At first I was as diffident as anyone else and wrote it in the form of an interview with a woman called Anya (who was really myself) on the subject of her (now long dissipated) good looks. My editor was not happy. I was forced to rewrite it in the first person singular. I still chickened out in two respects, though – I wrote it under a pseudonym (from Edgar Allen Poe, as usual) and I refused to provide Before and After photographs for the Independent on Sunday.

The article was then sold on to a women's glossy magazine which insisted (if I wanted my half of the fee) that I provide a photograph from my flaming youth and that they take a contemporary picture. Accordingly, I spent a very long, hot day in a studio and ended up looking, in my opinion, like a fifties housewife with what was virtually a bouffant hairstyle. No offence, they seemed pleasant enough.

I just hoped no-one I knew would see it.

For about fifteen years I rarely paid a train or bus fare. People just let me off. I never went food shopping – I didn't go into a supermarket until I was over thirty. I never had to buy meals or drinks unless I really insisted. Men gave me expensive drugs all the time. I wasn't trying to ponce off people or to prostitute myself. They just offered . . . Jean Cocteau said, 'The privileges of beauty are enormous', but it is hard to to make the damning admission that one is, or was beautiful, or to speculate on what the inevitable loss of such looks entails.

I was never a classic, or even a natural beauty. I was too small, and back then too thin and flat-chested – but youth, determination and artifice ensured that my combination of dark reddish hair, pale skin, big eyes, high cheekbones and pre-collagen pout conformed to a certain western ideal. Distinct, flexible, it has predominated for some forty years.

Facially, I was beautiful enough to obscure my other bad points. It would have been stupid to pretend I didn't know that many people were attracted to me. But conscious awareness of my looks made me feel superstitious and desperate. The hysterical emphasis on youth and beauty everywhere was a forcible reminder of their temporary nature. Everything I depended on was slipping away, day by day . . .

In the meantime I obeyed the usual rituals – I modelled (hats, cosmetics, kids, clothes), appeared talentlessly in films, accepted air tickets, travelled with rock bands, posed for artists and photographers. After university it never occurred to me – at first – to get a serious job. I had no confidence in any abilities beyond being decorative and I always lived with someone. There was always someone happy to look after me. I was not calculating or even practical about this and initally had to believe that I really cared for each lover. I preferred the scruffy and artistic to the purely wealthy and was often a zombie-like muse, absorbing the fantasies, projections and insults of some arty egomaniac. Like a lot of pretty girls, I endured some real bastards. Nice, unselfish men were usually much too diffident to approach. Also – particularly if your beauty is contrived – you feel a fraud and let men mistreat you. You know you are valued for something which is simultaneously deemed incredibly important and yet of little worth. Your position is a result of luck, not ability.

But things *are* much easier for the pretty girl. When you are indulged like that you acquire a sort of learned helplessness. It makes you very lazy with your life. You drift along like sea kelp. People would go to incredible lengths for me – driving me hundreds of miles on a whim, taking over all practical and unpleasant tasks. Many men expected sex in return but others, men and women who knew sex was out of the question, would still persist, for more obscure and complex reasons. People would try and persuade me to become an escort girl, service clients properly and make real money. But I felt I prostituted myself anyway, living partly off lovers. I despised myself. I did get jobs – they were constantly offered – but I couldn't get up in the morning. I'd always been out the night before. I survived – I was homeless for about a year so I would just go to a party and pick someone to live with for a while. Then this guy bought me some emeralds and a flat in Shepherd's Bush. Hardly *Breakfast At Tiffany's* . . .

The terrible pity is that you don't really know the power of your youth and beauty until you are older and it has gone. And it does go – no-one at forty looks as they did at eighteen, whatever they do.

I was terrified of ageing. I thought I was finished at twenty-five and at thirty I married, convinced I'd soon be worthless. Every day there were these sharp reminders. I read about three French TV commentators – beautiful women – who all killed themselves shortly after their fortieth birthdays. I couldn't forget it.

One time I was in a drug clinic and I used to watch from the window to see other women arrive. Some of them had been famous beauties in their time, top models, rock star consorts, and stars themselves. From a distance, with their long blonde hair, expensive boots, cuddling their saluki and shih tzu dogs, they still looked great, but up close they were old; skulls and ashes. It was chilling.

Every little sign that you are getting older is a dagger to the heart. You really feel it. The first time someone calls you 'Madam'. The first time a man's eyes don't follow you. The first time you like a guy and he is completely indifferent – no offers of a lift, a drink, not even a telephone number. The first year with no valentines and recalling the fifteen or twenty that used to arrive. The first sign of pity or triumph from a friend. The increasing callousness regarding your welfare. The growing anonymity – standing alone for the first time at a party. No more being whisked to the head of the queue and 'After you, please' and 'I expect we can find a spare seat', being automatically on the guest-list, having a backstage pass, not needing an invitation, being admired. You have to adjust to Real Life and about time too.

After thirty my shape changed. My shouders broadened and I lost the pipe-stem arms and thighs, the androgynous, adolescent silhouette necessary for fashion victimhood. After thirty-five the chin loses its definition, gravity takes over, the mouth turns down at the edges and awful lines score themselves from the edges of the nose to the mouth. In your mid-thirties you have to come to the decision whether to work at it (and it really is hard work by now), to exercise and have cosmetic surgery or not to bother. But by that time, you've been so spoilt that you don't have much self-discipline. The years of indulgence have taken their toll. And now you have to pay for everything – in every way. It is very easy to retreat into seclusion with drink, pets, drugs, TV or whatever floats your boat.

Regrets? I've had a few. I wish I'd been more hard-headed and had something to show for those years. I wish I'd restricted my charms to people who could have furthered a career. But with feminism barely established and no self-confidence it was difficult. Feminism created more options and made for better relationships with other women, but otherwise any pretty boy could have had the same experiences.

Now in my forties, I am still married, living in public housing and leading an ordinary working life. I don't resent younger people; after all I had a good innings. I can't say I've learnt anything heartwarming about the unimportance of looks – not in this society. My looks were part of me and, without them, I've never felt I am offering more than half a person. I hate it most when people see old pictures of me and say, 'God, I'd never have recognised you', because neither would I. And worse – if scientists do conquer ageing it will be too late for me. I always *knew* that would happen.

Conspiracy theory

Along with Hollywood, conspiracy theory also seems quintessentially American, although of course its roots predate the very discovery of that controversial country. I have a longstanding affection for conspiracy theory but am not really a total convert in that I believe that the fundamental cock-up theory governs most affairs. Still, I keep a large collection of conspiracy books behind a cunning false fish-tank in my library. The Guardian originally commissioned this quick run-down of the subject, but on seeing it, took fright, realising that if they showed their hand and published it then the pivotal role that The Guardian *had played in so many of these ongoing dramas might begin to come to light . . .*

'My God, can't I invent any preposterous paranoid fantasy that doesn't have some truth behind it?' Robert Anton Wilson, author

There are ancient, worm-ridden grimoires and bright new CD-ROMS that enable one to picnic on the grassy knoll and watch JFK's head explode; the world's conspiracy theories fill dark, never-ending miles of libraries. Additionally, the central figures and obsessions of conspiracy have fuelled the work of countless artists. Christopher Marlowe, Dr John Dee, Nicholas Hawksmoor, Richard II; alchemy, the French Revolution, fertility myths: all such alleged conspiracies and conspirators have inspired writers from Shakespeare to Iain Sinclair, from Peter Ackroyd to Lindsey Clarke. We may sneer complacently at the idea of midget aliens with almond eyes inflicting third-degree burns on Arizona house-wives, or leather-clad satanists harvesting children's organs for sale on Honduran human farms. Nevertheless, we all subscribe to conspiracy theory whether it's merely a weary nod at the turpitude of politicians and spin-doctors or a full-blooded belief that the Queen oversees a network of drugs distributed through St John's Ambulance Brigade, designed to undermine America's moral fibre.

Authors including Thomas Pynchon and William Burroughs have suggested that paranoia is the only sane response to an incomprehensible world. Conspiracy theories are part of a mind-set particularly well adapted to the present. The trickle-down from arts and science research tells us that nothing is stable, all is in flux, that God has gone off to play dice. Performance artists, musicians, painters and dramatists create work that ominously and suggestively confirms our powerlessness, whether it draws on snuff films or historical revisionism. Consider Damian Hirst's early assemblages of cages and torture instruments. Or Joe Coleman, self-professed geek who bites the heads off rats and whose paintings expose the running sores of a terminally dazed and confused society mired in virulent disease, sexual mania and medical madness. Fifty per cent of Americans do not bother to vote. Cynicism and distrust weave our national winding sheets as tiredly, stoically, we perceive the hypocrisies of public life, the not-so-hidden agendas of media and advertising and a morality that lavishly rewards the most shamelessly self-serving and power-crazed behaviour. If we tolerate so much, so openly, how extreme and venal can that which remains secret be?

Out there in cyberspace, the Net is awash with conspiracy theory, twenty-five per cent of it still debating the Kennedy assassination – with the assassination of Abraham Lincoln gaining ground fast. Improved telecommunications have vastly increased the conspiracy field, turning the world into a huge pinball machine whose lights flash and jangle with each scatter attack of new detail. And finally our fatal psychic millenarian mixture of credulity, scepticism, boredom and apprehension renders us susceptible to this tidal sewage of information and disinformation.

Of course, conspiracy theories go way back. Most contemporary secret organisations trace their lineage, quite incorrectly, to times immemorial, to Egypt, to the Knights Templar, to the Rosicrucians (hoax), or the Bavarian Illuminati and so on, but for sanity's sake, I focus only on the dominant contemporary theories.

So welcome to the secret societies, the cover-ups, the hoaxes, the double-blinds and the triple agents. Let the acronyms begin – CREEP, OSS-CIA, MI6, MK-ULTRA, NASA, IMF, TACT (Truth About Civil Turmoil), COG (Continuity of Government), FEMA (Federal Emergency Management Agency). One may dismiss conspiracy theory, one may respond, be amused, irreverent, annoyed, seduced, but altogether it can stand as a contemporary, wholly democratic art form, the stories and delusions of thousands of voices, building a fable, a fictive soap opera with familiar characters which attempts to counter the official version of our times.

Just remember – anyone important who is dead is actually still alive and vice versa. Every public figure uses doubles. Anyone murdered by a 'lone nut' assassin was the victim of a group and anyone murdered by a group was the victim of a single mastermind. As the Hell's Angels say, 'Three can keep a secret if two of them are dead.'

1 The Assassination of JFK

Still the front-runner. Whether Kennedy was killed by the FBI, the CIA, the Russians, the Mafia, the far Right, the far Left, anti-Cuban loyalists or a hairless tranvestite pilot with alopecia, we don't know. We do know that only Lee Harvey Oswald missed, that the Warren Committee was a scam and that the brain vanished. Journalist Paul Krassner mounted a widely believed conspiracy hoax that Lyndon Johnson ecstatically buggered the wounds in Kennedy's head as the body was flown to Washington on Air Force One. JFK responsible for a mountain of books and films, including Oliver Stone's *JFK* – which itself contains hundreds of 'subliminal images' including caged rats, Masonic hand signals and pictures of occult sex rituals – Don de Lillo's *Libra* and Norman Mailer's forthcoming *Oswald's Tale: An American Mystery*. JFK probably assassinated by a deep-cover alliance between Hollywood, literary agents and publishing houses. Spin-offs include:

a) *The murder of Lee Harvey Oswald* by Jack Ruby acting as a Mafia agent. Ruby usefully dying himself of cancer, natural or induced within two years. The sudden, unexplained deaths of another twenty-two witnesses to JFK's death or individuals questioned by the Warren Committee.

b) *The assassination of Robert Kennedy*. Ostensibly killed by Sirhan Sirhan in a hypnotic trance induced by military (east or west) mind control experiments. Sirhan's shots all missed. Actually shot by mysterious woman or security guard visible on film. John Lennon also killed by Mark Chapman linked to CIA-funded and neo-Nazi groups in similar pre-set trance condition. Refer to CIA experimentation RHIC-EDOM (Radio Hypnotic Intracerebral Control) and 'Operation Spellbinder' 1966 – 'Sleeper killer', unknowing control subjects who could be turned into assassins upon receiving previously implanted code word. There is extensive photographic documentation of electrodes implanted in the brains of unwitting subjects. Sirhan and Chapman 'examined' by same psychiatrist, Bernard Diamond.

c) *Chappaquiddick*. Mary Jo Kopechne learned about Kennedy Mafia involvement. She fled Chappaquiddick, was assaulted, suffered a broken nose and was left to suffocate for over two hours in submerged car. Subsequent cover-up involved everyone from Massachusetts legislature to Cardinal Cushing whose priests persuaded the family not to have an autopsy.

d) *The death of Marilyn Monroe*. With no barbiturate capsules in stomach, no injection marks and no drinking water, it appears a suppository was used. Alleged murder to avoid exposure of MM's link with Kennedys.

2 The Gemstone File

Early exposure to Gemstone has made this the most cuddlesome of conspiracy theories for me. Purportedly a vast file of letters penned by one Bruce Roberts, a crystallographer involved in the making of artificial rubies. His research was stolen by the Hughes Corporation as it involved laser beams and potentially fibre optics. No-one has ever seen the original document but for over two decades a synopsis, 'A Skeleton Key to the Gemstone File', has been reprinted, photocopied and circulated throughout the worldwide underground, with occasional additions. The compiler of the Key, Stephanie Caruana, claims to have read about four hundred of the thousand-odd original letters.

The Skeleton Key is a monolithic conspiracy theory covering all the main events in American politics from World War Two until Watergate. Essentially, Onassis is Mr Big. He makes millions in WW2 selling oil, arms and heroin to both sides without losing a single man or ship. He is in league with Rockefeller and I. G. Farben. Onassis kidnaps Howard Hughes, makes him addicted to heroin and ships him off to Skorpios, installing a puppet double in his place and thus acquiring Hughes Aircraft holdings. 1957 – Onassis liaises with Mafia to control presidency. J.F. and R. Kennedy later offed, having reneged on Mafia bargains. 'An old Mafia rule: if someone welshes on a deal, kill him and take his gun and his girl: in this case Jackie and the Pentagon.'

So the Skeleton Key goes on, year by year, crammed with specific points, some preposterous, some accurate. It veers between drunken, paranoid rants and oddly convincing detail. Some of it has been substantiated – particularly the sections involving CIA heroin trafficking in south-east Asia – although it remains riddled with holes, plagiarism and errors. Memorably, hundreds of characters – e.g. Senator Estes Kefauver – are offed with a non-traceable, apple-smelling, heart attack-inducing poison 'sodium morphate', usually administered in the form of apple pies . . . Scientists have searched in vain for this substance.

Jim Keith's book *The Gemstone File* reprints the Skeleton Key and examines the whole. In conclusion, it seems to be a patchwork of fact and crazy hoax – 'buried in the dross is a lot of hard fact' – which contains an underlying metaphorical truth regarding the takeover of post-war America by gangsters, corrupt politicians and other evildoers.

3 The Octopus

Son of the Gemstone File. Danny Casolaro, a journalist investigating an international power cabal (The Octopus) for his book *Behold a Pale Horse* was found dead in West Virginia, 1992. His research covered BCCI, Iran-Contra, secret weapons technology including bio-toxins, drug trafficking, CIA dirty tricks, murder for hire and money-laundering through the notorious Australian Nugan-Hand Bank. His strange 'suicide' occurred after he met the final informant who could confirm his theories.

4 UFOs

The people's favourite. A vast file which includes the much disputed 1947 Roswell case and many well-documented close encounters including the Cash-Landrum case. Here, three subjects who approach a 'spacecraft' in the road suffered severe burns and indications of radiation sickness. Are aliens trying to contact and abduct humans? Never-ending tales of military cover-ups. UFOs have given rise to countless films, books and speculations including the suggestion that they are all disinformation designed to draw attention away from secret weapons research and cheap energy sources. Affiliated to cattle mutilations – over 70,000 in the States alone, photographs revealing systematic hi-tech ex-sanguination and removal of organs – crop circle debates and Bermuda Triangle disappearances.

5 The Satanic Conspiracy

Despite the fancy names such as Ordo Templi Orientis (who owned the world's only occult petrol station), much modern satanism is merely a drizzle of second-hand Aleister Crowley prattle, drug use, sex 'magick' and out-takes from H. P. Lovecraft's fiction. Its real concerns remain properly satanic – power, money, sadism. Most frequently scapegoated is strange, black-cloaked British cult, The Process, an offshoot of Scientology, who decamped to the US and strongly influenced Charles Manson. The Process imploded in Mexico, allegedly fragmenting into numerous other groups. Most notable was the 'Four Pi' cult who harboured an 'occult superstar' and contract caller, Manson 2 aka William Menztner, who was convicted of the murder of depraved millionaire Roy Radin. Strong ties exist to the 'Son of Sam' case and a powerful occult network specialising in snuff films, kiddie porn, blackmail and the harvesting of human organs for sale. Usual suspects include Anton La Vey, head of Church of Satan and Col. Michael Aquino from US Intelligence, head of Temple of Set.

6 AIDS

A deliberately-engineered designer disease. Emerged full-blown (either by accident or design) in three US cities with organised gay populations before being exported to Africa and Haiti. No known virus has ever before targeted specific cells of human immune system. Aligned to undercover weapons research, biological and otherwise; including microwave radiation used at Greenham Common and the Russian Embassy and the mystery of the dead scientists, many of them employed at Marconi Defence and/or in SDI work. They might have gone to staff outposts on Mars or the moon for when the Earth becomes uninhabitable for elite groups.

7 Jonestown Conspiracy

An experiment in forced labour camps, an idea strongly promoted by senators like Newt Gingrich and Phil Gramm who feel that drug users, AIDs sufferers etc. should be isolated without constitutional rights. Also a trial 'Final Solution' for US black population in the event of racial disturbances. Ninety per cent of the dead were black and/or female and children. Little evidence of cyanide. Massive cover-up of original reports and autopsies. Part of long history of CIA/military intelligence thirty-year mind control programme MK-Ultra. Possible links to killings of Martin Luther King and Malcolm X.

8 Drugs Conspiracy

Drugs are the second largest international trading commodity after oil, yielding $500 billion yearly worldwide. The drug trade props up international banking, many governments and clandestine agencies. The 'War on Drugs' masks real wars in South America, helps suppress and distract US black population and allows considerable erosion of civil liberties.

9 White Supremacy

The most complex of conspiracies in that it involves a shadowy armer of plotters who are themselves dependent upon conspiracy theory for their beliefs. The many US groups, descended from the Ku Klux Klan include the Minutemen, Aryan Nations, White Patriots, and Posse Comitatus who have become increasingly aggressive and terrorist as the Oklahoma bombing indicates. They are fundamentally Hitlerian and draw on an eccentric variety of sources, many of them originally fictional such as *The Protocols of The Elders of Zion*, originally a satire on Napoleon II, and William Pierce's *The Turner Diaries*. They oppose what they believe is an international conspiracy of Jewish bankers, including the Rothschilds and Rockerfellers, sundry royals, groups such as the Knights of Malta, the Freemasons, the Trilateral Commission, British Intelligence. Anti-black, anti-Catholic, anti-Asian, all together they form an increasingly strong and complex, worldwide white resistance movement backed by centuries of anti-Semitism.

10 Political Correctness

A plot which receives confused support from both hard Left and factions of the Right to instigate strict censorship, ban pornography (and sometimes abortion). It imposes formidable strictures upon art and argument, forbidding criticism of ethnic groups, homosexuals and women, or discussion of ethnicity and IQ, negative impressions of homosexual experience, the Holocaust or any other historical revisionism that doesn't conform to a certain racial and sexual agenda or treating AIDS victims in the same way as victims of other communicable diseases.

So what does this farrago of folk-art signify? A furious hunger for storytelling certainly and a violent urge towards knowing truth and faith in a world that lacks both. Otherwise, especially considering how widely such tales are circulated and believed, they imply a slow, psychic crumbling of our traditional set-in-stone understanding of left wing and right wing. When the racist non-tax-paying Posse Comitatus are more hostile to federal government than any anarchists, when feminists find themselves joined with fundamentalists against pornography, when numerous libertarian figures have been fingered as CIA informants and the CIA has undoubtedly helped finance numerous arts projects, when intellectuals are passionately divided over Zionism and Islam, the political distinctions that have moulded all our psyches begin to blur and blend into more individualistic creative outlines.

But I've missed out God's Vatican bankers, Prince William as the Great Beast 666, the secret pact between the Beatles and the Royal Family – and have you heard? . . . whisper, whisper . . .

Mack! – The Knife!

Spin Magazine

This piece is from when I had a column in Spin Magazine *and was driven crazy by American fact-checkers wanting to know things like what exactly was the Newgate Calendar and how did I know and could I prove it, please? Scream!*

Anyway, you know how it is when you label files and you think you can't possibly forget what they refer to but you nearly always do? I was sure this was a non-fiction file. Anyway, it gave me the opportunity to write a little about one of my all-time favourite novels, Pimp.

When Ice-Cube sings about Iceberg Slim in 'Who's The Mack?' he is invoking one of the spiritual godfathers of gangster rap. For decades, alongside the musicians, black writers have been contributing their own versions of urban life. Although Iceberg Slim, aka Robert Beck, wrote many books, his classic is the autobiographical *Pimp*, originally published in 1969.

Pimp describes Iceberg's experiences as a top player in the pimp game in the 'terrible streets' of thirties and forties Chicago. Iceberg's prose is hypnotic, a dynamically demotic street argot as crazily animated as a break-dancer on PCP. Deciding 'I'm not going to be a flunky in a white man's world', Iceberg faced the stark choice that runs through all books on ghetto life – ignominy or crime. For many years he regarded pimping as the hipster's way of revenging himself on the white race. Iceberg Slim's adroit use of language has inspired generations of writers and musicians. One such was Donald Goines, who also portrayed black streetlife in books like *Dopefiend, Black Gangster* and *Daddy Cool* before being murdered by white men.

A similar novel published in 1968 and now re-issued is *Howard Street* by Nathan Heard (Amok). Written while Heard was in the penitentiary, it draws on the author's life in the ghettos of Newark. In what is essentially a work of social realism, Heard debates ethical issues and concludes that the pull of the hipster life and its all-pervasive cynicism will always prove more powerful than the meagre prospects of law-abiding conformity to white rules.

All these novels were beginning to raise issues that became omnipresent during the years of political protest and Panther politics. There was increased focus on the deprivation of black people within a white nation and the importance of recognising this common supremacist enemy rather then preying on other blacks within the ghetto. That these issues have become ever more poignant and diverse in the intervening years is made clear in Kody Scott's *Monster* (Atlantic) a book that has come roaring out of South Central LA like some massive bass riff. Scott's descriptions of gang warfare and his subsequent incarceration and politicisation within the California penal system were foreshadowed by the work of Eldridge Cleaver, George Jackson and George Carr in his 1973 autobiography *Bad* (re-issued this fall, A.K. Press). Scott, a born militarist and tactician, focuses deeply, narrowly, on gang dynamics in this extraordinarily clear and hard-edged autobiography, noting that most of the violence was Crip on Crip. He acknowledges the immense narcissistic power in being armed and dangerous in a world otherwise unresponsive to black youth and writes tellingly and movingly of the death wish that underlies gang activity: death being 'the only lasting peace . . . a reward' and he thus reveals 'the extreme expression of hopelessness' that constitutes gangbanging. *Monster* gradually develops into a powerful political tract as Scott surveys the ever-increasing drug wealth and weaponry in the 'hood and affirms his own commitment to the New Afrikan Independence Movement.

The language of violence sounds the same over in England and there too, to paraphrase Easy Z. the only colour most people care about is green. *Yardie* (Grove/Atlantic) by Victor Headley is a fast-paced ragga style thriller that describes the lives of the London 'Yardies' or Jamaican crack gangs who have revolutionised organised crime in London. D. is a chancer who lifts a kilo of coke from a syndicate and goes into business for himself, prowling the shebeens and reggae dance halls of Brixton and Hackney with his 'soldiers' and an Uzi. Detailed and authentic, *Yardie* was orginally published by a two-man operation and sold on upturned garbage cans outside nightclubs. It immediately found a young audience of readers – over 10,000 – well attuned to the life an old Dread in the book censors – 'Nowadays it's pure killing and fe wha? Vanity; gold, money, drugs, even woman' – and who can really disagree with him?

3

In the bag

Drugs and drugs and rock 'n' roll and some sex

'Happy people don't have to have fun.' Jean Stafford

I know that I am morbid. It seems to be partly an inherited trait and partly for reasons that, for now at least, should remain in my psychiatric file with the NHS. Some people say that I just have a sick mind. I am not sure what this means. How can anyone 'police' their thoughts? Thoughts just drift on, wandering and wondering. You can't suddenly say to yourself 'Stop right there!', unless you are going to throw up. For example, there are only three books that have upset me to the point of illness and only one of them is a real work of literature. That is *The Room* by Hubert Selby. I think it was the bits about fingernails. And the rape. The others are *Final Truth: The Autobiography of Mass Murderer/Serial Killer Donald 'Pee-Wee' Gaskins, as told to Wilton Earle* – a fairly self-explanatory title – and *Hogg* by Samuel Delany which I read relatively recently. With the latter it's not just that everyone goes to the bathroom in their jeans (both micturition and defecation) and gets others to lick it up, but even worse ingestions (from the anti-peristalsis point of view) are lovingly described.

I can remember quite clearly when I first realised that I was morbid and liked the night. I was quite small, in bed at home in Argyll, listening to all the owls and thinking about the old grave-yard up the road where my family had been buried for centuries. (So far back that there is a full-length stone figure of the one guy from the area who made it to the Crusades and home again. Less glamorously, the family was founded by someone known as Ardaig the Clumsy.) Anyway, I was just thinking about all their bones when the ceiling fell in. I was almost killed.

I did not attribute this to divine disapproval. From the outset, extreme hard-line Presbyterianism (no cooking, no cars on ferries on the Sabbath, religious books only on that day, plus the

Catechism to learn, with Church twice on Sundays and no music, only psalms) had always seemed so stunningly boring I couldn't think about it. Our house was on the shore and there was another island over the sound and I could see a white cottage on it so I just pretended I lived there instead.

Later, at school in England, I did get to love the *King James' Bible*, *The Book of Common Prayer* and *Hymns Ancient and Modern*. For the language, I mean.

Anyway, rather obscurely, the point of all this is that I really believe one must have an exaggerated sense of Right and Wrong, rather than an attenuated one, in order to be interested in evil. If one didn't have this blazing sense of duality one would surely be indifferent to wickedness.

The stuff I wrote as a child was all horror fiction. When I started writing fiction again I decided to begin with horror stories, partly because they came naturally to me and partly because it was genre fiction so I didn't have to fret about making Art or not. If Art appeared that might be nice but I wouldn't be *worrying* about it all the time. Some Art did eventually sidle in which meant in the long run that I got paid much less, literary fiction being extremely unprofitable compared to genre . . .

Methadone in their madness

The Guardian, 20 August 1994

This was my original 1994 title but of course the editor changed it. They always do. It was used later in Kevin Williamson's book about drugs legislation.

I wrote the following two lengthy pieces on drugs for Guardian Weekend. *Although the second feature was written three years after the first it was a sequel to it and followed up on the (very revealing) fates of the individual addicts introduced in this first piece.*

Both pieces were written out of sheer fury and frustration. I had seen what was going to happen when they started working towards changing the drug laws in the late sixties at the same time that the infamous Drug Dependency Units (DDUs) were being set up. Back then I had met a few addicts in London during my school holidays – mainly at Eel Pie Island and in Richmond – who were still getting their heroin legally from a doctor. But I only saw heroin once in the provinces before the law changed and stopped doctors providing heroin and cocaine for addicts. I knew about Prohibition. I knew there would be drugs everywhere soon once they were illegal. And now you can score from Land's End to John O'Groats.

The first piece was written out of pure, specific anger. All around me people were having their lives absolutely ruined by something which a century ago would have been of minor importance. All the media seemed intent on displaying their incredible ignorance and bigotry. What specifically annoyed me was that the media persisted in referring to methadone as if it were exactly the same as heroin and not a completely different substance which had caused a revolution in the use of drugs.

The second piece was also prompted by a specific fury. Everyone seemed to have forgotten history. Heroin had been demonised to the point where people gaped disbelievingly when I told them that in the UK, up till 1916, you could go into Harrods (or any other suitable shop) and buy heroin and cocaine over the counter. Now at least this *fact is reprinted constantly. Harrods also sold gelatine sheets soaked in morphine and cocaine during the Great War. The advertisement read: 'A useful present for friends at the front.' No doubt.*

Recently, in the wake of Arnold Trebach's mighty book The Heroin Solution, *other more sensible and humane studies have appeared in the US. They include* The Birth of Heroin and the Demonization of the Dope Fiend *by Th. Metzger. Such books make it quite clear that although those helpful Nazis at Bayer and IG Farben gave heroin and methadone to the world (and Zyklon B to the camps), it was the US which created the gigantic worldwide drugs cock-up we now behold. Metzger shows that the Dope Fiend is as much a mythic figure as 'the cowboy, gangster or rugged pioneer'. God's Own Medicine in the form of opium (both laudanum and paregoric) arrived in America on the 'Mayflower' with the Pilgrims in 1620. Their doctor, Samuel Fuller, brought his medical chest with him and it is documented in detail in the histories of the Founding Fathers. By the late 1800s ONE in TWENTY-FIVE Americans was a heavy user of opiates. Apart from war veterans, the average addict (or* habitué *as they were more kindly known then) was white, female, aged between thirty and forty and from the middle or upper classes. In order to trace how these innocuous users (one of whom wrote 'You don't know what morphine means to some of us, many of us, modern women without professions, without beliefs') transmogrified into the vicious Dope Fiend, it is necessary to understand America's very strange attitudes towards dirt, disease, contagion and threats to the American Way. Throughout this century the US has indulged in a curious psychic and cultural interplay between purity and pollution, which culminated in the very popular eugenics movement when they started madly sterilising anyone they considered defective (always those who were poor and thus less socially and sexually controlled than the middle classes would like). Countless groups were formed attesting to the American obsession with purity of all kinds – psychic, physical, social, sexual. (The American Society of Sanitary and Moral Prophylaxis, the American Social Hygiene Association and so on and on.) As they barrelled towards large-scale eugenics, they had to get rid of liquor on the way, necessitating The Women's Christian Temperance Union, originally formed in 1874. This spawned songs as horribly fascinating as later films such as* Reefer Madness. *They included the hysterical (in every sense 'Lips that Touch Liquor Must Never Touch Mine' – 'O John! How it crushed me when first in your face/The pen of the "Rum Fiend" had written "disgrace";/And turned me in silence and tears from that breath/All poisoned and foul from the chalice of death./It scattered the hopes I had treasured to last;/It darkened the future and clouded the past;/It shattered my idol, And ruined the shrine/For LIPS THAT TOUCH LIQUOR MUST NEVER TOUCH MINE' . . . Good Lord no, anything but that . . .*

The Rum Fiend, once vanquished (ahem) turned later into the Dope Fiend. The similarities in the hyperbole and hysteria are striking.

If the Nazis had not taken eugenics to its logical conclusion, the US might have sterilised itself out of existence by now and left us all in peace.

Incidentally, one of the more famous eugenics studies (facts were fudged and photographs altered in most of them, very similar to later anti-drug propaganda) was conducted on a family called the Pineys of New Jersey. The project was called 'Vineland' and one of its field workers produced a fanciful book which included a description of the

Piney nature 'Like a degenerate relative of the crab that ages ago gave up a free, roving life, and gluing its head to a rock, built a wall of defense around itself, spending the rest of its life kicking food into its mouth and enjoying the functionings of reproduction, the Pineys and all the rest of his type have become barnacles upon our civilization . . .' Somehow I feel that Thomas Pynchon read this and that the title of his novel *Vineland* was thus taken from the eugenics movement. It would be typically obscurantist of him. (Do I get a little prize or something?)

Anyway – since writing these pieces, the failure of the so-called War on Drugs and my increasing disillusionment with the US have convinced me that one way or another this darkness has to give.

I should make my current position clear. Obviously it is better if one can get through life without using drugs, both legal (antibiotics, insulin or as asthma inhalers, for example) and illegal, and without alcohol, cigarettes, patent medicine (Aspirin and Ibuprofen to start with), Flower Remedies or anything else. Few of us are that strong or that lucky over the length of an average adult life. Our present legal situation just makes things very much worse for what has always been a societal impulse, thoroughly documented since Homo Sapiens began drawing on the walls and jotting things down ('Homer, Homer, Homer & Homer Co.').

Twentieth-century Prohibition has poisoned the drugs, the users and the culture. I stopped buying any street/illegal drugs because the quality became so utterly dire that they were not worth the money. Everything was a pale ghost of its former self, thanks to the never-ending rapacity of organised crime. Crime bosses were able to buy up chemists who could approximate – say, cocaine – by using a variety of other substances – lidocaine, mannitol, procaine, quinine, strychnine etc. Crack (debased cocaine free-base) was the beginning of the end. It was vile, labour-intensive stuff, cut and stepped on so comprehensively that one had to wash it again and again. It was a testament only to greed, cold-heartedness and our drug laws.

Gradually, as older social users matured or aged out of recreational drug use, they were replaced by generation after generation of kids who basically were holding out money to be robbed. They had very high expectations of drugs, especially cocaine. They were completely ignorant about what drugs should be. Smokeable cocaine, in its free-base form is, for example, a very subtle drug and it takes time to know *it. Britain, unlike the US, has no real tradition of smoking methamphetamine (speed) which in smokeable form is known as 'Ice' or 'Crank'. It is very cheap and easy to make, so dealers can substitute it plus some dental 'caine and the kids get that Big Bang they are expecting – and that's it. It is just cheap tricks. They are being horribly exploited. Heroin has not fallen quite so low here as it has under organised crime in the States. Pharmaceutical heroin still appears occasionally. But really, all the street drugs are crap now. They've gotta step on it again, always. It all stinks.*

(A friend suggested that everyone in their late teens should spend a long weekend at an anti-rehab place. They would sample smaller and then slightly larger quantities of all the recreational drugs in their purest form. They would record their impressions in notebooks and on tape, and these they would keep. Hopefully, they would then have at least some yardstick by which to judge the alleged 'drugs' on sale and thus refuse them . . .)

I am not trying to be overly simplistic. Obviously there are many long, hard miles between taking a Disprin and being addicted to heroin. Psychotropic drugs, especially heroin, cocaine and crack, militate against the quality of life and ultimately undermine creativity. I would not recommend them to anyone, specially now the SSRIs and their successors the NASAs have arrived and can help dramatically with clinical depression.

Incidentally, when the police issue press releases to the media, they tend to exaggerate on a grand scale. They claim that a seizure is of ludicrous 'purity' (for example, cocaine hydrochloride – the sniffing kind) CANNOT be more than about ninety per cent pure, ever. They claim that the drugs seized are worth a dizzying amount 'on the street'. All such unlikely assertions are to justify police expenditure, time and effort. This is taxpayers' money they are wasting. They cannot very well send in a SWAT team and then say. 'Oh, we..ell, we got two grammes', can they? – although this is exactly what tends to happen in fly-on-the-wall TV docudramas. They also, of course, seize the alleged drug-dealer's money and assets, if there are any. It is not quite as bad as in the States where the 'profits' seized go directly to the local police department. Such an incentive, eh?

It is 4 a.m. Rick is sitting up, again, waiting for the doorbell to ring. Then he can cease his vigil, banish the chills and diarrhoea and go to bed. A solicitor, he is due in court at 9.30 a.m. His wife is an NHS professional. They have been heroin addicts for nearly two decades. They smoke it. They live in terror. They are terrified of arrest, of losing their jobs, losing their home, losing the care of their three young children. The black market devours their salaries apart from the mortgage payments. They can't go on, they can't get out. They don't want to be prescribed methadone. They don't want to be 'registered' addicts. They trust no-one. They endure. They suffer. Another all-night wait. *Ring*, bastard bell, ring, ring . . .

> *'Much as we all deplore the disclosure of personal*
> *confidential information we must accept that it will occur*
> *from time to time.'*
>> 'Bing' Spear, former Head of Drugs Inspectorate

Winston and Anna are in their early fifties and long-term hard-core heroin injectors. They used to manage when they were younger and Winston was dealing. Their council house is shared with Anna's teenage children from a previous marriage and the three daughters she's had with Winston. Then Anna took the fall for a cocaine bust and received a long prison sentence. Winston got his three small children back from care and brought them up haphazardly, moving around, one step ahead of the authorities. Now Anna is back, grey and broken, emphysemic, swollen with oedema. The little girls are grown. Winston is in hospital with bacterial endocarditis from polluted street heroin. They have no electricity. Their windows are broken and boarded, the front door nailed shut. Anna huddles by candlelight in a wreckage of rubbish, mattresses, moths, cats and ancient fur coats. She looks vague and puzzled. They have both been prescribed oral methadone for years. They are barely aware of it. They sell it.

> *'It's time to lock up drug users.'*
>> *Daily Express*, 17 April 1994

Chloë has a Double First and a prestigious job in a venerable institution. Unlike her colleagues she comes home to a high-rise flat with no phone. Then she goes to a local Burger King and waits for the man – usually another girl with the same problems. Often no-one turns up. She'll crawl to work the next day, trying not to throw up or let her bowels explode on the rush hour tube. Methadone? 'You can stuff that shit,' she says.

Toby is in gaol for the fourth time, serving six years. Middle-aged, he owns a large antiquarian bookshop. More prosperous than most addicts, he can buy large quantities at a discount, and like most users, he sells some to friends. A sitting duck for the local police, he has become a hardened recidivist because he prefers to smoke something other than a cigar with his coffee. Most of his 'assets' – i.e. savings – were confiscated when this reclusive bibliophile was surrealistically treated as a major dealer. 'I'm a junkie, not a criminal,' he says.

Why should we care about a few chronic heroin addicts with self-inflicted problems? There are good reasons for caring, and caring passionately, even on elementary humanitarian grounds. Unconcern duplicates denying treatment to an AIDS sufferer or a smoker with lung cancer. A century ago addicts could buy opiates freely in shops. Fifty years ago they could receive heroin and cocaine on prescription. But in recent years they have become a useful all-purpose demon, traduced, dehumanised. Addicts have no civil rights and no-one to fight for them. They can be forced to withdraw on remand without medication – 'an inexcusable piece of barbarism' – even when they hold a prescription for methadone. To those who've flirted with heroin for a few months, withdrawal may be only 'a mild dose of flu', but after several decades of heavy use, addicts rightly dread its horrors.

Today addiction elicits theories from everyone except those best-informed and least-consulted – the addicts themselves. 'It's all down to fashion', said one, quoted in Tam Stewart's *The Heroin Users* (1987). 'They convince you that you're one of those weak, dirty, degenerate people who've got problems,' says another, speaking of the NHS. 'Your experience is irrelevant. They are inflexible. Their minds are closed . . . You think they're motivated by compassion but it's power that turns them on.' Deprived of legal heroin, addicts are delivered gift-wrapped to hungry, vicious crime cartels who ensure that even the purest street heroin contains fifty-eight per cent of 'impurities'. The addict's health is always in danger. Prior to needle exchanges, HIV was widespread, and still is in prisons. It costs about £600 a week to maintain a heroin habit and addicts are locked into a dreary cycle of crime and imprisonment making it almost impossible for them to rejoin society when they finally 'age out' of their addiction, as most do. In addition, a junkie's child joins the 'At Risk' register in the womb if the mother is known to be using street drugs, although addicts tend to be much more conventional, caring parents than alcoholics. Their homes and possessions are targeted, not just by over-zealous police but also by so-called 'vigilantes', local thugs who trash and terrorise users and their families, seizing the drugs to sell round the corner, cynically applauding themselves for 'cleaning up the community'. Would you want to live like this? Well, of course you'd never be so stupid. But no-one sets out to become a hopeless slave to a drug. Of those who experiment with heroin most can walk away unscathed. A few however, once exposed, *do* become dependent and genetic research is only just beginning to discover possible causes. Professor Steve Jones, author of *The Language of Genes*, explains why possession of the D2A1 allele is now significantly associated with drug dependence: the dopamine D2 receptor is part of the brain's 'pleasure centre'. Drug-users appear to possess a much higher proportion of the A1 form of the gene than the one in six ratio found in the general population. So while an addict deserves help for a compulsion they cannot restrain, they may be able to exercise even less control over it than was suspected. But whatever the genetic outcome we urgently need to understand why Britain's heroin addicts have been consigned to this shadow zone of crime, poverty and disease. We need to act before further mindless emulation of US prohibitionist policies reproduces their war zones in UK cities.

Britain's illegal drugs trade is now worth almost three billion pounds annually. Two billion pounds' worth of property crime is drug-related. Drugs arbitrarily valued at £519 million were seized last year. Yet in 1950 there were just 306 known heroin addicts in Britain. By 1960 there were 437. Today there are nearly 25,000 known users. The street agencies estimate that there are easily eight times that number. How *did* this ever happen?

Incomprehension and dread characterise most people's view of heroin after decades of the media's misinformation and selective amnesia. Clean heroin is a benign drug, apart from its addictive potential. 'Cigarette smoking is unquestionably more damaging to the human body than heroin,' as Dr Vincent Dole famously stated. It is the laws that screw you up, not the drug, yet the public have learnt to blame the latter. Folk tales surround the subject – the 'slippery slope' from cannabis downwards, the necessity of constantly increasing the dose – all myths.

The sap of the poppy – opium – has been known for millennia. Homer wrote acutely about its characteristic combination of euphoria and numbness. For centuries opium was almost the only effective medication physicians possessed. Despite the invention of morphine (1803), the hypodermic (1843) and the first synthesis of heroin (1874), public consumption remained unregulated in the nineteenth century. From childhood, opium – used in laudanum and other medicinal compounds – was part of British life.

Charles Kingsley, writing in *Alton Lock* (1850), was untroubled by the drugs menace. 'You gooo into druggist's shop o' market day . . . and you'll see the little boxes, doozens and doozens a'ready on the counter; and never a ven-man's wife gooo by but what calls in for her pennord o'elevation . . .' 'But what is it?' 'Opium, bor' alive, opium!' Almost all the writers of the Romantic period used opium, although significantly very few became dependent. Opium was a universal panacea and the Empire showed no signs of toppling.

The twentieth century saw the US pioneering the long slide towards state control. The US's racist dislike of Chinese immigrants and their opium culture was speedily exploited by Britain. The Yellow Peril was threatening the English Rose and the 1920 Dangerous Drugs Act formalised wartime restrictions on opium and cocaine. Marek Kohn's *Dope Girls* (1992) gives a comprehensive account. However, Sir Humphrey Rolleston's report (1926) allowed doctors to provide heroin and cocaine to addicts. This was known as the 'British System'. Gradually the number of addicts fell. In 1958 there were 333 known addicts, including ninety-nine doctors, dentists and nurses.

Then the sixties erupted. The Establishment shivered with uncertainty and paranoia. By 1965 there were 927 known addicts and 2,782 by 1968. Crisis! The hastily reconvened Brain 2 Committee (1965) advocated changes that were to be dramatic and devastating. Two decisive factors caused this overreaction.

Some doctors, including Dr Petro and Lady Frankau, had been too generous, creating a small black market in pharmaceutical heroin and cocaine. Black markets in desirable goods are inevitable – whether antibiotics, televisions or heroin. Unfortunately no-one could foresee that this small 'grey' market in legal narcotics would be vastly preferable to today's immense, illegal black market.

The second authoritarian panic concerned recreational drug-taking by young people. Aghast, the authorities failed to notice that the lazy, Muppet-like hippies were disinclined towards slaughter and rapine under the influence of allegedly venomous drugs. Hippies usually took cannabis, other hallucinogens and a few amphetamines.

Extreme measures followed the Brain 2 Committee report. In 1968 GPs lost their right to prescribe heroin and cocaine for addicts. A special licence was now needed. (Today 108 doctors – mainly consultant psychiatrists – hold such a license although very few employ it.) DDUs – Drug Dependency Units – were set up instead, headed largely by ambitious consultant psychiatrists, mainly without previous experience of addiction. From the start the DDUs were vastly unpopular. Doctors who might just have prescribed heroin for a fifty-year-old lady dentist balked at handing out free, untaxed Ecstasy to her nephew with his waist-length hair, pink-tinted glasses, guitar and giro. No clear policy existed. Many doctors refused to be no more than legal drug-dealers. Others used the clinics to gain personal power. Some genuinely believed supplying heroin was unethical. (Cocaine, no longer considered addictive, was now out of the question.)

So, gradually, they adopted the US addict treatment system – methadone. Punitive medicine had arrived. Just when the 'British System' became universally recognised as a viable model for reasonable and tolerant drug management – it stopped.

Methadone treatment was popularised in America by Drs Dole and Nyswander in the early sixties. Invented in Germany during WW2, methadone (originally called 'dolophine' after Herr Hitler) is so often described as a 'heroin substitute' that people assume they are virtually indistinguishable. Wrong. What really excited the doctors was that it 'does not produce the euphoria, the feeling of exaltation which comes . . . from other narcotics'. The

Holy Grail! Methadone *is* supremely dull. The grandiose claims made for its efficacy in curing heroin addiction were over-optimistic and premature. Firstly, went the theory, unlike heroin which has to be taken frequently, methadone is very long-lasting and only needs to be taken once a day. Methadone *does* last much longer than heroin but any employed junkie can tell you it's perfectly possible to do without heroin during the day. Secondly, methadone is supposed to 'block' heroin and prevent one feeling it. This may be true of gargantuan amounts but on the ordinary, prescriptive dose of methadone this is a fallacy. Thirdly, although methadone is available in injectable ampoules, it is usually administered in a sugary green syrup and it was this that clinched its appeal. The idea was that the addict, stabilised on his legal morning gulp of methadone would settle down, get a job and come off drugs. Eagerly adopted in Britain, it didn't work like this. Offer a hard-core injecting addict a small cup of vile green glop and he could be forgiven for throwing it in your face. Addicts didn't want methadone, even though Britain was initially more flexible about providing it as ampoules.

Methadone's drawbacks were soon revealed; it is far more addictive than heroin, and more toxic. Withdrawal takes months. Even so, rapid reduction and abstinence became the aim. Dr Tim Willocks, novelist and addiction specialist comments: 'In a nutshell the only goal of treatment to date has been abstinence within two or three months and that's proved to be an impossible dream. Over eight to fifteen years most people do stop taking drugs permanently and within that time you can have people suffering a lot . . . contracting infectious diseases, having to steal, or you can keep them healthy and less socially disruptive by having maintenance.' Doctors liked methadone's low black market value. It wasn't going to create new addicts. Never mind that the burgeoning heroin black market was creating thousands of new addicts. Never mind that, denied their drug of choice, the addicts turned directly to this black market, which responded eagerly. Ignore the Iranian heroin pouring into Britain to create a new generation of 'scag kids' who smoked the stuff. Blindly the clinics pressed on, even though the vast majority of addicts wouldn't go near them. Clinic doctors were often high-handed in their treatment, demanding that addicts sign contracts guaranteeing that they would be 'drug-free' after a certain period. 'It's crazy,' says Dr Ann Dally, whose licence was temporarily revoked in 1987 after treating addicts more liberally. 'Where else in medicine can you promise and sign that you'll be better by a certain date?'

Methadone is a useful drug with several possible applications in treatment. Methadone maintenance *has* helped some addicts to become more stable. A few even prefer it if in injectable form. Some use it, supplemented with street drugs. Addicts differ as much in their responses as anyone else. But in general, oral methadone offered in small and decreasing amounts to every addict as a blanket policy, whatever their age or problems, has proved disastrous. The adoption of methadone treatment succeeded in turning the addict away from the clinics, arousing only cynical alienation towards sources of help and driving them inexorably towards an increasingly well-organised criminal alternative. The senior social worker at a central London DDU (his name withheld for fear of his job) was asked during this survey to estimate what percentage of his clients were taking illegal street heroin at least once a week. 'Ninety-five per cent,' he said.

As early as 1979 Terence Tanner, director of ROMA, a rehabilitative Housing Trust was lamenting, 'Those WRETCHED doctors . . . about 1972 they started moving off heroin to physeptone (methadone). Then off intravenous to oral. The result: the addicts go on the black market, lose their jobs . . . all this because the clinic doctors believe the addicts shouldn't have drugs.'

Fictional portraits of methadone are rare and invariably utterly damning. Vivid images are drawn from life in Paul T. Roger's *Saul's Book*: 'Kicking a methadone jones is ten times worse than kicking dope. You feel like someone's poking hot needles into your bones. You get cramps. You shit like a goose and it all comes out white. You think you're gonna die.' And this is the 'successful' reduction treatment favoured by our government? Dr John Marks has been a lone gunman holding off all critics for fifteen years at his Merseyside clinic whilst legally prescribing heroin, cocaine and other drugs under Section 7 of the 1971 Misuse of Drugs Act. Dr Marks claims that London has a death toll of ten to twenty per cent amongst addicts. 'The policy is CRUEL. They don't seem to care.' He also claims that a local police investigation of his methods suggested that his heroin prescribing has led to a ninety-six per cent reduction in local acquisitive crime.

An argument often raised by doctors who do not wish to prescribe heroin is: 'It would be like giving alcohol to an alcoholic.' Marks' answer describes the present situation very acutely. 'If you were an alcoholic in the Chicago of the 1930s and had just stolen your grandmother's purse to buy a tot of adulterated methylated spirits at an exorbitant price from Mr Capone, I would have a clear conscience in prescribing for you a dram of best Scotch whisky.'

However, methadone is NOT the sole culprit in creating the drugs mayhem we have today. While it has certainly played a part in the most simple, logical way – deny an addict their drug of choice and they'll go elsewhere – other potent factors are involved. Addiction figures were already rising rapidly by the end of the sixties before the DDUs opened. The conspicuous consumption of the decade brought pleasures to many people that earlier in the century were confined to the rich and powerful. (Diana Cooper, in the twenties, injects heroin but it ruins her complexion. A Hollywood star, Carmen Miranda, keeps her cocaine in her platform shoes.) The new dawning, the new democratisation of sumptuary bliss meant the wretched, rationed, British could start sampling everything from aubergines to sex and drugs. In a consumer culture, as William Burroughs has pointed out, drugs are the ultimate consumer item. They deliver (or should if they weren't cut to shreds) what they promise. Recreational drug use could not have been avoided in post-war life. Third World economies would inevitably have contributed to a changing drug scene. Greater drug consumption would also have brought a degree of crime and corruption. Such factors have to be considered when discussing a more flexible policy on opiates, as well as our position in the UN which presupposes agreement with other European countries on drugs legislation. But it seems obvious that the miseries imposed upon contemporary British heroin addicts could be much improved by more flexible prescribing policies and that the drug barons would lose by having some of their lucrative and reprehensible business removed and placed in the hands of those for whom concern for the addict was uppermost. Will Self, ex-addict and novelist, comments that 'the medical and pharmaceutical professions have attempted to enact closure over certain kinds of intoxicants' and regrets the impossibility of positive drug rituals developing within a society where the situation is polarised between alienation/ rebellion and prohibition/suppression, dichotomies which feed off one another.

Throughout the seventies and eighties life stayed grim for the British addict. In the early eighties I visited the head of one of London's DDUs to beg him to reconsider his methadone prescribing policy. Many of his patients, unable to obtain heroin, were injecting Diconal, an analgesic opioid. Crushed Diconal tablets resemble frothy pink milkshakes. Its insoluble filler can block veins so that gangrene and amputation sometimes follow. The DDU physician regarded me coldly and defended his policy, repeating robotically, 'Our records are excellent.' *His records were lies and his patients were dying.* Once in a methadone programme addicts are reluctant to lose a prescription that can be useful, both as revenue and in times of drought. Thus they frequently lie about their consumption of other drugs as transgression means termination.

Teddy, for example, lives in rural Britain. Addicted for over two decades he used to store his methadone in an old air-raid shelter, in case the bomb fell. When that was full he started burying it in a field. He complains that the older bottles now look sticky and undrinkable. He is 'a long-term addict stabilised on methadone'. Teddy has been using black market heroin all along *but no doubt his records are excellent.*

Finally, things are beginning to change. Two issues have tipped the scale – both threats to the community at large. The first was the HIV scare which led to needle exchanges and a more realistic approach to the debate. The second – and this is the real time-bomb – is the growing crime figures. Last year Raymond Kendall, Secretary General of Interpol, argued that 'Drug use should no longer be a criminal offence . . . I am totally against legalisation but in favour of decriminalisation for the user.' Lord Mancroft commented on Britain's prohibitive attitudes: 'This is the policy Britain has followed for thirty years and its failure is clear to see.' Commander John Grieve, Director of Intelligence at Scotland Yard said society had to 'think the unthinkable' and consider controlled legalisation and distribution of drugs because other anti-drug measures were not working. In the spring of this year there was an unprecedented outburst from police chiefs. Admitting that they have lost the war on drugs they suggested that ministers consider a controversial scheme to allow the nearly 25,000 registered addicts to receive heroin and other drugs on the NHS. A survey of 144 addicts in police custody revealed that those receiving NHS drugs spent just as much a day – about £100 – as those who were not. 'Providing addicts with heroin substitutes is a waste of time and money,' said the police doctors. Raymond Kendall stated that drugs were 'much less of a police problem than a social, health and welfare problem'. Earlier he stated that 'the prosecution of thousands of otherwise law-abiding citizens every year is both hypocritical and an affront to individual, civil and human rights'. Ex-Detective Chief Inspector Eddie Ellison, now retired, agrees: 'Imprisonment serves no purpose whatsoever.' Once Operational Head of the Metropolitan Drug Squad, he is outspoken in support of controlled legalisation. 'The current policy is failing badly.' He says, 'Almost without exception the major criminals in the London area are involved in drugs,' and goes on to cite the problems this brings: 'There isn't a drug squad in the world that hasn't become corrupt at one stage . . . There is no doubt at all that continuing prohibition will continue to put up the profits for criminals.' He acknowledges that this is an unprecedented situation: 'You've now got the enforcers, the police service having this dilemma (i.e. trying to enforce an unenforceable law) and identifying it to their political masters.'

The real war, the War *about* Drugs is now being fought between the drug professionals. It is a vituperative, back-stabbing fight.

On one side is a single-issue alliance of police officials, lawyers, doctors, ex-addicts, counsellors, writers and libertarians. They face a formidable phalanx of doctors defending a status quo defined by politicians unprepared to be labelled 'soft' on drugs before any forthcoming election.

The basic quarrel is between those wishing to continue throwing methadone at the problem, despite its proven failure[1] and those believing more doctors should be allowed to prescribe a wider variety of drugs, including heroin, without attracting Home Office wrath.

Within the methadone camp the current issues include: oral or injectable? Reduction or maintenance? Dosage? Policing addicts while they drink the horrible stuff, like in the US. (US addicts keep it in their mouths, spit it out and sell it. Very hygienic.) Urine testing for street drugs?

I spoke to Dr Michael Farrell, who along with Dr John Strang works at the Maudsley Hospital. They are both proponents of methadone treatment. He concedes that doses were previously too low. 'The evidence is that to get a good effect from methadone treatment you need doses within a specific range.' However, if I understood him correctly, he opposes giving addicts the specific drugs they require. He seemed to rely on the 'vast bulk of literature on methadone' without considering that some of it at least could be flawed. Dr Farrell took evasive action, saying that 'methadone prescribing is now boring, it's conventional, it's mainstream – and a lot of people on the margins don't like mainstream treatment'. This was aimed at the libertarians who wish to prescribe opiates other than methadone – as if they had not opposed methadone for decades but instead were, suddenly, perversely, espousing radical tactics for their own sake! Recently Dr Marks has made considerable progress by prescribing heroin and other drugs in smokeable form, in herbal cigarettes. This is encouraging news because intravenous injection, however safely performed, traumatises the system. I asked Dr Farrell whether he would rather see long-term addicts prescribed smokeable heroin or injectable methadone but he said my question was 'disingenuous' and wouldn't answer.

Currently, GP Dr Adrian Garfoot is appearing before a Home Office Misuse Of Drugs Tribunal charged with 'irresponsible prescribing'. Dr Garfoot is not 'marginal'. He'd never had any interest in drugs, never intended to be a drug doctor but faced with addict patients – older ones who'd done the twelve-step uselessly through every drug agency in the land – he responded with a realistic and humane sympathy which ought to be the ethical province of all doctors. He believes that GPs, as they were able to prior to 1968, should be allowed to prescribe the drug of choice to an addict – responsibly and with the emphasis on reduction. The sole alternative is purchase on the street.

Ultimately it comes down to cost. Oral methadone costs the

NHS £300–£400 per patient per year. Injectable opiates cost £1,000–£2,000 and opiate cigarettes or 'reefers' £300–£600. But substitution of the most expensive option would be less than the amount currently wasted in law enforcement. Jacob Veale in the Borough of Hammersmith and Fulham is succeeding dramatically in uniting the different services, with the intention of realistically helping addicts and protecting the community from crime. He says '£1 spent on an adequate (that is, flexible and not methadone only) prescribing service for an addict is £4 saved in community resources.'

I also spoke to Tim Rathbone MP, Chairman of the All Party Drugs Misuse Committee. Rathbone asserted that 'If we could turn the clock back to the time when they were invented we would have made nicotine and alcohol illegal. Absolutely!' – conjuring an image of the most joyless society ever known. He rejected any possibility that methadone treatment had contributed to the growth of the black market and speaking as if to a child said: 'The whole point of methadone treatment is to take people off the drugs that are found on the black market.' As he talked about the necessity for drugs education I recalled a teenager I'd spoken to last year, one of a local drugs posse, a sort of Deals on Wheels. He'd suffered a serious leg injury and been in awful pain until, he said, he'd taken some great painkillers. I feared he had sampled the product and asked what they were. He pulled out some Paramol. 'Oh – I thought you meant you'd done some smack.' 'Huh? That? That's a painkiller?' 'Well . . . yes.' 'Oh – I thought that was coke.' So much for Tory drugs education.

Rathbone appeared to devote his considerable energies to combating what he called 'legalisation' of drugs. No-one I spoke to, however libertarian, advocated legalisation of all drugs, or indeed any drug except cannabis. They advocated controlled decriminalisation. Universally, they wished to discourage drug use and prevent the unimaginable torrents of money being wrenched off rich and poor alike. They merely wanted a realistic, flexible approach to ensure that young heroin addicts in their teens and twenties received proper treatment and were detoxed and discouraged without being criminalised and that older addicts who, for whatever reason, needed heroin to function were allowed to have it and live peaceful lives without terror and disruption. These attitudes constitute a modest, reasonable goal and accord with my own.

I asked Eddie Ellison if we we nearing midnight on the subject. He laughed. By his standards we were well past the witching hour. 'There really is no option,' he said. 'It's all going to explode soon.'

The names of all addicts have been changed.

Methadone: The Forlorn Hope by Edward Jay Epstein. See O'Donahue and Richardson, *Pure Murder* (1984), pp. 88–92 for a summary.

There has only been ONE test comparing the prescribing of injectable heroin and oral methadone. Martin Mitcheson and Richard Hartnoll conducted a controlled study 1972–76. The results were equivocal although 'the methadone group tended to polarise towards more intensive purchase on the black market . . . There was no difference between the groups in terms of employment, health or death rate . . . Prescribing heroin . . . may reduce the degree of involvement in criminal activity, especially in terms of arrests and conviction rates.'

Chaos Theory: Drugs International plc

The Guardian, 1 November 1997

Saturday night. In Hastings, Flossie and Dave have switched off the video and are skinning up their last joint before bed. Their teenage children are out and their parents pray that they are only using Ecstasy, that it is not cut with poison and that they are not drinking too much or too little water. Whichever it is. They can't remember.

Daniel and Fiona are having a very informal dinner party in Brixton. The guests are like themselves journalists, or else novelists and critics. Everyone is drinking, doing lines of coke and sharing tokes on skunkweed. Downstairs, in the kitchen, two or three are chasing the heroin dragon on foil. Torquil, at almost fifty the oldest guest, ignores them and drags on his Silk Cut. He has the money and resources for a private heroin prescription – expensive but a fraction of the cost of impure street heroin. The younger users swear that they will never reach that stage. And they don't. They lose interest. Not everyone present is rich but no-one is poor. As recreational poly-drug-users, they will take whatever is around. They can afford to.

In a half-deserted old mining town near Newcastle, Kelly, Garnetta and Sophie sit, shivering on the car-seats which are the only furniture in the semi-burnt-out house. Most of the terrace is vandalised and boarded up. The girls are in their late teens. Kelly and Garnetta are old friends from the notorious Parkhead estates in Glasgow. They met Sophie, a chronically depressed college drop-out, somewhere in a club. Sophie's eyes are fixed hungrily on the small syringe full of cooked heroin which Kelly is plunging into a seeping, black hole in her groin, trying to avoid the encrustations of yellow pus. Smack is the only release from anxiety and misery Sophie has ever known. Tinfoil and bags for huffing glue left by local kids rustle on the floor. Garnetta's mouth is fastened on a hole punched in an empty drinks can. Her lighter shakes as she heats and draws deep on the mix of fag ash and powdered rock (crack). She hands it on. They live by shoplifting – 'It's not the money we want, just the drugs' and amateur prostitution. They are scared of pimps. They'd like to get to London but have boyfriends up north. Kelly wants to work in television.

What chains, what laws, what rules can ever bind the vast spectrum of British drug-users? Across the entire range of age, race, background and finance, they consume all possible combinations of all possible illegal drugs. So confused and contradictory are the myriad reports now that one might evoke the tired example of the blind men feeling an elephant. But if they were blind, they would never see what it was anyway. So with drugs. For all the vociferous opinions, who really knows exactly what they mean by the word 'drugs'?

Writing three years ago for *Guardian Weekend* on the failure of legislation and treatment to curb the rise of drug consumption I found everything to be very different. There was pronounced indifference, political and personal, all the way from cannabis to heroin. People were naturally protective of their personal drug use, but beyond that they were unconcerned. Heroin addicts went on suffering terribly from drug laws which denied them legal access to an expensive, physically addictive substance. No-one was much interested. Everyone vaguely thought that they knew what 'drugs' were – a diabetic dying without insulin was not someone on drugs. Nancy Reagan wasn't turning down anaesthetics for her facelifts either. The level of ignorance, both pharmacologically and historically, was incredible. It didn't seem clear to people that 'drugs' were an arbitrary selection of psycho-active substances that had been gradually outlawed over this century in Britain and the US for reasons to do with politics, class, economics and race, rather than any inherent qualities in the drugs themselves. Presented with riveting information such as the fact that one could buy cocaine and morphine over the counter at Harrods till 1916, or that the Royal Family ordered large quantities of heroin, cocaine, bromides, chloroform and adrenalin when at Balmoral from A. R. Clark's pharmacy in Braemar between 1897–1914 (all perfectly legal), listeners would back off carefully, obviously doubting one's sanity. There were few people to talk to. There were the rare doctors like Ann Dally and Adrian Garfoot who had tried hard to help addicts and been hauled up before the Home Office for their pains. Alternatively there were the entrenched Establishment doctors still hell-bent on imposing methadone 'treatment' on reluctant heroin addicts. So sublimely self-assured were such doctors at that time that they were often arrogant and truculent when interviewed. And then, most interestingly, there were the beginnings of a real debate instigated by of all people, a few influential police chiefs prepared to speak out and criticise the drugs situation as it stood. Most prominent amongst these law officers were Raymond Kendall, now Head of Interpol, who said then that 'Drug use should no longer be a criminal offence'; Commander John Grieve of Scotland Yard said society had to 'think the unthinkable' and consider controlled legalisation and distribution of hard drugs to addicts; most outspoken was retired Detective Chief Inspector Eddie Ellison, once part of the Metropolitan Drugs Squad, who condemned imprisonment for drugs offences, advocated controlled legalisation and said: 'There isn't a drugs squad in the world which hasn't become corrupt at one stage.' Then finally there was Keith Hellawell, Chairman of the Chief Constables' Committee on Drugs in 1994. The Committee admitted that they had lost the war against drugs and wanted ministers to allow all 25,000 registered addicts to receive heroin and other drugs on the NHS (as they used to). But even then Hellawell himself spoke with care: 'We've lost the war,' he said. 'Current policy has not stopped young people turning to drugs. It has not stopped the violence and other crime related to drugs . . . This is a cancer in our society.' It is not altogether a surprise to see Hellawell newly resplendent as the Drugs Czar as he has always been enough of a politician to leave his options open and hedge his bets. He can just about maintain that his new, government-sponsored traditionally prohibitionist policy is consistent. Just about.

Very few people back then seemed interested in following the delicate political and social changes that had presided over the growth of harsh legislation and extensive drug use, nor in considering feasible futures that might outlaw an obscene black market and the criminalisation of every kind of user. That it was a human rights issue seemed of little importance. Unfortunately this attitudinal change is not altruistic. Long-time campaigners against the current legislation say the same thing. For instance, Dr John Marks, the best-known opponent of current methadone-based 'treatment' methods: 'As prohibition is enforced so addicts turn to theft to buy drugs. Property is secured so they commit crimes against the person. City streets become uninhabitable. One of the main concerns of the public is safety. Everyone blames the addicts when it's the laws that have been so punitive against someone who wants to drink coca rather than tea or smoke opium rather than tobacco.' Dr Marks is echoed by Danny Kushlick, organiser of the increasingly high-profile lobbying group, Transform: 'The biggest reason for a change in attitude is the rise of property crime because of increased drug use.'

Fundamentally this is it. Terror and self-preservation have forced drugs into the forefront of our national consciousness. It is understandable. In a decayed part of Newcastle where the kids specialise in 'malicious ignition' – setting homes and cars on fire with aerosol flame-throwers – married pensioner, Barbara, says: 'I can't go oot on me oon, I'm frightened to leave the place. When I go oot Tom has to stay home, we take it in turns.' Another local, Marilyn, adds: 'You're waiting to be mugged, they're always after something.' Such stories are repeated in Leicester, Halifax, Salford, Glasgow, Liverpool. They all testify to the heartbreaking failure of national social and drugs policies.

Less vital but more apparent is a growing awareness of the obscene amounts of drug money flowing into organised crime. Interpol estimates the international drugs trade at just under one billion pounds every day. Each day in London fifteen kilos of black market heroin are consumed. Those to whom a million pounds is small change have few difficulties with infiltration and corruption of entire governments and customs departments.

What is much less well understood is exactly why prohibition has failed so drastically, why addicts are dying of disease on our streets or of drugs that are either filthily polluted or suddenly too pure; and why, too, armed drug gangs are shooting each other and anyone else in their path.

It was perfectly possible to foretell the ravages of the present scene not just three years ago but thirty, or even earlier. Prohibition against drugs has never worked – not in the US where it began, early this century, nor anywhere else. We are all of us now, drug-users or not, finally face to face with the results of the US's moral arrogance and malign influence.

At least we now have a debate on drugs. It is as if there is some psychic democracy at work when the time is right. In the years before homosexuality was legalised here Boston novelist Richard Yates, describing an American in London on a scholarship, wrote: 'He was dismayed to find how many of these people's innuendoes, winked or shouted, dwelt on the humorous aspects of homosexuality. Was all of England obsessed with that topic?' Yes, at that point.

Similarly there is no escaping the subject of drugs now. The broadsheets swap contradictory headlines on a daily basis; it is standard material (innuendoes and shouts) for comedians, comics and media. No-one lacks an opinion. Up, down and flying around there is an endless tumult of sound-bites: legalise . . . decriminalise . . . Deals on Wheels . . . Zero Tolerance . . . Just Say No! . . . medicinal use . . . methadone . . . late raves and early graves. A non-controversial chart-topper intones 'And the Drugs Don't

Work'; no-one believes that the tormented young songster is referring to Ibuprofen. (Does anyone remember The Doors being asked to change the line, 'Girl, we couldn't get much higher', for TV? Or BBC Radio's endless fussing over drug references in lyrics?) It is no longer even possible for a non-specialist to maintain a clippings file on the subject; an awesome blizzard of print downloads daily.

Today the number of policy groups, action groups, committees, reports, sub-committees, federations, institutes, alliances, foundations, enquiries, prevention cadres, policy centres, coordinators, reforms, working parties, advisory groups and inspectorates are mind-spinningly numerous and do as much to obfuscate the issues as to advance them. Everyone wants to speak out now. In fact no-one will shut up. Except of course for the Home Office who remain traditionally reluctant to go on the record, although this time around their coyness suggests confusion rather than disinterestedness.

Previously, any anti-prohibitionist not a specialist in drug affairs who advocated legal change was automatically assumed to be themselves a pretty serious drug-user. Any mention of decriminalising drugs and it was believed that you longed for the entire population to be able to rush into their local tobacconist, buy huge amounts of hemp, cocaine, heroin and opium over the counter (as indeed we could once do) and get totally wrecked. The very use of the word 'Prohibition' to describe current British and American drugs policies is new and is a description which inevitably evokes the total failure of US alcohol prohibition during the twenties.

There has been a lessening of stigma generally towards drug use with the creation of a new folk-devil. Paedophiles, after being left alone to teach and tie knots with children, are now subject to the terrifying process of cultural demonisation – look at a kiddy clothes catalogue one day and the next you'll be buggering the baby. This procedure closely parallels the ways in which public attitudes towards drug-users were manipulated and before that towards homosexuals and Jews.

But in re-tracing our steps towards an understanding of drugs issues, it must be admitted that the Oscar for changing societal attitudes must go to the Ecstasy generation. Ecstasy (MDMA) did what the hippies hoped LSD would do – as the ultimate feel-good virus it blazed straight through youth culture and into the mainstream.

A recent survey showed that one in three under-fourteens have tried an illegal drug. So, rather than squinting at yet more questionable statistics, I kidnapped a couple of Ecstasy kidlets who had grown up with drugs and lived through the rave scene. 'Eric' is a Cockney DJ in his late twenties and Jana his stunning, feline, honey-blonde Swedish girlfriend, age twenty-six. They were simultaneously mystical and matter-of-fact about drugs (like everyone else they dutifully included alcohol and tobacco amongst them). Regardless of legislation they felt that the use of drugs was theirs by right and a necessary part of a long period of self-discovery from adolescence onwards. 'Part of drugs is getting to know Mr Drug and how to handle it and what's in it for you in a personal sense,' said Eric. 'I smoked grass for the first time when I was thirteen,' he continued. 'I first got pissed on alcohol at eleven and tried cigarettes. It was something pretty much everybody did at that age. You were experimenting. It was an adventure. That's where it all starts for anyone. Curiosity . . . My older brother intoduced me to dope. Obviously I'd heard about it – it wasn't something alien. Everyone knew about getting stoned.'

Jana said that kids in Sweden tried drink and fags at the same age, 'but not drugs until they were a bit older. People stay longer as children in Sweden. We haven't got such pressures on us to grow up. The police came and talked to us in school and told us drugs were really bad. Then, when we were about seventeen, friends went abroad and we found our education wasn't accurate. Friends went to Ibiza for the Second Summer of Love and we got stuff sent from England. That was the main reason I came here – to try more! Yes, there are a lot more drugs in Sweden now. Definitely.'

As an eighties revival-mod, Eric graduated to speed: 'I got into dexeys far more than dope. You tended to drop into one culture or another – mod, punk, new Romantic, Goth. Each had its own house drugs. Being a mod represented how I felt. It's something that stays inside you. It's something you carry in your heart. It's a deep thing, not a fashion thing.' Towards the end of the eighties Eric's life started fragmenting: 'I really believed my youth was over. I was twenty. I'd look out at the Post Office Tower with tears streaming down my face. I'd basically given up and believed society's pressures. You were young and you express yourself, then it's over. Then this incredible, incredible fucking thing! This explosion! For me, spiritually the music saved me,' he continues. 'The two ran in parallel. Music and E.' Jana mentions the ancient puzzle, 'Youth cultures come with music and we don't have that in Europe.'

Eric carries on. 'I was moving very fast. Everything pumping along. From the indie to the rave scene. You seek to push the boundaries within yourself. My first real E experience was with Jana when we discovered hardcore. Es amplified the love we felt for each other to an extraordinarily high level. E is an absolute feeling. You can't go wrong 'cos you feel so good . . . When you've been split into different cultures it's a beautiful feeling when they blend into one another. Using E has become much more acceptable.'

They were both bitter about the media treatment of E. 'I think it's disgusting. Usual tabloid stuff. *The Sun* were very quick to jump on the bandwagon – Get Your Free Smiley T-shirt – but then someone dies and you get unhappy faces.' They were saddened by the Leah Betts tragedy and relieved when the tablets were finally exonerated.

They are cynical about government: 'They cash in rather than trying to beat the drug barons which they know they can't do. Drugs scare government – they don't like anything they can't control.' Neither can envisage drugs, 'except possibly cannabis', ever being legalised. 'They're frightened they'd lose votes. That's why Labour won't shift. I think all drugs should at least be made available from doctors. They should research more and see their potential.'

Eric has tried cocaine: 'It wasn't my drug, it made me feel too . . . Big'. Neither of them would take heroin – 'Sad people . . . needles . . . everyone asleep . . .' They would like their children to have a similar period of drug experimentation in London.

Both agreed – 'very much so' – that drug-taking would carry on, tacitly condoned to some extent throughout people's youth, winding down into occasional use, if any, in later life. 'I'll probably carry on puffing,' says Eric. He jumps up and starts spinning discs with fearsome dexterity on his mixing-desk. 'At first it was white people who were doing E. Then we started going to Jungle. Black people have been a lot more involved in making the music – Es made people realise there is a universal unity! For me it's done a lot of good to take drugs!' He turns up the bass – 'Happy hardcore,' he shouts. 'Everyone smilin', touchin' – wicked!'

Their equanimity, tolerance and firm belief that drug use is an integral part of recreational youth seems fairly representative. Such attitudes give context to *The Independent on Sunday*'s reasonable campaign to have cannabis legalised. It is now an unremarkable drug, widely accepted, with nugatory penalties for possession and apparent medical benefits. Does anyone still believe the crude propaganda of thirties films like *Reefer Madness*? Unbridled passions, maddened lust, seductive hallucinations – you wish!

An Alaskan Hell's Angel was outraged when visiting Amsterdam to find he could buy marijuana legally. It offended his sense of propriety. San Francisco is timidly following Holland and has a Marijuana Shop where it can be bought with a doctor's prescription and a coffee-house where it may be sedately smoked. Ageing Californians cry out 'I just thank the Lord for this drug', ironic considering that half the world, including India and Islamic countries, have been (and still are) consuming it uncontentiously since time immemorial.

New South Wales has recently announced the removal of all gaol penalties for offences pertaining to smallish amounts of cannabis and cultivation. They hope to institute penalties on the level of a driving fine. Over here Jack Straw's ad nauseam repetition of 'We shall not decriminalise, legalise or legitimise the use of drugs' is not dented by his recent stated intention of ensuring a consistent police response to cannabis offences. This is likely to strengthen cannabis prohibition and undermine the current, sometimes rather casual police attitude to small-time users.

There are those like addiction specialist, Professor Griffith Edwards, and now Keith Hellawell, who insist that scientists are becoming more, rather than less suspicious of the side-effects of cannabis. What about the very unpleasant side-effects of the millions of prescriptions for psycho-active drugs from the benzodiazepines (Valium, Temazepam, etc) onwards that are dispensed daily? After organised crime the pharmaceutical companies are the biggest dealers in the world and we know that their test results can be massaged. Hellawell also argues that 'unless supplies were untaxed or free there would still be large financial incentives for dealing' in cannabis. No government is going to sacrifice billions in revenue; there is a black market in everything – televisions, penicillin, cigarettes – but it is not this that has made war zones of our cities. How many bother to get their Camels that way? The standard anti-cannabis argument is why add to the problems we already have with alcohol and nicotine? But why waste massive resources and hand out criminal records over such a minor drug?

The most destructive aspect of the pro-cannabis lobby is their tendency to divid illegal drugs into 'soft' (i.e. harmless) ones and 'hard' (oh no, deadly, can't have that) ones. This trend can only isolate further those who are really suffering – addicts of crack or impure street heroin. Anyone seeing the results of bodily damage sustained by intravenous heroin users unable to obtain legal heroin will never forget it; arms and legs have been amputated after injections of Temazepam (jellies), crushed Diconal and methadone tablets; suppurating abcesses are caused by dirty street speed and heroin. This has little to do with choice or recreation. It speaks of deprivation, dysfunction and self-hatred. Nevertheless *all* illegal drugs are part of the same spectrum, from the matchstick thin joint to the syringe. A dichotomy is artificial. Of course the effects of drugs differ and they require differing degrees of decriminalisation. Life was once and should be again made tolerable for those who, with full and accurate education, still choose to take them. In the face of the total failure of drug prohibition and the suggested crimes against humanity that constitute the US's 'Zero Tolerance', the path increasingly being taken on the Continent and in Australia is one of gradual depenalisation (reduction of penalties for drug consumers), decriminalisation (non-enforcement of the crime of possession) and re-introduction of the old 'British System' of heroin on prescription for addicts. This particular model of harm-reduction cuts off vast-scale organised crime and saves lives.

Rosie Boycott's remark that 'Cannabis, unlike alcohol or heroin, isn't going to make anyone go out and kill, maim, murder or rob' is seriously distorting and typical of the way the dispute is conducted in free-floating soundbites. Alcohol, amphetamines, crack and possibly cocaine are the only common drugs that when abused may make someone aggressive. No-one on heroin maims or murders. Junkies rob when they have no access to legal heroin. Generally speaking no-one with legal, affordable access to their drug of choice goes around doing crimes at all, let alone carving people up. How many drinkers do you know who are murderers?

Crime and selling drugs are the only options for the ordinary, serious addict. A related issue is the constant confusion between 'users' and 'dealers'. One hears repeatedly 'Oh, I feel sorry for the addict but the dealers should be shot.' At street level – the level which overcrowds our prisons – the user and the dealer are usually the same person. Selling their drug is one of the few ways they can get more. By 'dealers' people really mean importers – that is, the richer barons of organised crime and the scions of corrupt governments, cosseted by cocaine-fuelled lawyers who ensure that they will never see a gaol cell.

If we just look at the other long-running contenders, the organic substances of coca leaves and opium, we see that they have been in widespread, legal use since records began. Such use survived the invention of the hypodermic (1843), the synthesis of morphine (1803), heroin (1874) and the use of laudanum (opium and alcohol). Cocaine hydrochloride (1855) came from the coca plant. All these new substances were favourites of countless nineteenth-century notables as well as ordinary working folk.

The US led the way in trying to prohibit the use of drugs and alcohol (they didn't bother with tobacco – after all, it came from Virginia) largely on moral and racist grounds. Opium was associated with Chinese immigrants, cocaine with Southern black labourers. They succeeded only in criminalising drug use and beginning their long, dismal, unwinnable War On Drugs.

Britain hesitated. Under the Rolleston Committee Report (1926) doctors were able to prescribe heroin and cocaine to addicts and cannabis linctus to patients as well. This was known as the 'British System'. There were few requests and few addicts, mainly middle-class and middle-aged, plus some *demi-mondaines* and portrait painters, a few Chinese in Limehouse, some wounded soldiers,' as Professor Griffith Edwards describes. Then, in the sixties when patterns of drug use changed, panic ensued,

the Brain Committee convened twice and in 1971 the still opera-
tive Misuse of Drugs Act was passed. GPs could no longer prescribe cocaine or heroin for addicts without a licence (forget
about cannabis). NHS Drug Dependency Units had been established (DDUs) headed by consultant psychiatrists. Heroin was
phased out and replaced with the non-euphoric American solution, methadone (physeptone). The DDUs became increasingly
punitive; injectable methadone was replaced by oral methadone
and then enforced reduction 'cures'. The main problem was that
addicts hated the DDUs and they hated methadone. They turned
to the black market.

A very powerful group of London doctors – known sometimes
as the 'methadone or Maudsley mafia' championed methadone
although it was highly addictive and much harder to withdraw
from than heroin. It seemed as if history was repeating itself;
heroin was hailed early on as a cure for morphine addiction and
cocaine for heroin dependency.

So nowadays almost every heroin addict – whether they inject
or not – is dependent upon the black market and suffers inordi-
nately. Of those I surveyed three years ago, two of the women have
lost their professional jobs (Rick's wife was a social worker and
Chloë a university lecturer). The other, Anna, is now dead of cancer of the mouth. (She complained of pain in her mouth and jaw
to her GP for **six years**. But, being a known, obvious junkie, she
was ignored and told to go away and lead a better life. Eventually
her dentist saw the tumour, by which time it was far too late. Is
this humane?) Her husband Winston, now in his fifties, has had
two strokes and is serving a three-year term for possession of a
small amount of heroin with intent to supply. Of the other two
men, both professionals, one (Rick) has gained a criminal conviction and is terrified of his employers finding out. The other, Toby,
was released from prison and is currently being prescribed legal
heroin. He has left London and is fine.

Clean heroin is not in itself a dangerous drug. Its great
drawback is the intense physical addiction that develops. The
lesser disincentive is constipation.

The redoubtable Dr John Marks on Merseyside has remained
the only high-profile NHS exponent of the British System. He has
survived efforts to discredit him and is now taken very seriously,

particularly abroad – a prophet being without honour in his own country. He is Drugs Adviser to the Liberal Democrat Party and has just been asked to head the Drug Addiction Services in New Zealand. He always continued to prescribe heroin and cocaine for addicts and recently weathered the terrible Widnes and Warrington tragedy. Marks treated addicts at those two clinics until his funding was finally revoked in 1996. Four hundred and fifty addicts maintained by Marks on their drug of choice were forcibly returned to methadone reduction and withdrawal. They were thus returned to the streets, to the black market, to prostitution, crime, imprisonment and disease. 'Now,' says Marks, 'according to the latest coroner's reports forty-one of them have died, crime has gone through the roof, drugs are everywhere, the police are going crazy, the local authority has protested publicly.'

Marks, certainly a sincere humanitarian, mentions that he always had the support of the Home Office and especially of the late, legendary and compassionate 'Bing' Spear, former head of the Home Office Drugs Inspectorate, now called, controversially, Action Against Drugs. It is presently headed by the much less sympathetic Alan MacFarlane who has stated that his priority is to stamp out the 'leakage' of prescription drugs on to the market. This is a bit like the Chancellor of the Exchequer saying that his priority is to tax the profits from car boot sales.

Marks believes that it was Griffith Edwards (who headed the Drugs Inspectorate at one time) who is responsible for 'the absurdly prohibitionist situation we have ended up in. His influence has cast a very long shadow. He chairs just about every committee that moves. I think he has a very strong effect on government policy.' Marks has never altered his own stance and says that the London doctors 'are hanging on till grim death. They have invested so much in saying how wonderful methadone is that they are going to have an awful lot of egg to scrape off.'

Professor Edwards was not as fearsome as he sounded. In fact, in contrast to other eminent London addiction specialists I've interviewed in past years, he could not have been kinder or more helpful in guiding me through the maze of governmental working parties and drug committees. An emeritus professor at London University, he is editor of *Addiction*, Chairman of the Prevention Working Group to the Advisory Council on the Misuse of Drugs and a member of the WHO's expert advisory group. He was modest in describing himself as 'a health scientist, on a good day'. He stuck politely but persistently to his famously conservative views. He added: 'I have enormously tentative views on my own evidence.' As regards heroin he says: 'Whether countries did or did not have heroin prescribing at that time (the sixties) is really irrelevant. It wasn't just that we mishandled it. The world got a drug epidemic.' And indeed the combination of youth culture and international travel created a society wholly different from that of the pre-war years.

He insists: 'It really is *banal* to believe that the government tried to inderdict the prescribing of heroin or doctors decided that prescribing it wasn't good news. They were still allowed to prescribe it.' Correct, in certain cases, under Section 7 of the Misuse of Drugs Act. He adds: 'I was at the time prescribing heroin and gave up because I thought it was no longer ethical to do so. I couldn't control its spill on to the streets, it produces drug craving and you don't get people better – you may stabilise a few people. I would like people to prescribe it still on rare occasions and responsible doctors do.' Well, almost never for addicts. 'But,' says Edwards, 'as a front-line treatment heroin is not as good as methadone which is much safer and much more effective – simply better medicine.' Deadlock. Marks says: 'The Home Office's own research shows that pure, pharmaceutical methadone is nineteen times more likely to kill you than street heroin.'

Methadone has its uses, mainly as a voluntary short-term reduction attempt. Forcing it on heroin addicts has never worked.

Edwards did not come across as a fire-breathing dragon of prohibition. It would be uncharitable to think that such doctors have recently acquired some public relations skills. Maybe I interviewed the others on bad care days. I have not spoken to the equally influential specialist, Professor John Strang, adviser to Labour on drugs both in and out of office but even diehard opponents of prohibition admit that he can be reasonable. Is it possible that such doctors, whose policies have been making life wretched for thousands of addicts, are sufficiently courageous and humane to admit that methadone shows indications of being discredited? Or are they engaged in expedient damage limitation and career protection? As a medical historian, Edwards must be well aware of the suffering, wastage and death imposed by powerful doctors in previous centuries – the fifty-year gap between discovering the cure for scurvy and eliminating the disease, the opposition to anaesthesia in childbirth and the atrocities committed in attempts to prevent masturbation. Psychiatrist Henry Maudsley (1835–1918), after whom the hospital was named, wrote of masturbation in terms virtually identical to recent anti-heroin advertising: ' . . . a mind enervated by vicious practices . . . moral degradation . . . they will actually defend their vice on some pretence or other'. Further standard writing on the subject sounds eerily recognisable: 'When young people . . . exhibit unaccountable symptoms of debility . . . with listlessness and love of solitude, look dark under the eyes etc, the possibility of vicious practices should not be lost sight of.' Familar? These attitudes were eventually followed by countless clitoridectomies to combat the odious habit. One woman was 'extirpated' for the sin of 'serious reading'. (*This really upsets me, as well it might!*)

Interestingly, Professor Edwards' current concerns are close to those of his complete opposite, reformer Danny Kushlick, founder of anti-prohibitionist group Transform. They are both increasingly troubled by rising drug consumption amongst the most deprived and under-privileged of the population. Kushlick notes: 'Whether it is tobacco, alcohol or crack, the link between social deprivation and problematic drug use is very clear. Poor people with little job training, hopes of employment or educational opportunities are living in a state of despair – and heroin is one hell of a drug for dealing with that.'

This is one of the cornerstones of our current drug chaos. The British System of providing heroin to addicts worked well when they were largely middle-class professionals. Would it work now for desperate, problematic users who have so much else to contend with? Well, it worked for Dr Mark's patients in the rundown neighbourhoods of Liverpool. And it stops addicts of every kind from 'dying like flies' as they are currently doing, says Marks.

As for the Labour government, the answer is certainly blowing in the wind. Marks says: 'Everybody thought something was going to change when Labour got in' and indeed many of the MPs are of an age to have inhaled. However, Jack 'Caliban' Straw – as he is known throughout the North-East – has exhibited all the intransigence, puritanism and lack of imagination common to those who have focused solely on socialist politics since adolescence. Drug-taking is invariably seen as bourgeois and decadent by life-long lefties. As H. L. Mencken said: 'Puritanism – the haunting fear that someone, somewhere may be happy.'

Another problem is that Labour must believe it was their fabulous policies that got them into office, notably 'Tough on crime, tough on the causes of crime.' Whereas of course they could have vowed to re-introduce rabies and still been elected, so disgusted was the populace with Conservative rule. It is possible to feel a shade of sympathy for them on drugs issues – buffeted by contradictory reports and specialists, challenged by thoughtful backbenchers like Paul Flynn and Brian Iddon, nervous of public opinion and a fickle, inscrutable populace, terrified of losing votes and faced with a full-scale debate on drugs despite their attempts to roll it up and put it away. No Royal Commission on Drugs has been convened, as many people had hoped. ('Too expensive,' says Griffith Edwards pragmatically.) 'Labour are a mixture,' ponders Dr Marks, 'but politicians all lead from behind. Or else they are puritans like Straw. I wonder whether Blair has gone religious or is a real Machiavellian chameleon who is just waiting for the right time?'

Some of Straw's suggested initiatives bear all the *hell*-marks of psychic torture: evicting 'dealers' and their families from council housing; returning addicts to the community but subjecting them to random urine testing. 'They'll be in the community but won't be using their drugs,' celebrates Straw, as if it were that simple – sitting around while your mates toke up in a damp council maisonette. There are promised inducements to prisoners who elect to remain drug-free – open prisons, short sentences, while refuseniks will have no probation, no remission and extra time added for 'dirty' urine tests, tests which are an automatic invasion of civil rights. Remember that most of these prisoners are small-time heroin addicts and are being deprived of something as necessary to them as water is to us. Unlike nicotine, heroin cannot be given up by a tremendous act of will – however much the user wishes to withdraw. Long-term addicts have to wait until the drug gives them up and they 'age out'. Forced withdrawal is agony.

Perhaps worst of all is the suggestion that doctors be shorn of their traditional freedom to prescribe the many drugs that still carry legal penalties and will only be allowed to give out – surprise! – oral methadone. This narrows treatment alternatives hideously at a point when they increasingly need to be tailored to the individual patient's needs; the 'British System' is only one alternative. And so it continues, from day to day, a dismal combination of indecision and ferocity.

Danny Kushlick points out that no-one appears to be trying to clear up the central misapprehensions about drugs – the confusion between recreational and problematic illicit drug use, the mix-up between drug use and drug policy which ensures that a moral stance governs legislation and the constant muddle between the effects of the drugs themselves and the effects of prohibiting them.

On the most urgent matter – the serious drug addicts who are dying all around from filthy street drugs and disease – there are currently the two international options, both marked by much squabbling, backtracking and in-fighting. There is the old US prohibition model – inane in the light of the vast consumer demand for something to get us through the night. Consider Dennis K. Hull of Florida, a heroin addict since age twenty. Now in his forties he has only spent nine months out of prison in his entire adult life. And the US is now upping the ante to 'zero tolerance' – increased resources (again) for police and customs, life sentences for supply, death for importation, more media and educational propaganda and enforced control of addicts through threats. Sounds civilised. Sounds desperate. Britain still meekly follows America – when will we learn to think for ourselves?

Many other countries are moving towards decriminalisation of some kind and re-introduction of the British System. Holland and allegedly Italy have decriminalised personal possession of small amounts of any drug, not without much Italian melodrama: inevitably, they eventually arrested someone rich who said they naturally bought larger quantities because it was cheaper that way. Dealer or not?

Switzerland has just concluded a very successful three-year trial of prescribing heroin to addicts and voted for its continuance. (The government found that during the trial crime was reduced by sixty per cent, the general and nutritional health of the addicts improved, as did their living conditions, their illicit cocaine and heroin use was dramatically reduced and it doubled the number of participants who were employed.) Rather joylessly, they made them inject in the clinic. Dr Marks has long foreseen that the main difficulty in accepting drug use is intravenous injection, even in the most legal, sterile conditions. He pioneered the very success-ful prescription of cocaine and heroin 'reefers' – cigarettes soaked in the required substance. Chelsea and Westminster Hospital here, recently running a small British System trial on tempting but inadequate amounts of heroin, rejected reefers partly because the National Addiction Centre was concerned about carcinogens! But Marks has always advocated that herbal tobacco be used – and as one will crawl through sewage to get one's gear – it seems unlikely that some stale rosemary and marjoram would deter anyone. Such reefers offer a very positive way forward. Had they been interna-tionally available it is possible that the viciously addictive, debased form of free-base cocaine, crack, might never have emerged. This is a good example of the negative effects of prohibition. Crack – too poisoned and adulterated to be ever prescribed – was designed for the urban poor and is decimating inner cities. Without cocaine prohibition we might never have seen crack. A legal, prescription alternative (free-base reefers?) might deter the cartels and lead to its demise.

Otherwise, 'Heroin maintenance is a proven method of reduc-ing the crime, disease and personal instability associated with heroin addiction,' says Dr Ethan Nadelman, Director of the US Lindesmith Centre, a harm reduction, drug policy think-tank. Such views have caused Australia to look towards stemming the black market and four of the territories are to begin an potentially extensive British System trial. This has been temporarily derailed by a short, sharp press attack (Christian fundamentalists every-where have opposed harm reduction although I can't recall the Bible ever saying 'Thou shalt not toke on huge doobies nor enjoy the fruits of the coca bush and opium poppy.'). Dr Marks sighs: 'Holland, Switzerland and Australia looked to Widnes. Now the Swiss have opened up and Liverpool closed down. Now the Dutch and Australians want to copy Liverpool and Spain and Italy to copy the Dutch. So it's a kind of domino effect. But it started with the British System and we were better off with our own original method which we abandoned to our great cost. It wasn't as if we didn't have an example of prohibition policy in the place where it originated – America. Unmitigated disaster!'

Society nowadays cannot really be compared to Britain during the pre-war years of the British System. But no-one seems to have come up with a more efficacious way of saving lives, returning addicts to work and cutting off the drug barons. Australia and the Continent are increasingly aware of this. Why not us, the instigators?

In 1996 Lewisham Community Safety Initiative convened a Citizens' Jury. For four days, sixteen people listened to experts debate the drugs issue. Finally fifteen of them voted that heroin should be provided for chronic addicts, noting that before hearing the facts nearly all would have considered it insanity.

What exactly are the benefits of drug prohibition? I am unable to see any. It does not stop those who want to from taking drugs, it just makes it much more dangerous to do so. All known human societies (except two, one of them in Iceland), after throwing the duvet down in the cave and stippling some bison on the cave wall have then rejoined the neighbours and got wasted on mind-altering substances. Shelter, food, sex, *World of Interiors* – off your face. That's the story. One man's morning glory seeds are another's bath-tub speed but the basic cultural model has never changed. In consumer societies governments cannot force bloating in one area and abstinence in another. Nothing is risk-free. Anything – legal or illegal – can be abused.

The only humane answer seems to be the decriminalising of non-addictive drugs and the prescribing of stronger ones to addicts while steering them in the direction of non-invasive use. The extra revenue can go to hospitals, schools and education, including realistic drugs education which might deter some people from embarking on a path that is no longer decadently, glamorously forbidden, but really rather dull.

Although we may not quite be at the stage of the old movie joke, 'More than any time in history man faces a crossroads. One path leads to despair and utter hopelessness, the other to total extinction. Let us pray that we have the wisdom to choose correctly', we are not far off. It is certainly past midnight. It seems that wincingly, crawlingly, very slowly, we are having to take tiny, halting steps through the maze of politics, morality and medicine towards decriminalisation, saving faces and eating words all the way until finally, perhaps, we will get back to where we once belonged.

TRANSFORM: The Campaign To Transform Drug Policy and Legislation, Box 59, 82 Colston St Bristol BS1 5BB

The Case of Anna Kavan by David Callard

(Peter Owen)
London Review of Books, 25 February 1993

I don't want to drone on indefinitely on the subject but the gifted writer, Anna Kavan, is a case in point when it comes to UK drugs legislation. Having been an addict since her twenties, receiving a regular, legal supply of pharmaceutical heroin from her (much-loved!) doctor, she was quite elderly when her doctor died. (The law changed in 1971.) A distinguished intellectual, she found it utterly humiliating to be shunted off to the Paddington (I think) Drugs Dependency Unit where she was surrounded by pin-eyed teenagers and condescended to by some wholly ignorant woman doctor, a classic exponent of what I term 'punitive medicine'. Talk of group therapy was vile enough but it was when they decided to change her intravenous heroin script to one of methadone that the lady vanished. She went back to her house in Chelsea and OD'd. Another one down. (Actually, history is inconclusive as to the manner of her death. Some say she died of a heart attack.)

When Kavan was younger she had written in her story, 'Julia and the Bazooka': 'Julia likes the doctor as soon as she meets him . . . He does not want to take her syringe away. He says, "You've used it for years already and you're none the worse. In fact you'd be far worse off without it." He trusts Julia, he knows she is not irresponsible, she will not increase the dosage too much or experiment with new drugs. It is

*ridiculous to say that all drug addicts are alike, all liars, all vicious,
all psychopaths or delinquents just out for kicks. He is sympathetic
towards Julia whose personality has been damaged by no love in
childhood so that she can't make contact with people or feel at home
in the world. In his opinion she is quite right to use the syringe, it is as
essential to her as insulin to a diabetic. Without it she could not lead a
normal existence, her life would be a shambles, but with its support she
is conscientious and energetic, intelligent, friendly. She is most unlike
the popular notion of a drug addict. Nobody could call her vicious.'*

And that about sums it up, I think. Well, at least for those who
don't give junkies a bad name.

During the war Anna Kavan worked for nearly two years at the
offices of Cyril Connolly's magazine, *Horizon*. Michael Sheldon,
in his book *Friends of Promise*, comments: 'Understandably,
Connolly was never comfortable with Kavan,' presumably referring to the fact of her heroin addiction of which Connolly was certainly aware. Friends and mentors over the years – Rhys Davies,
Peter Owen, Brian Aldiss – have made considerable efforts to dis-
pel such feelings of unease by stressing repeatedly how little her
drug addiction appeared to affect her; again and again, one reads
that 'She was of smart, cheerful appearance' and 'Neither in her
appearance or her behaviour did she reveal her incurable heroin
addiction.' Such loyal friends were all too aware of the insidious
demonisation of opiates in our society and did not wish her to be
regarded as a pathological case – although of course, in that
Kavan had lifelong access to clean legal drugs, there was no
reason at all why she should *not* appear cheerful, well-groomed,
hard-working and so on. It is not the narcotics themselves that
cause indigence, dishevelment and disease but the laws that
criminalise the addict. In a similar attempt to sanitise Kavan's
work the stories that deal directly with her addiction now never
seem to be reprinted. The Picador Classics edition of her selected
writings, *My Madness*, contains none of them. There are a number
of very moving stories such as 'Julia and the Bazooka' which deals
with her introduction to drugs, 'High in the Mountains' which
describes the effects of heroin and 'The Old Address' which
details obsession and withdrawal, which provide us with considerable insight into Kavan's personality and without which no more

than a partial analysis of her work can be made. Such attempts to distance Kavan from her drug, although well-meaning, are misleading. She was one of those rare writers who did not publish at all until she was habituated. Heroin was the centre of her existence; it was her lover, her religion, her salvation, and almost all of her later work charts the processes of addiction in an extraordinarily pure and crystalline form using again and again images – of cold, of ice, of forbidding landscapes, lowering castles and invisible watchers – in a manner that should be familiar to us from any study of the great addict writers of the Romantic period.

Naturally this presents the biographer with considerable problems. Kavan further complicated her biographer's task by destroying almost all her personal correspondence and all her diaries apart from those covering an early eighteen-month period. She changed her name several times, concealed her date of birth and in 1940 completely changed her appearance and literary style and adopted the name 'Anna Kavan' – a fictional character who had appeared in two of her early novels. Peter Owen has repeatedly encouraged the writing of a biography but the difficulties seemed insurmountable. Even her oldest and closest friend refused an invitation to write the book saying he did not know her well enough. Another close friend, Raymond Marriott, observed: 'She cast doubts, she lied, she fabricated, she spoke the truth, she was most honest. But where did it begin and where did it end?'

In such circumstances David Callard should be congratulated for completing the project at all. It is not a very satisfactory biography but she was not a very satisfactory subject. Callard's previous book, *Pretty Good for a Woman: The Enigma of Evelyn Scott* charted the life of a little-known American writer and radical, friend to Emma Goldman and Jean Rhys. Scott is less well-known than Kavan but Callard managed to produce a much longer and less sketchy account of her life than he was able to do for Kavan.

Helen Woods/Anna Kavan was born in Cannes in 1901 to a wealthy father and a frivolous socialite mother whose domination she was never to escape. As an infant Kavan claims she was sent away 'to a place where there was nothing but snow and ice'. Her upbringing was loveless and peripatetic. Her father died when she was fourteen, condemning her, she said, to 'lifelong loneliness'. Callard comments that her childhood was only a 'more extreme version' of the average Edwardian upper-class upbringing, quoting Raymond Marriott's observation: 'Many people have difficult childhoods. Some survive them and some don't. Anna didn't.' She married twice, first to Donald Ferguson with whom she spent two years in Burma and then, by common law to Stuart Edmonds, a wealthy dilettante artist. She had two children to whom she appeared indifferent; a daughter who died in infancy and a son who was later killed in WW2. She fictionalised both her husbands, Ferguson appearing most memorably as the sinister, sadistic Mr Dog Head in *Who Are You?* in 1963. She published her first six novels under the name 'Helen Ferguson', the first of which was published in 1929. Rhys Davies described them as 'conventional Home Counties' but Callard rightly finds them 'shot through with a sense of darkness and oppression' which foreshadows her mature work. All her writing, from first to last, was almost exclusively autobiographical.

Anna was introduced to drugs in London between her two marriages and was habituated to heroin by 1925. At this time Britain had an enlightened policy in regard to drugs. The Rolleston Committee of 1926 allowed doctors to prescribe maintenance doses of heroin to addicts so that they were able to function normally. This, known as the 'British System', worked well and the number of addicts actually declined for many years. Kavan maintained that heroin 'had saved my life and kept me from madness'. This comment, from an extremely intelligent and perceptive woman, is not to be taken lightly; it is almost undoubtedly true.

In 1938 Kavan suffered a particularly severe breakdown after the dissolution of her second marriage. Afterwards she resolved to accept her addiction and shed her old identity; she dyed her hair white-blonde, became Anna Kavan, a name that she had created earlier but which, by this time, seemed fortuitously reminiscent of Kafka. 'Why does the K sound in a name symbolise the struggle of those who try to make themselves at home on a homeless borderland?' she wrote. Anna Kavan's first book, *Asylum Piece*, appeared in 1940 and signified the birth of the literary style for which she is well-known – elliptical, experimental, haunting.

In the early forties Anna met the only man who was ever really of any importance to her. This was of course her dealer – or, in those days, her doctor. Dr Karl Bluth was a cultured man, a poet, playwright and essayist who had fled Nazi Germany. Bluth became an essential father-figure, mentor and in a strange way – in that he often administered her injections – a kind of lover to Kavan. He sympathised with her need for a shield against what were intolerable, suicidal depressions.

For the next twenty years Kavan lived a strange isolated life, supporting herself by renovating houses in Kensington. Disliking women, she was surrounded by a small coterie of homosexual men. Her career went into a long decline after the failure of what was for the times a highly experimental novel, *Sleep has His House*, in 1947 from which she was rescued by Peter Owen who in 1957 published *Eagle's Nest* and continued as her publisher for the rest of her life. Anna remained extremely close to Dr Bluth and when he died in 1964 she was so distraught that she attempted suicide: 'I was desperate, determined not to go on living.' He appears as a shadowy presence in many of her stories, and four of the stories in the posthumous 'Julia and the Bazooka' concern him directly.

Kavan's life has many parallels with that of Jean Rhys. Both were terribly damaged in infancy; both grew up gifted, suspicious, alienated. Both were addicts – Rhys was an alcoholic. Both at times referred to the hostile outer world of authority and bureaucracy as 'the Machine'. Neither made money from their fiction and both suffered long periods of obscurity from which they were rescued by kind and perspicacious publishers. Both achieved fame posthumously. Carole Angier, Rhys' biographer, tells us that Rhys suffered from 'borderline personality disorder', features of which are addiction, isolation and paranoia. For what it's worth, this diagnosis must also apply to Kavan. Until her death she kept a portrait of her detested mother. It was painted by Vladimir Tretchikoff – so its retention was an ambiguous gesture.

Kavan's greatest literary triumph *Ice*, in which she links the omnipresent threat of nuclear destruction to her own chilly emotional landscape, appeared in 1967 and was voted Best Science Fiction Novel of that year. Kavan responded positively to many aspects of sixties youth culture – the experimentation, open-mindedness and sartorial beauty – but ironically there was contained within it the seeds of her final anguish and destruction. The Brain Committee on Drugs reconvened in 1964 to take account of rising panic over youthful drug use. Vast and ruinous changes were proposed and eventually implemented. Addicts could no longer receive maintenance doses of heroin from their doctors but were forced to attend Drug Dependency Units. These were – and are – massively unpopular in that they adopted the American system of prescribing methadone, often in liquid form, rather than injectable heroin to addicts. Methadone is also an opiate but quite without the euphoric effects of opium, heroin or morphine. It can be useful during withdrawal periods but otherwise is of little interest to addicts. Few of them – some say as little as five per cent – have ever bothered with the clinics which they find inhumane, punitive and useless in terms of their needs. They all turned to the black market which responded generously, leading directly to the situation we have today: a huge addict population, criminalised, outcast, diseased, and a thriving black market controlled by organised crime syndicates. 'The entire supply and demand business has gone mad surrounding drugs,' wrote Kavan. In 1968 Kavan was assigned to one of these new Addiction Units, run by a woman called Dr Oppenheim, the last and possibly the worst of Anna's tormentors. Kavan became haunted by the fear that she might be transferred to methadone. She stockpiled heroin in case compulsory detoxification was enforced. She had difficulty getting needles. It is intolerably sad to contemplate this elderly and distinguished writer suffering the indignities of a clinic and the brusque attentions of a doctor, insensible of Kavan's gifts, who thought of addicts in terms of stereotypes. Tortured by fears which she ought not to have had to endure, Kavan died of a heart attack at the end of 1968. It is worth considering that under our present laws Kavan would have been denied the solace of legal heroin and would have written nothing. She would have been condemned to the hell of the black market or else have committed suicide. There are certainly living writers as needy, as gifted – but without that particular and occasionally beneficial option.

Kavan's life and art raise a number of interesting and important questions about the links between creativity, mental illness and addiction and about drug legislation, and it is unfortunate that Callard's book is not able to illuminate any of them. He does fill in many of the gaps in Kavan's life and he does produce some new and fascinating information – that she knew Aleister Crowley and had, of all people, Gerald Hamilton who was the model for Mr Norris in Christopher Isherwood's *Mr Norris Changes Trains* as a lodger – but as a biography this has many drawbacks. There are errors (Kavan's mother was the great-granddaughter, not granddaughter of Victorian physician, Richard Bright; William Burroughs did not have access to 'vast family wealth'). Callard does not appear to know that when Kavan fictionalised her second husband as 'Oblomov' she was referring to Goncharov's terminally lazy hero. He is inconsistent about Kavan's finances. There are lacunae – he seems unaware of the details of her period at *Horizon*. Callard does not attribute quotations and the book has no notes which makes it appear amateurish. He is no literary critic. He compares her early work vaguely to that of D. H. Lawrence and, taking his cue from Kavan's comments, sees the influence of Alain Robbe-Grillet and other *nouveau roman* writers in the later work. Callard maintains that 'the sensibility of an addict permeates and informs the work of Anna Kavan' but shows no understanding of what this means, again apart from the vague general knowledge that addicts dislike the cold and are uninterested in sex. Callard's book provides us with the missing chronology of Kavan's life but only the most fleeting, tantalising glimpses of her extraordinary powers as a writer.

There is no such thing as a typical addict and still less a typical addict who is also a professional writer. When we consider that all the Romantic poets (with the exception of Wordsworth) and most of the population of Britain took opium in the form of tinctures or pills during the nineteenth century, one can see the futility of relying on stereotypes. Kavan's ability to lead an orderly life and to write so productively and consistently recalls Wilkie Collins or George Crabbe, the latter, like Kavan an addict for forty years. Kavan was a dedicated writer – 'For years I've depended on my work as a *raison d'être*' – but she believed that her will to write – rather, her will to live – came from the heroin which protected her from a harsh and menacing world. This knowledge – that she is always obscurely threatened and survives precariously, subject to arbitrary forces – runs beneath the clear pellucid sentences of her mature style. Kavan rarely wrote directly about her addiction, but indirectly she rarely wrote about anything else. Despite their atypicality, such work as has been done on writer addicts (mainly by De Quincey and later by Alathea Hayter in *Opium and the Romantic Imagination*) does reveal that certain themes and experiences recur consistently and these can be observed with extraordinary clarity in Kavan's work. De Quincey understood that all experiences under opium are conditioned by the user's personality – their heredity, education, temperament, talent and imagination – but believed that opium dreams could be artistically productive, and Kavan was to insist on the dream-like quality of her work, particularly in relation to *Ice*. The early stages of addiction can be sufficiently euphoric as to encourage creativity; Kavan started writing steadily for publication soon after she became habituated. Most notably, long-term addiction results in a freezing, a petrifaction of all emotions and sensibility. 'There is a sort of vitrifying process that chills all sensibility,' wrote one commentator on Coleridge. 'Whatever is done is done in pale, cold strength of intellect.' Towards her death Kavan commented: 'I have not felt anything for twenty years.' The lack of warmth and passion in her work, its androgynous quality, the focus on an inner, rather than the outer world is all typical of addict writers, as is the bizarrerie of her imagination.

The inner world of the addict is one of signs and symbols; it has a recognisable landscape. It is Poe's Dreamland, Baudelaire's *paysages opiacés*, the world of Xanadu. Here certain images recur: outcasts, pariahs, quicksands, petrified landscapes, freezing cold, ice, mountains, castles, watching eyes. All this will be familiar to any reader of Kavan's work. She speaks of 'being frozen in nightmare paralysis'. The stories in *Asylum Piece* have all the paranoia of the addict: the sensation that eyes are watching the narrator in 'The Enemy', the house that lies in ambush in 'A Changed Situation'. The entire, obsessive novel *Ice*, is one of the great metaphors for addiction – 'A terrible cold world of ice and death had replaced the living world we had always known.' Kavan's book ranks with other notable images of narcotic thrall, Coleridge's icy, vampiric Geraldine or the 'Nightmare Life-in-Death' created when he amended *The Ancient Mariner*. This freezing horror remains the central image of heroin; to this day a Liverpool teenager can say 'It's got an icy fucking grip that just shuts on you.'

Kavan's world is hermetic, enclosed, self-obsessed, and the

suffering is endless. Although much has been made of the similar-
ity between her work and Kafka's, yet it is equally possible to see
the situation of the addict in her supplicatory narrators and their
tragic dependence on capricious, omnipotent powers. Her contemporaries, William Burroughs and Alexander Trocchi, were able
to find in addiction an appropriate metaphor for the alienation
and confusion of human beings in a consumerist technocracy.
Kavan's writing seems more secretive and encoded, its meaning
perhaps not always accessible even to herself. Ostensibly she comments on contemporary fears and soullessness yet her imagery
harks back to the past – her own past and the literary past.
Ironically, although she is seen as a defiantly modernist writer, yet
very often the cadences of her work recall the *fin de siècle*
Symbolists, or even Poe – a lake is 'a stagnant sheet of lava-
coloured water'. Her entire œuvre, despite the clipped contemporary sentences, corresponds extremely closely to the art of the
Romantic addict writers. Her work, far from being science fiction,
evokes the cold, ancient landscape of opium dreams and visions.
And within is always the figure of the child, fatally, psychically
wounded, just as at the epicentre of De Quincey's work lay a dead
child, sacrificed to the cruelty and inhumanity of the world.

Kavan's work can be read on a number of levels and it seems
possible that she constructed it, as she did her life, as a series of
what friends described as 'sliding panels' or 'Chinese boxes'. But
at its very heart runs her life's blood, the river of ice, the heroin.
The polarities of heat and cold she described, the fearfulness, the
despair, the sense of her own uniqueness – all are commonplaces
of the addict experience, rendered teasing and timeless in her
perfect prose. Roland Barthes wrote *Text Means Tissue*, referring to
the perpetual interweaving of meaning in words, but he could also
have meant that text in its perpetual, minute changes is equivalent
to real, living tissue. Barthes also imagined the paranoiac as
someone who would 'produce complicated texts, stories developed like arguments, constructions posited like games, like secret
complaints'. Is this not what Kavan bequeathed – a living tissue,
of lies, of truths, of codes and duplicities in which art and addiction were interwoven and which was literally the skin of her
soul?

Rock biographies

The Guardian, 12 December 1992

Let's lighten up a bit with some sex and rock 'n' roll. I'm starting to feel like a deejay here. Anyway – it does seem deeply stupid that recreational drugs are one of the prerogatives of youthful success, yet they're still illegal. As ever, it's not what you do, it's the way that you do it. Look at poor Boy George back in his narcotic era. Marianne Faithfull – what a drama queen! No middle-class lady junkie (and even less an icon/star) has to either live or sleep on the streets unless they choose to do so. (I mean, I used to sleep in graveyards sometimes but I didn't have to.) Ms Faithfull had a mother living not very far from London, who would not, I think, have refused a transfer charge phone call. Also someone will always find room for you in London. I have encountered both M. Faithfull and Anita Pallenberg (briefly, separately) and I always preferred the latter, even before I met either.

Michael Holroyd has yet to announce the definitive three-volume work on Prince (aka Sigil) but there is no doubt that rock biography, the bastard child of memoir, is now here to stay. The presses, running purple with prose, have delivered numberless books on the old guard: Janis, Dylan, Brian Jones, Jim Morrison, Keith Richards. Such stars have become omnipresent, like the sacred monsters of Hollywood's heyday. It was not always thus.

For a long time, publishers refused to believe that rock fans could read at all. One of the earlier examples of the full-blown form, *No-One Here Gets Out Alive*, a biography of Jim Morrison by Jerry Hopkins and Danny Sugerman, was rejected by thirty-five British and American publishers before going on to become a worldwide bestseller. Hopkins follows up this autumn with *The Lizard King*, another necrophile's paradise of musings on the 'surf-born Dionysus'.

Rock fans need to read and obsess over pictures. When

listening to CDs, or watching videos, they are always subservient to the reality imposed by the artist, always faintly aware of their own lowly status. Print allows the fan to drag the star into their own ambience and to achieve an illusion of control. The enormous popularity of the music press between 1970 and 1980 should have alerted publishers to this tendency; during that period the rock press functioned as a sort of church in which writers, fans themselves yet possessed of an ineffable hotline to the divinities, mediated between audience and star.

What the reader craves is access. Access to glimpses, gossip, secrets, drugs and sex. Many rock readers are as ghoulish as spectators at a drive-by shooting. They want to hear about Led Zeppelin stuffing sharks' noses up groupies or Michael Jackson's operations or Kurt Cobain's strung-out little baby. All too often what they actually get is hyperbolic PR or mind-numbing analyses of recording studio trivia and chord changes.

The rock biography usually falls into one of several distinct types. The first and most heartbreaking is the chronicle of an obsession in which a fan tries to achieve literary union with their beloved. Such books are marked by the writers being cut off from the web of contacts surrounding the artist and having to depend on secondary or discredited sources, and also by the execrable quality of the writing. For example, Mark Hodkinson in his otherwise tolerable biography of Marianne Faithfull, *As Tears Go By*, manages to announce: 'She was a vessel of optimism, finally free of heroin.' Duh? He is also horribly patronised by one of Faithfull's poseur boyfriends ('You don't get degrees at Eton').

Publishers are nowadays so eager to issue these automatic sellers and at the same time so disparaging of their content that the writing is virtually ignored. A book on Brian Jones, *Golden Stone* by Laura Jackson, is another casualty of such greed. It sinks beneath clichés that should have been swiftly blue-pencilled: 'Wickedly sensual, Brian's inbred elegance subtly robbed his bedroom eyes of any offence.' Neither, despite six years of research, does the author reveal anything about Jones's death, which was covered thoroughly two years ago by A. E. Hotchner in *Blown Away: The Rolling Stones and the Death of the Sixties*. She does however track down Jones's two sons, pictures of whom reveal that Brian would certainly have gone bald very young. Feeling as he did on the subject – and even nicknamed 'Mr Shampoo' – there was perhaps some mercy in his death.

A second category of rock biography contains what are probably the most interesting of the books. These are 'written' – usually with supernatural help – by someone who has had a personal connection with their subject. They have been chauffeur, session-player, drug-dealer or lover and have decided to kiss 'n' sell. Here you get the real sleaze as well as the most penetrating insights. The first sentence of Peggy Caserta's *Going Down with Janis* is a classic and says it all. 'I was stark naked, stoned out of my mind on heroin and the girl lying between my legs giving me head was Janis Joplin.' Why write more? This reveals, in the most basic, tabloid way, why Caserta's frenzied and jealous memoir, however inauthentic, will remain more appealing than the intelligent, dignified approach of Myra Friedman in the authorized biography *Buried Alive*. The attraction of course is human frailty, revealed not so much in the accounts of rock star excess as in the wretched, self-serving, special pleading of these narrators. The king of this kind of rock biography must be *Up and Down with The Rolling Stones* by drug-dealer to the stars, 'Spanish Tony' Sanchez. This tells a tale of greed and treachery so revealing that publication in Britain was delayed for over ten years by legal manoeuvres, even though none of the principals ever suggested that it was anything but accurate.

At its best this sort of biography can convey considerable understanding and affection. A good description of Keith Moon's life is contained in *Moon the Loon*, rendered in the guileless Cockney demotic of Dougal Butler, Moonie's 'man' and general factotum. A more recent publication, written by one of the last musicians to accompany Nico and documenting the final years of the Teutonic drama queen, is equally sympathetic. *Nico: The Last Bohemian* by James Young is a tender, lyrical book which simultaneously contributes an accurate picture of junkie life and its attendant black humour. Nico, in sad middle-age, is reduced to playing every toilet between Death Valley and Nuremberg for drug money, stuffing her stash up her 'tradesmen's entrance' at national borders and weeping hopelessly over her waning fortunes.

Less noble has been the writing career of cold-hearted hustler (and Fawn Hall spouse) Danny Sugarman, office boy to the

Doors and Jim Morrison groupie. *Wonderland Avenue* chronicles his time as manager to the post-Morrison Doors and then to Iggy Pop. He also serenades Guns 'N' Roses heart-throb, Axel Rose, in *Appetite for Destruction*, seeing in him a reincarnation of the Dionysian, shamanistic force that possessed Morrison and which Sugerman insists is the epicentre of rock 'n' roll. Another Jim Morrison book is *Strange Days* by Patricia Keneally, a well-written but highly irritable attack on all those who consider her less relevant to Jim's life than she does herself. A practicing Celtic witch, she 'married' Morrison in an occult 'hand-fasting' ceremony. Her book is high-toned gossip and she is vicious towards Morrison's common-law wife and 'cosmic mate', girlfriend Pamela Courson, now dead: 'She was a slut, a junkie, a whore and possibly a murderess.'

Once out of the personal memoir jungle there are the vast mudflats of the traditional rock biography. These are often predictable books, written by professional journalists, which provide a thorough if unexciting account of the artist's life. Veteran biographer Charles Shaar Murray, writer of the authorised biography of John Lee Hooker, points out that the pop culture vultures of the personal memoirs are incapable of accurate reportage whereas hard-nosed investigative journalists tend to have little understanding of rock style and music. Such journalists are, for a variety of reasons, usually unwilling to give offence and one rarely finds the extremes of hate and hagiography so prevalent in the less formal biographies. Here are all the standard works, most of them by Philip Norman. Here are the placid acres of Beatles books and the endless middle-of-the road biographies of groin-straining cock-rockers. Here are the interminable writings on Bob Dylan, none of them very revealing: a fascination with Dylan merely indicates that the author is self-obsessed and not really interested in anyone else at all. Richard Williams' *Dylan: A Man Called Alias*, contains more soulful, enigmatic pictures of the bard. Here also one finds the bland accounts of icons – Madonna, Michael Jackson – totemic figures so seamlessly media-conscious and self-controlled that books lie down in front of them and give up. And here one encounters the occasional gem: Steven Gaines' *Heroes & Villains: The True Story of the Beach Boys*, for example. Scandal too extends right into the field: both Led Zeppelin and Morrissey have feuded famously with biographers. Also, one wonders why it is, when so many bright and sensitive commentators on rock have been women – Lucy O'Brien, Charlotte Greig, Penny Stallings, Pamela Des Barres – that the ancient machismo of the rock world seems to be duplicated in the gender of its biographers. The 700-page *Penguin Book of Rock & Roll Writing*, manages to find just five women writers; editor Clinton Heylin includes Julie Burchill, Tama Janowitz and Deborah Frost's provocative Guns 'N' Roses piece 'Wimps 'R' Us'.

There are also those books like David Crosby's *Long Time Gone* and John Philip's *Papa John* in which the artist unburdens himself to some handy scribe. These two autobiographies are prolonged '*mea culpas*' in which the stars emerge from the Dope Olympics and begin their twelve-step exercises, moaning all the while about having been 'in denial'. Finally there are those writers, usually dedicated to necropop, who have succeeded in subverting the biographical genre to their own ends. One would have to include Greil Marcus' magnificent obsessions in *Lipstick Traces* and *Dead Elvis* as well as Albert Goldman's brutally seductive last rites. His *Elvis Presley* and *The Lives of John Lennon* are irreverent graveyards of vivid, faecal imagery. The best of all rock biographers is probably Nick Tosches. One of the fundamental conflicts in rock has been the split between Calvinist angst and the African musical heritage of the slave trade and in *Hellfire* Tosches sees this as being schizophrenically enshrined in the hysterical torments of Jerry Lee Lewis. Tosches' book *Dino* on Dean Martin purports to reveal the Mafia links behind the songbirds of the Rat Pack.

The jewel in the crown of all this white rock nostalgia must be Victor Bockris' huge tome *Keith Richards*. Bockris, an old-time Velvet Underground fan, is a serious writer who has always been drawn to the dark stars; the doomed, the damned, the ambiguous and the perverse. His doorstop-sized biography of Andy Warhol remains the definitive work on the subject. *Keith Richards* comes trailing that aura of black feathers and vomit so necessary to any discussion of the man, although the book is essentially a vast précis. Bockris has trawled through huge libraries of clippings to present the highlights. Although he struggles to be honest and fair to his readers he is inevitably compromised by dealing with a living subject and the book lacks the cutting edge he was able to bring to his consideration of Warhol.

What emerges overall from a consideration of the rock biography? Firstly, there is no doubt that the stories of the stars of the past thirty years comprise – particularly in Britain – a social record more vital and animated than any presented in fiction. Secondly, that the early rock stars – Elvis and Chuck Berry, the Stones, Hendrix – were considerably hardened by years of insult, neglect and persecution from an authoritarian society before record companies discovered their Midas touch. Now, every raggedy-ass newcomer is ecstatically endorsed long before they are ready for the rollercoaster ride of the biz. Lastly, most of the books contain accounts of Herculean drug use which makes it all the more tragic that Britain is taking so long to drag itself back to the logical pre-1968 ruling that heroin and cocaine should be available on prescription. In the meantime the credits have rolled on numberless victims of druggy outlaw chic and a mighty green torrent of money has been diverted to organised crime and spent sending gangsters' sons through Eton. And finally, although they differ in so many ways, the biographies are all agreed on one point. Every single artist is somehow 'mad, bad and dangerous to know'. Byron and the Romantics – rock on!

Punk

(with some reference to Jon Savage's England's Dreaming)
New Statesman

Having seen the Sex Pistols play their first few gigs (as everyone claims), I have a tender place in my heart for them. I remember them best when I went to the Patti Smith concert at the Roundhouse. Afterwards, at the reception, remembering that I lived with some very hungry people, I was just slipping a large pâté into my handbag (I thought of her as Pâté Smith thereafter) when all the Sex Pistols and their entourage slouched in and made every boy in the room with long hair feel like a total prat. There was a lot of furtive hair-cutting after that. Was it Jon Savage who said that J. Rotten sounded like a wailing mullah? He did, too.

Is there any far-flung hipster, flipster or finger-poppin-daddy who doesn't know the story of the Sex Pistols, pop's last great soap opera? Punk took a journey through ruins and rang down the final curtain. It is hard to avoid an elegiac tone. Punk, despite its brutal emphasis on the dynamics of the moment, was always really saying goodbye. The images of punk are scorched indelibly on to the narrative of the twentieth century: the skinny, hunchbacked boy 'hung onto the mike like a man caught in a wind tunnel', screaming imprecations. A monarch sailing serenely through her burned-out land, a safety-pin stapled firmly to her lip, No Future. Babylon. The winter of discontent. The late seventies were the millenarianist years, the apocalypso dancing and as such they tended to throw up archetypes.

Initially punk chucked a well-aimed gauntlet at the hippies who'd been looning around self-righteously for too long and at the rococo follies of fat-cat pop stars, face-down in bowlfuls of cocaine. Punk struck violently at self-image in a country whose dominant discourse had become pop culture, fashion and style, where the performative mode predominated and where one's entire socio-sexual life could turn on the width of one's trousers.

Although the sixties libertarians felt that they had written the book on bohemian excess, they were vulnerable. They had fought what they believed were ground-breaking battles – against sexual repression, against early adulthood and career conformity – only to find that nothing suited post-war consumer capitalism better than to keep everyone in a state of desirous adolescence. Altogether their madcap psychedelicised rhetoric had developed inexorably along the lines of earlier periods of societal revolt. The radical wing had led to Stammheim and the Baader-Meinhof deaths. The mystico-religious aspect was now poised to deliver the almighty Technicolor yawn of occultism, astrology and assorted gibberish that was to become known as 'New Age'. The final wing were the urban nihilists and decadents of Velvet Underground persuasion and it was they that fuelled the punk psychodrama.

Malcolm 'I was out to sell lots of trousers' McLaren was with Vivienne Westwood, owner of World's End boutique SEX.

Inspired by the Parisian Situationists and Lettrists, who in the fifties had memorably decoded and subverted the capitalist spectacle, the SEX partners settled on sexual fetish clothing as being the most confrontational. Later McLaren was to present himself as an all-seeing combination of Svengali, Fagin and Colonel Parker, who had masterminded the Sex Pistols through adroit media manipulation, but in reality English punk evolved haphazardly after McLaren visited New York in 1975 and noted well all that was going down at CBGB's club. There were the New York Dolls, a trashy satin 'n' tat outfit who 'liked to look sixteen and bored shitless', Television with their chopped-off hair and zomboid stares and The Ramones, the original dumbo one-chord wonders. It was all there – drop-dead urban chic and romantic nihilism. McLaren came home, gathered some aspiring musos from the disaffected deviants hanging around the shop and launched the Pistols on a search and destroy mission. All togged up in their bondage pants, with Day-Glo hair, they were presented as the children of nightmare, a self-mutilating *danse macabre* against which all previous reflexes of shock horror and outrage were to be wholly inadequate. Then The Clash flounced on as urban guerrillas in paint-spattered militia wear, prattling of sten guns in Knightsbridge. The songs thrashed it all out. They were bored. They were pretty vacant. They had no future. They had no fun. There were no utopias. Teen histrionics nothing! This was Dole Queue Rock, hard-core Attitude and, once the whole caravan got going in a blur of televised expletives and a confetti of fanzines, it was a tabloid heaven of photo opportunities – the ones that never stop.

The US never overcame its soporific quaalude consciousness long enough to achieve the *Sturm und Drang* of British punk. It was clear that the pure philosopher's stone of punk lay in London and that its essence was rage, a rage that ran far deeper than class resentment or *pro situ* mouthings. John Lydon aka Johnny Rotten emerged as a shambling, shamanistic ghoul. Suitably demonised, he was a conduit for national stress and subliminally recognised as an archetypal figure with links to the Ranters and Diggers of the past. It was a time of great unrest, rising unemployment, nameless anxieties and unvoiced doubts. The Queen's Jubilee might have served as a soothing salve; the mirrored tower blocks and the empty shipyards waited, silent in the sun, but Lydon cast a leprous shadow, speaking with terrible force of waste, loss, corruption and decay. Quite unconsciously the British punks, with Lydon as their figurehead, had tapped into the deepest fears of the national psyche, the tremulous terrors of a people whose national identity had been eroded throughout the post-war decades and who were now, in the most profound sense, at a loss. And thus, seeing their worst fears made flesh, the good yeomen of England turned on the punks and tried to rip them to shreds. British punks in fact tended to be mildly patriotic and suffered as scapegoats for an identity crisis they shared.

Punk, amorphous and protean, managed briefly to unite a vastly disparate cast in a moment of high-tension theatre. Its strange blend of radical politics, right-wing imagery, sexual fetish material, taboo flouting, puritan disgust, art and irony described a nexus of paradox which, further burdened by issues of class, race and identity, was primed to implode. Negativity and nihilism also involved a countdown to oblivion and record companies and the media added their own divisive agendas. Punk had been balanced on a razor's edge; it was the last gasp of the post-war youth cultures, the final powerful co-ordinated cult and simultaneously it took the first baby breaths of the cynical entrepreneurial culture that became known as Thatcherism. After the Sex Pistols broke up and Thatcher came to power, her aggressive dominatrix politics a curious mirror of punk style, it was time to shape up or ship out into a neo-hippie twilight of political opposition or heavy, comforting drug use – memories are made of hits.

The Clash etc

A Riot of Our Own by Johnny Green with Gary Barker, illus. Ray Lowry, foreword by Joe Strummer
The Independent, 30 August 1997

My tender feelings towards Mr Lydon and Co were greatly exceeded by my love for The Clash, who never wrote really stupid lyrics. When I was working at Compendium Bookshop they were over

*the road at Rehearsal Studios and they ate in the same caff as we did.
And so it came to pass when their road-manager with compañero
Johnny Green published his inevitable book of reminiscences* A Riot
of Our Own: Night and Day with The Clash *that on reading it I
found I had crept into it twice, once anonymously and once, well,
onymously. I won't embarrass Johnny Green here with any of my own
reminiscences as he was quite sweet about me, viz: 'It was run by a
drug-dealer, who was living with an old friend of mine. My friend's
way of dealing with the world was to take to her bed for weeks at a
time. She would hold court, propped up by pillows, in her nightdress'
etc. etc. etc. And later – 'a friend, Liz Young, is the girl in the film*
(Rude Boy) *who gives Ray Gange a blow job in the toilets. After
filming, Ray said to her: "How about doing it for real?" She said
"You must be joking." Actually the conversational interchange wasn't
quite like that and that's why we have* Rashomon.

*Oh, well, if I can't write such things here, where can I? It's my
book and I'll cry if I want to. Anyway, it's not much to be proud of . . .*

The Clash were a potentially world-class, killer rock band who
became major casualties of the long, confusing battle that has
constituted five decades of youth culture. Time was, youth and
leisure being a new invention, that uncertain steps were taken
until ideas, art, influences and creativity coalesced into the
amorphous mass bohemianism that came to define being young.
In the earlier post-war decades, all this activity, whether propelled
by usury or utopianism, had a profound, ineradicable effect on the
dominant culture. Gradually, inevitably, it was distilled down to
its most basic and automatic impulses – energy, style, sex, dance,
speed, loads of laffs and chemicals, in short, ecstasy; a shiny, teen
'n'twenty Disneyland bubble of delirium bobbing atop real life
where you pay for all the rides and retire sweat-sodden after a few
years to strap on the unchanging manacles of marriage and
mortgage, progeny and progress. The Clash were shot down in
the great fight between youth as a credible, creative, potentially
subversive force that unnerved and destabilised and youth as
largely passive style consumers, amusing, profitable and non-
sensical.

The Clash combined these oppositional forces and walked a
razor-blade. They were both scary, awesomely talented punk

musicians and very cute children who looked great and wanted to play with all the toys of carefree success and excess.

This is their story, told from the seamy trenches of those old wars by their ex-road manager and partner-in-crime. Johnny Green was a big, truculent guy, a closet-intellectual, his appearance deceptively mellowed by large specs which made him look, as Joe Strummer says, 'like a librarian in Macclesfield'. However, a river of pure madness and mayhem raged through his personality, fed by rich tributaries of sarcasm, irony, rogue chemicals, fags and booze.

Some hold that my having been vaguely privy to the events of this book equips me for pronouncing upon it. Is it authentic? Yes. It is as true as a sequence of memories from a single perspective can ever be. Here it all is, London calling from the top of the dial – the low-life liggers, the bags of cash, the cops, the coke, the quarrels, up and down the Westway in and out the lights, the great bass speakers, the driving rain and reggae, expectation, expectoration and the cosmic live gigs when the hottest garage band ever revved it up to bone-breaking levels of intensity. There were warring managers, the winding-up of fellow soldiers Tom Robinson and Richard Hell and becoming less bored with the USA.

Others may consider that familiarity with the material obviates objectivity. So let me add that the very authenticity of the book ensures intervals of monotony, known as 'touring'. Rehearsing and recording have conversational limitations and this is largely *Boys' Own* territory, with female roles pretty much restricted to certifiable nags and slags.

But overall, this is a witty tribute to the only lastingly listenable punk band. Weep for the lost lyrical promise of Jones and Strummer. Relive the exultant perversity of 'London's drowning and I – I live by the river.' And down they went.

The Dark Stuff: Selected writings on rock music 1972–1993 by Nick Kent

(Penguin)
The Guardian, 31 May 1994

*For a long time my favourite journalists were Nick Kent,
Charles Shaar Murray, Julie Burchill and Ian Penman.*

*Enough said. I'll still read anything they write. Even if it's in a
computer magazine.*

Long, long ago in the early 1970s the *NME* employed journalist
Nick Kent – a writer as deadly and accurate as a Gaboon viper.
He performed sterling service in providing a lifeline for all those
disaffected provincial deviants who longed to emulate him and
hang out with, like, Iggy and Keef and Lou and David. Back in
those days before show business and public relations knocked
rock 'n' roll into its present bland shape there was less distinction
between star singer and star writer. It was no secret that Kent got
closer to his idols than anyone else – and he was at heart, like all
great rock writers a consummate fan – nor that he followed them
all the way into the primal soup of dedicated decadence that produced the big bang of the burning, chaotic rock years. Iggy Pop
described Kent as 'a great palsied mantis', dressed in 'tattered
black leather and velvet guitar-slinger garb', his nose 'perpetually
dripping' from a 'perpetual drug shortage'. Lou Reed called him
'the Judy Garland of rock'. To Peter York he was 'fabulously thin
and pale . . . the most exquisite, grimy neo-decadent get-up in
London'. A legend in other people's lavatories, an idol amongst
idols.

When Kent turned his pinpoint pupils upon a rock star the
subject would ultimately receive a printed combination of the kiss
of death and an eternal welcome to the Human Wreckage Hall of
Fame. He worked like a hellish negative of *Hello!* magazine –
the worst that could be printed appeared accompanied by the

statutory curse of infamy. A whisper of substance abuse, the miasma of psychosis and Kent would appear – affable, convivial, understanding. Consider the majority of his subjects, self-selected for this collection: Lou Reed, Iggy Pop, Guns 'N' Roses, Shane McGowan, The Happy Mondays. Syd Barrett, Brian Jones, Keith Richards . . . *What do these have in common?* All together now . . .

The articles here tend to be later ones, written in the eighties and nineties, but they draw on earlier work to provide an overview of the dark star in question. Many have been extensively, subtly re-ordered and rewritten. Kent rewrote, he has said, because the pieces sounded 'terribly clichéd' (doesn't all earlier work seem unsatisfactory to a writer?) – and because the now fully reformed journalist 'disliked the puerile way I wrote about drugs'. This suggests drastic revisionism. However, I seem to recall a thin scarred vein of the perception that chemical excess destroys talent – whether authorial or musical – faintly, puritanically present in the earlier work.

This book therefore lies somewhere between the original journalism and a new anthology. Nevertheless, all that a fan might wish for is here. Kent was a superb interviewer, capable of annihilating his own ego to the point where his subjects hanged themselves. And don't think that the rock writer's life is all indescribably hip, long days of wine and neuroses. It's hard work transcribing hours of taped obscenities, guitar whines and mumbled margarita orders, panning for that speck of intelligible response.

Kent was always compulsively readable and remains so. He gives good gossip – after all, he was there – acute insights and a surprising degree of satire. There is no more authentic account of the ballad of Sid and Nancy, nor has anyone else written with such reflective humanity on the way power eroded the souls of the Stones.

Kent conveys the acne and the ecstasy of the adolescent spirit of rock or what he calls 'the mixing of the Byronic and the moronic' to perfection. Ironically his very professionalism renders the author himself opaque and there are few autobiographical glimpses.

The new, rehabilitated Kent, Paris-based with girlfriend and child, now intends a biography of Neil Young whom he regards as one of the few artists of integrity in the business. As he quotes from Young, one can perhaps catch a glimpse of the elusive writer himself, keeper of the crypt. 'I've been running all my life. Where I'm going – who the fuck knows? The way I feel now I can keep going for a long time.' Let's hope Kent writes forever.

Damage

The Guardian, 3 December 1993

The following is only peripherally an interview with rock band Gallon Drunk. It is really (quite obviously) all about the late, great, much-loved and much-lamented Robin Cook aka Derek Raymond, one of the nicest guys you could ever hope to meet.

And now you can't. When, when will they be able to download personality and keep people (well, let's say only very nice writers) on disk after they are dead? Like in Greg Egan's Permutation City?

An old woman is hurled out of a northbound car to die on the hard shoulder of the M1 as the night rain washes over her. A Ford assembly-line worker butchers a child on a Hanwell estate. A pensioner and a Spanish prostitute perish together in a decaying Empire Gate mansion block. These are the sort of deaths that do not interest anyone very much. They rarely make the papers. They hold no opportunities for promotion. They are the murders that the unnamed narrator of Derek Raymond's 'Factory' series of detective novels investigates. This man, embittered and humane, works out of a West End police station – the 'Factory'. Working for a department called 'Unexplained Deaths' he sees all around him wreckage, waste and agony.

These are hellishly bleak and desolate novels. They turn over London as if it were some vast refuse tip, revealing all its most scarred and Godforsaken corners, its most rancid and pitiful secrets. They are powerfully compassionate books in which the narrator seeks justice for the most loveless and wretched of the city's inhabitants. They belong recognisably to the Chandleresque genre of *noir* fiction and film which helps to explain why the novels are so highly esteemed in France. In Britain they are heirs to the less familiar territory of Patrick Hamilton and Gerald Kersh. The first Factory novel, *He Died with his Eyes Open*, appeared in 1984 and the fifth in the series, *Dead Man Upright*, has just been published.

Many of the observations in the novels are based on personal experience. Derek Raymond's real name is Robin Cook. An entertaining, haunted-looking man, he has served on the bohemian front line for decades and is an habitué of the Coach and Horses in Soho.

Born in 1931, Cook always detested his privileged background. He walked out of Eton. He was, he wrote, someone 'who was sick of the dead-on-its-feet upper crust he was born into, that he didn't believe in, didn't want, whose values were meaningless'. He was seeking to carve his way out and 'crime was the only chisel I could find'. Cook joined various other upper-class rakes who were beginning to assault the rigid, seemingly entrenched icebergs of polite British society. These were razor-sharp fifties wide boys, artful dodgers of whom British gonzo journalist, Nik Cohn, wrote: 'It became chic to cut corners, to gamble and dabble in illegalities and carry an air of mystery, to know gangsters by their first name.' Although Cook was closely involved with a number of criminal enterprises – 'I was bent, that's all' – he had enough detachment to write a series of satirical novels about those days. The first and best-known of these was *The Crust on its Uppers*, originally published in 1962 and re-issued last year by Serpent's Tail. Cook eventually wandered abroad but completed two years as a London mini-cab driver before settling in France in 1974.

In France Cook worked at a number of desperate, dead-end jobs – as a roofer, as a driver, in vineyards – and wrote nothing for a long time. He says: 'I'd been working on the land for five years when I wrote *He Died with his Eyes Open*. One of my neighbours said to me: "You're fucked. You're forty-eight. Call yourself a writer? You'll be a day labourer for the rest of your life." It hit me and I thought, "Come on, see if it will still work."' He says that he intended the book to be a one-off and that it was largely autobiographical. In retrospect it is an ironic book. The detective narrator is seeking the murderer of a man who initially appears to be little more than an alcoholic dosser. The character of this victim corresponds closely to Cook's own. The book was very well received and his publisher encouraged him to follow it up. Thus it was, having effectively killed himself off, Cook emerged with a new writing career, a new identity as Derek Raymond and a huge number of new fans.

It was the fourth book in the Factory series, *I was Dora Suarez* – over which a publisher memorably lost his lunch ('Threw up all over his desk apparently') – which was to bring Cook real notoriety and renown. Painful to read, it was carefully researched and the writing of it caused Cook great distress. Its poor, doomed victim, Dora, is an AIDS sufferer working in a private sex club where much of the erotic entertainment features small rodents inserted into the anus. Her killer, Tony Spavento, is not only so sexually disturbed that he kills others but also ritually mutilates himself. Many of these details Cook obtained from police reports.

Throughout the Factory series Cook had shown an increasing interest in the psychology of the psychopathic murderer, and in his autobiography, *The Hidden Files,* published last year he discussed the 'vile psychic weather' of his novels. No serious novelist can animate evil without having a profound belief in its opposite. 'Tenderness, compassion,' he says, 'if you haven't any of that you might as well not bother writing novels at all' and it is this sense of pity and of pathos that most deeply characterises his books. His most recent novel, *Dead Man Upright,* is virtually a textbook of sexual psychopathology. Cook says that he has met psychopaths and 'They were flat. There was no reaching them. There's a dimension missing. There's no depth.' Ultimately such blankness and self-absorption can only stun the imagination and Cook now intends to take the Factory series in a different direction.

Cook's most recent venture has been more unusual. In the wake of Hubert Selby's work with Henry Rollins and William Burroughs' recordings with The Disposable Heroes of Hiphophrasy, he has been involved in recording extracts from *I was Dora Suarez* with a musical score by two members of London band Gallon Drunk, James Johnston and Terry Edwards. Gallon Drunk's last album *From the Heart of Town* showed a preoccupation with the seedy world of London's dispossessed very similar to Cook's own. Lyricist, James Johnston, works not unlike Cook, picking up fragments of conversations from street and bars.

Johnston was already a fan of Cook's work and stresses how much he enjoyed supplementing the text 'in the most subtle ways possible'. Terry Edwards initially found the project more troubling, saying that his original reaction to the book was 'shock and horror. The murders are graphically portrayed and it's very disturbing.' Edwards was also concerned about the focus on sexual violence and the way the book had to be extensively edited. Little is left but the murders and the policeman's revenge, a very violent revenge carried out as Edwards says: 'on a severely mentally disturbed person. However, I've spoken with Robin about this and the idea is that evil permeates good, that it permeates the detective and he becomes as mad as the killer.' Cook was initially taken aback at the idea of reading to music. He describes his voice as being 'like an iron parrot'. However, his reading poignantly conveys the pain and bewilderment of the novel, and the music, which is simple and plangent, communicates the ambience so effectively that the aural version is very much more affecting than the written one – and it *is* a very strong and alarming piece of work.

Cook, Edwards and Johnston met up originally in the Coach and Horses and seem to have been there for some time now, leaving journalists with interview tapes that have to be held to the ear like an alcoholic seashell. All three are happy with the final collaboration. Cook was particularly pleased at their interest in his work and the fact that there seemed 'to be no age gap at all' – which means he has been attracting disaffected bohemian readers for over thirty years now.

Hanged, drawn and quartoed

New Statesman, 2 October 1998

I am going to work up to this confession gradually. I read to relax as well as work but the last thing I want to read for fun is any more deeply avant-garde US writing. So I read poetry, proper old poetry up to Yeats, Eliot and Auden. And I read horror fiction. And I read true crime and friends can get quite disapproving. So I subjected myself to a rigorous moral whatsit and decided that, as I had never had the remotest sexual thought or fantasy concerning murder or mutilation or blood or rape, I read it for the reasons I thought I did – 'satiable curiosity and ordinary fascination with wickedness. It's all those details – I don't mean about crimes but about how real people live. All those days of eating boiled mutton in 90°F temperatures which must have helped send Lizzie Borden completely round the bend. And exactly where people keep everything in a trailer. You used to get all these sorts of details about everyday life in novels but you don't any more, they're too artistic.

I started reading true crime completely by accident – I had of course read Truman Capote's In Cold Blood *and Norman Mailer's opus on Gary 'Let's Do It' Gilmore,* The Executioner's Song, *and thought that the former was greatly over-rated and the latter unbelievably turgid. (Even The Adverts did it better – 'Gary don't need his eyes to see/Gary and his eyes have parted company'.) I was living then in Camden and teaching at a college in the West London suburbs so I had to go to Victoria every day and get a train. On the way back I always spent ages in the station bookstall and one day I bought a book called* The Nutcracker *by journalist Shana Alexander. It was super-captivating, about this loopy ex-Vassar alchoholic who adored George Balanchine and got her two sons so hopelessly screwed up that when she asked them to kill her father (a skinflint auto-parts millionaire) they did. Or one of them did. These kids were deeply deranged, many sandwiches short of a picnic – they were ultra right-wing and put out a family 'zine full of share prices and adverts for panty liners. It was just so weird that I kept on reading true crime, only to find, as with all genre writing, that a good book was a jewel beyond price.*

Still, there are a few.

Ever since the Newgate Calendar was first issued in the seventeenth century, villains have been 'hanged, drawn and quartoed' in order to satisfy the naturally macabre urges of the human mind. More recently, there has been a huge boom in true crime publishing and it has become one of the most profitable areas of the industry. Publishers and booksellers alike attest to the fact that much of this new true crime readership is made up of women and there is a possible reason for this, apart from the obvious fact that such books articulate the violent rage and murderous fury that women are still expected to repress. McLuhan's 'global village' is a misnomer in that it bears no relation to to the open scandals and secrets that littered small communities in the past. Everything in the 'global village' is filtered: it is censored, re-formed, written and re-presented via the media. True crime, in that it is written, certainly belongs to the mediatised world but, now that the novel has largely deserted family life for areas of metaphysical speculation, it is only in true crime that one receives the sort of artless insights into domestic life that were once a daily reality and have since been superseded by urban secrecy.

Bad true crime writing is dull and formulaic. Speedily written, it is usually culled from newspaper reports and frequently perpetuates misinformation. Good, or even excellent, true crime writing is very rare – one might think of Truman Capote, Brian Masters, Darcy O'Brien. It too follows a pattern but a cunning and delicate one wherein the author spends years researching the background to a community, the psychology of those involved, and if possible, comes to know the perpetrators. Unfortunately it all tends to get tarred with the same brush and all too often excellent work is dismissed alongside the trashiest hack 'n' slice paperbacks. Genre writing is like parties – one has to attend to all the bad ones to be there for the great one. And so I have been surprised in one month to encounter two books destined to become classics in the field, plus others that suggest that the standard of true crime writing is slowly beginning to improve.

Alexandra Artley's book, *Murder in the Heart* (Hamish Hamilton), does not really deserve to be called true crime. Appropriately introduced by Brian Masters, it is one of the most extraordinary and sensitive books ever written about a crime, an examination of 'one small family gone completely mad'. In 1988 the Preston police responded to a call which led them to a chilling, morbidly neat little terraced house and the corpse of a man shot twice in the chest. Surrounding him were three grieving women, all wearing gold wedding rings. One of them was Tommy Thompson's wife, the other two his middle-aged daughters.

Tommy Thompson had been a tyrant and a sadist who had sexually abused his daughters. For forty years his wife and children had been terrified, mute and captive. Thompson's two daughters were convicted of murder and received a suspended sentence. Artley set herself the task of interpreting and understanding this family's suffering. She goes deep into the background of those involved, presenting along the way a compelling portrait of the small Lancashire mill towns during the post-war years. She consults everyone with whom the family had any contact and has the wisdom to include herself in the narrative so that her responses, frustrations and breakthroughs become as engrossing as the original story. Her research is impeccable – Thompson's widow and daughters wrote their own account of their lives, documents of infinite pathos, which Artley utilises with great delicacy and precision. She speaks to dialect experts, quotes local poets and has consulted a vast library on sexual abuse. This is a stunning, extremely moving book in which Artley bears witness to domestic agony and reminds us that there are other Tommy Thompsons still lurking behind pristine front doors. The only comparison in Britain is with John Cornwell's 1982 *Earth to Earth*, another account of a solitary, reclusive family – and Artley's is the superior work.

The other new book destined to become a classic is entirely different and will appear in a form that may deflect the serious reader for some time. *Final Truth: The Autobiography of Mass Murderer/Serial Killer Donald 'Pee-Wee' Gaskins as told to Wilton Earle* (Mondo) is a devastating and ferocious publication. 'Pee-Wee' Gaskins was born in rural South Carolina in 1933 and executed there in the electric chair in 1991. In the interim he proved to be one of the most violent criminals America has ever seen. Before his death he dictated these tapes and stipulated that they should be transcribed verbatim and published. Earle's editorial interference has been kept to a minimum. This is Gaskins' authentic white trash voice, sardonic, relentless, devious and wholly without remorse. Knowing electrocution was inevitable Gaskins opts for what seems to be, by and large, the truth. He confesses to a number of murders of close relatives which were previously unsuspected and to sexual practices so vile and extreme that they make the book a heart-stopping and shocking experience even for this gutter-fixated bibliophile. There has only been one previous book of this sort, the – very similar – autobiography of Carl Panzram published in the 1940s. Gaskins' revelations appear to render redundant much of the interminable library on sociopathology and psychopathology. Gaskins' background, although deprived, was not at all unusual for the time. It would appear, as Nelson Algren once put it: 'Some cats just swing like that.' Throughout history there have been individuals who found sexual pleasure in observing acute pain but such practices were restricted to those of great wealth and power. Nowadays our pleasures are democratic and will remain so until brain chemistry is better understood, and more awkwardly, subject to legislation. This is a very serious book, indispensable to psychiatry and criminology. One might hesitate to recommend it to others, although fortunately murderers rarely seem to do much reading.

Another unusual, but much less dramatic book is Ann E. Imbrie's *Spoken in Darkness: Small-Town Murder and Friendship Beyond Death* (Bloomsbury). Imbrie, now an English Professor at Vassar, grew up in Ohio and was schoolfriends with another girl, Lee Snavely, who became a junkie and a prostitute and later fell victim to serial killer Gary Taylor. Imbrie takes the opportunity to meditate upon the lives of provincial women who grew up in the sixties, and their relationships, particularly with their mothers. She considers the reasons for her life taking such a different path from Lee's and in general offers a tentative feminist model for true crime writing. This is well-researched, well-written, but ultimately hampered by Imbrie's own distance from Lee's chosen world.

Beverley Allitt killed several children in Grantham Hospital and of the two books on the case, *Murder on Ward Four* by Nick Davies (Chatto) and *Angel of Death* by John Askill and Martyn Sharpe (Michael O'Mara), Davies' is by far the best. One of the tragedies of this case was that the mental illness, 'Munchausen's syndrome by proxy', which drives carers or parents to hurt others was so little understood in Britain. It had been amply documented in a near-identical Texan case, that of Genene Jones, and if true crime were not so maligned and little read by professional people in Britain lives might have been saved.

The first book on Waco, *Fire and Blood: The True Story of David Koresh and the Waco Seige* (Fourth Estate) by David Leppard is a premature pot-boiler, as evinced by his appalling chapter on offender profiling and the psychology of Koresh. This is a very complex subject, involving hundreds of people and every level of the US government and no book written in six weeks can even begin to do it justice. The *New Yorker* published a drawing of a Waco T-shirt bearing the legend 'The Seven Seals Of David Koresh' and beside it were printed seven badges of American law enforcement bureaus – ATF, FBI, DEA and so on. 'Complex' is just too mild a word for the Waco Kid's apocalypse.

Happy like Murderers by Gordon Burn

(Faber & Faber)
New Statesman, 2 October 1998

Unfortunately, Gordon Burn, whom I like, always viewed me with some suspicion after I pointed out that in his first novel, Alma Cogan, *it was not actually Alma Cogan who sang 'The Little Drummer Boy' on the Christmas album Hindley and Brady played in the background when they tape-recorded their abominable treatment of Lesley-Anne Downey. It was Ray Conniff and his Singers, a medley called 'We Wish You A Merry Christmas'. Thus Alma Cogan had no conceivable connection, even given poetic licence and a passport, with the Moors Murderers which somewhat undermines one of the novel's themes. It's still an excellent novel and I still think he's a good writer although not at his best in the book that follows.*

I can't reprint any more of this stuff. That's it.

True crime is an aspect of publishing so successful that it has been striding around the books market like a booted dominatrix for the past two decades. Nothing new in this, of course, apart from the technological scale. Punters have lusted for details of crimes and perpetrators since the days of the Newgate Calendar and the Red Barn murder dramas. Earlier still, songs and oral accounts of atrocities always functioned as popular – very popular – entertainment.

Nowadays, moral uncertainty has clouded these simple pleasures. Critics look at the business of turning crime into entertainment as distasteful, a twisted and sleazy form of vulgar voyeurism that helps inure an already affectless public to further horror and violence. Thus critics endorse only the most elitist true crime, even though Truman Capote's brief interview with Manson assassin, Bobby Beausoleil, is more vivid than the whole of *In Cold Blood* and Norman Mailer's *The Executioner's Song* is frankly boring. As with any specialist subject – thrift shopping, party-going – genre reading requires that you endure a ton of slurry if you are to be there for the gold nugget; in this case perhaps Shana Alexander's *The Nutcracker* or Steven Levy's *The Unicorn's Secret*.

Essentially critics will deign to notice true crime writing only if it is extremely restrained and inexplicit. Even the laudable Brian Masters is far too graphic for some and poor old Colin Wilson just cannot be mentioned in polite company.

The reason for this excessive prudery and unease is that our society has outlawed death to a point far beyond taboo. Few of us ever see death. Our media censors all the realities of death. Films inevitably glamorise and thus distort it by the mere intervention of cameras and physical beauty. If we had all been exposed to the gallows and the plague, or even only, as I have been, to police photos of what a bomb really does to human flesh or a molester to a child victim then we might all grow up and stop treating death like the Victorians treated sex, with prurience and unease and embarrassment and knee-jerk morality. Murder and torture are the most distorted aspect of death's persistent reality. Murder and torture in all their stinking, hellish, heartbreaking contempt for life are the ultimate perversion of what we are. As such, they and every other form of death demand our full knowledge and attention, our understanding and respect, our awe. Instead we are 'protected' from all that is disturbing and ultimately it ceases to disturb and can only titillate.

We have invented the invisible death, the clean death, the superficial death. Death – 'He's the ruffian on the stair' – is none of these things.

So who reads or writes true crime? The majority of its readers are women, presumably in automatic response to Joe Orton's *pensée*: 'Life being what it is, one dreams of revenge.' Some readers of true crime apparently find it sexually exciting. (One can easily test this. If your private sexual fantasies include murder then you are using true crime as pornography.) In general, however, I think that the largest group of people drawn to crime, horror and the macabre do not have – as is generally supposed – a stunted moral sense but the reverse. They have a grossly over-inflated awareness of good and evil, a veritable Mr Atlas of a conscience. They usually come from very religious backgrounds, either Catholic or Calvinist, and this ingrained Manichaeanism is what gives evil its terrible resonance and, at times, appeal for them. Without a vibrant sense of its dualistic opposite, wickedness would inspire only indifference. (Aleister Crowley, in full flight from the fundamentalist Plymouth Brethren, is a good example as is film director, John Waters, or master moralist, Stephen King.)

The final group of true crime devotees are people with an obsessive interest in the everyday details of ordinary lives. Now that novels no longer provide such social realism, one of the few places you can learn about the minutiae of domestic lives is in books of true crime – whether it be Lizzie Borden's frenzy-inducing diet of warmed-over mutton or Denis Nilsen's bedsit desolation with his dog.

Theoretically someone could belong to all these groups but it seems highly likely that Gordon Burn inhabits the final one. He is interested in people and place to a degree that makes him an extremely competent journalist and in his best fiction, such as *Alma Cogan*, a hugely animated, powerfully evocative novelist.

The case of serial killers, Fred and Rosemary West, is surely iconic by now and needs little introduction. Twenty-five, Cromwell Street, Gloucester, may have been razed and ploughed with salt but it stays with us all as psychic real estate. This is the sixth book I have read devoted solely to the Wests. (Have those who violate the social contract no civil rights at all? Is their privacy legally void?)

Burn's task has been to do something different, something individual with the now familiar facts – priapic cheeky chappie and jobbing builder, Fred, all tall tales and compulsive sexual innuendo; his sullen, schoolgirl wife Rose, coming straight from an incestuous home to be groomed by Fred into enthusiastic pros-titution, bisexuality, inter-racial sex and terminal sadomasochism – a deadly union consecrated over the disarticulated bones of their many young girl victims in the cellar and the sacrifice of two of their own large brood of children and stepchildren.

So what does Burn do? Firstly, taking a tip (whether wittingly or not) from that literary master of mutilation, Dennis Cooper, Burn dismembers the body of his own text. Eschewing chronological order, he fractures the narrative for rhythmic emphasis, ensnaring the reader in an appalled and continuing awareness of the breaking up of flesh.

Essentially Burn seeks to convey, impressionistically, the ambience of the Wests' home and personalities and through them to present an accurate image of the ocean of wounded humanity that comprises the contemporary underclass. Here is all the living debris; rootless, shiftless, drifting, dazed people. Strugglers and stragglers and strivers. Unplanned pregnancies. Little stabs at happiness. Desertions and divorces and extended families so complex that even the Old Testament couldn't document them. Young and old, casualties of the breakdown of family, medicine, education and employment, mutate into vulnerable cynics on the wrong side of the law and the social services. Burn seeks to show how the Wests both embodied and manipulated this new world for their own demonically delicious conspiracy. And in all this he succeeds admirably. The book is far closer to Nick Davies' *Dark Heart: The Shocking Truth about Modern Britain* than to any of the other books on the West case.

Burn often writes in a non-standard, staccato demotic that mimics the pace and rhythm of his characters. Fred West – 'Ducking in, ducking out . . . He hated anything official. People in uniform and briefcase-carrying nosey-parkers. He would extend the house incrementally jerry-built and screened-off from the street. And in this way he combined two of the things that gave him most pleasure. Making and constructing. And making a monkey of. Pulling the wool over. Putting one over on. The chisel. The blag.'

Even more cleverly, Burn understands absolutely the role of repetition in the dialogue of these lives and uses it constantly, artfully. Ceaseless patterning and repetition are basic to the semantics of those like West who are illiterate but verbal, uneducated but imaginative. Burn has a fine ear and is great at getting right in there with the detail. He maps obsessively the geography of the Wests' patch and their fetishisation of objects and places – five-bar gates, bus-stops, dildos. Burn can schmooze along with anyone so we have the whole picture of Rose's extended and dysfunctional family, all the family life of one of their few mercifully surviving victims, Carol Raine, and a great deal of the lives of the previous owners of number Twenty-five. The trouble is, very little of this is relevant to the dynamic of the Wests' marriage and murders.

Burn is far more of a sociologist than a criminologist. In roundabout fashion he does provide all the basic facts but they are merely a précis of the earlier books. The single new and unlovely fact he unearths is that Fred, living in Glasgow, apparently used to rub his mixed-race baby stepdaughter, Charmaine, against his groin, announcing that he was sexually exciting the infant to orgasm. Later he killed her.

Even sociologically, Burn ignores what seems to me the most revealing societal aspect of the West case. The Wests provide an intriguing link between George Orwell's vision of the old-fashioned, domestic, very English murder with neighbours twitching curtains, endless cups of tea, mutilation between meals and the new post-war, hi-tech world. Twenty-five Cromwell Street bulged with porn videos, Readers' Wives, contact mags, fetish catalogues, hand-held cameras, Polaroids, bugging devices in the bedroom. Fred, the classic harmless little man next door, was a peeper and voyeur; he films Rose brutally assaulting teenage runaways, then brings them a nice cuppa to calm them.

Burn just does not know enough about criminology. He calmly records the two very serious head injuries West suffered in the late fifties with no apparent awareness of the current furore regarding the incredibly high incidence of severe head injuries amongst serial killers, as propounded by Elliot Leyton and other theorists. Burn also regards the missing digits and toes of West's victims as an ongoing mystery although word is that West was galvanised by an apocryphal, rural folk tale at the age of seven – a local person was allegedly buried alive and tried to claw their way out, tearing their extremities. With his propensity for total eroticisation this memory may have hardened into fetish when an early girlfriend apparently had her fingers sliced off by a pane of falling glass.

Burn also relies overmuch on certain books such as Maria Tatar's *Lustmord* whilst ignoring others that might have been more pertinent.

Of course Burn has a thesis which is that West fetishised things, particularly his tools, which slimed oil (as if it were his real sperm) over every surface. Simultaneously he treated people as objects. 'The ability to . . . turn people into things is something that Fred West had to a murderous degree.' Well, yes. This is not news on the psychopathic front.

Burn doesn't even directly draw our attention to passages in the Fred West tapes where he segues into referring to knives or tools as 'he' and bodies as 'it'.

Most frustrating of all are the times when Burn leads up to some potentially original or intriguing insight and backs off. He comments on the 'private . . . complex, almost subliminal language of signals and cues . . . codes' that operated between Fred and Rose but takes only the simplest steps towards decryption. Similarly, Fred's obsession with his house 'with entrances and thresholds', together with his compulsive need to explore orifices and holes and his sick, DIY surgical fetish about the interior of the vagina, is allied by Burn to his constant drilling, compulsive work habits and the fitting of things into other things. Such topics are so thought-provoking that Mark Seltzer in his recent *Serial Killers: Life and Death in America's Wound Culture* devotes an entire chapter to boundary issues and the role of architecture and construction in the life of the killer, citing H. H. Holmes, John Wayne Gacy and others. Seltzer describes 'An extraordinary absorption in place and place-making that becomes indistinguishable from programs of self-making and self-construction. The violence and horror precipitated by the radical failure of distinction between subject and place – by the reciprocal topographies of subject and context – are absolutely crucial in understanding cases of repetitive violence.' Had Burn been more willing to pursue such avenues we might have learnt something new about West.

Burn seems to have a curious unease with theory. He proffers names like Otto Dix, George Grosz, Jung and Dr Schreber with a sort of aggressive bashfulness, like a child displaying a stolen toy. His previous true crime book on Peter Sutcliffe, *Somebody's Husband, Somebody's Son*, was a classic in the sense of the information it uncovered and the brutal crudity it conveyed. But it took Nicole Ward Jouve in *The Streetcleaner* to take the sort of intellectual and intuitive risks with those facts that ultimately crystallise into original ideas, however many kooky missteps there may be along the way.

There was nothing new to uncover in the West case, and, avoiding risks, Burn preferred to do what he does best, that is, write very well. Consequently, this book with its impressionism and imagery and muted streams of consciousness is, like its Damien Hirst cover, essentially style-driven. The title, once seemingly slick and brash, looks perfect now. The Wests were happy like murderers and Burn goes no deeper than that. Fred West went far, far deeper into the soil, and the dark, and the womb and the extremes of the physical life. Burn should have done the same, in the intellectual and artistic sense. He doesn't. But then Fred was 'emotionally null. Morally delinquent. A moral vacuum . . . a moral blank' and Burn isn't, so perhaps it was an impossible task.

The Goth of Small Things: Poppy

The Independent on Sunday

I obviously have one or two things in common with Poppy Z. Brite which is probably why I was sent to interview her. I liked her a lot, I think she is a courageous writer and I love her home town, New Orleans. We even thought of buying a house there – you could still get those great, cracked, wedding-cake-in-the-rain versions of Tara then for $30,000 in the Garden District. It is a very evocative place – Nelson Algren, John Kennedy O'Toole, Tennessee Williams – but I just don't see how anyone gets any work done. It is incredibly hot and humid too and full of washed-up half-remembered names like Warhol's scriptwriter, Ronnie Tavel. A friend, writer Seth Morgan, crashed there and died on his Harley and that made it more depressing. Johnny Thunders died there as well. Although you can see the original streetcar with 'Desire' on its front destination and the huge (live) snakes in the Voodoo Museum are lovely. Oh, well. More recently Ms Brite seems to have gone over the top a bit, to no useful purpose . . .

Poppy Z. Brite agrees with me – 'I don't like vampires very much.' She's right. They're predictable, familiar and they chew through the bytes on the PCWs of a thousand mediocre horror writers. Yet Brite's first book, *Lost Souls*, appears to be a horror novel about vampires. The fact that it's also a symbolic first novel about a youth subculture is indicative of the strange state of American fiction at the moment. 'What I wanted to write about,' she says, 'was the Gothic subculture of which I was an observer and participant at the time and vampires are such an essential icon in that – and that's how they turn up in my book.'

Brite's work is strange, unclassifiable. It's called horror. At the moment new American fiction seems divided into two distinct camps. On the one hand phalanxes of would-be Raymond Carvers stride out of the universities and creative writing courses like the workers in *Metropolis*, eager to hit the keys on stories about blue-collar folk in mobile homes. On the other hand are a diverse group – some well-known, some less so, some new and brilliantly talented, united only by their focus on urban life and their alienated outsider backgrounds. One could include Darius James, Darryl Pinckney, Bob Flanagan, Pagan Kennedy, Sapphire, Gary Indiana, Suzette Partido, Diamanda Galas, David Trinidad – and on. And on. These are writers from the streets and cities rather than the colleges. They have a dizzying circus of background experiences and their writing reflects this. They have been prostitutes, sex workers, hackers, incest survivors, professional sado-masochists, performance artists, AIDS activists, fanzine collectors, social workers and drug addicts. Poppy Brite herself has been a candymaker, mouse caretaker, artist's model and stripper. There have been attempts to label these writers – 'Generation X', 'New Narrative' and so on but with only their subversive outlaw sensibility in common it is hard to pigeonhole the work. Like Brite they tend to concentrate on the fringes of contemporary experience. Their spiritual godfather is the incomparable LA writer Dennis Cooper – 'Dennis is probably my favourite author' says Brite – whose novels on language, desire and death have made him a grunge Georges Bataille.

The horror genre is naturally one of the most fertile fields in which to find vivid new writing. It is an area where writers can develop, particularly if their themes are excessive and extreme. Later, however, the genre can become a ghetto. Patrick McGrath, who was like Brite a Penguin Original horror writer, is one of the few to have crossed over to 'serious', i.e. literary fiction.

Last year Kathe Koja's *Skin* was published in Britain. Classed as a horror novel it gained very little recognition. Koja, like Brite in *Lost Souls*, was describing a contemporary youth cult. *Skin* is a petrifying, innovative investigation into the youth cults that favour body art – piercing of the flesh including genitals, tattooing and scarification. Her heroine, Bibi, reaches insane extremes and ends up half-human, half-android: ' . . . little head heavy with hooks and chains from ear to nose and nose to lip . . . bristling shiny with hooks, spined with them, hooks in her ears and tusked tiny at nose and lip, anemone steel all over and down her bare back the thready spill of chains . . . like strange metal hair surrounding the raised scars . . .'

Kathe Koja is published in America by the same Abyss imprint of Delacorte that publishes Brite. They also publish Tanith Lee, Melanie Tem and Brian Hodge. Both Brite and Koja are more than horror writers – they have strong styles, write about obscure aspects of contemporary culture and are classified in too limited a fashion.

Poppy Z. Brite was born in 1967 in New Orleans and moved back there to live in the old French quarter last year – 'those exotically named, haunted streets – Ursulines, Bienville, Decatur'. New Orleans is a far cry from Kensington on a rainy day which is where I met her this week. Brite is a tiny girl with a pretty, feline face. Her Japanese-black hair is artfully cut into a fringed bob which hangs as thick, heavy and burnished as a block of shining wood. She is dressed all in black. Her short skirt is made of worn antique velvet. She wears a large, translucent crucifix. In her room Poppy holds my cassette recorder gingerly like a polite child with an unwanted biscuit but very soon, in conversation, proves herself to be far from fragile. She is competent, professional, very much to the point.

'I've been writing forever. I submitted my first story at age twelve.' When she was eighteen she sold a story to *The Horror Show Magazine*, a prestigious, selective Californian publication edited by David Silva and she says 'became a horror writer almost by default'.

Although Brite spent the first six years of her 'tempestuous' childhood in New Orleans, she left after her parents' 'ugly' divorce and moved to North Carolina with her mother. There she eventually attended college for about two months but dropped out to write *Lost Souls*. 'I think college is deadly for writers,' Brite comments, adding that she reads a lot and is good at educating herself.

Lost Souls was written in 1987–88. It finally appeared, after revisions, in 1992 and has just been published in Britain. Looking back, she says it seems to her 'like a very young book, a late teens, early twenties book, half-depressed, half-elated, a mixture of joy and despair'. She continues: 'After *Lost Souls* came out I think everyone expected me to be this pale, suicidal little Gothic, ghostly girl. They were about seven years too late!' She does admit to extreme depression and alienation at the height of her Goth involvement and says she was 'into cutting my wrists for fun, playing with blood and all that'.

The heavy Gothic sub-cult with its vampire make-up, graveyard clothes and black nail-varnish was originally a British invention which spread more slowly to North America 'in the mid to late eighties – and it's still going on now,' Brite says. She claims that the American version is 'less steeped in gloom and doom' and that she has come to believe that Goths 'do not necessarily court or worship death, *they just refuse to fear it*'.

Lost Souls is set partly in New Orleans and partly in Brite's fictional North Carolina, town, Missing Mile. It focuses on two sets of boys. Molochai, Twig and their leader Zillah are real vampires, rocking around America in their black van, satiating themselves with blood, torture, raucous music, candy and a rainbow cornucopia of drugs. But these are less traditional vampires (no sleeping in coffins) than extreme, immortal fantasy Goths with their 'dark blots of make-up' and hair in 'great tangled clumps'. We meet them in New Orleans at Mardi Gras 'where the liquor flows like milk, strings of bright, cheap beads hang from wrought-iron balconies . . . The sky is purple, the flare of a match behind a cupped hand is gold; the liquor is green, made from a thousand herbs, made from altars.' The boys in Missing Mile are musician Steve and his friend, a strange, gentle psychic called Ghost. The link between the two groups is the teenager named Nothing, Zillah's half-vampire son who tracks down his father and finds himself equally sexually drawn to him and to Ghost, men who represent the light and dark – or the human and non-human – sides of his personality.

Both *Lost Souls* and Brite's early stories are replete with *fin-de-siècle* imagery – ashes, roses, decay, spilt wine, opium, incense and candle-light, blasphemy, androgyny, extreme perversion and demonic beauty. So strong is this mood of decadence and corruption, heightened by the visionary lyricism of adolescence, so overpowering is Brite's aura of intoxicating vapours, rags of clouds and lace and skeletons with moonstone eyes that I believed she was deliberately resuscitating the 1890s and comparing its maddened millenarianism to the extreme behaviour characteristic of the end of this century. As Phillippe Jullian writes about the 1890s in *Dreamers of Decadence* (1971): 'There were no perversions that they did not know and no profane ecstasies that escaped them. They looked to morphine or the whip, to little girls or fairground workers to plunge them into delirium.' Brite disabuses me of this notion. She was just observing Goth behaviour and writing down her fantasies, she says. She acknowledges an interest in Poe, Baudelaire and Rimbaud ('I've always been interested in death and gore and pain. I wanted to be a coroner when I was little') but she has never read, for example, Huysmans. So much for critics. Goth culture is certainly influenced, if only unconsciously, by the decadent strategies of the past. As Brite says: 'With the Symbolist poets it's not so much that they are a stylistic influence but that we are coming from the same place.'

Far stronger than any 'horror' in Brite's work is the highly erotic male homosexual sex. *Lost Souls* was nominated for a Lambda Award for outstanding gay-themed fiction. Brite is one of the very few women writers who can create a fictional portrait of an extremely sexually attractive man. 'Zillah was the most beautiful of the three, with a smooth, symmetrical, androgynous face, with brilliant eyes as green as the last drop of Chartreuse in the bottle . . . He wore his nails long and pointed and he wore his caramel-coloured hair tied back with a purple silk scarf. Wisps of the ponytail have escaped, framing the stunning face, the achingly green eyes.'

'The male characters have never been a problem for me,' says Brite. 'It's the female characters that really make me stretchy.' She says there are many women she loves and admires, 'but as a gender they don't fascinate me the way men do'.

She states: 'Biologically I am a woman writer but it's never the way I've thought of myself. Ever since I was old enough to know what gay men were I've considered myself to be a gay man that happened to be born in a female body and that's the perspective I'm coming from.' I sympathise with this feeling and ask Brite whether she's ever thought of taking it as far as transsexuality. She says no, that she wouldn't make a very good man being only five foot tall and anyway penile implants don't work well.

Brite talks about her personal life, declining to go off the record. 'I have no off-limits subjects as far as interviews go. You can print anything I say.' She continues: 'I live with two boy-friends. They are both bisexual and we have a three-way relation-ship. One of them, Chris DeBarr, is a chef and some-time poet and political activist. The other, Chris Lee, is primarily a mage – his main art form is ceremonial magic. He's half Chinese, a musi-cian and practises martial arts.' They live above a second-hand bookshop in Royal Street, a part of the French Quarter that is, Brite says, about seventy-five per cent gay.

New Orleans, the Crescent City, is extremely important in Brite's personal mythology. She remembers being taken as a child to St Louis Cemetery No 1 where the great nineteenth-century voodoo queen, Marie Laveau, is reputedly buried. St Louis No 1, standing innocently beneath that blazing blue sky must be one of the spookiest places on earth. There is a startlingly accurate description of it in *Lost Souls*. The dead were buried above ground because the land was waterlogged, and they lie in little white houses or mausoleums. It is easy to get lost along the endless winding pathways.

When I myself was there, there was a grey dog that kept lead-ing me back to Marie Laveau's tomb which was covered with red crosses chalked in brick. It had dried flowers, ribbons, cigarettes, small change and candles piled before it and was surrounded by supplicants muttering their incantations and requests.

Inevitably Brite gets compared to Ann Rice – a much more tra-ditional horror writer who also lives in New Orleans. Brite com-ments: 'I think it's pretty silly. I haven't really read her work and what little I have I didn't care for. It didn't really speak to me per-sonally. I can see how the comparisons have popped up – we've both written homo-erotic vampire novels set in New Orleans. She's pretty oblique about the sex though and I'm anything but.'

Brite felt she had no alternative but to succeed as a writer – 'I knew that if I were still alive at age twenty-six I would be a successful writer. I didn't have a back-up plan, I wasn't fit for anything else. It was either make it as a writer or die.' Seriously? 'I might very well have killed myself in despair. I don't think that there's any sort of other life I could stand. You know if you have the talent. You know if you have the drive.'

Brite has completed her next novel, *Drawing Blood* – 'It's a haunted house love story. It has to do with underground comix and computer hackers.' Brite emphasises that she 'always follows her obsessions' which are a virtual guide to the fetishes of alternative fiction. They also include 'serial killers, Japanese dismemberment videos, jazz, death rock, seventies glam metal and psycho-industrial noise'. Brite says it has been reaching the gay market in the States – 'I'd just as soon be known as a gay writer as a horror writer. I don't like being genre-ised. I don't mind being called a horror writer but I'm not crazy about it either because it inevitably means that a lot of people who would like my books are never going to pick them up. After all, almost anything that Dennis Cooper has written could be called horror.'

Brite deserves to transcend all labels and already has an astonishing variety of fans in America. Her psyche is perhaps strangely poised between the ordinary, functioning world of Missing Mile, North Carolina, which provides her work ethic and psychological stability and the haunted dream world of New Orleans which contributes her exotic content.

We discuss Louisiana voodoo for a while which Brite has described in a previous story as 'a slapdash recipe concocted of one part Haitian graveyard dust, one part juju from the African bush, a jigger of holy Communion wine, and a dash of swamp miasma'. Then we spend the rest of the time talking about the parking problems in New Orleans. They are really terrible.

Pornocopia by Laurence O'Toole

(Serpent's Tail)
New Statesman, 14 August 1998

OK. Here's some sex.

Sex! What is it good for? It keeps us in a constant state of existential tension because the sexual urge towards propagation of the species is a primal one, locked deep in the primitive part of the brain-stem – our rat-brain, our lizard-brain. The ancient sexual impulse is in constant conflict with our more civilised, higher states of consciousness, those which nurture thought and value personality. Sexually we are at war with ourselves because in nature we are of value solely because of our fertility and any other gifts and attributes, however outstanding, are as dust. This dichotomy has caused centuries of dissent and discussion with the Catholic Church still insisting that sex should be procreative only. However, during this century, the confusing dialogues surrounding sexuality have multiplied almost to infinity. The arrival of reliable contraception, the democratisation of pleasure with heavy emphasis upon non-procreative sexual pleasure, the claims of feminists and other minority groups, growing awareness of sexual abuse, a disenchantment with the theories of Freud and the ubiquitous nature of new technologies – all these and innumerable other issues have contrived to whip up a maelstrom of muddle.

Just one example can illustrate all these cross-currents: nature's brutal design once saw to it that women rarely outlived the menopause which ended their procreative usefulness. Longer lifespans have confounded this but left many women adrift without the sexual or maternal role, so that grandmothers clamour for babies and ageing women battle to retain their youthful sexuality with HRT, silicone, surgeons' knives and cosmetics – all on sale in a rapacious market-place.

It seems ironic that a society which pullulates daily with sexual issues should need yet another book on the subject and that it should actually prove to be both a useful and instructive one. In *Pornocopia* Laurence O'Toole wisely restricts himself to the pornographic image. Had he included the history of erotic books his publication would had to have come equipped with wheels and batteries for transportation. (He remarks 'Books have gradually ceased to function in public demonology as dangerous cultural packages', an observation which, although debatable, presages a future simultaneously freer and sadder for the bibliophile.) As it is, O'Toole only has to cover magazines, films, TV, computers, cable, video and compact disc technology.

Well, at least this limits his task to this century. Initially O'Toole briskly disposes of an ancient canard by quoting critic Charlotte Raven: 'What is erotica if not pornography wearing a veil?' He also states: 'It is the asssertion of this book that porn is as much art as is any other kind of expression.'

The author's most significant achievement lies in his making quite clear something about which many people are ignorant – that 'hardcore porn is virtually illegal in Britain'. It is not illegal to possess it but illegal to import it, distribute it, sell it, publish it and so forth. Later in the book he makes it quite clear how the myth of hardcore availability in Soho arose, how different is the reality which usually involves cheating a customer who cannot complain and how recent changes have made it even more difficult to procure.

O'Toole also makes it very clear that Britain is one of the most highly censored countries in Europe and 'In terms of pornography Britain is the most censored nation in the western world.' A combination of bad laws and fuzzy wording – 'indecency', 'deprave and corrupt' – allow moralists almost unlimited powers over what we see. We are blighted by shoddy softcore mags and movies; films on TV are cut crudely with no regard for continuity. And even in the book world, works are cut, huge quantities of material especially 'zines and art books – not even necessarily sexual, merely subversive or deviant – are not printed here or even imported, as independent booksellers have long since tired of wrangling with Customs. If someone like myself who cherishes the bizarre, wants to read about the American who fell in love with his John Deere tractor, wrote it love letters and died having sex with it, it is possible for them for them to do so legally but it would probably be too much trouble. O'Toole makes clear that the practice of making things too difficult to bother with is very effective censorship.

O'Toole contrasts our situation with that of America, where nationwide, hardcore porn is legal (excepting child pornography), although a patchwork of conflicting state laws make using the mails a problem. In a pluralistic society such as the US there is a demand for not just straightforward hetero hardcore (full-frontal genitalia, erections, intercourse of every sort and 'pop' – or 'cum' – shots) but also a market for numberless sub-genres of film and video: bondage, gay, corsetry, amateur and even lesbians-who-smoke – and so on and on. Britain is a similarly heterogeneous society and O'Toole considers it ludicrous that we are 'protected' from seeing consensual sexual acts when there is no scientific proof that doing so harms people and considerable evidence that seeing images designed to arouse can bring sexual pleasure and variety to many including hetero and gay couples as well as those isolated by illness or with particular tastes. One person's porn is another's yawn. US sexologist, John Money, argues that our reactions to erotic input are created in infancy. This seems correct. Watching a *thousand* hardcore coprophilia films could not turn or 'corrupt' me.

Considering that everything in our society (unfortunately including children) has been gradually eroticised by advertising – perfumes, soft furnishings, coffee – it does seem more than ridiculous that we are all held in thrall here by the mythical 'young person' who must be protected whatever the cost to our intellectual, emotional or artistic freedoms.

One of the best reasons, O'Toole argues, for bringing Britain into line with the majority of Europe regarding hardcore is that it would demystify the subject and remove the last urban myths of white slavery, peepers in plastic macs, violence and underage girls drugged into submission. Early in the book he clashes with the anti-porn feminists, including obviously Catherine MacKinnon and Andrea Dworkin, and her demented definition of porn as 'Dachau brought into the bedroom and celebrated'. That particular weird alliance of feminists, the Catholic Church and the Moral Majority always seemed sick, the equivalent of resuscitating the angel in the house within a joyless puritanism that did much to turn women against feminism. O'Toole also describes the UK 'Liberty' wars and the formation of Feminists Against Censorship.

O'Toole has done a great deal of research onsite at Van Nuys, California, the mini-Hollywood which churns out flash, semi-arty high-end hard-porn and has its own stars, ceremonies and awards. The industry seems rigorously regulated, especially regarding age. Some directors like John Stagliano with his 'Buttman' series have become pop culture heroes. Women are obviously essential to the industry and participate (voluntarily) not just as performers but as directors and in all the other roles of the film process. O'Toole interviews some of the women but when invited to witness one of the sex scenes being enacted on a closed set he makes his excuses . . .

O'Toole also covers CD-ROMs and cyberporn while we wait to see whether the Net will be overrun by commerce and censors like Net Nanny and Cyber Patrol or will retain pockets of real freedom and anarchy.

Writing about sex tends either to be couched in high-end, doctoral-level theoretical jargon or to be dim, raunchy and sticky with that famous Italian suppository, innuendo. A clear, comprehensive history of the pornographic image in the west, providing a guide to the laws and the porn wars was badly needed. O'Toole answers all possible questions and clarifies many shamefully murky areas. Sex will never bring about a revolution but people seem to like it. Why deprive them?

Just remember if you and your loved one film yourselves frolicking *al fresco* in Greece, complete with pop shots and reverse cow-girl (work it out) and bring the video home, you could end up in court.

Fashion, style and memory

New Statesman, 1 January 1999

I think this was the only time I was ever asked to write about fashion. Style, yes, fashion, no, although I have always found it an interesting, if profoundly odd, subject. The book titles below are self-explanatory. Jane Mulvagh wrote me a very kind note after this was published saying she hadn't known about Cedric in Love In a Cold Climate. *Thank you, if you see this.*

Vivienne Westwood: An Unfashionable Life by Jane Mulvagh (Harper Collins) and *The Ossie Clark Diaries* ed. Lady Henrietta Rous (Bloomsbury)

There is a famous encounter in Nancy Mitford's *Love In A Cold Climate*. Cedric, a droll, flamboyantly camp social climber visits narrator, Fanny, a slightly dowdy young aristo married to an Oxford don. 'Aha!' notes Cedric immediately: 'So now we dress at Schiaparelli, I see!' Fanny says that her scarlet jacket was a present and expresses horror at the waste of money when, expertly, Cedric prices it. 'Simply silly . . . there's only a yard of stuff in it, worth a pound, if that.'

Cedric retorts 'And how many yards of canvas in a Fragonard? . . . Art is more than yards . . .'

In these brief lines of dialogue Mitford summarises a gulf that exists to this day. Our society seems permanently divided between those who throw around words like 'genius', who believe that couture is high art, worthy of museum status and serious study and the others – Fanny's spiritual descendants. To them it is all too silly; it's frivolous, immoral and the money would be better invested in third-world school books. Apart from a few protean stylists who can move painlessly from catwalk to thrift shop, fashion, for the majority is either bliss or blight.

In this context it is interesting that in both of these large books, each devoted to the work of a significant clothes designer, the clothes themselves do not occupy centre stage. They are the chorus, the supporting cast, the backdrop. A biography of a European couturier (even the recent, relatively racy one of Yves St Laurent) is forced to focus primarily on the designs. There is not much else. But Ossie Clark and Vivienne Westwood were English artists first and fashion designers second. Over here, we are far more interested in character than clothes. We prefer flamboyance to fabric. In the UK the context of fashion differs considerably from its European counterpart. Fashion here is more animated and inclusive, is less cerebral, hierarchical and distanced than in

Europe. Thus Clark and Westwood functioned primarily as personalities. They are each emblematic of a particular period in post-war culture.

Ossie Clark's name evokes an familiar pantheon of imagery – prettiness and privilege, spun-sugar rebellion, Mick 'n' Bianca, Twiggy and Bailey, white butterflies, Moroccan lamps, dim rooms swagged and draped with ethnic tassels and fabrics, a fog of incense, rose-coloured spectacles and those early cocksure, thundering chords of the Beatles-Stones-Who soundtrack.

To an even greater extent Westwood represents a paparazzi paradise: designer to the original London punks, she's there too, professionally sullen with her bleach-blonde spiky crop, ripped fishnets, mohair jerseys and all her other provocative, confrontational, hard-edged, asexual clothes; later, there's Vivienne picketing for culture in flesh-coloured tights and a strategic fig-leaf, or greeting royalty in a totally see-through lace dress. Flash! The mini-crini. Vivienne swaying around in her rocking horse shoes, hectoring anyone on declining educational standards. Flash! Naomi Campbell tumbles off Vivienne's ten-inch platform shoes.

Originally, untramelled by *idées reçues*, the untutored Westwood could always pull off a dazzling visual statement, particularly when in partnership (and love) with Malcolm McLaren. Alone, says author Mulvagh, she could not inject 'contemporary reference'. 'The semiotics of the street did not impinge on her isolated sensibilities . . . McLaren had a brazen, feet-on-the-ground, finger-on-the-pulse modernity.'

Mulvagh's biography is thorough, well-informed, straightforwardly (rather than theoretically) intelligent and very readable. Naturally she must traverse ground already over-excavated, but she succeeds in illuminating Westwood's contradictory character. Remote from politics or anarchy, Westwood's innate attraction was to a 'heavy-handed . . . romantic historicism'. Mulvagh displays tact and respect in documenting Westwood's life post-McLaren, particularly in regard to that journalistic banana-skin, Westwood's guru-self-styled professional intellectual, Gary Ness. Helplessly drawn towards male mentors whose ideas she respected, Westwood remained under the doubtful influence of Ness for years, apparently unable to discern that his self-conscious, self-serving ideas of what constituted an 'intellectual' were hopelessly warped and unbalanced – for example, his whole-sale rejection of all twentieth-century culture. It seems almost inconceivable that after associating with McLaren, Westwood could start parroting Ness' weirdo anachronisms.

Mulvagh succeeds in balancing praise and pathos in this poised assessment of Westwood, pointing out how 'extremely impressionable'Westwood is and noting that she is very much better at research and reproduction than originality in design; a debatable contention.

With both these books there is some sense of surfeit, of over-load. They both concern the very recent past, decades which have already been cannibalised, sucked dry, analysed to death. For the computer-literate bibliophile there is little challenge now in cultural research. There is no more 'search' in research. It is all available. Every last detail and minor character.

The Ossie Clark Diaries is a much more slapdash book, despite its stylish graphics and great photographs. Perversely, this hap-hazard quality makes it more appealing and more in tune with its content than Mulvagh's professionalism.

There is a disarming forward by 'Lady Henrietta Rous' – 'I could never understand why he [Clark] was never helped more radically by his extremely famous, rich friends.' There are some truly appalling mistakes and typos (designers 'Tuffin and *Foule*'!).

The body of the book is composed of Clark's day-to-day diary entries. The resulting minutiae has a salutary effect in demytholo-gising the sixties and early seventies. It shrinks the starry cast of famous names into bite-sized chunks of real life. So these leg-endary people get tired and bored and sick; they quarrel and sleep and get divorced and cry. Vividly, unpretentiously, Clark records his decline from prince of the fashion pack, Hockney model and consort of the cool into forgotten, miserable penury. Clark was murdered by his last boyfriend in 1996.

This is a sad morality tale running from innocence through excess to waste and ruin. Clark's sudden, well-deserved success, his lack of business acumen in the newly-emerging fast-paced society and his narcotic self-indulgence provide a more accurate and familiar fable of the period than the lives of tougher stars who endured and thrived.

Both Clark and Westwood displayed a lack of interest in

commerce and professionalism typical of real innovators. Today, professionalism alone – however mediocre the product – tends to leave talent and chaotic creativity far behind. Both designers have had countless, and much more commercially successful imitators. Thus, these books, in celebration of two English eccentrics are valuable. Lest we forget.

A very successful virus

The Guardian, 16 May 1998

This is probably the most important feature I've ever written, not that anyone took much notice. It was published in Weekend Guardian *and concerns the terrifying worldwide spread of the recently-isolated Hepatitis C virus.*

I wanted to place it far away from the drugs pieces because there has been an attempt to dismiss it as a problem that only affects drug-users (a bit like the early days of HIV/AIDS and gay men in the States). In fact ANYONE can contract Hepatitis C – from a dentist, from a toothbrush, from a piercing, from an innoculation and, until recently, from a blood transfusion.

I was born in Nigeria, West Africa, where I spent much of my first decade. I was immunised at primary school there – before the invention of disposable syringes – and because my surname begins with 'Y' I always got the last jab. I developed what they called 'jaundice' in my teens and again in my early twenties (long before I met anything risky, apart from dentists). I always tired easily (which is probably why I spent so much time in bed!). In my thirties I became very ill with what they had started calling 'Hepatitis Non-A/Non-B'. They estimated my life expectancy at five years but the virus went into remission for a long time, not appearing again until the beginning of 1998. This time it was back with a vengeance. Despite being a virtual non-drinker, I had developed cirrhosis. I have been really ill ever since, although my hospital, the Chelsea and Westminster, is nice. The first time I went I thought it was a cross between an art gallery and a mall. Actually, it was a mall – I bought a pair of velvet trousers there.

The Hepatitis C virus is now quietly acknowledged as their biggest public health threat by Australia and the States, also the leading cause of liver transplants. Our Department of Health have, quite wrongly, been keeping silent on the subject while thousands, maybe millions, of people in the UK are suffering from terrible fatigue, possibly due to Hep. C – or HCV – as it is usually known, and they get told they have Myalgic Encephalitis or it's all in their mind or something. GPs here are very ignorant on the subject. Get tested! Although there is as yet no immunisation or cure, yet there is plenty of information on how to prolong your life and deal with the symptoms (See below).

Our government will have *to wake up because the threat is also economic. People tend to become symptomatic in their thirties or forties, at the height of their earning powers and borrowing. I lost my job. All your stamina just drains away. There is also a terrible shortage of donor organs in the UK. Every day, hearts and lungs and livers and kidneys are burnt and buried when they should really be giving life and happiness to very ill and miserable people. In some European countries it is assumed that everyone is an organ donor UNLESS they carry a card to the contrary. That is much better than the wishy-washy system we have here where it is hard to be* aware *of, let alone* acquire, *a donor card.*

If Bill Gates is really going to give his zillions to medical research it should go to cancer research which is grossly underfunded and Hep. C research. Both are terrible plagues. Two out of every three people get cancer and one in every three dies of it. Almost every one of my friends who are now dead (apart from the AIDS victims) died of cancer or Hep. C. Give us the money now! For research! Please . . .! *A Hepatitis C Charity has just been founded. Otherwise, there will be so very much more suffering. And it is a horrible disease.*

It is no secret that Mike S. did a lot of serious partying when he was young. He totalled his Dad's car twice before he'd even left school and was laid up for months – traction, transfusions, the lot. Then at college Mike was known as 'the nearest thing to a goat with three A levels': he shagged the girls and made them cry, tried every possible drug in every possible way, sank lakes of lager – but all that was long ago. For the last fifteen years he's been, well, a model citizen. Huge house in Esher, even bigger mortgage, an alarmingly pretty wife, two great kids. Up until about two years ago he was expecting to become a partner in his firm of industrial architects. He felt that he'd escaped free and clear from his misspent youth. He'd had an AIDS test when he got married, of course. Completely clean. But then, this weird thing. He started to feel really terrible if he drank. Not just a hangover, but seriously ill. He seemed to be tired all the time – so chronically fatigued that some days he could hardly put one foot in front of the other. He had aches and pains. Headaches too. He spent a fortune dragging himself round specialists and they all disagreed. He was depressed, they said. He was stressed. He had Chronic Fatigue Syndrome. He had ME. He had arthritis. Finally he meets a liver specialist – a hepatologist – and gets the correct diagnosis. He has Hepatitis C. What? Sorry, they have only recently isolated the virus. Medically there are not many options. It could have been his blood transfusions. It could have been his drug phase. Sorry.

Mike is very ill. He loses his job. And worst of all his teenage daughter, Ashley, already has cirrhosis of the liver. Mike's wife is also infected and she's passed it on to the kids during childbirth.

Mike is aghast. He says: 'I almost wish I'd had AIDS back then and I'd have saved everyone all this agony.'

Unfortunately Mike's story is not unusual now. One hears variations on it almost every day.

Hepatitis C is a virus with a very long incubation period – anything from about five to over thirty years. So that night you decided to go for it in downtown Houston and get a tattoo of Death in a ten-gallon hat, or the time you had to have dental treatment in Kerala, or thought you'd try fixing just one speedball, just once – it can come back on you. It seems very cruel.

No-one wishes to be alarmist about it but there is no doubt that Hepatitis C is potentially a major public health problem. In one of the only two books as yet available on the subject, authors Richard English and Dr Graham Foster, write: 'For the community as a whole, Hepatitis C is a viral time bomb which is slowly destroying the health of large numbers of the world population.'

Until the present decade, patients with chronic undifferentiated liver problems were described as having Hepatitis Non-A/Non-B. Then in 1989 the tiny but very persistent and adaptable Hepatitis C virus was isolated. In 1991 an antibodies test was made available so a positive reaction to that could be followed up by the Polymerase Chain Reaction (PCR) test plus the standard liver function tests and biopsies.

Hepatitis A and Hepatitis B are well-known hazards, particularly B, although the majority of sufferers from both illnesses recover and there are now vaccines for them both too. There is no vaccine against the Hepatitis C virus, generally known as HCV, and as will be described, western medicine offers only one controversial and unpredictable potential 'cure'.

Hepatitis C may have been around in the Orient for as long as 4,000 years and is considered to have made its jump into the west during the Korean, Vietnam and Second World wars.

So what exactly are the symptoms of Hepatitis C and who is vulnerable to it? HCV is a blood-borne RNA virus, a member of the 'flavavirus' family. Genetically, it is completely different from the HIV/AIDS virus which is a retrovirus. Hepatitis C and HIV should never be confused. They potentiate totally different diseases and, whereas HIV is usually transmitted sexually, this is rarely the case with Hepatitis C. Former and current intravenous drug-users are vulnerable to both viruses but cases of dual infection are uncommon. The Hepatitis C virus is, however, extremely infectious, virulent and extremely resilient. It is genetically unstable and this, ironically, constitutes a strength in that its very mutability and heterogeneity render it resistant to drug therapy. It is thought that no more than twenty per cent of patients may mount an immune response strong enough to minimise the damage. The rest proceed slowly, chronically and often asymptomatically until some aspect of the disease eventually manifests itself. In fact hepatic viruses are on the increase – there are now hepatitises from A through to N.

Matthew Dolan is himself an HCV patient who wrote and published an indispensable guide to the illness, *The Hepatitis C Handbook*, and set up the first HCV support group in the UK in 1994. He is highly aware that once symptoms do manifest themself, they sound so vague and general that they could be ascribed to almost anything – which is one reason, along with the limited medical awareness, why HCV is so often misdiagnosed. 'It has been mistaken for all kinds of other conditions,' Dolan says. 'It's been systematically misdiagnosed. It's diagnosed as depression, it's diagnosed as arthritis, it's diagnosed as kidney disease, it's diagnosed as alcoholism, it's diagnosed in many cases as everything but what it actually is . . . People with Hepatitis C are often exhausted by the time they get a diagnosis.' Dolan points out that the most frequent misdiagnosis is one of Myalgic Encephalomyelitis or ME – a condition many GPs still find hard to accept. ME is also known as Chronic Fatigue Symptom, or Post Viral Fatigue Symptom. Recent research suggests that as many as forty per cent of diagnosed ME sufferers may really be Hepatitis C Positive but no-one has ever thought to test them. (In any case, the two conditions are not mutually exclusive.) Women in particular have often found it hard to obtain an HCV diagnosis and are frequently fobbed off with accusations of malingering, neuroses or menopause.

Symptoms of Hepatitis C may sound nebulous but are usually absolutely devastating for the sufferer, quite unlike anything they have experienced previously in terms of depression or fatigue. Dolan says: 'The classic set of Hepatitis C symptoms are: exhaustion; malaise; depression; indigestion; intolerance to alcohol; attacks of mental confusion usually known as "brain fog".' He continues: 'When we talk about exhaustion here, we're talking about the feeling that one has been completely disconnected from a power supply – that you have to stop whatever you're doing when you get an attack. You have no option. It's not about being a bit tired and just having to take it easy. If you're driving a car, you have to stop. If you're going somewhere, if you're doing something you have to say "Excuse me, I need to lie down." Other common symptoms include 'flu; pains in the liver region; night sweats; diarrhoea; headaches and itchy skin. Once symptoms are established they may come and go for a long time (it is an almost infinitely various and subtle disease) depending on the circumstances and behaviour of the individual. Ultimately the disease may progress into Chronic Active Hepatitis, that is, increased inflammation of the liver, cirrhosis (whether one drinks or not), liver cancer or non-Hodgkin's lymphoma, another type of cancer. Liver failure may also ensue and include encephalopathy which means impaired mental function or bleeding varices, a medical emergency signalled by the vomiting of blood. Other associated conditions are Crohn's Disease, lupus, aplastic anaemia, kidney disease, rheumatoid arthritis and thrombosis. In short, as Dolan says: 'HCV is a chronic condition which can take a number of varied clinical courses and which will cause varying degrees of debilitation. Sufferers may develop a range of directly life-threatening conditions. Their life expectancy may be lowered and their quality of life reduced.'

The British Liver Trust estimates that about one per cent of the UK population, that is, some 600,000 people, have already been diagnosed with Hepatitis C and the numbers are growing daily. To date, few people here have actually been tested for it and those who have are mainly in high-risk groups. Matthew Dolan adds that this means that some two million families are already affected: when one or two of the family breadwinners are out of commission, naturally everyone suffers.

Australia has been quick to identify HCV as probably the most common, current life-threatening infection to the general population. It is also the most likely single cause for future liver transplants. This latter statistic has been endorsed by the British Liver Trust as applying to the UK as well. Director, Christopher Buckler, claims that more than forty-five per cent of calls to the British Liver Trust information line now concern Hepatitis C.

The Centre for Disease Control at Atlanta estimates that some five to seven million people in the States are already infected with HCV, and some researchers put the number as high as nine million. Country singer, Naomi Judd, herself infected with HCV, spoke on the Oprah Winfrey Show in March 1998. Calling Hepatitis C 'the silent killer', she identified it as 'an emerging, urgent health crisis in America – the biggest health emergency we have got' and 'the number one cause of death for liver disease'. Worldwide, she said: 'It is now pandemic.'

Despite the enormous concern expressed by those who are aware of the disease, there is still a high level of ignorance regarding its potential amongst doctors and health workers in this country. Those receiving a diagnosis may be told not to worry about it and find that their symptoms are still being minimised. This is partly because no-one wants to hear of a new plague after AIDS and BSE and partly because, as HCV is a relatively recent virus, the statistics can vary. However, there are indications that we have all underestimated the inherent threat of viruses worldwide and that AIDS is only the tip of a viral iceberg. Our changing attitudes are evinced by the concern regarding the transplantation of animal organs into humans.

Additionally, the very success of governmental procedures against AIDS has made everyone complacent. Lorraine Hewitt, manager of a South London publicly-funded drugs agency, the Stockwell Project, says: 'Especially worrying is the superstitious belief by planners and funders that HIV is vanishing and there is a stealthy dismantling of HIV drug and sexual health prevention services. Important needle-exchanges and services in London are being reduced or closed. Given that HCV is an infinitely more robust virus than HIV/AIDS, and entirely blood-borne, this is a horrifying trend.' Hewitt also points out that '*No-one* that the Stockwell Project has referred for testing has yet proved to be Hepatitis C negative.'

Naturally, drug workers were some of the first to be aware of the dangers of Hepatitis C because past or current intravenous drug-users (IVDUs) are at risk from both HIV and HCV. But the Hepatitis C virus is vastly more threatening to IVDUs than AIDS to the point where it is now estimated that ninety-five per cent of long-term drug injectors will have the Hepatitis C virus. The average prevalence of HCV amongst the drug-using community is about sixty-five per cent and this applies to those who have injected once only. However, this has tended to create a climate in which *only* IVDUs are seen as potential HCV victims, and this is very far from being the case. One HCV patient, George, remarked bitterly: 'With any new disease they make out that it is sexually transmitted or transmitted by drugs. They put a stigma on it, they want to keep it under wraps so that they don't have to put any money into it.' In fact, in about twenty to forty per cent of Hepatitis C cases, the carrier has no idea at all how they may have been infected, or so they claim. This may just be politic now that medical records are no longer sacrosanct but available to employers.

Hepatitis C is extremely contagious where there has been any blood-to-blood contact and certainly some groups are more at risk than others. But the people in high-risk groups are extremely varied and comprise a large cross-section of the population.

I was apparently infected with Hepatitis C during a routine primary school inoculation in Lagos, Nigeria, where I was born and raised. In my case the disease has now progressed to cirrhosis. Composer Peter de Havilland was infected with Hepatitis C by a blood transfusion at the age of ten. And then, many people, such as Mike S, mentioned at the start of this feature could have been infected with HCV in one of several ways.

Matthew Dolan has made it very clear that those at risk from Hepatitis C include not just drug-users but any hospital patients who received blood transfusions or blood products prior to September 1991. Additionally anyone who has travelled very widely and had numerous inoculations, or medical treatment abroad could be at risk. Army personnel, colonials, and those vaccinated, particularly when abroad and before the invention of the disposable syringe in 1965, may be vulnerable. There is also a risk from tattooing, ear-piercing, body-piercing, electrolysis, acupuncture, vaccination programmes and barber shops, especially considering how hardy and long-lasting HCV has been. Drug workers, hospital workers, dentists and those at risk from needlestick injuries may also become infected. Any inadequately sterilised hospital equipment – EEG needles, air filters in oxygen masks – may harbour the virus. Some seventeen per cent of dentists are estimated to use inadequate sterilisation procedures which may allow HCV to linger in blood spray. In the home, shared razors and toothbrushes are good candidates for transmission. One of the most vexed points is how long HCV can live. In inhospitable conditions, outside the body, the AIDS virus will survive for less than a minute whereas with HCV there have been claims that it can remain at large and infectious for up to three months.

There is still some controversy about the extent to which Hepatitis C is sexually transmitted. As one fashionable Kensington GP put it, apparently 'nice, quiet, married sex' carries a very low risk. The euphemisms 'rough' or 'traumatic sex' are heard quite often, meaning practices that involve or could cause bleeding. In long-term relationships where one partner has HCV, it is considered unlikely that they will infect the other. Despite this apparently low risk, HCV *can* be sexually transmitted, although it is more likely that partners infect each other through sharing personal items such as toothbrushes, razors and scissors. More worrying is the likelihood of mother-to-child HCV transmission during the birth process. It seems that HCV is not transmitted from a carrier to the foetus, but even so, birth transmission may be the fastest growing section of the patient population.

HCV is a very successful virus. The real worry is its durability and toughness which is why measures which have successfully prevented AIDS have proved inadequate against it, particularly amongst the addict population. Needles immersed in bleach for thirty seconds and then boiled for twenty minutes can still carry active Hepatitis C. It is not enough not to share needles. With HCV all drug-taking paraphernalia is potentially lethal, including spoons, barrels, swabs, filters and tourniquets. No cleaning method can absolutely guarantee protection.

There are already some attempts to ghettoise Hepatitis C as a junkie disease and dismiss it with the sort of 'you brought it on yourself' stigma to which AIDS was subjected in the early years. This must be strongly resisted in that, theoretically, absolutely anyone may acquire the Hepatitis C virus. To try and differentiate between 'guilty' and 'innocent' sufferers from disease is as spurious and inhumane as mourning the student murder victims of the Yorkshire Ripper and ignoring those who were prostitutes.

Growing concern has not yet been reflected in public awareness or the provision of funds. Christopher Buckler says: 'The British Liver Trust is acutely aware of the many issues that face people with HCV and is actively working on a number of fronts to improve information, treatment and support for sufferers and their families. Arguably the most important of these is our on-going dialogue with hepatologists and the DoH to get guidelines in place which will ensure standardisation of treatment for all patients.' At the Stockwell Project, Hewitt comments on 'the authorities' passivity towards this epidemic. . . . The ACMD and DoH should be focused on Hepatitis C in the way it was on HIV.' Writer, Paul Wells, says: 'An early response – far from being alarmist – is the only alternative.' Addiction specialist, Dr Colin Brewer, of the Stapleford Clinic notes: 'I think HCV does represent a serious epidemic of liver failure and certainly quite a few of my patients have significant liver disease as a result of Hepatitis C. Some patients have died from it. I have far more patients with Hepatitis C than we have ones with HIV.'

However, all is not completely bleak on the Western Front as regards HCV. Dr Iain Murray-Lyon, a consultant at Charing Cross Hospital, is an internationally recognised gastro-enterologist and liver specialist. He knows as much about Hepatitis C as anyone in Britain. He remarks on the tininess of the virus. 'It had to await new techniques, it had to await molecular biological techniques before they had the methods that were sensitive enough to pick the virus up. Technology had to catch up with the knowledge that there was a virus.' Nevertheless, Murray-Lyon says: 'I don't think there is any reason to panic. It's not in terms of a "pandemic". The biggest problem in the world seems to be in Egypt. Maybe fifteen to twenty per cent of the middle-aged population there is infected. It is thought that it was spread by the use of needles in the eradication campaigns for bilharzia in the sixties and seventies.' He considers the UK population generally safe from HCV 'unless they're indulging in some unsafe practice'. Murray-Lyon continues: 'It's much less infectious than Hepatitis B, because there are such tiny amounts in the blood. Sexual transmission is unusual. You can't get it from sneezing or sitting next to a patient on a bus. So it's usually toothbrushes or razors, or you could get it potentially from the dentist, I suppose.'

He adds: 'It's perfectly true that the majority of people in the community who are Hepatitis C positive are unaware of it. It's perfectly valid to say that the majority of people who are Hepatitis C positive are undiagnosed.'

He acknowledges that they have many patients who have taken drugs briefly in their youth but have long since cleaned up when they are diagnosed HCV positive. 'Then,' he says, 'there is the question "Did I pass it on to my wife?" and "Has my wife passed it on to the children?" We have a number of patients where the mother has come in, she's had a short spell of drug addiction and in comes the daughter, aged sixteen, who's got it and has cirrhosis. Horrible! Appalling. You can imagine the guilt that people go through in situations like this. The mother has a teenager with a living time bomb. The other aspect that keeps popping up as a great concern is the guilt that people feel who were blood donors for many years, not knowing that they were passing on Hepatitis C. And that really hurts people a lot.'

Murray-Lyon continues, 'I think public awareness can be raised but I don't think there's any cause for panic on a population basis. I think there's cause for concern on a personal basis. There was a case recently where an anaesthetist apparently transmitted the virus to a patient through the equipment. So one can't be too careful about the equipment being used in hospitals and the sterility.'

Sterilisation and hygiene are at the heart of of HCV prevention rather than sexual issues, as was the case with AIDS. Professor Tedder, Head of the Department of Virology at University College comments: 'I think the potential for the spread of blood-borne viruses is still considerable and an awareness that you could stop them with good hygiene in and outside hospital is well worth having.' But promoting Dettox is much less sexy than publicising condoms.

Murray-Lyon goes on to comment on the single biggest controversy in the Hepatitis C field. Currently, short of liver transplantation, western medicine offers only one main treatment for HCV patients. This is the antiviral drug, Recombinant Interferon Alpha, essentially a massive immune supplement, notorious for sometimes producing quite horrendous side-effects and for being a most uncertain and unpredictable attempt at a cure. This is a tremendously complex subject as Dr Murray-Lyon makes clear: 'It depends on whom you're treating with Interferon. We know that some HCV sub-types (or genotypes) respond poorly. We know that the more advanced the liver disease is, the less likely you are to respond, so cirrhotics respond very poorly. And it depends on how much virus you have in the body. The higher the viral load – and we can measure that now – the less likely people are to respond. Also Interferon can make people very depressed and we have had to stop a few patients on Interferon because of profound depression. I haven't personally had any suicides on it, but there have been suicides, yes.' He mentions that 'sensitive flowers' – arty, creative people – do not seem to respond well to Interferon.

Murray-Lyon will go no further than saying 'Interferon *can* be a cure' but many people have been much more emphatic. Naomi Judd, as spokesperson for the American Liver Trust, claimed that Interferon was definitely the cure, was in fact 'the only game in town' and that she herself had been cured of HCV by it. The actual figures are much less heartening. Of every hundred patients selected apparently at random at least ten per cent will be contra-indicated for Interferon and at least ten per cent will drop out of treatment. There is about a twenty per cent likelihood of patients achieving a 'sustained response'. This means that HCV remains undetectable in their blood and livers for six months following the completion of treatment. However, some ten per cent of such patients will relapse in the subsequent eighteen months. So the chances of one actually clearing the virus for five years are in the region of ten to thirteen per cent. 'Temporary response' means that liver function improves during treatment but the virus re-appears.

Some patients allege that the drug companies are all too aware of the coming Hepatitis C wave and are promoting Interferon (now usually given in conjunction with Ribavirin) madly as a cure. In short, that they are concentrated on profit rather than preven-tion and cure. Peter de Havilland is a composer and lyricist who has recently completed the score to the Levi's/Turning Point animated drug information film *Drugs World*. He says: 'Interferon was a drug in search of a disease. They tried it on cancer, they tried it on AIDS, they even tried it on the common cold. All it actually cures is leukaemia in cats.'

Matthew Dolan adds: 'I feel it's oversold, the drug therapy, and that a number of patients are prescribed drug therapy who are not suitable. The benefits are maximised and the pitfalls minimised. I've seen some of the damaged patients. Doctors concentrate on very narrow clinical indicators. They will wet themselves if they can achieve a reduction in the viral load and completely ignore the fact that their patient is now suffering extreme mental anxiety, has aching joints and completely unmanageable fatigue. But the real-ity is that the drug companies have no choice but to behave the way they do. They have to make a profit because they're obligated to their shareholders. These people are not disinterested, benign boffins. They do it because they're employed to. Their objectives are the development of products which they can argue are effec-tive, but they must be profitable as well. All the drug companies are piling into the Interferon market – Glaxo, Wellcome, Angen – and they're all trying to differentiate their products in different ways. Schering-Plough has been the dominant player, but there is Roche too.'

Peter de Havilland provides an animated, scary account of his long struggle with HCV and Interferon. 'I contracted Hepatitis C when I was about ten. I was given a load of blood products after an operation and about six weeks afterwards I turned yellow, was vomiting and felt as if I had been poisoned. They ran tests and said it was nothing to worry about; at the very worst it might be Hepatitis Non-A/Non-B. Some years later I came down with several very bad attacks of glandular fever and consequently missed a lot of schooling. When I left I went to America – physically I seemed better but I certainly couldn't party like my friends did. Gradually I developed extreme exhaustion, night sweats, diarrhoea, so back in the UK I had an AIDS test. Negative. I was also an active alcoholic and drug-user. Even so, having a glass of wine shouldn't send you to the bog for two days. It all trashed my career. I was signed to the Virgin contemporary classical label. I went into business with Boy George and Jeremy Healey and basically I fucked up. I was so sick all the time. I got sober in 1993 but many friends who stopped drinking at the same time were making remrkable physical recoveries and I just didn't feel healthy. By 1994 I had piercing headaches that could last for weeks – this terrible feeling that someone had shat inside my head. My doctor said it was all anxiety. I think he had me down as a decadent, middle-class worrier who'd taken too many drugs. I couldn't sleep, I felt foggy, I was depressed, I had night-sweats and rashes all over my body. Basically I'd had these symptoms on and off throughout my life. Eventually I was diagnosed with Hepatitis C.' De Havilland observes: 'This is a very elusive and subtle virus which affects every aspect of your life. For example it is potentiated by stress. People tend to get into trouble with HCV in their mid-forties just as they're coming to the most financially productive time in their life which is very stressful in itself. The virus sends you into this screaming vortex of despair, spiralling down towards the disenfranchised underclass which Labour are so blind to. People lose their jobs, their homes . . . One of the worst things is the stripping away of self-respect and dignity, of having to burrow through Kafkaesque reams of bureaucracy all the time. A lot of people like myself get caught in a dreadful poverty trap because of this illness. I had a liver biopsy – a very invasive procedure. My biopsy site haemorrhaged and I was in bed for two weeks. After the biopsy my liver never really recovered. I've had a lot more pain since then. At this time (1996) the doctors were saying that Interferon promised a fifty-fifty chance of remission for patients who hadn't progressed to cirrhosis. This was just semantics – they meant being free of the virus for a year before it re-appeared. Anyway I elected to go on a drug trial. I was lent out to the Royal Free, who were overseeing the drug trial for Schering-Plough. Professor Dusheiko and his team presented it optimistically. I didn't realise there were people making their professional names on this illness. They can be very high-handed in their manner and appear to have an almost religious belief in Interferon which I expect is in direct proportion to the amount of money Schering-Plough (or whatever other drug company) is giving to their teaching and research hospitals. It was synonymous with the way doctors in the US embraced Prozac.

'I was seriously ill. They were really looking for people who weren't ill. The more sick people there were, the more likely their statistics would show up in a bad light. They targeted people with little or no liver damage, or those they knew had just become infected and they targeted younger people and people with certain responsive HCV genotypes.

'Initially we were at a private hospital and then we went home and continued taking the drug. I was on three million units of Interferon twice a day; that was then the standard dose. Now it is six million. I was also given Ribavirin.

'After the first injection I was in a semi-coma with a temperature of 104° F but they said I'd be fine once I got home. They said I was the only person on this trial with such a bad reaction. I found out later this was untrue. Many people were having problems with vision, suicidal depression, pain in joints, hair falling out. Just before we went to write down our reactions in a book they'd say: "Oh, you're just excited about being on a trial" . . . They took our blood all the time.

'At home I felt as if I had Spanish flu. I was throwing up, all my bones ached, my temperature remained very high, I was manic and suicidal. I'd go to the hospital and complain and they'd say: "It should get better next week. Don't worry." Eventually my mother was so worried she flew in from abroad. My whole face was swollen up like a melon. I was taken suddenly off the drug which is wrong – you get a post-Interferon crash – you spiral down, you go through complete and utter physical and mental anguish. I developed double pneumonia. They screwed up. All they were interested in was getting the blood out of you for their research and for you to keep your mouth shut.'

'Schering-Plough,' says de Havilland, 'had an outside clinical consultancy company to oversee the trial so as to seem unbiased. They said I had dropped out with "attitude problems" which was a lie as most people found it very hard going and dropped out. Their supervisor was arrogant, supercilious and trivialised everybody's feelings. There was no professional social worker. We were not treated like human beings. We were not accorded respect. It was always implied that if we didn't toe the line, we wouldn't get our reward, our carrot of receiving the Interferon/Ribavirin combination free for a year. They said if we didn't get that, there was no way we would get better.'

Claire M. took part in the same 1996 clinical trial, although as an Interferon 'responder' her experience was very different. She says: 'I contracted Hepatitis C about eighteen years ago when I dabbled in drugs as an IVDU. I was diagnosed about two years ago. I was asymptomatic and I hadn't touched drugs during those eighteen years. I'd moved on from there. I'm thirty-seven.

'I didn't want to report my status to my GP. I thought it could have bad implications for me in terms of perhaps my mortgage, or even my job. I did a lot of research and felt that Interferon in combination with Ribavirin was the best option, so I started looking around for a means by which I could have the treatment without revealing my condition to the GP. I had Chronic Active Hepatitis with mild inflammation, plus moderate to severe liver damage. I wanted to be shot of this. It just seemed too much of a consequence of my previous life. I found out that the Royal Free was running a pharmakinetic study looking at the interactions between Interferon and Ribavirin and needed volunteers.

'The trial was one month. It was quite hard going in that you had to be a guinea-pig and give a lot of blood. It started at a private hospital and you had to go back quite often for tests. I was screened. They did all the checks.

'I think it was a pretty arbitrary selection of patients, although they wouldn't have anyone who was taking drugs. They told us from the outset that it wouldn't be a study that would do us any good – it was for purposes of pure research, but obviously they had to offer a carrot which was that after this first month you could receive six to twelve months of Interferon/Ribavirin – free. It is usually expensive.

'I was worried that I'd have problems with my thyroid, with depression and that I'd feel really awful. After the first injection it felt like a really, really bad bout of flu but it was quite manageable.

'It is not very pleasant giving oneself injections in the stomach but it was no worse than feeling pretty rough.

'I think most of the others fared reasonably well, although that first month was quite arduous. They had one group on Interferon alone, including me, and one on Interferon/Ribavirin. I took three million units three times a week at home for the month. At the end of the month my liver function ALT tests had gone down from about hundred to twenty-three but I hadn't cleared the virus, although there was a huge reduction in my viral load. I continued with three million units of Interferon three times a week and five tablets a day of Ribavirin for the next six months. The Ribavirin had a very drying effect on my skin. Apart from that I don't think it made much difference really. I didn't go on feeling flu-ish. Paracetamol helped. I didn't work at the time as I was being very cautious. After six months I had cleared the Hepatitis C virus and my ALTs were twelve to sixteen. After six months I was still negative for HCV and I opted to continue for another six months because I thought I'm not going to do this again and there wasn't a great deal else they could offer me afterwards. Only four people were left of the original group by this time. At the end of the year I was still HCV negative and my ALT score was twelve.

'I don't feel vastly different now. It's not like I've come off it and returned to some wonderful state. I feel OK. Over the year my hair thinned a bit – not balding or anything, but thinned.

'That's started to grow back. I lost about half a stone on the treatment and my appetite's coming back. I'm working part-time, although it's really full-time!'

Although Claire scoffs at Murray-Lyon's contention that 'sensitive flowers' do not respond, there is no doubt she is temperamentally very different from Peter de Havilland. Claire concludes: 'I can't believe that the drug companies actually want to harm people. They're getting their information from consultants who definitely want to help their patients. The trouble is the GPs don't know about HCV, they are waiting for guidelines from consultants who need funding – and the consultants are waiting to hear from the government.'

However, as Matthew Dolan's *Hepatitis C Handbook* makes clear, there are alternatives to drug therapy, ways of living with the virus and maximising one's health and immune system. He provides a very practical, efficacious list of western herbal treatments, vitamins, minerals and amino-acids, available from chemists and health food stockists. He comments: 'The HCV community here is very closely linked by the Internet. People are savvy. The information is out there. The world is changing.'

One of the most positive ways forwards for HCV patients lies in the region of Traditional Chinese Medicine (TCM) which has recently achieved significant results in treating liver patients. TCM has been practised in China for 5,000 years, a country which has always had a very high incidence of hepatic problems.

If the HCV community in London has a sage or avatar it is John Tindall, who at thirty-six is the Director of the Gateway Clinic. He is spoken of with near-reverence by his clients and personally he projects considerable contemplative strength. The Gateway, funded by Lambeth Health Authority, is an extraordinary institution, extremely democratic, friendly and informal – a huge contrast to the rigid hierarchies of hospitals. It appears to be run on broadly Buddhist and Taoist lines and patients can receive Chinese herbs on the premises and on prescription, as well as acupuncture, acupressure, massage and other holistic treatments. They may also attend Qui Qong classes, a meditative healing exercise.

Whether one believes literally in the TCM concepts of qui (energy), yin and yang, sees it as a metaphorical model or is entirely sceptical doesn't matter at all. It still works. Dolan says: 'I was completely sceptical; I thought that Chinese herbs were linked to witchcraft and that it was all psychosomatic. Then, after about five weeks into treatment, I experienced this surge in my energy levels; I felt that I was being restored to my normal function. Eventually my viral load dropped dramatically. My hepatologist was gobsmacked and didn't seem to want to acknowledge any possible link between my taking the herbal medicine and the huge drop in my viral load. It is a fair conclusion that Chinese herbal medicine can alleviate symptoms in many patients, I would guess seventy per cent or more. You see, this virus is constantly diversifying and mutating and this presents a serious problem to the immune system and to those trying to come up with anti-viral solutions. Chinese herbs and western drug therapy are the two strongest central approaches to treatment. Chinese medicine matches broad range formulations, sometimes involving up to thirty different herbs, which can act in a synergetic manner against a whole array of symptoms. Western drug therapy works in the absolute opposite way which is to take one substance and refine out the so-called active ingredients to try and get an antidote. Between these two techniques we've probably got quite a rich primary attack against the virus.' Both Dolan and Peter de Havilland feel they have benefited enormously from their attendance at Gateway and I could find no patient there who disagreed with them.

John Tindall trained as a physiotherapist and acupuncturist. He spent time in the States working in prisons, with alcoholics, and on Indian reservations. He also did postgraduate studies in China where 'I really started focusing on dealing with virology and immunology, dealing with HIV and Hepatitis C and developing an acupuncture and Chinese medicine programme for these specifically.' He started using Chinese herbs to treat patients at the Landmark, an HIV/AIDS unit.

In 1991 the Gateway Clinic opened. It had initially been funded by Tindall himself. He says 'Today it has 1,000 patients on its books; we treat sixty patients a day. We have 300 HIV clients – a quarter of those take no conventional drug therapy so each one is saving the NHS £25,000 p.a. We have 250 people with Hepatitis C, only ten of whom continue to take Interferon or Ribavirin. Other patients include those with drug and alcohol problems, gynaecology, dermatology or rheumatology patients and others. The waiting room is always full – young people, old people, different nationalities, different problems. Everybody's treated exactly the same but the treatments are all individual. We get results here – we probably work harder and faster than any other health clinic around. People like it too.'

Tindall notes the rise in the number of liver patients and says: 'Hepatitis C can affect every single part of your body. It can affect your breathing, your liver, your eyes, your headaches, your muscles and joints. A western medic might say "Those symptoms don't relate to Hepatitis C." In Chinese medicine we would say: "If one organ is out of balance, all organs can be out of balance." In Chinese medicine when we say "clear away toxins" that's the same as western medicine saying "reduce viral load". When we say "We need to harmonise yin and yang", this is equivalent to "raising the immune system".'

Although some western clinicians remain doubtful, Dr Murray-Lyon is highly receptive to Tindall's successful treatment of liver patients. Tindall says: 'He's very keen on sending patients here; he's very keen on us designing a herbal formula to deal with the side effects of Interferon/Ribavirin.' Tindall, with Matthew Dolan, is also trying to develop Chinese products in tablet form that could be taken by hepatic patients all over the country. The biggest problem is acquiring funding for trials that will be acceptable to the western medical community. The drug companies have little interest in financing such research because the Chinese formulations involve large numbers of herbs and are thus unpatentable. This funding is desperately needed and, were I a wealthy philanthropist, I would have no hesitation in backing the research now being carried out at the Gateway Clinic.

Although Tindall has HCV patients who have lived with the disease for thirty years 'because their lifestyle was good', he does say: 'If public education about Hepatitis C is not raised, then the medical profession and the government will be pushed into facing a reality about many things – inoculations, immunisations, surgery that has backfired on people.'

Dr Murray-Lyon himself says: 'There is a growing interest in Chinese and other traditional medicines. I've no doubt that they can help symptoms – patients come back to us saying that they feel better. I'm quite an admirer of John Tindall's clinic. What the component is in his clinic, be it the drugs, be it his personality, be it acupuncture and different forms of therapy – I don't know what it is that is helping but it is certainly a help. We are presently trying to get some studies together to examine whether or not his herbs actually affect the virus.'

So, where are we now? We have lots of sick, puzzled people and many uncertain, ignorant GPs. We have the prospect of increasing numbers of Hepatitis C positive patients, particularly in prisons and in cities with major drug problems such as Glasgow, Liverpool and Edinburgh. We have the Newcastle solicitors, Deas, Mallen, Soutar, coordinating the action for some seventy-five to eighty patients bringing suit against the National Blood Transfusion Service under the Consumer Protection Act. These are people who were infected with Hepatitis C through blood transfusions given in the 'window period' between 1 March 1988 and 30 September 1991. During this time, other countries including Australia, the US and Canada took action to screen blood supplies for HCV as soon as it became possible to do so.

Anthony Mallen says: 'I hate the scaremongering of so many lawyers. But we have an obligation to say that we are co-ordinating the claims and if people get in touch with us we can put them in contact with a solicitor.'

What else? We have a government and DoH seemingly wholly uninterested in the problem and its potential for economic and social devastation as people become symptomatic and lose their jobs. Indeed, the government shows indications of extreme cold-heartedness towards the disabled. Erin O'Mara who is twenty-eight was sexually infected with AIDS and also has Hepatitis C, kidney malformation and seizures. In 1996 she was granted a permanent Disability Living Allowance of £320 per month. This has just been wholly revoked under new Labour directives, leaving her with only Income Support.

Current drug-users who are HCV positive cannot obtain the usual range of treatment. There seems to be a harsh form of triage at work. They are not offered Interferon, neither has any injecting drug-user received a liver transplant. Martine Paule Delattre, forty-eight, has become so desperate that she has deliberately infected herself with AIDS in recent weeks in a hazardous attempt to receive kind medical treatment. She is an epileptic whose Hepatitis C has progressed to liver cancer. Terminally ill, she has, in essence, been told by her hospital – the Middlesex – not to present herself for treatment whilst still injecting street heroin.

How do we propose to deal with the issues arising from this debilitating liver disease? In retrospect it seems that we have all been extremely naive over the last fifty years in that vast numbers of people have been traversing the planet daily with no regard at all for the viral implications. John Tindall agrees: 'Yes, absolutely. Just look what's happening to the world ecologically. The world's immune system is being messed up so the ecology of the people on it is being messed up. The Chinese have an understanding of the macrocosm and the microcosm: what is out there will be reflected inwardly.'

Call 020–7582–5226 for HCV advice and information.

For a list of all UK HCV Support Groups, including those of the British Liver Trust – and also for information pertaining to the Hepatitis C Charity – send sae to: Box 13036, London NW1 3WG.

The Hepatitis C Handbook (by Matthew Dolan © Catalyst Press, £12.99) is available from Central Books. Call 020–8986–5488.

John Tindall is currently practising three days a week in Britain 8 a.m. to 8 p.m. at Yuan Clinic, The Green Healer, 7a Clapham High St, London SW4 7TS Tel. 020–7622–9079.

4

UK literature

British writing in the 1990s

New Statesman, 12 July 1999

Since I wrote the following piece, fictional matters have changed yet again, quite dramatically. I have tried to outline recent shifts in the Epilogue.

We have been warned regularly, for almost a century now, that the Death of the Novel is nigh. This dire prediction has always been confounded; like a charred and dusty phoenix, the novel has risen again and again from the ashes of doubt and doom.

But now, for the first time, something seems different. I can find almost no new UK fiction that I wish to read. The near-unbearable excitement of entering a bookshop has gone, as has the joy of leafing through publishers' catalogues and wondering how I can possibly wait months until certain proofs are available. In common with other serial readers, I know I have been driven to re-reading old favourites and catching up on classics.

There may of course be personal reasons for this fretfulness. Perhaps after a lifetime of non-stop reading, I am just burnt out. Or it could be that long-term reviewing of fiction – which certainly has a insidiously destructive effect on one's relation to text – has taken its toll. It may be that writing more means reading less and missing good novels. Perhaps not being so unhappy any more reduces the desperate need for fictional escape. However, I am not altogether convinced by any of these rationalisations. In the past, somehow, whether by intuition, recommendation or constant experimentation I always managed to find novels that could be treasured.

I am not suggesting that there is no-one at all in Britain who is currently writing readable fiction. There are a number of writers producing perfectly sound work. There are under-rated writers like Frank Kuppner and Brigid Penney. There is the brilliant Alan Warner, the admirable Iain Sinclair and the very inventive Will

Self. There is Stewart Home whose whole life seems to be becoming a conceptual artefact and the rather different, but equally quaint Martin Millar. The writers who give me most pleasure are probably those who produce impeccable short stories – Shena Mackay, Jane Gardam, Claire Boylan and Georgina Hammick. There is Robert Irwin. Terry Pratchett is a notable humorist. We are hardly bereft of creativity.

And yet . . . with the occasional exception, often by one of the writers cited above, there is very little that, well, seizes the soul. The last truly great writer, Samuel Beckett, doesn't really count because of his nationality. Some of Graham Greene provides enduring joy, but there is no point in looking back if we are to diagnose the current problem. The bookshops are full of candy-coloured fluorescent fiction which I do not want to read. Nor is my complaint a solitary one.

The symptom is clear enough. Most of what passes for literary fiction in Britain is just not very good. It is far less easy to disentangle the reasons for this state of affairs as they are longstanding and culturally complex.

The hegemony of American fiction over the last fifty years has done nothing for our self-esteem. The British renaissance that critics struggled to keep afloat in the fifties has ultimately proved to have sheltered only two good writers, Philip Larkin and Ted Hughes. More recently the growth of critical theory in academia has distanced some readers from wishing to attain an understanding of literature. Also people do not read enough good books – real books, old books, classics. Such reading plus the inevitable acquisition of grammar, rhythm and vocabulary that accompanies it is essential for a writer. People probably do not have the time to read novels now – recreational reading used to be the past-time of a leisured middle-class that no longer exists.

Our culture is increasingly a visual one which tends to adopt the standards of the cinema. Thus publishers have started behaving as conservatively as studios, gravitating towards manuscripts which can be likened to a previous, successful work. The fiscal bottom line dominates more in publishing and editors have less time in which to read new and obscure work. The cult of commissioning books from those who are celebrities in other fields is a complete waste of time too.

Critical standards are also extremely low. It might have been understood that *The Horse Whisperer* and *The Bridges of Madison County* were not serious books but *Cold Mountain* which was barely any improvement, was greeted ecstatically. They are all bad books. Not Good Bad books – like *Gone with the Wind* or *Valley of the Dolls*, just bad.

It seems that there is a deep need for fiction as reassurance, fiction which mirrors the heartwarming values of the cinema, fiction that is neither imaginative or challenging. Sentimental books are in demand – witness the success of *Captain Corelli's Mandolin*. Perhaps this is understandable in a highly stressed and uncertain world (not that it's ever been otherwise) – but it does nothing for literature.

There is a positive embracing of mediocrity which can result in quite ludicrous hyperbole. Neither of the recent novels by Vikram Seth and Salman Rushdie is particularly commendable and yet one would think that Homer was giving a reading in Books etc. for all the fuss.

There is a terrible paucity of both passion and imagination in fiction. The spate of confessional, autobiographical semi-fiction has discouraged an appreciation of the powers of imagination in both writers and readers. This cult of disclosure is one indication of the ways in which our lives are less interior than they used to be, less eccentric, less inclined towards dependence on our own imaginations. We live in a crowded world – perhaps it is inevitable that homogeneity of vision prevails. Perhaps the need for poetry and mystery is shrinking; after all, whatever one feels about religion, one just needs to look at what they have done to the King James Bible and the 1662 *Book of Common Prayer* to see a platitudinous democracy of the imagination in action.

God help us if, in future, all our language is similarly reduced to the level of a maintenance manual.

———————

There were some more points I wanted to make in the above essay but there wasn't room. Firstly, the literary landscape is not wholly bleak and drear apart from the authors I mentioned by name. In London, Victoria Hull – Director of the Clerkenwell Literary

Festival – has shown considerable imagination and vision in host-
ing, all year, literary events which make every attempt to break
with the usual dismal atmosphere of Readings and Signings. In
combining drama, discussion and fiction with club culture, DJs
and theme nights, Hull has worked to ensure that literature should
not be restricted to the middle-aged and middle-class. She is also
adept at combining established writers (A. L. Kennedy, Peter
Ackroyd) with newer and I would suggest, more animated scribes,
including Steven Wells, Tommy Oudo, Billy Childish, Chris
Savage-King.

Also, in Brighton, for many years the redoubtable Polly
Marshall has been pursuing a similar policy in her club 'Do
Tongues'. She has often featured American writers – indeed it is
hard to think of any competent authors working in English who
haven't read there.

Writing is deemed of so little interest in the UK that even the
writers only get a modicum of attention (compared to, say, film
actors who have yet to make a penetrating observation). But the
people behind the writers, those putting on events as above,
organisers, editors – they get absolutely no credit at all.

Secondly, I *have* read a novel I enjoyed this year, [published
March 2000]. From Bantam Press, it is *Danny Boy* by Jo-Ann
Goodwin. Although its plot – teenage junkie lads from Doncaster
on the run in London – sounds as predictable, lightweight and
lacking in subtext as any of the dross which passes for contemporary fiction, *Danny Boy* is in fact a much quirkier and more
engaging work. To divulge more would spoil the book, so I won't.

The third point I wanted to make was something too inchoate
for précis. It seems to be that almost everything in our culture mil-
itates against the individual imagination. The very names 'popular' or 'mass' culture indicate that they exist to tell us how to think,
how to feel, what to want, what to expect. All aspects of the media,
from fashion, to interior decor, to arts criticism seem to exist to
tell people who they are. Thus, increasingly society has been
developing an attitude which feels that only someone who has personally experienced something is in a position to write or talk
about it: hence all these books, whether fiction or factoid on
incest, marital breakup, depression, drugs, football or one-parent
childrearing. Such works contain the implicit assumption that the

author must personally be qualified to attempt such subjects. This is complete balls. Everyone experiences things very differently – thus a divorced woman with no imagination or lyric gift can plod through her banal perceptions of the trauma, whereas another writer, never divorced but with more creativity and vitality could provide a riveting fictional account of a marital breakdown. It just doesn't follow that because someone has done something, or can do something well, that they are therefore equipped to expound upon it. As I remarked, when has an actor said or written anything interesting? Never.

People seem so unsure of who or what they are that they make themselves into a collage of other people's opinions and expectations and then hang about waiting for these expectations to be fulfilled in novels and films.

All this constantly, subtly, downgrades the power of the imagination. Clichéd thinking is running rampant. One small example – virtually everyone seems to believe that a wretched ritual called 'wining and dining' is conducive to the development of romance. Why? I hate eating, I hate eating in public, I hate eating and talking and I hate restaurants where exploited people with every right to dislike me might be blowing snot all over my gnocchi. Even when I used to drink I didn't like it. I cannot but suspect that on a much grander scale, in a billion scenarios, people are doing things they don't particularly enjoy because they feel they should, e.g. lots of sex, strenuous holidays abroad, buying new cars, attending bad movies, being bored. And so on. They shouldn't.

The other tendril slowly paralysing the individual imagination is more obvious and can be seen at its most extreme in the US. The psychic straitjacket known as Political Correctness has, at its best, contributed to some much-needed progress. In Britain its manifestations are less strident but nevertheless any mode of thought (particularly a political one) imposed on the intelligentsia is, by definition, counter-creative. Taboos have their exits and their entrances – the elderly taboos of sex and drugs have been routed. They have been replaced by the very stringent taboos of politically correct thinking. In particular, everyone must make obeisance to the Three Major Taboos – sexism, racism, paedophilia.

No aspiring novelist would dare to flout the rules regarding sexism and racism in their books. Would a literary novelist even consider representing a vastly unpleasant person of colour or one who was thoroughly evil – say, a serial killer? I certainly can't think of any examples but I am sure that if they exist there will be some *ironic distancing* involved, as a clue that the author is only flouting the rules of political correctness in a manner so self-conscious that it ultimately inverts the context and re-establishes the status quo.

With paedophilia, you just can't win. A.M. Homes gets into trouble for writing about paedophilia in *The End of Alice*. Larry Clarke gets into trouble for making a film (*Kids*) which is *not* about paedophilia but is assumed to be as his actors are so young. *Kids*, I thought, was a useful and realistic film which should be shown in every school as it reveals so explicitly the differing attitudes of teenage boys and girls towards sex. No chance. Just more froth and fluff and outrage and shrieks of 'Child porn ahoy! Lynch him.' N.B. I AM NOT ADVOCATING CHILD PORNOGRAPHY. I AM OBJECTING TO THE MYTHS AND DEMONISATION SURROUNDING WHATEVER GROUP IS CURRENTLY ACTING AS SOCIETY'S SCAPEGOAT – whether it be junkies, homosexuals, Jews, gypsies, paedophiles, etc.

The very fact I have to spell this out indicates how far we have sunk.

Anyway, in essence, creative writers *must* be able to write about whatever they want without fear of censure. Additionally, our imagination is the most powerful force we possess. Don't distrust it. Use it.

The aftermath to the essay published above in the *New Statesman* was most interesting and curious. I received a letter from an editor at a new, mail-order publishing house. She had divined, quite correctly, that what I was complaining about was not being able to find books to *love*. My library is full of books I truly love but it is very hard to find new ones now. Anyway, she enclosed a copy of one of their recent publications, *Fidelity* by Susan Glaspell, originally published 1915. I knew Susan Glaspell as the American writer of a classic short story, 'A Jury of her Peers', and I did indeed love *Fidelity* when I read it.

I was particularly intrigued by these publishers, Persephone

Books Ltd, as their founder, Nicola Beauman, is a critic for whom I have enormous admiration. She wrote the wonderful (and much-loved) book of criticism, *A Very Great Profession: The Woman's Novel 1914–39*. Apparently Nicola Beauman had long wanted to be able to reprint books she loved which had been forgotten.

I wrote to thank Victoria Wallace, who had sent *Fidelity* and she sent me two more of their publications: *William – An Englishman* by Cicely Hamilton (originally published 1919) and *The Victorian Chaise Longue*, a horror novel by Marghanita Laski (originally published 1953), for which I had been searching for decades. I read both these novels consecutively, at one sitting. They were extraordinarily absorbing – and very good. The books themselves are utterly beautiful – grey softbacks with the most incredible endpapers, designs chosen from the period of the novel and intended to enhance and echo the themes of the book. So if you, like me, are short of real fiction – the sort that blots out the world – suggest you contact: Persephone Books, 28 Great Sutton Street, London EC1V ODS Tel: 020–7253–5454, fax: 020–7253–5656, e-mail: sales@persephonebooks.co.uk, www.persephonebooks.co.uk

They also publish a magazine, *The Persephone Quarterly* which has criticism, woodcuts, details about the novels and about upcoming publications. All the books cost £10 each or three for £25 which I think is a bargain nowadays.

I am very, very bad at answering letters and acknowledging books sent to me. The fact that I wrote long letters back to Persephone Books indicates very clearly how much receiving these publications meant to me – and how happy I was to encounter a publisher with such an admirable set of priorities. Books must be loved – with discrimination.

In the Fifties by Peter Vansittart

(John Murray)
The Guardian, 1995

*I thought I might attempt some thematic unity now. You may
or may not have read my earlier maddened diatribes in this book
about the 1950s – a decade so awful that the very thought of it makes
me tear wallpaper off with my teeth. Anyway, I believe the review
below to be my last outburst on the subject so let's get it over with.*

Open any fashion magazine just now and somewhere there will be
a certain sinister sihouette. That particular women's costume,
tightly cinched at the waist with its calf-length, New Look skirts
and its perky accessories – a little hat, matching gloves, and pastel
bucket bag – can induce powerful feelings of panic. Such fragmentary, infantile images as I retain of a fifties Britain infrequently
visited, recall a miasma of misery and tedium that seemed to
emanate from the very pavements. Gigantic adults, wide thick
trousers, bumpy feet in white, open-work sandals; a stifling sense
of corsetry and social tensions. Men with unbelievable hair like
that of the young Kingsley Amis – crimped in tight waves across
their skulls. Boredom and inanition hang in the air with pipe
smoke. Some of this may be hindsight: the general sense of constant, tiny, razor-sharp class skirmishes, a simpering attitude
towards the monarchy. At the time the very air seemed loaded
with a cloying mixture of female servility and the sharp, no-
nonsense barking of men's voices, lapsing now and then, particularly on radio, into a contemptuous, jolly approximation of
familiarity, patently fraudulent. This is certain – that the rudeness
and hostility of professional men towards women and children
darkened every encounter: the casual sadism of doctors, the stiff-
upper-lip mockery of dentists operating without anaesthetics,
everyone smug and secure in the belief that children had no emotional life.

Peter Vansittart quotes from those whose view was wider than from the pushchair and whose responses were equally negative; Sir Peter Hall castigating 'the miserable fifties', a Times journalist writing of 'The sheer nastiness of 1950s Britain, a lace-curtain-twitching society . . .' Vansittart's retort is placid – 'I remember it differently.' During the decade he was in his thirties, a published author, a schoolteacher with an avid interest in contemporary literary life.

For a long time it seemed that all we could stomach of fifties memoirs were those louche accounts of Fitzrovian bohemians, denizens of Hangover Square, as evoked by Dan Farson, Julian McLaren Ross and various biographers. Although Vansittart mentions those perpetually toping troupers, Nina Hamnett, Francis Bacon, the Roberts MacBryde and Colquhoun, Dylan Thomas – he was not really one of their number. Vansittart himself has little interest in the conventions – 'traditional decencies, little-man fortitude, public-school leadership and self-deprecation, the absurdity of foreigners and contemporary art' – attitudes which persisted in the provinces throughout most of the sixties.

The value of these memoirs is the unpretentious, cosmopolitan intellectual enthusiasms they convey. He covers a great deal of ground, looking closely at the politics and attitudes of writers then still surviving such as Pound, John Masefield, Henry Williamson, Wyndham Lewis and T. S. Eliot before later considering the Angry – well, Mildly Irritated – Young Men, Kenneth Tynan and the *nouveau roman*. For his quotations and anecdotes Vansittart depends partly on his old-fashioned, useful 'commonplace book', a diary/notebook in which one recorded anything of interest. He is not in the business of dropping names, nor did he move in elevated circles; he describes himself as 'a small-fry hanger-on' and his memories have a modestly pleasing spontaneity and idiosyncracy – he records Aldous Huxley having to eat curried mice in India; the trial of an African who killed someone whom he believed had transformed his friend into a peanut. Vansittart attends a droll mescaline party presided over by a Cockney magus bedizened with earrings.

Overall he seems to have felt a great optimism and hope for the future. 'I felt that we now had not only the will but also the apparatus for a more humane attitude towards crime, health, sex, women and children, colour, other countries.' He documents the founding of the NHS and the ICA but his coupling of women with children in this brave new world is revealing. If one didn't know otherwise, one could assume from this book that women at the time were on a par with cats – attractive, silent, unsuited to public life. There are notable exceptions – Rebecca West, Bridget Riley, Muriel Spark – and Vansittart, who is merely recording the times, applauds the emancipation of women. Yet he seems to have little imaginative empathy with the dismal and restricted lives of the majority. He records flatly a Scotland Yard Commander's words: 'Not all murders are serious, some are just husbands killing their wives.' He deplores the hanging of Ruth Ellis – and indeed that of Derek Bentley – but lacks outrage, seemingly more interested in political affairs and suffering abroad than in the monstrosities and corruption at home.

Vansittart and his contemporaries focus on international politics and allow politics to inform their aesthetics. This is the sole instance in which Britain with its decreasing intellectual cosmopolitanism seems more parochial now than then.

Vansittart's chapter on Youth is very uneven. He taught at a progressive Summerhill-like school – Burgess Hill – where adolescents experienced freedoms quite divorced from those of their contemporaries. Recalling Colin MacInnes as 'white-haired, rheumy eyed', declaring 'I am a teenager', Vansittart obviously had some intuition that *Absolute Beginners* was Marylebone Road magic realism, no more than semi-accurate. He notes correctly the influence of American literature on the young – Kerouac's *On The Road*, Ginsberg's *Howl* and Burroughs' *Naked Lunch* but the quotation attributed to the latter is from Kerouac.

Despite its range and versatility the book damns itself with faint praise. Although engaging, it has a tepid quality. Vansittart seems to think the fifties were quite nice. 'On the whole I remember a pleasant enough decade.' The mild politeness of this phrase is sufficient to summon the mean-spirited ghosts of the fifties and keep the home fires of hatred burning.

'When will you pay me?' say the bells of Old Bailey

New Statesman, 10 May 1991

Before I go all regional, I'd like to include something about London – that most strange and enduring of cities, and my home for over twenty years. Unfortunately the following was the nearest I could find to a paean.

The London novel is as old as the novel itself. From Defoe to Dickens there's been high life and low life, the drawing-rooms and the docks, the fires, the plagues, the intrigues and the pox. Now, the city generates its own quasi-fictional mythology. Dr Johnson strolls to the chop-house, Jack the Ripper doffs his topper, Rossetti sobs outside the apothecary's, Holmes and Watson go whispering by in a hansom, Fagin's children are crying as a cold rain falls on Greenwich and a river fog creeps over the cobbles. Metafictional, hyper-real, it is a formidable heritage. The city has seen them all: dandies and yuppies, mods and pot-boys, villains, cutpurses, adulterers and anarchists. These are the people of the abyss. This is where the ghosts go.

Mother London has continued to spawn her chroniclers and the inter-war years produced a mighty list of city scribes. The genteel agonies of Patrick Hamilton's great trilogy *20,000 Streets under the Sky* and the low-life dives of early sleaze merchant Gerald Kersh, were followed in 1956 by Samuel Selvon's *The Lonely Londoners*, the first account of West Indian immigrants encountering the cold heart of Notting Hill Gate. This in turn had a vast influence on the books of Colin MacInnes. After MacInnes, the deluge; in the seventies and eighties downtown dykes and uptown clubbers were all equally eager to record their own versions of metropolitan roulette. Stockwell, Whitechapel, Soho and Brixton. Dyer, Simmons, Bracewell, Millar, Elms, Pullinger. How the fingers flew.

So as the Thames rises higher and Dungeness seethes ominously to the east, is London finally burning? How fares the London novelist today with the clock hands at five to twelve?

'Sweet Thames! run softly, till I end my Song.' Edmund Spenser wrote it and and T. S. Eliot nicked it – for one of those great *Waste Land* riffs. It's a wonder Stewart Home, organiser of the 1988 Festival of Plagiarism and a writer with a profound commitment to intertextuality, didn't pinch it for himself but, then, it is representative of a ruling-class culture he abhors. The Thames runs – not so sweetly, not so softly – through his novels. They are political rants that leap out at the reader like a maddened Rottweiler on speed, making straight for the soft, pink, liberal underbelly. *Defiant Pose* (Peter Owen) has an indefatigably bonking anarcho-skinhead hero, in this case a real child of Albion, whose handle – Terry Blake – underlines the book's allegorical intent. Home's devotion to pulp literature and in particular the novels of Richard Allen (*Bootboys*, *Knuckle Girls*) impel him to insert large chunks of ludicrously repetitive sex and violence into the book in parodic imitation of formula writing. The fact that this is a somewhat arty trick in itself becomes lost in the general bourgeois bashing. Blake loathes everyone except heroic street-hardened proles like himself, 'wimmin' and black people. Still, the furious energy and aggression of the writing is very welcome. Home is also one of the few writers prepared to engage with the issue of – hush, whisper who dares – *class*, or rather to pick it up, scream at it and tear its head off.

The very talented Patrick McGrath has little interest in the modern world. *Spider* (Viking) follows his elegant Gothic pastiche, *The Grotesque*, and is a much more serious, sombre book which attempts to deal with aspects of McGrath's own childhood, lived in the shadow of Broadmoor. It is 1957 and his eponymous hero has just got out of an asylum. Lunatically wrapped in brown paper to avoid seepage, Spider records the events that led to his incarceration. The narrative voice is, as ever in McGrath, tricksy and suspect. McGrath's London is a vague, smoky, downtrodden place, redolent of the rich, seamy smells of the pre-plastic age; liver and onions, flannel, sawdust and beer.

Sam North's weird *Chapel Street* (Secker & Warburg) is located in the heart of London but it could be on the moon. A selection of insubstantial characters with improbable names languish in a rundown boarding house. One recalls that ultimate fictional wet week, Lawrence Durrell's *The Black Book*; a classic of boarding-house *angst*. Durrell's manic attack on 'the English death' – the wretched warped lives of the inmates – make North's book seem pallid by contrast. North eviscerates his characters in a languid way, narrowly examining their sexual relations and asking questions like 'Why did Skim embrace disappointment?' As if we cared . . .

As London novelists go, there are still too many absolute beginners.

Celtic writing: *Trainspotting* by Irvine Welsh

(Secker & Warburg)
The Guardian, 1993

Although I don't have the accent – due to a peripatetic upbringing and an English boarding school – I am nevertheless completely Scottish. (I miss my village in the Highlands so much in fact that last October I bought half – the upper half – of a miniscule fisherman's cottage there, which looks out to sea. I'd be there now if I didn't have this book to finish.) Anyway, partly for reasons of national pride and partly because Scottish writing has comprised the only real literary advance we have seen in the nineties, I am going to begin this section with the Celtic writers.

When I first read Trainspotting *all my inexplicable, far-sighted, incredibly spooky pre-cognitive Celtic visionary qualities surfaced en masse to tell me that we had a bit of a show-stopper here. So I begged and begged* The Guardian *to let me do an interview with Irvine Welsh. They refused. Frequently. Finally, in order to shut me up, I suppose, they agreed that I could interview him for some special* Guardian Edinburgh Festival *pull-out, on the basis that Welsh was reading from* Trainspotting *at that year's Festival. So I think I must have done the first broadsheet interview with him.*

We actually did the interview in London, at my flat. Welsh came round with his wife, Anne. He was wound up very tight; very suspicious. He seemed to radiate distrust of the media and to be determined to dislike me and everything he assumed I stood for. (I think he may have expected someone a bit more professional – with big shoulders and Proper Hair – who didn't live in a dump like a condemned second-hand bookstore.) Anyway, whatever. But right from the start Welsh was extremely sharp about the press and very canny in all his dealings with them. He never really gave anything away – particularly regarding drug use. Thus, considering the nature of his fiction, he has been able to avoid becoming a cartoon and been able to maintain his dignity and integrity and get on with his life. As I said, he is very canny indeed.

I met him again later, in less strained circumstances and he seemed like a great guy, affable and seriously mental. Still, what do I know really?

Welsh's contribution to literature was a classic of artistic revolution. It had all the constituents of artistic upheaval, whether we are talking about Punk or Impressionism. Firstly, the prevailing style of art, music, writing – whatever – starts to seem increasingly entrenched and bourgeois and to have little or no impact on people's lives. Nor is it capable of representing ongoing cultural changes. So some visionary young artists (like the Pre-Raphaelites) decide to debunk the whole charade and start creating art that is more vital, animated and representative of the Zeitgeist. So they get back to basics and draw, or write, the truth of their culture, as they see it. And this is a revelation!

In this manner, Welsh must be credited for dragging all the socially excluded back into literature and seeing that British literature finally reflected contemporary Britain. Of course he was not the only one – and there have been thousands of imitators since. But his is the clearest trajectory and – thanks to the film – the best-known.

It is a bit depressing for me to consider that Welsh's household name stardom rests on a film. Books alone just can't cut it any more, it would seem. Suppose one of Alan Warner's books had become a hit movie. He would be a lot better known, wouldn't he?

Sad, very sad.

What follows is (a) a review of Trainspotting *just in case you haven't heard of it . . . (b) the Edinburgh Festival interview and (c) something on one of Welsh's later books.*

Irvine Welsh's first novel smashes into the neat shopfront of contemporary literature like a runaway car on a ram-raid. It is a brutally confrontational book, born out of the rage that fuels so many of the disaffected in Conservative Britain, those whose voices are perpetually marginalised by an anodyne tide of pointless journalistic punditry.

Trainspotting is set in Edinburgh, a city where the gap between go-ahead gentrification and subversive squalor is now probably wider than at any time since the days of Burke and Hare. The book embodies the sort of post-punk nihilism that was the norm for urban cynics too poor or too repelled to participate in the illusory largesse of the 1980s. It also suggests how pernicious and divisive is the much-vaunted notion of an 'underclass', that stereotypical image of a country split between orderly taxpayers and a multitudinous shower of crack-addicts, criminals, welfare witches and winos brawling at the gates. Welsh certainly speaks for the urban tribes and the travellers, the druggies and the alienated youth but he knows they are no inarticulate rent-a-mob and that 'the street' is not some romantically cool kingdom but a prosaic place where people live.

The novel is centred on the old dockside area of Leith where the ghosts of a lawless past meet the empty promises of enterprise culture. It consists of a number of vignettes, as loosely aligned as the group of friends whose lives are documented therein. Many chapters take the form of interior monologues, thus pitchforking the reader into a desperate immediacy – the claustrophobic tensions of family, the macho rivalries of pub and club or the near incommunicable torment of searching for drugs when you're strung out. Insofar as the novel has a controlling voice it is that of Mark Renton, a streetwise intellectual and junkie who laceratingly charts the daily round of drink, drugs, dole and theft for himself and friends, Sick Boy, Spud and Begbie. Dialogue and monologue are rendered in dialect, without which it would have been impossible to present the rhythms and stresses of present-day Edinburgh demotic. It is revitalising to encounter Scottish dialect in such an uncompromising setting, free from either regional whimsy or the self-conscious deification of working-class life often associated with determinedly left-wing writers. Welsh is no sentimentalist and his large cast of proletarian characters are frequently presented as being brutal, thick and opportunistic, domestically abusive in private and riddled with racial and sectarian bigotry in public. The drug-users in the book are less prone to these sort of drunken, brew crew excesses and it is clear that the repressive attitudes towards drugs which made Edinburgh a byword for harshness in the eighties and gave it the highest HIV rate in the country were quite pointless and merely compounded the suffering of those already condemned to adulterated substances, disease, petty crime and the vagaries of an unstable black market. Welsh is the first British fiction writer to make clear the distinction between heroin, available on prescription until 1968, and the much-loathed heroin substitute, methadone, which has been the state-sponsored substitute since that time – 'It's this methadone, though, it's a fuckin' killer.' The adoption of this American system of methadone maintenance merely encouraged the growth of the black market, and the drug-ravaged face of today's city, which Welsh documents so acutely, is testament to government policies monstrously ill-conceived, tragically shortsighted and ultimately fatal.

As with the punk music so beloved of Mark Renton, *Trainspotting*'s raw power cloaks much unevenness and uncertainty. The novel is both contrived and careless, artless and artful. Passages of painstakingly authentic detail – the social realism of magistrates' court or family funerals – are followed by episodes of Alfred Jarry-on-junk faecal farce or theatrically overblown sequences of psychic assault and battery, designed to maximise shock value. The huge cast of characters and their nicknames can be disorientating and some chapters remain isolated as self-contained short stories without being integrated into the whole. Nevertheless, as with a song lyric, the overall mood or tone remains consistent and indeed the novel has both the advantages and disadvantages of a blast of sound from a garage band; well-directed rage and vehemence combine with headbanging dissonance and the vacuity of adolescent angst.

Welsh's considerable achievement lies in the documentation of a way of life that has become an enduring necessity for huge numbers of people and which has been minimally represented in fiction: a life of poor accommodation, indifferent health, scams, deals and fantasies of escape, provisional sexual arrangements, long days with the curtains drawn in hard-to-let flats and the video on, with the dope and the lager and the speed or the smack. Welsh evokes this landscape with considerable vitality and humour and also manages to suggest the massive contempt and indifference with which so many people regard the societal structures as presented through government, courts and media. In this sense the book resembles a busy narrative painting in which the traffic of Jacob's ladder is pitched between Saughton Prison and Tollcross and which indicts all those whose failures of judgement and legislation have let this come about.

Interview with Irvine Welsh

The Guardian, 1993

OK, here's the interview. I've never completely grasped the metaphor about Leith Station that Welsh outlined in the first paragraph. Still, it's what the man said.

The Edinburgh docks are at Leith. Once, like nineteenth-century Limehouse, or the great Glasgow shipyards, Leith was an exotic, cosmopolitan place from whence the Victorian merchant princes reaped their spoils. Now, even Leith Central Station has been demolished. Irvine Welsh, first-time author of the novel *Trainspotting*, says he imagines present-day Edinburgh – yuppified, gentrified, host to Festival follies – as a sort of ghost train roaring through a ghostly Leith Station, fizzing with streamers and champagne, rocking past platforms lined with skeletons. Now, in reality, no trains come in and none go out. And the same is true for the people of Leith.

Trainspotting is a hard-edged furiously abrasive novel, a violent contrast to the complacent world of the Edinburgh Festival. It forces the reader to take note of this other Edinburgh, the city of low pay and no pay, of boredom, aimlessness, self-hatred, sectarian violence and heavy, persistent drug use. The novel is also named for the pointless activity of trainspotting, analogous in its futility to attempting to 'nullify your life' with heroin. 'What happened in the early eighties,' says Welsh, 'was that you had a massive explosion of heroin in Edinburgh – you had all this cheap Pakistani heroin coming into the city and into the housing schemes.'

The last great drug novel to come out of Scotland was Alex Trocchi's *Cain's Book* in 1963. Welsh is careful to dissociate himself from the existential angst of writers like Trocchi and Burroughs. 'The junkie in Trocchi and Burroughs' fiction was by and large a culturally middle-class figure – a member of the intelligentsia, a rebel who saw society as not having done anything for them, so they're into this drug that's their own, a symbol of their rebellion. There's always been that sort of bohemian type drug subculture. But in Edinburgh, in the eighties you're talking about people who wouldn't normally be involved in the heroin scene, people who didn't have that Trocchi-esque attitude of setting themselves up in opposition to society. It was just people who really didn't have a fucking clue as to what was going on . . .'

Much of *Trainspotting* is interior monologue written in streetwise dialect as heavy as the fog round Arthur's Seat. Welsh says he couldn't imagine presenting characters who thought in received pronunciation – 'A living language is there to be used. It shouldn't be hidden, shouldn't be pushed aside, shouldn't bow to pressures regarding standard English.' The novel follows the lives of a group of Leith boys, friends since childhood, as they mature precariously through crime, addiction, alcoholism and ill-starred sexual encounters. Bitter, tragic and farcical by turns, it is a wholly authentic account of contemporary street-life – the uneasy alliances and small-time smack deals, the sudden random violence interspersed with drug-induced bonhomie. On the first day of the Edinburgh Festival, the book's primary narrator, Mark Renton, is found dredging through his own shit, his arms scabbed and weeping, in a bookie's lavatory searching for the opium suppositories he has inadvertently expelled. Despite the comprehensive drug use detailed in the book – 'Dope, acid, speed, E, mushies, nembies, vallies, smack, the fuckin' lot . . .' – Welsh actively resists classification as a drugs novelist: 'I'm not writing a textbook on drugs or drug legislation . . . I wouldn't be comfortable becoming a spokesperson for anything; drugs' spokesperson, underclass spokesperson. I don't think you can write anything definitive if you do. It's only your truth as you see it.'

Irvine Welsh was born in Edinburgh in 1958. He left school at sixteen to become an apprentice TV mechanic before drifting through a series of manual and clerical-professional jobs. He cites the primary influence on his writing as having been punk music: 'Iggy Pop was always my main man. And the Sex Pistols,' Welsh says. 'I used to muck around in bands but I never had much musical ability so I used to write songs about five pages long – like a story.' After paying his dues in bands such as Pubic Lice and Stairway 13, Welsh wrote *Trainspotting* – 'over quite a long period as just sort of wee pieces of things'. Part of it was printed in an anthology of new Scottish writing which gave him the confidence to write it all up together as a book. Whilst acknowledging the work of Glasgow writers such as James Kelman and Alasdair Gray, Welsh notes that 'there's been a massive explosion of writing in Edinburgh and East Central Scotland. Kevin Williamson's *Rebel Ink* magazine, the underground magazine, features a lot of new writing, much of it very good.' Welsh agrees that the Glasgow writers tend to belong to an older, more bohemian generation whereas the new Edinburgh writers are younger and more punk-influenced. 'Growing up through the punk era made a great impression on a lot of people. A lot of the Glasgow writers are concerned with work and the alienation from work and now you've got a generation who've grown up with the dole queue and YTS schemes – there is no work. The rave kids coming up now – they know that work's a pile of shit. Because of the industry in Glasgow there's a kind of machismo about work – that dignity of labour thing. Many of the older Glasgow writers are aligned to industrial socialism. I think work is a horrible thing. People should avoid it at all costs.'

Welsh feels that many of the older Glasgow writers have little understanding of some of the issues raised in *Trainspotting*. 'I've always found the treatment of someone who's got drug problems a bit offensive in Scottish literature. In classic Scottish fiction such as William McIlvanney and Alan Spence you see the junkie coming into their books as this sort of shadowy cardboard cut-out figure who's there to undermine or subvert decent Scottish working-class values – Alan Spence has this guy standing outside a playground trying to push drugs to kids!' In *Trainspotting*, Welsh says, 'I wanted to show a broader network. I wasn't really interested in telling the story of one or two people with drug problems so much as showing that such behaviour always takes place within a context. It's not isolated. Such behaviour has repercussions for the individual and for the people surrounding that individual. I didn't want to present the junkie as isolated and cut off. I wanted to focus on the relationships and the cultural pressures surrounding these characters. Obviously there are extremes of behaviour that people can get into, extremes of anti-social and fucked-up behaviour and I didn't want to spare that.'

Trainspotting has a number of other dominant themes, including domestic brutality, poverty, AIDS and sectarian violence, issues which he again feels have been neglected by many writers whom he otherwise admires. 'In traditional Scottish fiction there's been this kind of reverence for working-class culture. There's a lot of glossing over of sectarian and domestic violence – it's all portrayed in this creepy, sentimental way. The Orange Walk for example – it's seen as a big sentimental thing with nothing sinister about it; just a symbol of the working-class community. I wanted to react against that. I wanted to show that there's a lot of ugliness and a lot of negative things in all cultures. I'm not about putting any kind of culture on a pedestal. I'm not about trying to sanitise it.' Welsh suspects that a lot of people might see *Trainspotting* 'as a kind of indulgence, an orgy of self-hatred, and feel that I'm attacking the culture I've come from and grown up in, but I don't see it that way. I think you have to say that sectarianism and domestic violence are ugly things. They're ugly and they're wrong. You can't make a joke about a woman with a black eye 'cos her old man's had one too many or a man wi' a beer glass in his face 'cos his skin's the wrong colour or he's of a different religious or footballing persuasion. You can't portray it as just a big laugh.'

Welsh himself has moved on from the negativity and nihilism that surrounded the end of punk into an identification with the more knowing and sophisticated world of rave culture and house music. He points out that the proliferation of musical styles and the lack of a star system make it harder for the rave kids to be coopted by the capitalist music industry, unlike punk, which ended up doing no more than supplying a hungry media with extreme shock value. Similarly, many other younger writers, both British and American, derive their primary creative impulses from music and popular culture rather than literature – 'Music, television, magazines and comics have always influenced me more than books.' Welsh even says: 'I don't see myself as a writer. I don't want to be a writer. I'm just somebody who's written something and might write something else if I've got anything to say.' Apparently he has. Another book of stories *The Acid House* – 'more surreal and fantastical' – will be out next year.

In the meantime, *Trainspotting* stands as a crazed, splenetic rant against the sleek, self-congratulatory Edinburgh of the Festival. Welsh's is the voice from the pit, from a thousand freezing nights waiting to score drugs, a thousand long days in front of dying televisions, a voice from the dark side that seems to say: 'We're out there, we're everywhere, we're always there. It's *you* with your one-act plays and your private views and your four-hour lunches and your evening launches who're the ghosts. You'll pass on. We'll remain.'

The Acid House by Irvine Welsh

(Jonathan Cape)
The Guardian, 8 March 1994

The following review of The Acid House *is not supposed to be an example of Build Him Up, Knock Him Down journalism. I still think Welsh is one of the best writers of the last decade. The very faint doubts I express at the end of the piece are trivial compared to attacks on his subsequent work by those who feel he's never surpassed* Trainspotting.

I suppose it's all a bit like what Somerset Maugham wrote in The Colonel's Lady: '*Then because he was a critic he thought he should criticize.*'

Irvine Welsh's first novel *Trainspotting* smashed into the neat shop-front of contemporary literature last year and quickly established an entire Drug Brutalism section. Welsh's uniquely valuable contribution has been his unparalleled ability to represent the real lives of most people in Britain today – lives of poor accommodation, indifferent health, scams, deals and fantasies of escape, long days with the curtains drawn and the video on, with the dope and the Carlsberg and the speed or the smack.

Insidiously, unbelievably, the idea of an 'underclass' has come to permeate Britain – the notion of a country split between orderly taxpayers and a raging shower of crack-addicts, welfare witches and winos. An image of near-Dickensian wretchedness – vicious truanting children, amoral gaol-bird parents – has become fixed in the national consciousness. Welsh has always understod how pernicious and divisive this concept is and how much more subtle are the currents of British life.

Crime writer, John Williams, in his new book *Bloody Valentine* writes: 'People . . . fail to understand that a certain amount of sex 'n' drugs 'n' reggae represents a lifestyle that is actually attractive, that people freely choose to become part of it, finding it more like life than living on a Librium-fuelled housing estate.' Welsh understands implicitly that deprivation is relative. Accordingly, his work has a wide-ranging compassion and humanity, wholly unshackled by conventional notions of success or failure and balanced by his total lack of sentimentality. His characters are often uncompromisingly presented as being brutal, thick and opportunistic. Again and again one comes back to the vivid representational qualities of the work – to its realism.

In *The Acid House* Welsh often challenges this quality. This is a collection of stories by a writer in the process of development, stories by someone who is trying to find a voice that will extend his range beyond semi-autobiographical material. The result is patchy as Welsh plays with numerous approaches to short fiction – experimental, fantastical, conventional, typographically innovative, dialect, non-dialect. Welsh's writing has matured considerably since *Trainspotting* – there is less rage and dissonance, less of the head-banging vacuity of adolescent angst. The flow of personal emotion is better integrated with the hard man dialogue. Welsh seems intent on proving his imaginative versatility, proving that he is not a one-note author. But the most successful stories remain those in which the principal persona is someone probably

not very far from the author's younger self – a Scottish man drifting around Edinburgh, London and Amsterdam, dabbling in
drugs and petty crime. Although similar to the vignettes in
Trainspotting, these new stories are more highly structured, more
obviously fictive.

Two of these stories with their Scottish narrator stand out
as near perfect. 'Eurotrash' – 'a grubby map of all the places
you didn't want to go: addiction, mental breakdown, drug psychosis, sexual exploitation' and the all too brutally authentic
'Stoke Newington Blues'. Here, in a few lines of needle-sharp
dialogue, Welsh delivers a complete character analysis of a whining female junkie as she complains about a possibly imaginary
rape: 'It hurts, Euan. It fucking hurts inside. The gear's the only
thing that takes the pain away. I'm dead inside. No man can
understand.'

Welsh is often much less successful when experimenting with
the more traditional type of story. His portraits of people other
than small-time criminals are uncertain. However, his wit and
vitality suggest that he will ultimately be able to conquer different
fields – the fantastical, comically inverted 'Where the Debris
Meets the Sea' proves that he can master more ambitious, highly
satirical material. Overall it seems likely that this collection of free
kicks will go a long way towards establishing him as a writer of
considerable range and ability.

Welsh is the most gifted of the younger writers working in
Britain today. I hesitate to express my one slight reservation about
his work, a criticism that initially seems extremely bland. Welsh, by
his own admission, although always a storyteller never really
intended to be a writer. 'Music, television, magazines have always
influenced me more than books,' Welsh has said and this is part of
what gives him such perception when exploring contemporary
consciousness. But this lack of reading inevitably means that he
attempts subjects already used in short stories. Here 'Vat 96'
echoes a Roald Dahl plot and two others correspond closely to
obscure stories by Fitzgerald and Tennessee Williams. This is
obviously done in complete innocence – there are countless ways
of dealing with the same themes and Welsh's style is unmistakably
his own. But it does raise the issue of how much a writer should
read and to what purpose. There are those like Martin Amis who

feel that one cannot read or write well without a (preferably Oxbridge) education in the literary classics. There are those who feel the opposite, that academic ignorance is essential for true creative vision. William Burroughs probably got it about right: 'I have never known a writer who was not at one time an avid reader. Some knowledge of what *has* been done in writing is, I think, essential . . .' Welsh now evidently reads more and this collection shows him trying to discover what sort of writer he could become, his natural talent for dialogue and social comment having been established. But for me there has always been something very faint, something almost inexpressible lacking in his writing, although whether this has anything to do with his literary background is unfathomable. Harold Brodkey wrote: 'The essence of art is that it does not ever consist of a single voice without some evidence beyond that voice: art involves at least one convincing voice plus at least one other genuinely existent thing.' It is this 'one other genuinely existent thing' that I find missing in Welsh's work.

Morvern Callar by Alan Warner

(Jonathan Cape)
The Guardian, 1999

Of all the new, younger Scottish writers, my own personal favourite is Alan Warner. This is because he grew up not far from where I did in Scotland, thus much of his fiction is littered with references that I know well. No-one has ever written better about that part of Scotland either – that early, southerly part of the Highlands before it becomes the true, untamed (although rather touristed) Highlands and Islands. Morvern Collar and The Sopranos are, I think, two of the best novels of the nineties.

(Because of yet another space crisis at The Guardian *this review was cut to the bone, more remorselessly than any other piece. I was quite fond of the review, mainly because I liked the book so much, but I barely recognised it on publication. This is the original, uncut version.)*

Critics have performed grotesque contortions in recent years trying to avoid using a word which Alan Warner has invoked to describe his first novel. Symbolist, symbolism. Warner has claimed in interview that literature is necessarily symbolic. It is probably true that whether one calls it imagery or the subtextual, most literary fiction contains conscious references to themes and meanings which are not immediately apparent. Certainly, in this respect, Warner's novel is peculiarly rich and resonant. Warner also succeeds in sustaining a first-person narrative by a character other than the author and in writing about contemporary youth culture without becoming instantly dated – both notoriously difficult feats.

Morvern – the narrator – is a girl working in a dead-end supermarket job in a desolate, chillingly beautiful west of Scotland port town. At the start of the book she comes home to find her boyfriend has cut his throat. Morvern cries a little, unwraps the Christmas presents he has left her, lights a Silk Cut and goes on with her life, saying only that he has gone away. It transpires that he has left some forty thousand pounds in the bank. Morvern is able to go to Europe and move deep into the pulsing heart of the rave scene.

Beneath this simple structure is an architectural warren of patterns, oppositions, tensions and, indeed, symbolism. Morvern's unnamed home town could be one of many – Thurso, Oban, Dunoon. Referred to only as 'the port' it becomes emblematic of life for many young people on the Scottish coast; a life of narrow expectations and ruined futures enacted against a background of hypnotic natural beauty. There is nothing to do after work except get 'mortal' in the local bars. The local characters, as seen from Morvern's wry perspective, are both comical and heartbreaking, tormented by boredom: 'for a crack me and Mockit injected whiskey into each other's temples . . . we were steaming out the mind totally mortal within ten seconds . . . After that we put liquid LSD onto our pupils using the eyedropper . . .' Morvern observes this desperation; she sees her foster father, Red Hanna, an old-style Communist grown bitter after a lifetime on the railways; she listens to the memories of her friend Lanna's granny. It is this exceptionally strong sense of place and history that prevents the book from drifting into a mindless recitation of Ecstasy-fuelled sexuality when Morvern breaks away.

Then there is the strange business of Morvern's boyfriend. Warner has stated that he was striking both at the convention of an omniscient narrator and at the *Boy's* [Boyse] *Own* tendencies of some recent Scottish writing in killing him. 'I wanted to kill the male! Right away. I'm dead,' he has said. But the death of the author is not so easy to arrange. Morvern refers to her late lover throughout as 'He', with the capital letter. At one point she winches his body so that it is hanging over a model He made of his nearby childhood village and crashes the corpse down on the miniature house . . . This struggle between the god-like author and his creation is carried further. 'He' has left a novel written on his computer, with a farewell note instructing Morvern to send it to certain publishers. Deleting His name, she substitutes herself as author. The book's acceptance provides Morvern with another escape route but, as with the posthumous largesse that finances her travels, it is all orchestrated by the dead man.

Eventually driven to dispose of the corpse Morvern does so in a way that evokes the myth of Osiris. This is a theme carried through to the end of the book when Morvern returns to Scotland, both traumatised and exhilarated. She is also pregnant: 'The child of the raves'. Her child is fathered by the European youth culture that Warner makes clear has a terrible, apocalyptic edge to it; the ambient DJ who plays deep in the catacombs of Spain is called Sacaea after a Babylonian festival in which prisoners were permitted several days of total debauchery before being executed.

Morvern's deadpan, dispassionate prose is visually vague – 'I tied the reddish scarf onto my head and put the greenish socks on' – but highly responsive to physical and aural stimuli: the sudden shock of bottled water on her sweating body, the voluptuous coating on of nail-varnish, the chink of ice cubes as dusk falls. And always the music 'You heard the trancey ambient getting louder . . . swirly bass patterns coming out the bins . . . Stretching up fingers to touch the ever-so-occasional laser needles you could feel how high up your legs your skirt might be with the pounding, pounding of hardcore all round you.'

Morvern is a compelling creation, elusive, enigmatic and opaque. Both ordinary and extraordinary she is impossible to forget, whether exhibiting her sparkly knee (acquired in a childhood fall on to some Christmas glitter) in a port bar or swaying endlessly to the great heartbeat of the sound systems beneath Europe. Dispassionate and cool, she never flinches when recording bodily necessity or sexual need. Despite her sensuality and drunken hedonism she has a very dark and ominous aspect. Ironically, towards the end of the novel it would seem as if she finally outdistances her creator and expands into a tragic, mythic dimension all her own.

Morvern gleams out like onyx from the centre of what is a vivid, macabre and lyrical book. Although his subject matter is not dissimilar, Warner's book has a density quite lacking in the Bret Easton Ellis school of 'And then we fucked, and then we drove and then we killed someone and then we did some drugs,' a form that exists solely to emphasise affectless emptiness. Morvern's character incorporates a certain amount of that listless, meaningless spontaneity – it is a relevant cultural marker – but otherwise Warner peoples that vast internal emptiness with what it actually contains: memories, character, feelings and all the fragmentary flotsam of the unconscious, personal and primal.

The Sopranos by Alan Warner

(Jonathan Cape)
The Guardian, 1998

In Scotland, the adjective 'fey' has a precise colloquial meaning: it denotes someone with a degree of psychic or prophetic ability. It indicates a visionary streak and extra-sensory perception. Alan Warner's spooky ability to inhabit the hearts and minds of teenage girls can be considered fey in the extreme. In his stunning first novel, *Morvern Callar*, Warner used this uncanny talent to establish the unforgettable character of his eponymous heroine. His next book, *These Demented Lands*, descended into hallucinogenic incoherence. It was overly ambitious and Warner's idiosyncratic combination of learning and lyricism lurched out of control. Now, however, he has been able to balance out the different aspects of his formidable talent and produce a novel that is wider in scope than *Morvern Callar* without surrendering any of the telling detail and observation that characterised that book.

In *The Sopranos*, Warner returns to the setting of *Morvern Callar*, his home town on the west coast of Scotland that he always terms 'the Port'. The novel spans one day in the lives of six school-girls from the Port. As part of the choir for their school, Saint Mary's of Perpetual Succour, they travel by coach to Edinburgh (referred to only as 'the Capital') to participate in an inter-school singing competition.

Despite the admonishments of the nuns in charge, school is naturally the last thing on their minds. They are properly con-cerned with divesting themselves of uniform, donning tiny skirts, exposing pierced navels, getting the perfume and make-up and nail-varnish on and hitting the town's pubs, clubs and record shops with all the furious force of their youth, beauty and frustra-tion.

Warner's evocation of the day is largely in dialogue and he is a master of teen demotic. Whether weepy, bitchy, giggly or obscene, Warner provides every nuance of their characters through conver-sation in a sustained tour de force. He doesn't even use dialect over-much, but establishes the exact tone and pitch of their exchanges through rhythm and speech pattern. It is just as though one were eavesdropping.

No male writer has ever mastered the rituals of make-up in the way Warner has. (Most of them still confuse mascara and eye-liner.) In fact, no writer – male or female – has ever expressed the grimy physicality of female adolescence with such acuity – the reckless drinking, the vomiting, the time spent squashed up in cold lavatories, smoking and changing clothes; the tissues and tan-gas and Wonderbras; the endless impedimenta of cosmetics and haircare to be lugged around in plastic bags.

Throughout the long day's pilgrimage, Warner manages to touch on all the classic themes of fiction – love, lust and death, class, sexual identity and sexual deviation – and finally to resolve them with a peculiar spiritual grace. Although the adventures and reminiscences of the girls are scatological and hilarious, these do not obscure the deep tensions and realities of their lives. Orla is dying of Hodgkinson's Disease. Kylah wants to leave her rock band. Michelle, back home, is pregnant – 'Pure and intense she's devoured the few opportunities for the wee bit sparkle that was ever going to come her way.'

One of the book's most lengthy, poignant and sensual exchanges is the long conversation between Kay, an English university-bound outsider and Fiannula, the rowdy, beautiful leader of the Sopranos in-crowd. Gradually, over eighteen tequilas, several gins and Bloody Marys, the two girls overcome their mutual distrust and share their sexual uncertainties and predicaments. The bright sun shattering on the pavement, the dark cool bar, the chink of bottles and ice, the anxious counting of money – it is all as vivid and complex as life itself, as real and immediate as prose can be.

Despite the rather crass Spice Girls'-type cover picture this is the most profound of Warner's books. His sense of place and atmosphere remain extraordinarily intense. The girls want to get back to the Port that night because a nuclear submarine is in the bay and the sailors might be ashore. As darkness falls, 'above, moonhusk, hung like an abandoned wasp-comb'. The land itself 'was massively ancient . . . the exposed cliffs below the glacial glens showing time wasn't finished with the world here'. Such descriptions are both powerful and accurate. My family home is not far from the Port. During sporadic schooling there, Free Presbyterian relatives forbade me talking to what Warner calls 'wicked wee Catholic heathens'. But of course their concerns are exactly the same as those of Protestant schoolgirls – and of schoolgirls everywhere. In critical terms this means that the book has universal application. More straightforwardly, it's just brilliant.

Poor Things by Alasdair Gray

(Bloomsbury)
The Guardian, 3 September 1992

Another controversial and provocative Scottish novelist. I have included this piece not so much because I am an admirer of Alasdair Gray's work (I am) but because in purely technical terms this is a good book review. This is what you are supposed to do: 1. Bit of

*general/background info'. 2. Brief plot summary. 3. Larger issues
emerging from plot. Author's intentions. 4. Original crit. if possible. 5.
Neat summation of above. (Also insert quotations throughout.)
Ultimate Purpose: an opportunity for the reviewer to show off.*
    So that's it then.

Alasdair Gray is the elder statesman of a provocative group of
Glasgow writers which includes James Kelman and Tom Leonard.
Some say that these are super-talented, hard-drinking, sophisticated artists, others that they are superannuated, hard-drinking,
prolier-than-thou beatnik losers. Gray's own output has certainly
been uneven and eccentric. His books are striking artefacts, copi-
ously illustrated with his dramatic Yellow Book-ish drawings and
bedizened with mock blurbs and reviews but his writing has at
times frustrated the most ardent fan. His last novel was *Something
Leather,* a small stew of provincial vitiation which puzzled and
polarised critics. However, there is no doubt that this new book is
his most substantial since *Lanark* in 1981. He has finally managed
to unite a number of apparently irreconcilable obsessions – with
women, fiction, politics and Scottish history – into what is a
bibliophile's paradise of postmodern precision.

Poor Things is presented as a series of Victorian documents. The
main narrative is contained in the memoirs of one Archibald
McCandless, Scottish Public Health Officer. Gray is intent upon
pastiche and McCandless' story is a ghoulish gem of Glasgow
Gothic. As a student, McCandless' mentor was the gifted surgeon
Godwin Bysshe Baxter – a name which alerts readers to the
Frankenstein link. McCandless claims that in 1881 'God' Baxter
re-animated the drowned corpse of a beautiful young woman,
implanting within her the brain of her own unborn foetus. 'God',
a deformed grotesque with a gentle and intellectual soul, names
his creation Bella and falls ably to the task of education and nurture. However, the combination of Bella's innocent polymorphous
perversity and lush physical maturity creates problems and she
flees, continuing her education in a Paris brothel. Increasingly distressed by injustice and oppression she returns to Glasgow fired
with socialist zeal, marries McCandless and becomes a doctor.
A long letter from Bella follows this heartwarming piece of
bizarrerie in which she indignantly repudiates McCandless' story

and offers an alternative, ordinary explanation of her association with Godwin Baxter. As a sensible suffragette she dismisses her husband's tale; it is representative of 'all that was morbid in that most morbid of centuries, the nineteenth' and she attributes it to the unwholesome influence of Gothic 'ghouleries'. Nevertheless, there are as many puzzles and ellipses in Bella's account as in the rest of the book and consequently hours of pleasure for the dedicated literary sleuth tracking the 'real' story down the labyrinthine ways of the several narratives. Other letters and Gray's own 'Notes Critical and Historical' enlarge the playful web of clues and factoids. Fact and fiction are continually intermingled and destabilised throughout the narrative. The maps, drawings and engravings that accompany the text range from Glen Baxter-like absurdities to the sombre morbidities of (inevitably) *Gray's Anatomy*.

Of course Bella, emblematic of the 'New Woman', has to reject anything that is redolent of the melodramatic hysteria and erotic repressions of the previous century. Bella also embodies other intriguing and powerful archetypes. She is that male fantasy figure, the pliant *volupté* with the docile mind of a child. At the same time, reared to break cultural bonds, she is the male nightmare – untrammelled female sexuality, the devourer, the vagina dentata. She is a woman so sexually free and complete that she threatens the very essence of every man she confronts. In her pre-Godwin life, we learn, Bella was another symbolic figure, the mistreated and neurasthenic Victorian lady. Finally, no matter which version of Bella's life we 'believe', its thrust is the same – towards enlightenment, education, Socialism, feminism and sexual freedom. Divided neatly into body and brain, she is both the past and the future. Furthermore, in Bella's very being is an image of the novel as literary device: the 'body' of the text is the neo-nineteenth century narrative powered by the tricksy, contemporary brain of the author.

This complex structure allows Gray enormous scope in which to survey the new world birthing itself from out of all the misconceptions and neuroses of the Victorian age. Gray also adheres closely to postmodernist literary concerns. At every turn we are dutifully reminded of the artificiality of fictional process and the fictionality of historical process along with the instability of the authorial role. This literary trickiness has become a commonplace through the works of such as E. L. Doctorow or D. M. Thomas. Many of these fictional games have grown stale, partly because they necessitate an excess of control which is inimical to the imagination. *Poor Things* succeeds so well largely because Gray's obsessions are sufficiently powerful to enable his characters to transcend literary theory; rather than acting like mannequins with a message, they become fully animated and memorable, less parody than loving re-creation, or homage to the dying art of character construction. Thus does Gray successfully combine the best of the old and the new – a narrative that is as gripping and ordinarily readable as books used to be, together with an organising spirit that is informed, but not overwhelmed, by the penetrating yet somewhat lifeless dictates of theoretical exercise.

Terry Pratchett – Interview and introduction to the Discworld

The Guardian, 23 October 1993

I must have a break from Celtic Gothic.

Although Nicci Gerrard claimed recently that she had never met a woman who had read any of Pratchett's Discworld novels, I have most certainly read them all. And found them very funny. Gerrard was suggesting that they are Boys' Own *type books with nothing in them to interest girly readers. This is not so. They are for everyone.*

Terry Pratchett seemed to be a very kind and incredibly well-organised man. After this was published he sent me a map of Ankh-Morpork; he'd adapted Yeats and written across it 'Tread softly because you tread on my streets.' . . .

'It was a night so dark and stormy that even clichés had crept away to seek cover. The heath was blasted, lightning rent the sky, the heavens opened and the tempest raged. Three gaunt crones were crouched around the inexplicably blazing fire. The wind whipped at their blackened rags as they hurled their imprecations into the storm.

Ancient curses rent the air as the foul rites continued. And as the cauldron bubbled an eldritch voice shrieked: "When shall we three meet again?"

There was a pause.

Finally another voice said, in far more ordinary tones: "Well, I can do next Tuesday."'

Anyone familiar with the work of Terry Pratchett will find such a scene instantly recognisable. This combination of generally familiar lore with a cold douche of the prosaic, the homely, the familiar and the down-to-earth is the cornerstone of his style. It has seen him through ten years of prodigious invention, during which time he has created, in formidable detail, an entire other world – the Discworld.

Pratchett has been producing two to three books a year for some time now, interspersing his Discworld novels with children's fiction. There is often something faintly depressing about the mountain of statistics that accompany a bestselling author. There is the ritual repetition of the millions of copies sold, the innumerable translations into obscure languages, the flurry and scurry of foreign rights and options and spin-offs when all the time one is aware that when the dust settles what will probably crawl out is a few rather indifferent paperbacks. Although Pratchett is undoubtedly a Publishing Phenomena in exactly this sort of way, the end result is something far more appealing and has been achieved by a less usual route. His fame and popularity have spread slowly, without the intervention of either Hollywood or *Hello!* magazine on the one hand, or regular high profile reviews and the chitterings of literary editors on the other. His reputation arose slowly, often endorsed by dedicated non-readers – 'kids in leather jackets with NOZZER or SCAZ on their T-shirts,' as Pratchett has said – who then passed the books on to Nozzer's Mum and her friends. By now his army of fans transcends all boundaries and must include as many professors as it does neo-punks. But for his publishers the facts are the traditional ambrosial record of bestsellerdom. The Discworld novels have sold over four million copies in the UK alone. Since *Mort* was published in 1988 every single new Pratchett novel has gone into the bestseller lists. In November 1991 he was at number one in both the hardback and paperback bestseller lists with *Moving Pictures* and *Witches Abroad* and again in May 1992 for *Reaper Man* and *Small Gods*. He has received the Writers' Guild Award for Best Children's Writer of the Year for *Johnny and the Dead*. His sales are exceeded only by writers such as Catherine Cookson and Frederick Forsyth. His keeping company with such names is the first thing that is likely to generate confusion about the quality of Pratchett's work.

There is a persistent belief nowadays that writing which is very popular cannot simultaneously be any good. Very often of course it's not very good – much populist fiction is conventional, predictable and unimaginative – but there are notable exceptions, just as Dickens and Mark Twain were popular exceptions to the tides of late Victorian dross. Pratchett's situation is further complicated by the genre limbo he inhabits, somewhere between fantasy and humour and additionally by the ambiguous status accorded humorous writing in this country.

Terry Pratchett in person seems to have achieved an ironic detachment from all such literary scuffling. He is a slight, silvery figure, diffident and unpretentious. In conversation, however, he is emphatic, fiercely protective of his Discworld characters and very much more amusing than one would expect a comic writer to be. He was born in 1948 in Beaconsfield, near where one of his heroes, G. K. Chesterton, lived (whom his grandmother remembered as 'a big, fat man with a squeaky voice'). He re-created his idyllic fifties rural childhood in his 1990 fictional collaboration with Neil Gaiman *Good Omens*. Pratchett went straight from school into local journalism and then spent eight years working as a press officer for the Central Electricity Generating Board. Describing this he has said: 'It was my job to say: "Radioactivity? What radioactivity? Oh, *that* radioactivity."' When his fourth book and first Discworld novel, *The Colour of Magic*, became successful he gave up the day job, had a farewell party in a nuclear power station and devoted himself full-time to writing.

Despite some ambivalence about 'literary wankers in London', Pratchett doesn't feel that on the whole he has been badly treated by the critics – 'although anyone connected with the *Sunday Times* will always shove a knife in me and jump up and down on the handle'. The *Independent*, after all, has called him 'One of the best and one of the funniest English authors alive.' *The Times* has described him as 'the best thing since Wodehouse'. As a genre writer, however, he feels he bears 'the mark of Cain'. It is ironic because Pratchett's books bear very little relation to what is usually termed fantasy. I find fantasy, or 'sword and sorcery' as it is sometimes known, almost completely unreadable. Indeed, although Pratchett wouldn't thank you for the term, much of his work is a deconstruction of the self-regarding solemnity of Tolkien and his successors in the fantasy field. Such books usually involve maidens fair, wizards wise, brigands brave and lots of other inverted pseudo-medieval nonsense. Pratchett does admit to a detestation of what he calls the 'Ho, landlord! A pint of your finest ale' school and has no time for 'fluffy elves and beautiful unicorns'. On the Discworld everything is far more real than ideal: Pratchett's wizards tend to be strikingly incompetent and his dragons prey to all sorts of distressing illnesses that prevent them from flaming properly, from Slab Throat to the Black Tups. In fact, Pratchett is so opposed to feyness and fancies that he asserts with considerable passion: 'I *really hate* elves. I hate the elves in our own society, the style without content.' One of the Discworld novels, *Lords and Ladies*, is devoted to revealing elves as Pratchett sees them – empty, vapid, cruel, stylish poseurs – and in this, as in all the other books in the series, Pratchett is using the Discworld as a framework from within which he can comment in depth on the workings of human nature in our own world. Although he has described himself as 'a fantasy writer who doesn't like fantasy', he doesn't reject the job description: 'It's a honourable trade.' What he does contest is 'all the tired old assumptions of post-Tolkien fantasy. The classic fantasy universe swallows a lot of givens which ought to be examined – whether, for example, having a king is a good thing – and we swallow a lot of givens in our own society and I think you should take a second look at them. I think you should question the natural wisdom of wizards whether they're modern wizards or fantasy wizards.'

Pratchett's work is actually far more in the tradition of classic British humour than anything else. 'It was,' he says, 'far more satisfying to concentrate on the humour you get from character development and the interplay of characters rather than simply setting out to write a funny fantasy sitcom.' The names that come to mind as one reads the books are those that Pratchett has admitted as influences – Beachcomber, The Goons, Michael Bentine, Alan Coren, Keith Waterhouse and Sellars and Yeatman's *1066 & All That*. The Discworld novels are particularly reminiscent of this latter classic, so much so that Pratchett often seems to be purveying All The Myths You Can Remember. The comparison with P. G. Wodehouse is also apposite, although Pratchett astutely points out that Wodehouse's work bears very little relation to the way people actually behave: 'The charm of Wodehouse is that it all beautifully takes place in an aquarium somewhere.' He adds: 'I've always enjoyed and respected Wodehouse and so I get embarrassed at Wodehouse comparisons. I have to say that the Fry and Laurie TV series spoiled him for me – reading the books is a pleasure, seeing them portrayed on the screen is an invitation to socialist revolution!' Nevertheless, there are strong similarities. Both writers create a complex fantasy world peopled by eccentric and memorable characters. Readers can join the books at any point in the series. Each novel is a cat's cradle of humorous commentary within which the writers can play with language and point up the ludicrous nature of linguistic conventions. Neither writer is academically respectable and yet their books have given more joy to a wider cross-section of people than any number of more obviously cerebral, po-faced, fly-by-night allegories.

So what is it that makes the Discworld so different, so appealing? Well, for one thing it is an intensely visual place. The Discworld is flat and sits on top of the broad and star-tanned shoulders of four elephants which are carried through space on the back of a giant turtle: 'Great A'Tuin, the turtle comes, swimming slowly through the interstellar gulf, hydrogen frost on his ponderous limbs, his huge and ancient shell pocked with meteor craters.' The great turtle slides through space 'like an endless tortoiseshell hairbrush'. The Discworld is described, tellingly, as 'world and mirror of worlds'. Around its Rim, the ocean pours off endlessly into the night, at its Hub rises the glittering peaks of Cori Celesti, home of the gods. Cori Celesti is a ten-mile high column of cold, coruscating fire. The gods live on the top, in a place called Dunmanifestin. Do they spend their time playing idly with the fates of men? Not really. They are more likely to be arguing with other mythological creatures such as the Ice Giants over the

lowering of property values in the celestial regions or who has forgotten to return the lawnmower.

Over the Disc can be seen the greenish-purple flickers of
octarine, the pigment of the imagination and the colour of magic.
The Disc has a strong magical field and runs on magic rather in
the way our world runs on electricity; that is, it is not annoyingly
obtrusive but it is always there and one would certainly notice it if
it went.

The Disc is a very large place and many of its countries and
kingdoms are eerily familiar although they tend to be mired in the
time we are most likely to recognise them. Djeylibeybi is unavoid-
ably Egyptian, although they are still building pyramids. Ephebe
and Tsort are strongly reminiscent of the classical worlds of
Greece and Rome. Sto Helit, Quirm and Lancre are small rural
kingdoms. ('Lancre Castle was built by an architect who had
heard about Gormenghast but hadn't got the budget.') There are
a number of faraway places – Klatch, sea-girt Krull, the Great Nef
desert and the Tezuman Empire which boasts a particularly horrible little god called Quetzovercoatl, the Feathered Boa, and is
recognisably Aztec.

However, most of the action in the books takes place around
the great city of Ankh-Morpork – 'When a man is tired of Ankh-
Morpork he is tired of ankle-deep slurry.' Ankh-Morpork is the
essence of cities, the archetypal city, the sort that never sleeps,
where all the cuisines of the world collide, sometimes quite violently. Here, 'under night's damp cloak assassins assassinated,
thieves thieved, hussies hustled. And so on.' It has its palatial mansions and an inner-city no-go area called the Shades. It also has its
Tourist Brochure, 'Wellcome to Ankh-Morpork, Citie of One
Thousand Surprises', with a handy extra section entitled 'Soe
you're A Barbariean Invader?' Perched on the banks of the Ankh,
a river so silted that 'even an agnostic could have walked across it',
Ankh-Morpork is overseen by the ascetic, Machiavellian Lord
Vetinari who administers 'not so much a reign of terror as the
occasional light shower'. Vetinari is in fact no tyrant but an intelligent despot, devoted to the organisation of his city and a considerable improvement on previous incumbents such as
Psychoneurotic Lord Snapcase. Even crime is organised; in addition to the more ordinary guilds – the Merchants', the Guild of

Fools and Joculators – there is a Thieves' Guild and an Assassins' Guild.

Pratchett is at pains to point out that the details of his invented world are not so ludicrous as one might think. The belief that the world travels on the back of a giant turtle 'is one of the oldest myths of the planet. The American Indians believed it. Primitive Eurasians believed it. Someone recently sent me a Bantu legend about the world going through space on a turtle.' He agrees that it's odd – 'When you see a turtle it's not the first thing you think of.' He says the elephants are 'a kind of Indo-European subset. And from Indian myth. They turn up a lot. I took the Discworld more or less from stock and added details of my own, but if it's complicated it's because the human imagination is complicated.' Pratchett is very interested in cities and the way they work. 'Everything we are is derived from the fact that we are citizens.' He suggests that Ankh-Morpork is 'pretty much an early Victorian city. No-one's invented steam or electricity yet.' He feels that a city is the mirror of a civilisation and that 'civilisation – obviously city-based – has to be defended against the things that undermine it'. But Pratchett is certainly not going to make any grandiose claims for his invention. 'I'm a writer of mildly humorous fantasy. I'm bright enough to know that if Ankh-Morpork existed it would be rife with disease and crime. It works on the Discworld, what else can I say?' He does point out, however, that: 'There were thieves' and beggars' guilds in China. If you were having a posh celebration you sent the beggars' guild some money – an anti-invitation – or else all these beggars with their interesting running sores would be coming up to your guests.'

Ankh-Morpork is also home to the venerable pile of Unseen University, the premier college of wizardry on the Disc. And within the university is the Library, the greatest collection of magical texts anywhere in the multiverse. Like all good libraries and bookshops it defies the laws of space-time and is said to go on forever. Pratchett says it is based on a bookshop he remembers from childhood which was a tiny cottage on the outside and endlessly huge indoors. Naturally the aged books of occult lore in the library have a life of their own. Many of them leak raw magic and this sometimes forms a critical Black Mass. Some of the larger grimoires have to be kept in chains. *The True Arte of Levitatione* has spent the last century in the rafters and *Ge Fordge's Compendyum of Sex Majick* is kept in a vat of ice. The Library and its Librarian – who was changed into an orang-utan in a magical explosion – play a very important role in the Discworld books. Pratchett says with amusement: 'I get a lot of letters from librarians which say "Your books are very popular with boys who don't like reading. Later we can try and introduce them to **real** literature!" . . . They claim I have raised the status of librarians! There is a vogue for them wearing OOK badges' – 'ook' being one of the few things the Librarian says. One of Pratchett's most notable and important achievements is the way that he has made books – and libraries – interesting and exciting to a whole generation of adolescents who otherwise would have been more than likely to ignore them.

However exotic and jokey they sound, all the books are about people behaving in recognisably human ways. They may be called demons or wizards or trolls but they behave like bureaucrats or academics or next-door neighbours. As he says: 'With probably the minimum amount of changes I could set them in medieval Germany or eighteenth-century Ireland – although you wouldn't get many orang-utans as librarians . . .' Pratchett's imagination is eclectic and the novels are not only inventive but informative about everything from quantum physics to the behaviour of camels. Pratchett may parody history and myth but at the same time he resuscitates it and animates it for his readers.

The Discworld was introduced in the early books through the arrival of Twoflower, its first tourist. Accompanied by his ambient Luggage – 'half suitcase, half homicidal maniac' which was capable of eating people *and* producing clean shirts, Twoflower behaved in the irritating way of tourists everywhere. Gradually the novels gained momentum and began to revolve around certain key characters and to tackle more ambitious and serious themes.

The most popular of the Discworld characters, the one that receives the most fan-mail, is Death. Death is a traditionalist – he always speaks in capital letters and describes himself as AN ANTHROPOMORPHIC PERSONIFICATION. He chooses to appear in the expected guise complete with black robe and scythe, although he deviates from tradition in the matter of his horse. 'Death had tried fiery steeds and skeletal horses in the past, and found them impractical, especially the fiery ones, which tended to set light to their own bedding and stand in the middle of it looking embarrassed.' Death rides an ordinary white horse called Binky. Death is a bleak, mordantly humorous personality. He doesn't actually kill people – fate decides all that – he just turns up and ushers them onwards to wherever they think they are going. Pratchett always makes it very clear that heaven and hell and gods – especially gods – are human creations, sustained and animated by belief and hope. This is probably why Death – albeit in a benign form – so dominates the books and gives them their sense of stoicism, of optimism achieved against very considerable odds. This too is what renders them more than lightweight entertainments. Death is an inescapable reality, not a myth, nor a fantasy, nor a religion. As Death so often says: 'THERE IS ONLY ME.'

The other overpowering characters to emerge from the Discworld are the three witches, Granny Weatherwax, Nanny Ogg and Magrat Garlick. About five hundred miles from Ankh-Morpork are the wild Ramtop Mountains and the village of Bad Ass. It is in these parts, which function as a sort of distillation of rural Britain, that the witches have their small and incredibly quarrelsome coven. Pratchett admits to an especial fondness for the witches, particularly the headstrong and irascible Granny Weatherwax. He says: 'Granny Weatherwax often speaks for me.' He describes her as 'an incredibly mentally stable lady but there's a lot of harshness about her'. He continues: 'The beautiful thing about the three witches is you know that as soon as you put them together they'll be having a row. They need one another but they get on one another's nerves all the time.' Granny Weatherwax, for all her skill, rather distrusts magic and prefers to use hard-headed common sense or elementary psychology to get things done. Nanny Ogg, although equally tough, is very different. Having had a lurid amatory history in her youth she now rules an extended domestic empire, surrounded by downtrodden daughters-in-law. She is vivacious and vulgar, partial to strong drink and more than likely to be found dancing on the table, showing her petticoats and singing rude songs such as 'The Hedgehog Can Never Be Buggered At All' or 'A Wizard's Staff has a Knob on the End'. (Pratchett speaks ruefully of the number of versions of these rural classics he has been sent.) Magrat Garlick as the youngest witch has New Age inclinations and sends off for mail-order occult jewellery. She despairs of the two other witches' rough-and-ready approach to magic. When during an Invocation in the wash-house Nanny Ogg intones '*I invoke and bind thee* – with the balding scrubbing brush of Art and the washboard of Protection', Magrat sighs for sigils and octagams and incense.

The witches are the main players in three of the best Discworld novels *Wyrd Sisters*, *Witches Abroad* and *Lords and Ladies*. *Wyrd Sisters* plays with the plot of *Macbeth*. One of the pleasures of the books is the way in which literary classics – *Great Expectations* or *Tom Brown's Schooldays* – float effortlessly through them in a manner that would be pounced on as intertextual in another author but is never allowed to become strident or alienating in Pratchett's work. In fact it is difficult to summarise many of the Discworld books without sounding pretentious in a way that would certainly horrify Pratchett. *Witches Abroad* examines the nature of narrative causality in fairy tales (see?) and *Guards, Guards* is the Discworld version of a private eye novel. *Pyramids* and *Small Gods* both look at the tyranny and sadism of established religions. *Lords and Ladies* is an attack on the emptiness of style and glamour and *Reaper Man* considers the death of cities and the growth of suburban mall culture. *Men At Arms*, which Pratchett describes as 'a police procedural novel', returns to the members of the Night Watch introduced in *Guards, Guards*. The Watch has become an Equal Opportunity Employer with a troll, a lady werewolf and a dwarf added to the ranks. Pratchett does not approve of species-ism.

Whether one finds the Discworld books amusing seems to have nothing to with educational background, intellect, or even sense of humour. Many people, friends and couples who otherwise agree on almost everything, find themselves fiercely at odds over Pratchett's books with one combatant complaining furiously that they are childish, no better than watered-down Monty Python and certainly inferior to Douglas Adams, while the other laughs helplessly. Certainly Pratchett has managed, over the course of a very large number of books, to entertain without ever being offensive. His books are never sexually or racially abusive. They find their humour wholly within the quirks of contemporary human nature. That is not to say that the different types and species in the books – trolls, vampires, ghouls, wizards, dwarfs and barbarian invaders – do not moan and insult and criticise one another, but this is achieved without the undercurrent of malice and contempt that was once thought integral to wit. The Discworld novels project extremely strong values – respect for the old, decency, generosity, honesty, lack of pretension. They are exceptionally humane, compassionate and principled books.

Pratchett is reluctant to make any claims but he does murmur that Granny Weatherwax once said she didn't know much about Good and Evil but she did know right from wrong and he sort of goes along with that. He does express regret that the word 'decency' has become so devalued. 'The reason I feel embarrassed about using the word is it seems to have been commandeered by a certain sort of person. "Decency" is said, but what is heard is "Flog 'em within a inch of their lives and send 'em home."' When pressed he admits that his books project 'a low-grade, generalised respect for other people' and that 'if there's any messages in the books, then they're simple enough: think for yourself, don't put your faith in dreams, don't trust in the wisdom of wizards'.

Pratchett has strong feelings for his readers, which he says dates from his journalism days. 'You're always aware of the readers out there.' He undertakes tremendous signing tours each year and personally answers every single one of his deluge of fan letters. This combined with his enormous fictional output suggests incredible energy and discipline. Pratchett is aware that, because the books seem light-hearted and funny, people assume that they are easy to write. Of course they are not, as anyone who has ever tried anything similar knows. Pratchett says: 'I enjoy doing it. I can't think of anything I'd rather do but it *is* hard. It ought to be hard. It's much more enjoyable if it is.' This streak of puritan discipline, together with a certain degree of forcefulness, indicates that Pratchett is a more wintry character than the novels suggest. He describes himself as 'the most amiable sort of bloke normally' and this seems true enough but he also projects a dogged, persistent sense of shrewd, hard-headed realism. This is mirrored in his extremely diffident attitude to his wealth. He obstinately refuses to be seduced by its allure, other than in the most practical way. 'Even if I got a big, fast car I would drive it like an old grandad,' he says. He lives quietly in the same Somerset cottage he has inhabited for many years, along with his wife Lyn and daughter Rhianna. This sharp contrast between the lavish extravagance of his imagination and the careful, ironic practicality of his attitudes is what gives his work its sharpness and originality. This balance of extremes is found in all his fiction. His first children's book *The Carpet People* was published when he was twenty, and Pratchett says of writing for children: 'You can pick big things which you can tackle at a small level, at a very local level.' This is a good description of the essence of Pratchett's books. They almost all involve the creation of a strange and minutely-detailed universe, wherein odd beings behave exactly like ordinary people. Pratchett is always examining large themes in a local environment, aware that the immediate world around them is what defines people and makes them behave as they do. He recalls 'an image that impressed me no end when I was about eleven. I read about these frogs in South America, in the cloud-forest, that spend their entire life-cycles in a flower. They lay their eggs in the flower and the tad-poles grow up and become little frogs which hunt around the pool in the flower.' Without sentiment, without whimsicality, Pratchett seems to endlessly recreate that flower and study the miniature universe it contains.

People who need people

The Sunday Times, 26 June 1994

I am trying to avoid reprinting book reviews unless there seems to be a compelling, general reason to do so – perhaps (with luck) the review raises points of persuasive interest or contains information otherwise unavailable. But overall I prefer to reproduce features as reviews are, by their very nature and form, bound to date and become irrelevant to everybody apart from extraordinarily anal and obsessive academics.

The following was written right at the start of the now-omnipresent vogue for 'This Book is my Life! I Lived it and then I Wrote it Down. Every detail is TRUE!!!!' style of writing. Initially this trend sparked off a number of moving, middle-brow articles (like the one below)

*fretting about What Is Fact? What Is Fiction? and their inter-
relationship before everyone got tired and let the deluge of factoid,
autofiction, diary-novels and books of emotional journalism just wash
over them. Another day, another confessional novel . . .*

I do wish *more people would take note of Fran Leibowitz's
inspiring words: 'If you have a burning, restless urge to write or paint,
simply eat something sweet and the feeling will pass. Your life story
would not make a good book. Do not even try. All God's children are
not beautiful. Most of God's children are, in fact, barely presentable . . .'*

Marilyn Monroe dyes her pubic hair blonde with a toothbrush.
John Kennedy screws Marilyn Monroe in the Bates Motel. John
Lennon goes to work for the DHSS. John Bunyan cuts Izaak
Walton's fishing line. Fergie falls for Ross Perot. Hemingway
hunts Bigfoot. The real Jack the Ripper was a runaway combine
harvester. The real Jack the Ripper was ritually murdered by five
Jewesses in Nazi Germany. And so on.

Where has all this – and much worse – happened? In fiction.
Two recent books could hardly be more different, apart from their
central literary device. Peter Lefcourt's *Di and I* is a first-person
fantasy affair between Princess Diana and a Californian screenwriter. In the other corner is the gravitas of *Art and Lies* – Jeanette
Winterson invents modernism using Handel, Sappho and Picasso
as mouthpieces. Other recent work also utilises the same convention – the use of 'real' people in fiction. Allen Massie's *The Ragged
Lion* purports to be Sir Walter Scott's lost memoirs. In *Eating
Pavlova*, D. M. Thomas continues his prolonged linguistic flirtation with the Freud family. Peter Ackroyd, an old hand at this, will
soon publish *Dan Leno and the Limehouse Monster* featuring
Victorian clown, Dan Leno, George Gissing and Karl Marx
involved with a murderer predating the Whitechapel killings by a
few years. Saucy Jack must have been too common for the fastid-
ious Mr Ackroyd.

Has an established post-war American literary fashion suddenly infected British writers? Far from it. Real individuals have
featured in storytelling since its earliest, oral days. Homer (or
Homer and Co) entertained with heroic deeds in legendary wars,
myth, fact and folklore all intermingled. Odysseus may have been
ruler of Ithaca.

Even after the next fifteen-hundred-year-long ecclesiastical innings when the emphasis was, with some exceptions, on spirituality in art, the Elizabethan dramatists weighed in as before with plotlines culled from faded fables and chronicles of doubtful historicity – with a nod to the divine right of kings. This mixing of the factual and the imaginary continued into the rise of the novel. Defoe's *Robinson Crusoe* (1719) was allegedly based on the adventures of Alexander Selkirk.

The novel reached its apogee in the nineteenth century, peopled now by largely imaginary characters. Some great novelists did use 'real' people in their books: Dickens' Madame Defarge, the pitiless 'tigress' given to 'knitting shrouds' at the foot of the guillotine in *A Tale of Two Cities*, existed. Walter Scott's novels were crammed with portraits of late sinners and saints. Both he and Victor Hugo were fascinated by Louis XI's cruel, devout and duplicitous character. Strictly speaking, all such books belonged to the slowly evolving genre of historical novel. Although R. L. Stevenson's *Kidnapped* was again an historical account, we might nominate his descriptions of Alan Breck Stuart, the murder of the Red Fox and the trial of James of the Glens as the first modern presentation of real characters in fiction – for their animation, immediacy and the perennial importance of these issues to the Scottish people.

By the twentieth century writers were becoming increasingly coy. The libel shark had begun to stir. Everyone knew that Somerset Maugham's Charles Strickland in *The Moon and Sixpence* was Gauguin, that Evelyn Waugh's Lord Copper was Beaverbrook and Scott Fitzgerald's Last Tycoon, Irving Thalberg. So what brought the rush of real, contemporary individuals into fiction in the post-war years? It was mass comunications and the steely onward march of the Structuralists, Post-structuralists and Deconstructionists. 'Il n'y a rien dehors le texte' declaimed Derrida – if all the world was text and all its men and women mere significations, anyone was up for grabs. But libel lawyers did not warm to literary theory. They pounced on intertextuality when Kathy Acker inserted a chunk of Harold Robbins into a book although she had been left untouched when revealing the duplicity of autobiography in *The Adult Life of Toulouse-Lautrec*. Thus a certain class of person developed whom one was likely to encounter in literature. They were usually – but not always – dead and the author had to tread carefully. While one could rely on the Clan of the Cave Bear not to sue, a lesbian novel starring, say, Sylvia Plath would be certain to incur the wrath of the Hughes Estate.

These real figures in literature, whether quick or dead, tend to be iconic – that is, near-deified and so grotesquely famous that they or their descendants would hardly stoop to sue. Thus we have the British royals as in *Di and I* – a book that hovers between the satirical and the saccharine. The author deserves credit for being the first writer to react appropriately to certain adolescent pictures of the Princess in Andrew Morton's book – those which emanate all the awesome power of the nymphet, the pre-adolescent immortalised by Nabokov. 'You have to be an artist and madman . . . to discern . . . the slightly feline outline of a cheekbone, the slenderness of a downy limb . . . the little deadly demon among the wholesome children; *she* stands unrecognised by them and unconscious herself of her fantastic power.' Generally, Sue Arnold's mocking foghorn message about societal inequality in *The Queen and I* reflects our mass disenchantment with the Royals as does Adam Mars-Jones in *Lantern Lecture* when the Queen catches rabies from one of her interminable corgis. Nowadays, in most cases the author comes to bury rather than to praise former heroes and heroines. Alternatively they sprinkle the text with assorted Lenins, Jungs, Freuds and Einsteins to lend intellectual cred to frail work. The highest seriousness involves inserting yourself into your novel, as does Martin Amis and a hundred low-rent imitators.

There are certain icons, certain books and certain writers who inhabit this strange limbo where fact and fantasy bleed one into the other. E. L. Doctorow's *Ragtime* (1976) is usually considered the definitive book of this type. It includes Houdini, Harry Thaw, murderer of architect Stanford White, and perennial favourite Sigmund Freud. But Thomas Pynchon had already inextricably fused reality and illusion. In *Gravity's Rainbow* (1973) the real – Jack Kennedy, Duncan Sandys, a nomadic Namibian tribe called the Hereros and Werner von Braun all succumb to a confetti of frenzied invention.

Amongst the most frequent icons are: Marilyn Monroe –

immortalised in *The Immortals* by Budd Schulberg. Marilyn also appears in Bill Morris' *Biography of a Buick*, along with Joe di Maggio, Neal Cassady, Jack Kerouac and Elvis Presley. Jack Kennedy is the other great icon; both Don de Lillo's subtle and delicate *Libra* and D. M. Thomas's rather more crude *Flying in to Love* deal with his assasination. ('Ten thousand dreams a night . . . are dreamt about Kennedy's assassination,' writes Thomas). Margaret Thatcher appears to have achieved iconic status, appearing in Mark Lawson's gratingly convincing *Bloody Margaret* and in Ian MacEwan's *The Child in Time* where she confesses, most improbably, her love for a virtual toyboy of a politician. Jack the Ripper is another familar fictional standby, infesting countless books and stories including Iain Sinclair's *White Chapell, Scarlet Tracings*. There are also novels about his victims, including one by Hilary Bailey and Paul West's *The Women of Whitechapell*. Criminals in general are favourite fodder; E. L. Doctorow's *Billy Bathgate* concerns Dutch Schultz, and William Burroughs went for the throat with *The Last Words of Dutch Schultz*. Bugsy Siegel ('He just crosses to the shady side of the street now and then') appears, with a host of past Hollywood greats in Gavin Lambert's wonderful book *Running Time*. Bugsy too, oddly disguised as the Fisher King in the stricken land of Las Vegas, appears in Tim Powers' *Last Call*. Denis Cooper's *Jerk* is about serial killer Dean Corll. Gordon Burn links Myra Hindley with his eponymous *Alma Cogan*.

Pop stars, notoriously litigious, appear less frequently, unless dead. Numerous horror stories present a shambling, rotting band – Jimi and Janis, Brian and Morrison – playing forever . . . *somewhere* . . . An exception is the Almodóvar-like Spanish novel *Desperately Seeking Julio* by Maruja Torres – which also includes Thatcher, the Reagans and Mitterrand – and has Iglesias consulting a magic swimming pool as to who is the greatest star of all. Amongst other women writers Angela Carter presents Baudelaire's mistress Jeanne Duval, Tama Janowitz uses Andy Warhol and Pat Booth Robert Mapplethorpe.

Irvine Welsh's recent story 'Where the Debris Meets the Sea' features Madonna, Victoria Principal, Kylie Minogue and Kim Basinger lusting after Edinburgh rough trade hunks. Presented with this experimental gem, Minogue personally expressed some bewilderment about the nature of desire and textuality but seemed relieved to be in such luscious company.

Authors closely associated with the use of real individuals in their work are T. Coraghessan Boyle whose masterpiece *Water Music* stars Regency explorer, Mungo Park. Boyle's novel *The Road to Wellville* mocks Dr Kellogg and the early health food industry. The Texan author Howard Waldrop is the greatest unknown practitioner of the art, capable of having Proust, Jarry, Dreyfus, Picasso, Rousseau and Satie all filmed by Georges Meliès within one story. In Britain Peter Ackroyd has established himself with novels about cabbalistic architect Hawksmoor, Oscar Wilde, Chatterton and Doctor Dee (another fictional favourite). Jeremy Reed mines a predictable, repetitive seam with novels starring Rimbaud, Lautréamont and Antonin Artaud.

Why are none of these known as historical novels? Hush, whisper who dares – postmodern irony and self-consciousness together with frequent juxtapositions of the 'real' and the fictional define this contemporary form. 'Historical' novels are innocent genre fiction, free of such literary conceits – and conceit.

There are novels about Marlowe, about Hitler in Liverpool, about Scott of the Antarctic, about Elgar on the Amazon, Gilles de Rais, Marie Laveau the voodoo queen, Oskar Schindler, John Updike – *U and I* by Nicolson Baker – Brecht – *Loving Brecht* by Elaine Feinstein. The villain in the Flashman books is the great-grandfather of Michael Ignatieff. To further confuse matters, two fictional characters have crept into the pantheon and are treated exactly as though they had lived and (one of them) died – Sherlock Holmes and Dracula. Factions within fiction.

I, me, mine: Fiction and autobiography

The Guardian, 21 April 1995

Whereas the previous 'think-piece' – as I believe they are non-euphoniously called – was about Very Famous People (JFK, Marilyn) turning up in fiction, this one is the other way round. It is about people whose main claim to fame is having been the model for a very well-known fictional character. (The classic example is Neal Cassady, model for Dean Moriarty in Jack Kerouac's On The Road.*)*

Incidentally, considering the list of books at the end of this piece, can anyone think of a novel of equal stature (i.e. as good as, say, The Bell Jar*) and written in the same fictional-memoir mode which has appeared in the years since I wrote this and which should be added to the list? I can't.*

The good ship Gossip has recently been anchored off Literary Cove. Does Martin Amis' new novel really chart the course of his mid-life crisis and his intimations of mortality? Did Julian Barnes serve as source material for one of the characters? Did Nick Hornby's *High Fidelity* really detail the author's unwilling maturation, his own acceptance of monogamy, his marriage? Fiction, with its teasing combination of autobiography, fantasy, revisionism and comment has always provided a trap for the unwary. Now, with reality and illusion indissolubly mingled, has the novel, in symbiosis with the dominant culture, fused the real and hyper-real so seamlessly that no-one can claw them apart?

The novel has consistently provoked debate about the original identities of narrators and characters . . . 'When I was a little boy,' said Isaac Bashevis Singer, 'they called me a liar but now I am grown up they call me a writer.'

Stendhal took the opposite view, laying less emphasis on invention: 'The novel is a mirror walking along a main road.' Whether seen as licensed mendacity or helplessly representational, fiction has also received the full blast of critical theory which asserts that even autobiography is fictive and that authors inevitably, impotently, transmit a collage of experiential and artistic influences. It is now accepted that the intervention of language must always renegotiate the experience portrayed. Having sex is not the same as writing about it. Knowing someone is not the same as describing them. In Paul De Man's words: 'A fundamental discrepancy always prevents the observer from coinciding fully with the consciousness he is observing.'

Additionally the author is no longer regarded as autonomous but rather as a medium transmitting the ectoplasm of an imagination that cannot be 'original' but is the composite of a multitude of other artistic influences and images which render texts necessarily interactive.

But rumours of the author's death are greatly exaggerated. The novel, so pliable, so endlessly adaptable, endures. Authors continue to unite autobiography and fantasy and to act as literary Dr Frankensteins, fleshing out their characters with the traits of lovers, family and friends. Looking back through literary history one sees countless examples of this process. Astraea in Alexander Pope's 1733 *Imitations of Horace*, was based on one of the earliest women authors, Aphra Behn. Annie Besant, socialist and birth-control campaigner, appears in works by George Bernard Shaw and Pinero. Lord Byron appears, thinly disguised, in at least six novels including Thomas Love Peacock's 1818 *Nightmare Abbey*. Impressed by his portrayal as Mr Cypress, Byron sent Peacock a rosebud which the author promptly mounted in a gold locket. Even Captain Ahab in *Moby-Dick* had a precursor, one Owen Chase, who survived by cannibalism after his ship was overturned by a sperm whale.

Authors model characters upon those around them for a vast number of reasons ranging from fascination to lust, hatred and revenge. The originals often react badly, something the author can be too naive or ingenuous to anticipate. Thomas Wolfe was surprised when his small-town family and friends were wounded by their fictional counterparts in *Look Homeward, Angel*. Proust when writing *Remembrance of Things Past*, pumped up on bull's adrenalin and pausing only to shit on a portrait of his mother, failed to foresee that it would offend some of his aristocratic friends, however subtly they were portrayed.

F. Scott Fitzgerald relied heavily upon autobiography in his fiction, utilising his wife Zelda constantly. (A friend described her succinctly as 'A small-town Southern belle. Chews gum, shows knees.') Fitzgerald's novella *The Rich Boy* is an excellent example of the tangles that surround fictional portraits. The hero, Anson Hunter, was based on Fitzgerald's schoolfriend Ludlow Fowler. In 1925 Fitzgerald wrote to Fowler 'I have written a story about you called "The Rich Boy" – it is so disguised that no-one except you and me and maybe two of the girls concerned would recognise, unless you gave it away, but it is in a large measure the story of your life, toned down here and there and symplified [*sic*]. Also many gaps had to come out of my imagination. It is frank, unsparing but sympathetic . . .' Besides illuminating the nuts and bolts of character construction this has a sequel. Fowler asked for two cuts – a sex scene and a reference to his heavy drinking. These were duly made and the story published. Today the cuts have been restored. The essential point is the passage of time.

No-one now minds that Delmore Schwartz was the source for Bellow's *Humboldt's Gift* or that D. H. Lawrence was depicted – usually very malevolently – in at least ten novels, including works by H. G. Wells and Aldous Huxley. One can swim confidently as far along as the fifties Beat generation when the same cast – Ginsberg, Burroughs, Neal Cassady, Gregory Corso, Herbert Huncke – were endlessly eulogised and recycled, barely disguised, in each other's work. But if I were to start speculating that a contemporary novel was essentially autobiographical or that it contained a screamingly obvious portrait of so-and-so, well, the lawyers could start unscrewing their Mont Blancs.

We may be less prudish now but threatened litigation can still cause an entire print-run to be destroyed. Similarities between Q. C. Savory and J. B. Priestley meant that Graham Greene's *Stamboul Train* was withdrawn for reprinting. Sometimes an author reveals sources as did Iain Sinclair when he cited legendary demon booksellers Martin Stone and drif field as inspiring characters in *White Chapell, Scarlet Tracings*. More common is the coyness displayed by Robyn Sisman – at Oxford with Bill Clinton – whose new novel *Special Relationship* describes an Oxford affair with someone who later runs for President. Horror writer Poppy Z. Brite's new novel *Exquisite Corpse* with characters based on Jeffrey Dahmer and Dennis Nilsen was initially rejected by both her English and American publishers – presumably not so much through fear of litigation as that readers might lose their lunch.

However, the fictional practice of imaginative disguise coupled with the 1952 Defamation Act under which publishers must establish that the words were not defamatory, or that no reference to the plaintiff was intended and no circumstances were known by which he or she might be thought to be referred to, tend to render suits impotent. Fiction is notoriously slippery territory. Sue Townsend cannot have known that an Adrian Mole lectured at a North London polytechnic. In 1971 Stephen Vizinczey sued a

German magazine which identified him with the hero of his *In Praise of Older Women* and was awarded derisory damages of one halfpenny – without costs. But authors and publishers remain cautious, although Evelyn Waugh maintained that no original, however obvious, would take offence if they were portrayed as attractive to women. Isherwood, however, always used to obtain written permission from his originals.

During her lifetime Sylvia Plath published *The Bell Jar* – a highly autobiographical account of her first nervous breakdown – under a pseudonym. Wisely, because the originals of her fictional protagonists were appalled. Even her mother, the redoubtable Aurelia Plath, wrote: 'As this books stands by itself it represents the basest ingratitude.' One Jane Anderson who had recognised herself as a lesbian mental patient in the novel sued for six million dollars (settled out of court) when the book was filmed. More recently, playwright John Guare, inspired by a New York conman who pretended to be Sidney Poitier's son, wrote the play *Six Degrees of Separation*. The astute young crook took him to court only to have the case thrown out.

It is near impossible to determine the truth quotient of writing which wavers between autobiographical and biographical reference and that which is purely fictional. Very often the damage is less legal than personal. Hugh Walpole's final years were destroyed by Somerset Maugham's portrayal of him as Alroy Kear in *Cakes and Ale*. Julian Barnes has reportedly terminated relations with Amis, although whether he objects to the depiction of Gwyn Barry in *The Information*, is defending his wife, ex-Amis agent Pat Kavanagh, or has other reasons is unknown.

So writers lie – or keep very quiet – about their real-life originals. Dickens, Tolstoy, Maugham, Meredith, Wells and Waugh were all economical with the truth at the time. Contemporary novels abound with real protagonists: the works of Dominick Dunne, Jacqueline Susann and Jackie Collins somehow spring to mind. Jeffrey Archer says: 'I fear all the people in *Not a Penny More, Not a Penny Less* are still very much alive (crooks included)' and then shuts up. The real identities of Cliff Lewis in Osborne's *Look Back in Anger* and Artemisa and Helena in Gore Vidal's *Two Sisters* are well known . . . and so on. Martin Amis has apparently claimed that only minor writers use real people for major characters – presumably discounting Proust, Tolstoy and Dickens, let alone his novelist contemporaries.

Twice this century there has been an uproar over the publication of a novel in which the characters were recognisable. The first was in 1926 when Hemingway's barely fictionalised account of his American friends in Paris, *The Sun Also Rises*, was published. 'For those who know the stamping ground of the American expatriates in Paris', wrote a contemporary journalist, 'it will become speedily patent that practically all of these characters are based on real people.' Publisher Harold Loeb, fictionalised as Robert Cohn – the book 'hit like an upper cut', he said – suffered from the anti-Semitism and distortion of the characterisation. The others, including Lady Duff Twysden as the louche Lady Brett Ashley, generally seemed rather flattered and started trying to live up to their newly glamorous reputations.

The other case was very much grimmer. Truman Capote had failed to write his Proustian opus about 'the very grand and the very rich in a wine and roses stratosphere'. Such fragments as existed of *Answered Prayers* appeared in *Esquire* in 1975–76 and stirred a hurricane of horror in the *haut monde*. The society poodle had turned and rent them. Capote's mind, by now on the endangered species list from drink and drugs, promiscuously mingled fact, fiction and gossip. A few characters were barely disguised – Tennessee Williams appears as Mr Wallace, living at the Plaza Hotel, the room littered with turds from his English bulldog. Wallace rents the narrator from a male escort service; ' "How about it?' he said . . . Roll over and spread those cheeks." ' The narrator explains that he pitches but doesn't catch. ' "Oohh" (says Wallace), his way-down-yonder voice mushy as sweet-potato pie, "I don't want to cornhole you, ole buddy. I just want to put out my cigar." ' Many other characters, including Colette, the Kennedys and Gloria Vanderbilt lack even the flimsy protection of a pseudonym. The composer Ned Rorem, named, is described as 'an intolerable combination of brimstone behaviour and self-righteous piety . . . his skull was criminally contoured, flat-backed, like Dillinger's; and his face, smooth, sweet as cake batter, was a bad blend of the weak and the willful.' Capote also raked over in salacious detail an old society murder case, hushed up after a wife shot her husband. The widowed murderess received an early copy of *Esquire* and killed herself. Throughout *Answered Prayers* Capote mocks and traduces those who had been his closest friends. 'They're too dumb,' he said. 'They won't know who they are.' They did and so did the rest of the world. Capote's expulsion from the Olympus of society blighted the rest of his life.

There are many weird tales to be found amongst those who inspired fictional characters. Jean Rhys provides the only fictional portrait of composer Philip Heseltine, aka Peter Warlock, in 'Till September, Petronella'. Rhys' affair with Ford Madox Ford provoked the two couples involved to three novels and a memoir, including Rhys' classic *Quartet*. The awful Harald Petersen in Mary MCarthy's *The Group* is based on her first husband Harold Johnsrud. Djuna Barnes' Dr Matthew O'Connor was Dan Mahoney, an alcoholic, transvestite abortionist. The Great Beast Aleister Crowley, drinker of cat's blood and practitioner of sex 'magick', appears as Oliver Haddo in Maugham's *The Magician* and Dr Trelawny in Anthony Powell's *A Dance to the Music of Time*, a lengthy work which shows clearly how thin is the veil between autobiography and fiction. World-class paranoid Wyndham Lewis constantly struck at enemies and publishers in his novels. Huxley, Lawrence and Waugh all regularly regurgitated their contemporaries.

But of all the muses, the most fascinating are those who, although not known as public figures, were personalities so enthralling, destructive and seductive that they feature regularly in the fiction of their day. One such was the epicene, venomous old Etonian, Brian Howard, the model for Anthony Blanche in Waugh's *Brideshead Revisited* and Ambrose Silk in *Put Out More Flags*. He also appears in Wyndham Lewis' *The Roaring Queen* and was satirised by Cyril Connolly. Waugh describes Blanche's adolescence: 'Criss-cross about the world he travelled, waxing in wickedness like a Hogarthian page boy . . . he dined with Proust and Gide and was on closer terms with Cocteau and Diaghilev; Firbank sent him novels with fervent inscriptions; he had aroused three irreconcilable feuds in Capri; he had practised black art in Cefalu; he had been cured of drug-taking in California and of an Oedipus Complex in Vienna.' Hyperbolic . . . comical – but you get the general idea.

But king – or queen – of the muses must be Denham Fouts.

Immortalised as Paul in Isherwood's *Down There on a Visit*, he also appears in Capote and Gore Vidal's work and in countless memoirs. A Florida angel with body odour so divine that people swiped his hankies, he was a myth known as 'Best Kept Boy in the World'. Bisexual courtesan to the rich, he had a scorpion tattooed in his groin, a huge dog called Trotsky and was known to shoot flaming arrows down the Bois de Boulogne. His innocent, schoolboy looks – 'as though youth were a chemical solution in which Fouts was permanently incarcerated' – masked moral corruption. Isherwood writes: 'His handsome profile was bitterly sharp, like a knife edge . . . And goodness, underneath the looks and the charm and the drawl, how sour he was.' His cynicism ran unimaginably deep; 'He thought that the world was made up of whores,' said a friend. Beguiling and deadly, he became a junkie and died on the lavatory in Rome.

This century has seen gradual but profound changes in fiction. The day of the highly imaginative, action or adventure story, thriller and horror combined, written by talented authors seems largely to have gone. Conan Doyle, Rider Haggard, Nathaniel Hawthorne, Henry James, Rudyard Kipling, Robert Louis Stevenson, all wrote work that would now be viewed in some sort of genre capacity - sci-fi, thriller, fantasy. Genre is what most people read. From modernism onwards fiction diverged. What is known as literary fiction developed, which very few people read. Literary fiction seems to have evolved entwined like ivy in tandem with literary criticism, so that it is no longer possible to tell which one is the parasite. Literary fiction tends very often towards the self-referential, the paradoxical and the autobiographical. Informed by the tenets of theory it plays with narrative and narrator, with life and fiction. There is a sense that the unrestrained play of imagination and the telling of stories is somewhat vulgar. Literary fiction has become more akin to poetry, as if only the most devout aesthetic studies and the most rigorous self-knowledge will lead to philosophical truths and ideas. This is supposed to compensate for lack of money. Feminism too produced a surfeit of confessional literature, lightly tethered to polemic. Much of the brat pack, slaves of Manhattan-type fiction published in the eighties gave the impression of being highly autobiographical. Recently I met a novelist highly regarded on the West Coast, part of the recent

Los Angeles–San Francisco artistic renaissance. I discovered that her fiction was almost exclusively autobiographical. I mentioned that I'd always kept a diary and she urged me to change names and publish immediately. 'You've done all the work,' she said, sounding faintly resentful. It had not occurred to me. Perhaps, archaically, I thought that fiction needed some shred of inagination.

It is often hard now to avoid the impression that mind-wrenching imaginary invention belongs to William Gibson, Harlan Ellison, Philip K. Dick – genre – and that literary fiction has become psychotherapy, necessarily autobiographical. The large-scale, furiously imaginative writers still exist – Pynchon certainly, William T. Vollman, T. Coraghessan Boyle, John Irving – but they often, particularly Boyle and Irving, seem somehow in danger of losing their literary respectability, of being too enjoyable, sleeping with too many readers as it were; their texts no longer serious literary spinsters but comfortable whores.

Genre writing naturally contains some excellent authors more than capable – in this context – of all the authorial tricks of source, pseudonym and comment. Fantasy writer Elizabeth Hand produces a devastating critique of Andy Warhol's Factory and its suicidal allure within the context of a fairy tale *The Erl King*. This novella describes Warhol and his acolytes – faintly disguised – as having sold their souls for fame: – 'It was a standard contract – souls, sanity, first-born children . . . How else would they have ever got where they did? Superstars! Rich and famous! And for what reason? None of them has any talent – none of them – but they ended up on TV and in *Vogue* . . .'

Meanwhile much literary fiction continues withdrawn and inward-looking. Ironically, the pace of public life and the huge pressure to achieve – something, anything – contributes further to escalating autobiographical tendencies in fiction. Fame is short and life long and the simplest way for the young author to grab attention is – if English – to write a sensitive *roman-à-clef* about being an Oxbridge junkie or, if American, a sensitive account of adolescence as a deprived small-town lesbian. Anything will do – your sexual fantasies, your breakdown, your stint as a chef or merchant banker. Furthermore, in Britain there seems to be something akin to a positive fear of the imagination at present. Fiction which strays outside the narrowly personal will inevitably encounter the grim social and political realities, the demons, of a country in the grip of self-loathing, lost between past and future in a post-imperial identity crisis.

Contemporary confusion between fact and fiction is further fed by a media so consistently ravenous for material that its profiling of writers leads the public to confuse them with their art. (Scott Fitzgerald, Hemingway and Truman Capote are earlier examples of authors who came to believe their own publicity and allowed it to further muddy art that was deeply psychologically autobiographical in any case.) Secondly, readers and critics of serious fiction are now sophisticated to the point of prurience; crudely psychoanalytically aware, they read looking for the goods on an author.

Fiction is not an account of life but a view of life. The material drawn upon, although it represents spiritual and psychological autobiography, is re-ordered so that it becomes more emotionally and artistically authentic than the original experience. There seems no doubt that both *The Information* and *High Fidelity* are novels in that they correspond to this definition. Amis' contention that he is both Tull and Barry – the two protagonists – seems more reasonable than any alternative. Real-life originals may provide details and sparks of character but once marinated in the authorial blender they become homunculi, property of the author which is why different fictional representations of the same person tell us more about the author than about the original muse. The most frequent response to Hornby's *High Fidelity* is 'Oh God, I know people just like that!' which suggests that his characters are truly archetypes, culled from various sources and brilliantly reconstituted so that they evoke facets of many, many different friends and relationships.

When William Burroughs said 'Every word I write is autobiography. Every word I write is fiction', he captured the perennially elusive quality of the debate. The issue remains, remains, like all the best novels, ultimately enigmatic.

Fictional portraits

Lady Ottoline Morrell
Aristocratic eccentric draped in theatrical costume. Friend and patron to Bloomsbury Group. Portrayed as:

Mrs Aldwinkle in *Those Barren Leaves* (1925) by Aldous Huxley;
Lady Caroline Bury in *It's a Battlefield* (1934) by Graham Greene;
Lady Virginia Caraway in *The Aesthetes* (1927) by J.W. Turner;
Lady Septuagesima Goodley in *Triple Fugue* (1924) by Osbert Sitwell;
Hermione Roddice in *Women in Love* (1920) by D. H. Lawrence;
Priscilla Wimbus in *Crome Yellow* (1921) by Aldous Huxley;
Part model for Clarissa Dalloway in *The Voyage Out* (1915) and *Mrs Dalloway* (1925) by Virginia Woolf.

Lord Beaverbrook
Eccentric, maverick newspaper proprietor of the twenties.
Lord Copper in *Scoop* (1930) by Evelyn Waugh;
Lord Raingo in *Lord Raingo* (1926) by Arnold Bennett;
Lord Ottercove in *My Sinful Earth* (1928) and *Doom* (1929) by William Gerhardie;
Lord Mondmark, in *Vile Bodies* by Evelyn Waugh;
Lord Westerleigh in *The Return of William Shakespeare* (1929) by Hugh Kingsmill;
Sir Bussy Woodcock in *The Autocracy of Mr Parham* (1930) by H.G. Wells.

Dora Carrington
Artist. In love with homosexual author Lytton Strachey, she committed suicide after his death.
Mary Bracegirdle in *Crome Yellow* (1921) by Aldous Huxley;
Betty Bligh in *The Apes of God* (1930) by Wyndham Lewis;
Minette in *Women in Love* by D. H. Lawrence (1920);
Greta Morrison in *Mendel* (1916) by Gilbert Canaan.

William Burroughs
Spectral presence. Author of *The Naked Lunch*.
Frank Carmody in *The Subterraneans* (1958) by Jack Kerouac;
Bull Hubbard in *Desolation Angels* (1966) by Jack Kerouac;
Wilson Holmes in *Vanity Of Duluoz* (1968) by Jack Kerouac;
Old Bull Lee in *On the Road* (1958) by Jack Kerouac;
With wife Joan Vollmer as Will and Mary Dennison in *The Town and the City* (1950) by Jack Kerouac.

Herbert Huncke
Beatnik, junkie, raconteur.
Elmo Hassel in *On the Road* (1957) by Jack Kerouac;
Junkey in *The Town and the City* (1950);
Huck in *Visions of Cody* (1960) and *Book of Dreams* (1961) by
Jack Kerouac;
Herman in *Junky* (1953) by William Burroughs;
Ancke in *Go* (1952) by John Clellon Holmes.

Novels

Autobiographical and semi-autobiographical:
Nightwood by Djuna Barnes
Maiden Voyage by Denton Welch
The Bell Jar by Sylvia Plath
Voyage In The Dark by Jean Rhys
Tender is The Night by F. Scott Fitzgerald
Post Office by Charles Bukowski
Cain's Book by Alex Trocchi
Diary of a Drug Fiend by Aleister Crowley
He Died with his Eyes Open by Derek Raymond
Queer by William Burroughs
Postcards from the Edge by Carrie Fisher
The Painted Bird by Jerzy Koszcinski

Top novelist held in kiddy porn drugs case!!

The Guardian, 12 April 1995

*This is really the only kind of non-fiction I enjoy writing –
general, non-academic articles about books and literary history with
room for all the anecdotes and quotations that I like best. And this is
exactly what editors like to cut most – general literary chat. They can't
see the point. They don't think it is relevant. I suppose that is precisely
the attraction for me – that it has no point, apart from amusing other
book-lovers.*

*In this essay I muse on the unstoppable rise of the biography, a
phenomenon that made literary editors rather fretful. It made everyone
else in publishing happy though.*

The most priapic and prurient allegations against writers, artists
and musicians continue to pour off the presses and find a ready
market: Eric Gill practised serial incest, James Joyce was a
coprophile, Daphne du Maurier a lesbian, Charles Dickens an
adulterer, John Lennon a murderer. The general attitude amongst
publishers seems to be 'Dead at last? Let the wild rumpus begin!'
This gives the unfortunate impression of the deceased artist as
carrion beneath a squabbling cloud of vultures pulling out long,
juicy titbits and clutching cheques in their scaly, scrabbling claws.
Meanwhile the biographers and critics fuss and fret amongst
themselves, denouncing each other, scrutinising the publisher's
advances, mounting self-serving defences and condemning those
who have gone too far. Such debates can be summarised as: *They*
are bottom-feeding, muck-raking tabloid scum, *you* are an
American academic with the soul of a laundry list, *I* am a noble
seeker after truth, dedicated to illuminating the author and the
text.

That the results of the biography boom should be huge, som-
bre-looking tomes hung about with all the accoutrements of the
academy always seems curious. One would expect sleazy paperbacks, their covers strewn with wanton women, wild-eyed men
and hypodermic syringes, bannered like B-movie posters:
'Lesbian Tease! Poison Penpal!' (Jane Austen); 'Recovered
Memories! Child Sex Ring!' (Virginia Woolf) or 'Classic Bitch!'
(Charlotte Brontë).

It was not always thus. Although some of the very earliest biographies, such as Suetonius' *Lives of the Caesars* (1 AD), were
bawdy, gossipy and wholly unreliable, such tendencies soon gave
way to idealised accounts of lives of the saints. It was not until the
seventeenth and eighteenth centuries that biography in England
truly became animated and individual, culminating in Boswell's
classic, influential *Life of Johnson* (1791). However, most of our
own century has been spent in forms of increasingly extreme
revolt against the biographical forms that dominated the mid-
Victorian period. These were often characterised by an extreme

prudishness and gentility that completely eclipsed the subject. Sex, scandal or anything disgreeable that might affect the surviving family of the subject was excised. Besides love, there was a great deal else that could not speak its name.

During this century there have been two major revolutions in the art of biography. The Bloomsbury Group, dedicated to scatological conversations and rejection of Victorian respectability, influenced Lytton Strachey, who re-assessed the form in a number of biographies, notably *Eminent Victorians* (1918). He restored to biography much of the selective subjectivity, impressionism, emotional impact and critical acuity that it had surrendered.

During the post-war period, as western society gradually relaxed its strictures on sexuality and deviation, Michael Holroyd published his great biographies of Lytton Strachey and Augustus John. In these, published between 1967 and 1975, he quietly but firmly asserted the right of the biographer to pursue the subject into the most intimate highways and byways of their life. Recently Holroyd released a sort of director's cut of his Lytton Strachey biography suggesting that, as time passes and more people die, it is not inappropriate to reveal yet more details in the interests of illumination and authenticity.

However, all this was accomplished with dignity and discretion. And indeed the majority of famous contemporary biographers – Richard Ellman, Richard Holmes, Norman Sherry, Christopher Sykes, Claire Tomalin – write with equal sensitivity. Their revelations lie deep within somewhat academic, thoroughly well-researched books.

The changes that have arisen lie in different areas. Biography, particularly literary biography, has become an overcrowded field – largely because many readers who used to enjoy classic, serious novels have switched to biography where, in contrast to modern fiction, they can be assured of an instantly comprehensible plotline (birth to death) and the presence of characters with incontestably human attributes. On such a crowded stage, publishers, publicists and critics of such biographies have been forced to emphasise the most salacious details of the book in their charge in order to ensure attention. Secondly, some biographers, for similar reasons, select subjects whose traumas and quirks fall into the narrow field of the predictably sensational – sexual deviation or perversion, mental instability, addictions of various sorts. Thus it is that a minor, albeit good writer like Patrick Hamilton has had three recent biographies. He was – oo-er – an alcoholic. By comparison a great writer like Flannery O'Connor who can only chalk up disease, dying young and the undeniable eccentricity of making dresses for her chickens languishes uncanonised. No sex? No drugs? No advance. Thirdly, if one can't find a suitably fallible genius, there is always the option of writing about those who didn't do much themselves except hang about being bohemian or self-sacrificing as partners to the great – Caitlin Thomas and Chester Kallman, the unruly, promiscuous partners of Dylan T. and W. H. Auden respectively, or Nora Barnacle, a muse long-suffering enough to finally marry Joyce.

Finally, there are those biographers who have a personal agenda and no more. The saga of Rudyard Kipling's biographers runs the gamut from Victorian reticence to postmodern open season. Early biographers such as Charles Carrington found Kipling's daughter, Elsie Bambridge, and other sources reluctant to see either Kipling or the embattled Carrie Kipling presented in even a mildly critical light. After a long, literary decline, Kipling is once more in favour but largely with biographers who wish to accentuate his mental morbidity and sadism or those like Martin Seymour-Smith who are determined to prove him homosexual.

The underlying issue in modern biography is not so much whether exhaustive domestic detail affects our response to a writer's work – it doesn't – but as to whether more controversial revelations do. Does knowledge of Joyce's emotional rapport with toilet paper sully the final, great cadences of *The Dead*, for example? Yes, in the same sense as a name or a song once associated with someone disagreeable is forever slightly tainted. Yet, at the same time, no, in that there is a choice for the reader. One can surrender oneself to what the writer intended, *or* one can regard art as a psychoanalytic key to the author. The fact that these alternative readings are not indivisible creates the tension of the contemporary biographical debate.

Overall these issues these testify to a culture that has become incredibly impoverished in terms of what is deemed interesting, that is, sufficiently shocking to make an impact. Laundry lists make careers but shocking – for a while – makes reputations, and money. Anything more subtle than sexual peculiarity, madness preferably with violence and self-destruction on the side, and addiction is deemed of minimal interest to the public. It has been left to fiction to explore all the real deceits, ambiguities and stratagems of the biographical progress – those areas which are really fascinating in accepting that a biography says as much about the author as about the subject. Carol Shield's *Mary Swann*, Alison Lurie's *The Truth About Lorin Jones* explore such areas as do three great short stories: Alice Munro's 'Dulse' has a woman fling the fact of Willa Cather's lesbianism at an elderly, respectable lover of Cather's work. 'Meneseteung' explores further the relationship between biography and fiction. Perthaps most pertinent of all is Jane Gardam's 'The Sidmouth Letters' in which an academic descendant of Jane Austen's refuses to read and then destroys a packet of her famous relative's love letters in order to keep them out of the hands of a mendacious, academic American careerist. Would such highmindedness force us all to regress to Victorian hypocrisy? It seems that we cannot both have our urinal cake and eat it too. In ignorance there lies both bliss and maddened frustration.

Short story selection

The Good Book Guide.

Although this is, sadly, not a feature on the short story (I would have gone on FOREVER) I have left it in as being what I think is an informed and irresistible guide to books of short stories by someone who has certainly read all the ones listed here and (for my sins) many, many more.

A powerful short story has an almost visceral impact. Reading a selection of first-class stories is akin to watching rockets go off, one after another and seeing them explode in an iridescent shower. One can only gasp and wonder. There have been many theorists of the short story who have pointed out how closely stories resemble poetry with their compression of experience and how important it is for each story to have a central unifying principle and how every word must contribute to the underlying meaning. All this theory does little to describe the experience of reading a brilliant story for the first time. In my selection I have tried to concentrate on writers whose work will evoke that authentic sense of shock and awe; the magical qualities of the firework display.

Flannery O'Connor *The Complete Stories* (Faber)
Flannery O'Connor may well come to be seen as the finest short storywriter of this century although she published relatively little and died young. Her stories were written between 1947 and 1964 and largely set in her home territory, the rural deep south of America. Many of her best stories are centred on an overwhelming moment of spiritual illumination in the lives of ordinary people. Her other great theme is an exploration of the clash between opposing temperaments: again and again the educated 'artistic' sensibility with its attendant affectations is contrasted with the limited, simple world of the small-town philistine. The grotesque, disturbing quality of her work can be seen in her great 'A Good Man is Hard to Find'.

Truman Capote *A Tree of Night and Other Stories* (Penguin)
The landscape of the American South with its lonely bayous and trailing Spanish moss seems to have influenced a number of writers – O'Connor, William Faulkner, Tennessee Williams – whose work is often described as Southern Gothic. This was Capote's background too and these early stories have a lush, haunting quality very typical of the region. Spooky children and dreamy adolescents drift like wraiths across the pages.

Jane Gardam *Showing the Flag* (Abacus)
Nothing could be further from these stories of American outsiders than the work of Jane Gardam. All her collections have been masterly but her recent *Showing the Flag* is one of the most poignant. Kensington shabby gentility, Wimbledon widows who've outlived the days of the Raj, order, discipline, the stiff-upper lip; Gardam understands the English middle classes all too well. She deftly exposes their rites and rituals, always discerning beneath the well-mannered surface the tremulous, pitiful hopes and fears of

those who have been trained to control themselves and others at all times.

Jean Rhys *Tigers are Better Looking* (Penguin)
Jean Rhys was a writer well-qualified to expose the cold heart of England. Born in Dominica, she came to England with high hopes only to be repelled by greed, snobbery and hypocrisy. She battled these qualities throughout her long, peripatetic life and her best stories are small miracles of formal perfection. This collection is deservedly a classic. 'Till September, Petronella' is as perfect a description of between the wars English bohemianism as one could hope for.

Matthew J. Bruccol *ed. The Short Stories of F. Scott Fitzgerald* (Scribners)
Scott Fitzgerald has been badly served in regard to his stories and this stunning collection is long overdue. Too often Fitzgerald's stories have been dismissed as slick commercial exercises. In fact, with the exception of *The Great Gatsby*, they tend to be less flawed than his novels. Fitzgerald was incapable of writing badly and there is not a single poor story in this book. One can trace his obsession with the Southern belle – based on his wife, Zelda – from the early 'The Ice Palace' to the poignant 'The Last of the Belles'. These are unforgettable, heartbreaking tales. As the golden years of the twenties waned Fitzgerald's stories turn to marital breakup and disillusion and the note of nostalgia and regret for the passing of youth that characterises his work becomes ever more bittersweet.

Ellen Gilchrist *The Blue-Eyed Buddhist and Other Stories* (Faber)
Ellen Gilchrist is yet another writer from the American South, this time contemporary. Her stories often deal with the stresses and dilemmas of modern life – illegitimacy, divorce, drugs – but her prose has a mannerly Southern grace. Her writing is flexible and spirited. This collection contains her best-known stories and is an excellent introduction to her work and her own favourite fictional characters.

Alice Munro *The Beggar-Maid: Stories of Flo and Rose* (Penguin)
Many of today's best short story writers are women. Amongst them Alice Munro has a deservedly high reputation. For those unfamiliar

with her work this very early book introduces all her major themes. A series of vignettes traces the life of a Canadian woman from dirt-poor rural childhood through a failed marriage and into middle age. Munro's concern is human nature and all its poor deceits and stratagems. Perceptive and humane, her insight is formidable.

Donald Barthelme *Forty Stories* (Futura)

The books selected so far contain traditional stories in the sense that plot and characterisation operate according to familiar fictional models. It would be a pity to omit a more experimental work. Barthelme's stories challenge easy assumptions about literature. They raise questions about our interaction with the text and about the ways in which writers use fact, history, fantasy and autobiography in constructing a story. Their surreal quality echoes the strange juxtapositions of modern life and its arbitrary sensory overload. Try 'Porcupines at the University', the story of how forty-five thousand porcupines try to enrol in higher education. This is a gentle welcome to the postmodern world.

James Kelman *The Burn* (Secker & Warburg)

James Kelman is undoubtedly one of Britain's best younger writers and *The Burn* is his third book of stories. As a Scottish writer he has succeeded in restoring regional literature to the mainstream. His strong, rigorous prose and angry, frustrated characters are forcible reminders of the disenfranchised voices of Britain.

Alberto Manguel, ed. *Black Water: The Anthology of Fantastic Literature* and *White Fire: Further Fantastic Literature* (both Picador)

It has been impossible to include the many excellent short story writers working all over the world. However, these two vast anthologies provide a wonderful introduction to hundreds of writers of short fiction. Manguel is an exceptionally sensitive editor and his selection ranges from Gabriel García Márquez, Kenzaburo Oe and Isabel Allende to A. S. Byatt and Julian Barnes. These anthologies are the sort of rare books that transport one back to the dream days of reading, 'the land of lost content', when the everyday world would fade into a myriad of magical imaginary universes.

Home is where the art is

Commissioned by *The Guardian* in 1994; unpublished

*Obviously there are writers in Britain whose work I really do
like. One of these is Stewart Home who, a bit like a magic lantern
show, manages to be Dadaist, Marxist, Postmodernistically Nihilist
and Ironic without Overt Situationism, Bardic and probably Ludic
(whatever that means), all at once. His public life is like that of those
conceptual artists who live in a glass bowl for ages and everyone
watches and marvels.*

*This is more an attempt to analyse, even psycho-analyse, the urges
that power Homes' art rather than a critique of the work itself. It was
a kamikaze mission.*

*I did this interview ages ago so it will be somewhat out of date as
Home is constantly invading new territory. It'll be Poland next.*

Americans often ask about the literary underground in Britain;
'Well, there's Stewart Home' is one, desperate response. People
say a literary underground here is impossible now in that publishers will print anything, however extreme. Characteristically, Home
spits at this notion: 'It's complete crap. There *are* tame, pretend-
underground writers and the literary establishment likes feeling it
can take anything on board. Garbage!'

Home has indeed driven quite a few interested publishers
away, shaking, sweating and once, throwing up. So, what is he
really up to? Home is a conceptual artist, installationist, theorist,
novelist and all-round cultural terrorist. Intellectually he is cunning, elliptical and contradictory. Always two steps ahead of his
questioners, he can parry and undercut any analysis of his work
with his lethal combination of post-everything irony and his
extensive, eccentric range of references. Age cannot wither nor
custom stale his infinite variety act. In person he is crop-haired
and cherubic with an impeccable, self-conscious, late-skinhead
dress sense. He is also affable, amusing, kind and well-balanced,

far from the Rottweiler-on-amphetamine act that characterises his performances and prose. He has received a considerable amount of press coverage, almost all of which ends in questions about his intentions. Is he a post-punk prankster, a Loki of the metaphor or a serious subversive? No-one can decide. He has been called 'an egomaniac on a world historical scale', a charge he accepts delightedly. Yet this 'egomaniac' went on Art Strike from 1989 to 1992, producing nothing and refusing an invitation to appear on the Jonathan Ross Show. Iain Sinclair voices the suspicion 'that Home's major project is Stewart Home' but Home spent years with the self-referential, avant-garde Neoist group inciting artists – including himself – to work under multiple pseudonyms, usually either 'Karen Eliot' and 'Monty Cantsin' and thus attack the hegemony of originality. He is the promotion-hungry 'instinctive auto-didact' who sent friends to interviews in his stead. He rants against the cultural elite yet is as likely to appear in a Chelsea drawing room as at home on the hapless no-go Teviot Estate. Always these imponderables, these dichotomies. Everywhere there are incongruities, inconsistencies, curve balls, mazes. Where does one start to deconstruct a slippery, rabid deconstructionist, bent on out-manoeuvering critics? Someone who oscillates wildly between sincerity, put-ons and nihilism, someone who is always prepared to grin and say agreeably 'My main interest was in fucking things up.'

There are some certainties in his turning world. Home was born near Merton and his artistic roots lie deep in Britain – but in the sense of a William Blake rather than a patriot/nationalist. Despite his skinhead persona he always stresses that his own long-ago skinhead group was racially mixed. In particular London is his *locus sigilli*, his inspiration. 'My books have one character which is London,' he says. 'London is a melting pot and that's what makes it so exciting.' His opposition to 'high culture' is unwavering. 'The well of British culture has been poisoned. There's this safe, boring, dull, stupid cultural establishment – they either wait till things are burnt out and then they take them on board or else they're so desperate for an infusion of new blood they'll vampirise a bit.' Ignoring his own considerable cultural knowledge and speaking of his raging, splatter/sex novels he continues: 'The iconography of the skinhead – you can't get anything that's more opposed to high culture. Attempts have been made to assimilate punk in the high art discourse but it's quite problematic for skinhead youth culture to be taken up by high fashion. That's why it's such a good icon for me because, rather than saying I want to unite high and popular culture, I'd rather smash the two pieces together, like splitting the atom, and create something from the resulting wreckage.'

Home's career as a 'cultural worker' began in several 'crap' skinhead/punk bands. Then, announcing. 'I have no artistic talent whatsoever', he became an artist, or rather demonstrated that anybody could parlay themselves into the galleries. He started with the usual junk, industrial music, tape loops, gobs of recited Situationism, people as artworks, then graduated to installations, arranging random objects in a bizarre way. Familiar? In 1988 he published *The Assault on Culture (Utopian Currents from Lettrisme to Class War)* and lo he was in *The Observer* and *Artscribe*, television beckoning. Simultaneously he had been publishing his anarcho-artzine *Smile*, arranging yearly 'Festivals of Plagiarism' and bonding with the Neoists, a post-post-parody of avant-garde movements. Iain Sinclair has astutely pointed out that the avant-garde serpent has eaten its tail – 'The documentation of non-activity is necessarily extensive.' Or alternatively, nothing happens until it is documented and preferably, publicised.

Although Home continues the production of contentious mail-art and participates in quasi-sardonic conceptualism – like the recent attempt to levitate Brighton Pavilion – he has essentially detonated his art career. And who is to say that a deconstruction of the puerile fiscal values and vanities of the gallery system is not as valid a work of conceptual art as any other? Had he capered on, he could have made money, being of an original and enterprising bent, but there is a bedrock streak of intransigent morality in Home. He'll play but he won't profit if it means compromise.

Home then rediscovered a book by seventies youth pulp fiction author Richard Allen (*Skinhead, Knuckle Girls* etc and recalling his teenage enthusiasm for pulp, embarked on a series of novels and stories between 1989 and 1994 (minus Art Strike). *Pure Mania, Defiant Pose, No Pity* and his latest *Red London* all mix the repetitive smash 'n' grab, sex 'n' violence of pulp fiction with input from his own considerably more intellectual armoury in an attempt to achieve the nuclear fission, the cultural wreckage of head-on collision. These cult novels, despite their faithful army of fans, have been seriously misread and dismissed as shock–horror, anarcho-punk rantings. More soberly, they are largely sophisticated satires supported by their infrastructure of loathing for the cultural establishment. Home mocks the Pro-Situationists with whom he's been associated – 'a moronic sect' – and also his own pulp writer heroes; not only are Home's characters polymorphously perverse, in the most obscene and confrontational ways, but his 'skinheads' are often – apart from their ultra-violence and presumably their Herculean, indiscriminate sex lives – miniature versions of Home himself, vegan, eco-friendly, non-racist, nonsexist and given to obscure political and theoretical musings. Home admits that initally he was 'obsessed with intertextuality' but that, unlike Kathy Acker, he wanted to 'pull different things in very carefully so that you couldn't see the joins'. He says now 'The early work was more accessible because I was mixing up "high culture" such as bog-standard bits of poststructuralism with the pulp novels, so I just had two basic sources. As I developed I put in more and more from other sources. You can see with *Red London* I've wanted to bring in the horror and fantasy pulp fiction.'

Although all the novels are similar, a whirlpool of references with Home himself at the epicentre, *Red London* is by far the best and most elaborate. He decodes and mocks the tradition of a book about a forbidden book. He satirises the obscure Scientology offshoot cult, The Process, and another cult, The Temple Of Psychick Youth. He establishes London more vividly as a site of resonant energies, reflecting his current interest in the London Psychogeographical Society. His imagery – skinheads, riots, sex – are more lucidly metaphorical and iconic. He pursues his interest in conspiracy, Freemasonry and mind-control further towards the occult whilst making very clear in conversation: 'I've no interest in Wicca or Paganism or Satanism. I've no particular literal belief – their significance arises from the fact people *believe* in *them*. I see the occult as a system of symbol manipulation but so is literature and culture.' He adds perceptively: 'The avant-garde fakes its modernity. The occult fakes its antiquity. You can't have one without the other. They are flip-sides of the same coin.'

The more closely one studies Home's fiction, the more dense

and complex it becomes. Admired by writers as various as Dennis Cooper and Iain Sinclair, initially it seems to walk a tightrope – pulp parody spliced with arcane references and a contradictory approach to high art. Home slags off cerebral culture whilst himself being articulate and widely read. He maintains: 'The contradictions in my work are deliberate – they generate the tension.' However, in *Red London* the philosophy, politics and pulp fiction unite to clarify his ongoing rampant attack on the 'introspection' and 'politeness' of 'dead' British culture.

But what drives this courteous, non-smoker, non-drinker ever onwards in his furious, frenzied creation of labyrinthine texts? Home cannot be analysed emotionally – he affects disbelief in the unconscious – but the tools of psychoanalysis can be applied to his intellect. Most men are very simplistic in their male pride whereas Home's is extremely subtle. His will to power is extraordinarily strong – a psychopathology of the intellect that suggest Genghis Khan-like qualities. But as a pleasant individual Home lacks the desire to slaughter thousands. These punishing urges turn inwards and focus upon the only possible subject, Home himself, and by extension his imagination and the mischief it can create. This will to dominate is orchestrated by a mind all too sensitive to postmodern intellectual fragmentation. Thus, intellectually, he has become highly skilled at parlaying his stock of enthusiasms into an 'art' that repeatedly asserts his own self, power, autonomy and individuality in the face of a world where such concepts have been degenerating. His union of acceptable contemporary positions – anti-sexism and anti-racism – plus his appropriation of a quasi-skinhead persona and uniform, with all the buttoned-down, orderly intellectual retention it represents for him, means that he can keep his psyche united, and rise above vexed issues. The accusations of egomania are correct – as he'd be the first to agree – and Sinclair said of Home's pulp hero Richard Allen 'his underlying programme [is] fascistic' but the maintenance of Home's ego in a fractured world is an artistic and intellectual necessity for him. The fascist persona is the flip-side of the libertarian coin. You can't have one without the other. Additionally, to survive socially and artistically while retaining power and control, he ironically undercuts the pedagogic and dictatorial qualities that drive him while irony enables him to mock his own will to power. Artists are egotists. Many people – including Home – are ambitious but his unceasing force and energy suggest violently obsessive drives.

Philadelphia's libertarian, Ira Einhorn, described himself as 'a planetary enzyme'. (He was later discovered to be a murderer.) Home is *sui generis* but his self description suggests, more lyrically, the same thing. He wants, he says, to be 'a numinous object'. No wonder the Victoria and Albert collects his work.

The most radical gesture

New Statesman

> *While we are on the subject it never does any harm to run over Situationism once again.*

The Situationist International in a Postmodern Age by Sadie Plant (Routledge)

When one sees old photographs of the Lettrists and Situationists with their spiky hair, spotted scarves and dark glasses, strolling along the boulevards, it is hard to believe that these are pictures taken during the fifties and not the Punk rock era. It would seem that some people are, to use Jean Baudrillard's phase, just 'born modern'.

The Situationist International, founded in Paris in 1957, was an astonishingly prescient revolutionary political movement. The key texts they produced were Guy Debord's *The Society of the Spectacle* and Raoul Vaneigem's lively and extravagant *The Revolution of Everyday Life*. Drawing on Marxism, Surrealism and Dada, they were the first to define the 'spectacle' of post-war consumer society. In the post-war boom, commodity relations spread to all aspects of life so that people became alienated not only from labour but from their own selves, their own desires and pleasures. These, assisted by an increasingly dominant media, were repackaged and sold back to them as part of the 'leisure' industry. We ceased to participate in our own lives and became spectators, totally passive consumers. We live still in 'the society of the spectacle' only now it is a spectacle grown monstrous and bloated, a blizzard of communications, information-technology, and virtual realities which together create what Baudrillard has termed the 'hyper-real'. The illusions and simulations that surround us (Euro Disney, Heritage Britain, film), all dominated by economic relations, constitute this hyper-real. 'He not busy being born is busy buying,' said the Angry Brigade and they were right.

The Situationists believed that the spectacle could be deconstructed or 'detourned' by playful acts of subversion which would restore 'authenticity' and 'meaning' to people's lives. They refused on moral and artistic grounds to cooperate with the demands of commodity exchange and envisaged a world free of mediation and hierarchy. The Situationists had an enormous influence on the events of May '68, and although they personally opposed terrorism, continued to influence a wide variety of revolutionary responses to capitalist homogeneity: the Angry Brigade, the Red Brigades and 'Metropolitan Indians' in Italy, King Mob, Punk and Class War. Sadie Plant's book is particularly useful in bringing all *pro situ* activities up to date: she includes the 'Art Strike' in operation at present, the Post-Serious International, the recent Festivals of Plagiarism and the story of Tony Wilson's Manchester nightclub 'The Hacienda'.

Situationist theory obviously rested on a utopian vision of 'authenticity' beyond the spectacle, and ironically it was Situationist sympathisers like Jean-François Lyotard and Baudrillard who did the most to freeze any revolutionary potential. As the philosophers got to work on the failure of May '68, poststructuralist and postmodern theory evolved and rendered meaningless the Situationist distinction between the 'real' and the spectacle. Post-structuralism argues that there is no 'reality' beyond that which appears in discourse and that the 'individuality' that the Situationists sought to reclaim is a fraudulent subjectivity which is itself only produced by a network of discourses. Baudrillard came to believe that political intervention in the spectacle was impossible; the hyper-real was seamless, there could be no 'real' behind the spectacle as both reality and meaning have slipped away forever in the deluge of signs, simulations, images and representations. 'The desire for revolution is also the desire for an autonomy, singularity and pure intensity which renders it impossible,' he decided.

And so it ends in a standoff between those with a nostalgia for the lost days of truth, meaning and liberation and those subsumed by language games and the glittering seductions of a tireless, ever-accelerating spectacle.

An analysis of Situationist theory is long overdue and Sadie Plant's thorough, rigorous account finally gives the credit deserved for the Situationists' enormous contribution to post-war theory and revolutionary politics. They had immense insight and a real capacity to rouse people to action from within the numbing blandishments of the hyper-real. 'How can you live in a world in which you pay for everything?' asked Vaneigem.

Three UK Writers: Jonathan Meades, Will Self and Michael Bracewell

Here are some novels that I did like. I have been allowed to keep in three reviews of contemporary English writers. The reasons for my liking Pompey *are thoroughly – extensively even – detailed in the review, I think.*

Pompey by Jonathan Meades
(Jonathan Cape)
The Independent on Sunday, 25 April 1993

If Jonathan Meades' first collection of stories, *Filthy English*, dipped a prissy toe into the churning sewer that underruns English gentility then his new novel flings itself orgiastically into the mephitic effluence. Meades is obsessed with 'the terminal Englishness whose highest virtues are found in unrocked boats, in what's beneath the carpet'. He lifts the carpet, rocks the boat and produces panoramic seasickness, a vast involuntary technicolor yawn of fictive projectile vomiting.

Pompey has a story and is well and tightly structured although a synopsis makes it sound like magic realism written on some brain-shredding drug. In the wretched aftermath of World War

Two Guy Vallender, a fireworks manufacturer from Plymouth (Pompey), fathers four children by different mothers. Locally there is Poor Eddie, his legitimate child, a gimpy geek with a talent for healing and 'Mad Bantu', son of a black prostitute, hopelessly damaged *in utero* by abortifacients. There is also Bonnie, the golden girl, born of Guy's quick coition with his sister-in-law, who matures into a rabid junkie and star of dog fuck porn films. The final child is Jean-Marie, a faggy little leather boy conceived in the black-market blackout of post-war Belgium. The narrator is one 'Jonathan Meades' (oh no, just when we thought it was safe to go back into the library), cousin to Bonnie and Poor Eddie, who reveals the ways in which these four, ignorant of one another's genesis, poisonously and tragically interweave their lives.

Meades sees conventional mores as a thin tissue of skin stretched over a societal obscenity of suppurating intestinal tubing. His first target is physicality and decay and he pursues crotch-rot and colostomy bags, teratology and scatology with all the zeal of a brain-damaged bloodhound. Sex is 'rubbing offal' and vomit 'tummy mud' in this cruel bottom feeder of a book. In addition he relentlessly pumps up the volume on other contemporary taboos, torturing them into hyper-real bizarrerie. There is a cannibalistic pygmy hunt in the Belgian Congo which allows a foul sex and blood-borne lentivirus, HoTLoVe, to make its fatal leap on to humankind worldwide. There is a parodic evangelistic sect, headed by Ray Butt, ex-racist and sexist comic and now a raving legless torso, to whose church Poor Eddie lends his weird skills. And of course there is Pompey itself, little England vexing us to nightmare, a rocking cradle of disease, sleaze, venality and lubricity; the final dystopia for human wreckage.

Meades' vocabulary is insane: 'sporades', 'glabella', 'spelaean' (three times) 'ichthyomorphic'. A field is 'bounded by wire on whose barbs flocculated spermatozoa of paste-white wool'. Waves are 'tympanic majuscules'. And yet in this context such overheated over-writing is strangely effective, sledgehammering the reader into submission. This florid word-salad contains more than a pinch of Amis *fils*: Fate is 'a bad barman', asthma 'bad music' and 'bad meat' is everywhere. Meades flagellates language and blackmails it into comedy in an attempt to represent human experience and all its boiling tributaries of thought, image and memory with a visceral immediacy.

An army of greasers and grotesques stream through the book, shaking it all about in a hokey-cokey from Hell and here the fireworks analogy is particularly apt (and frequently employed.) The novel has all the vigour and animation, all the bravado and brio of a fireworks display but after the vulgar beauty has faded, we face a grey ash of burn-out, a misanthropic dawn which prompts the old question: 'Was it worth it after all?' Is there enough compassion and humanism here to balance the detailed pyrotechnical linguistics of loathing?

Throughout this faecal gumbo there are flickers of pathos and mourning like methane gas blowing over sewage. Without such glimmers of pity the book would be no more than a savage, splenetic rant against some mindless deity of cancer and despair, the god that says 'The joke's on you.' The English novel desperately needs its senses violently deranged and this pus-encrusted piledriver of a novel, cousin to Scarfe and Steadman, might just provide a kickstart.

My Idea of Fun by Will Self
(Bloomsbury)
New Statesman, 10 October 1993

I always find Will Self to be fantastically inventive and funny. His The Rock of Crack as Big as the Ritz *deserves classic status.*

'Typhoid and swans,' said Dr Hannibal Lecter, 'Typhoid and swans – they both come from the same place.' Lecter was shaking his fist at the infinite, denying a benevolent deity. Similarly, Will Self's new novel rejects the simplicity of binary oppositions and refuses to acknowledge the easy certainties of good and evil.

My Idea of Fun tells the story of Ian Wharton, a boy with the gift of eidesis, or photographic memory. As a child he comes under the corrupt influence of a man he learns to call The Fat Controller. This is a person who seems to be immortal, who has powers 'awesome, inhuman . . . even godlike'. An Edwardian vocabulary, and in certain guises, his loud, 'fairground barker' personality are strongly reminiscent of the portrait of Aleister

Crowley in Anthony Powell's memoirs. The Fat Controller instructs Ian in the basics of magical lore – the tarot, astrology, alchemy, the Kabbalah – whilst simultaneously deriding them as 'a pathetic attempt to use proto-scientific methods to . . . apprehend the transcendent'. Ian's eidetic abilities become so pronounced that he is able to enter into his own mind pictures, to experience directly the bizarreries of time-travel, telekinesis, teleportation. Ian is convinced that these powers will cease if he has a sexual relationship – The Fat Controller tells him his penis will drop off if he inserts it into a woman. Depressed, the grown Ian consults a psychiatrist, Dr Gyggle, who initally convinces him that it has all been an elaborate hysteria. Ultimately, however, Gyggle and The Fat Controller are seen to be in league and Ian's soul is lost to the most ferocious Dionysian abandon.

This is a novel that can be approached in a number of ways. The least charitable reading would be that Self is no more than an upmarket Clive Barker who has stippled his Faustian horror show with intellectual credibility – the shades of Proust, Nietzsche, Bulgakov, Milton, Jonathan Carroll and other restless ghosts twist uneasily in the slipstream of his turbo-charged imagination. However, this seems unlikely. The book is not prurient or voyeuristic. Its shocks are relatively mild and its structure too complex, detailed and convoluted to exist merely in the service of some meaningless personal surrealism. It seems more probable that Self is attempting something quite different, that he is trying to deal with the neglected subject of the precise relationship between the writer and the world; that the book offers a rubric of creativity and that Ian is a blank screen upon which is projected a creative psychodrama. Ian's visual memory can be seen as a cathexis around which the creative process is necessarily structured and it is significant that the first image he conjures up in detail is that of a philosopher. The Fat Controller calls himself a 'mage' and this seems to refer to image or imagination as much as magic. Ian's corruption into murder and other fine arts is part of the necessary insertion into the cesspool of the creative imagination, suggestive of the utter amorality of the artistic process. Ian suffers both from being cut off from the world and, simultaneously, from being drenched with its imagery. Such feelings, so common to creative neurasthenics, are exacerbated by the contemporary barrage of media and product overload. What Ian calls 'my calculus of personal ritual' is a way of subduing and gaining power over an inchoate and threatening world. Ian's very impotence, his fear of genitality, is indicative of the way in which novelists are doomed to fuck only the products of their own imagination. Seen like this, the book becomes a fiendishly clever allegory, a parable for the rites of the imagination. The Fat Controller is, in one incarnation, 'The Brahmin of the Banal', giving him a tortuous identity. He is the evil of banality and the artist who accepts his most poisonous remedies and follows the darkest road of the imagination loses forever the balm of the ordinary, the everyday. He is the animus at the centre of all things, both the mechanistic and the numinous, a metaphor for the shamanistic animism that can creatively illuminate a prosaic reality. Ian of course is not an artist. He is, interestingly, a marketing manager, but his existence, from the sublime to the ridiculous, is as a palimpsest for the authorial imagination. This interpretation becomes harder to sustain midway through the novel when the tone changes and The Fat Controller comes to represent some all-encompassing conspiracy theory of the unconscious. For Ian's wife, Jane, The Fat Controller is explicitly identified with 'the Dionysian other, Pan, Priapus', that impulse both sensual and demonic contained in Self's sinister interpretation of the word 'fun'.

The Fat Controller's vocabulary parallels Self's own use of language. It is described as 'an explosion, a lexical flash, irradiating everything in the immediate area with toxic prolixity'. His 'word-seam' is 'the very fount of knowledge itself, a mulchy conceptual bed' and this *correspondence* between author and mage suggests the inevitable spider web of links between creativity and language.

The entire book suggests a sensibility which, appalled by life, frustrated and embarrassed by its limitations, has taken refuge in extreme knowingness, a profound, ironic rejection of the simple, the obvious and the innocent in favour of a spinning, unemotional complexity where ideas perform the functions of character. As such, the book is a dark labyrinth, elusive and allusive, codified by some punk Prospero into an endlessly beguiling theorem of the unconscious. Whether we actually apprehend 'the bare-faced cheek of the infinite' or merely the mordant chic of an esoteric jester – *The Tempest* in a teacup – we certainly find ourselves cheek-to-cheek with some very rough magic.

The Conclave by Michael Bracewell
(Secker & Warburg)
New Statesman, 2 October 1992

I have always liked Bracewell's work too and feel that it tends to get a much more superficial reading than it deserves.

Michael Bracewell is ill-served by the jacket copy to this novel which promises that he charts the 1980s through an examination of 'offices, commuting, shopping, art, house prices, cars . . . kitchens, postmodernism, debt' and so on. This sounds as though Stephen Bayley might have written the book and does nothing whatsoever to suggest that this is, by any standards, a superb piece of work.

The Conclave looks at the thirty years of Martin Knight's life from 1960 to 1990. It is the story of the insidious seduction of a soul by a number of complex forces so deeply intertwined with recent developments in British life and worldwide technocratic consumerism that it is wholly impossible to make any simplistic judgements about them. Martin Knight is an apparently ordinary young man from the outer suburbs of London. He is by temperament an aesthete. Despite his interest in the arts, Martin's mind is 'not right for such Subjects'. He becomes a succesful systems analyst during the eighties until the Crash and ensuing recession wash him up on the bleak tides of debt and unemployment. Martin is someone who, as he develops, comes to 'mistake luxury for beauty and extravagance for art'. The novel explores, with great subtlety and delicacy, whether such a development or seduction is inevitable in a world where art and commerce are indivisible. There is here a faint echo of the way in which Charles Ryder is aesthetically ravished in Waugh's *Brideshead Revisited* and his artistic integrity compromised by the 'charm' and beauty of privileged English life. 'Charm is the great English blight,' Ryder is warned. 'It kills love; it kills art.' Martin, like Ryder, becomes a snob in that peculiarly English way wherein aesthetic good taste cannot be disentangled from class and finance. Neither Waugh nor Bracewell allow their heroes to be unambiguously destroyed by such ambitions. At the end of *The Conclave*, Martin, facing ruin, still clings to his discerning dreams; his plans for his unborn child include expensive sequinned hats as well as 'galleries and concerts'. The intricacies of money, taste and education close around him like a fist and Bracewell is far too astute to dismiss Martin as an empty consumerist shell or unequivocally mock his aspirations.

Bracewell has little interest in the predictable outrages of bohemia. His choice of characters is fuelled by humility and compassion and the elegance of his writing never obscures its clarity and unforced simplicity. He is adept at revealing the pretensions, fears and yearnings of unexceptional people, an artistic credo tellingly outlined in his previous novel *Divine Concepts of Physical Beauty*. Herein, writing of his hero he says: 'but beneath this bland surface there must exist something more . . . where the banal translates, if not into poetry, then prose gone mad, and the standard takes on a unique meaning.' This recalls Virginia Woolf writing on the creation of character: 'What one must do to bring her to life was to think poetically and prosaically at one and the same moment . . . that she is Mrs Martin, aged thirty-six, dressed in blue, wearing a black hat and brown shoes; but [also] – that she is a vessel in which all sorts of spirits and forces are coursing and flashing perpetually.' Bracewell has that bisexuality of the imagination so essential to the creative writer and both his male and female characters receive the penetrating attention that Woolf describes.

Bracewell's evocation of the 'self-assured, cosmetic renaissance' of Britain in the 1980s is unsurpassed. At the same time he is able to bring an intense, heightened lyricism to his writing on the beauty of London and the south. This combination suggests that Bracewell has brought back to the English novel something of inestimable importance: a mind wholly in tune with the times. For years the documentation of middle-class lives has been carried out by novelists who have been, to a large extent, out of touch with the huge changes in consciousness that have characterised recent decades. Bracewell has a deep understanding of the ways in which popular culture and stylistic cool inform contemporary lives and he is able to integrate this into his dissection of a certain stratum of modern society.

Additionally, although Bracewell is fully aware of postmodern literary concerns, unlike many other writers he feels no need to hang out the flags of such knowledge and wildly signal his technical sophistication and literary self-consciousness. Rather it is as if, having considered the aims and limitations of the novel, he is now able to write in a way that never sacrifices readability and never equates intelligence with literary conjuring tricks. In this way he re-animates the English novel in a manner which is quietly revolutionary. It is immensely encouraging to think that the sun may be setting on all the recent trouble, strife and anxiety that has beset the novel and that writers like Bracewell here, or perhaps Donna Tartt in America, feel able to restore to the form those elements of entertainment, illumination, unabashed intellect and perception that once rendered the serious novel so irresistible.

In *Brightness Falls* Jay McInerney similarly tried to encapsulate the 1980s and failed because of his inability to integrate classic realism with the multi-textured chaos of commodity fetishism and consumer homogeneity. Bracewell has surefootedly negotiated such pitfalls and written a novel of significant profundity. I read it at one sitting – 4 am, 5 am – and felt that Bracewell's future was wholly assured.

Censorship

New Statesman

And there is, inevitably – censorship

Literary censorship is always a hot and sexy topic. Every *pisseur de copie* in town moans about Brett Easton Ellis' *American Psycho* and Helen Zahavi's *Dirty Weekend*: Ellis' book is the most repulsive ever written. Zahavi is pathologically disturbed. We must reassess the censorship laws. Where have these people *been*? It is disingenuous – if not plain ignorant – to assume that the two novels in question are isolated cases deserving of such histrionic attention. Books of pornographic violence are nothing new. Additionally, it is risible to advocate increased censorship in a country with an infallible tendency to prosecute works of undeniable literary merit.

In the last two years alone new translations of De Sade's *120 Days of Sodom*, Apollinaire's *Les Onze Milles Verges* (Peter Owen) and Octave Mirbeau's *The Torture Garden* (Dedalus) have burst upon an apathetic world. If age did not confer a patina of respectability they could be considered a mite trashy. In any case it is misleading to suggest that we have untrammelled literary freedom in this country. There is constant, quiet, relentless editorial trimming (the Apollinaire text was cut), authors are forced to drop explicit scenes and English editions of American books are regularly shorn of their more provocative passages; Richard Price's *The Wanderers* arrived in the UK *sans* its famous 'venereal sandwich' sequence.

In addition, although the glory days of struggle between police, customs and the radical bookshops are largely over, this is because such shops nowadays operate a careful buying policy which eschews controversial material. Forbidden Planet say they act 'with extreme caution'. The Book Inn was recently prosecuted – and acquitted – for stocking Re/Search's *Tribal Primitives*, an investigation of piercing and tattooing accompanied by bland photographs of wrinkly genitalia sporting small brass rods. Savoy Books in Manchester are awaiting a decision on David Britton's *Lord Horror*, a book which outrages current taboos on racism.

Ellis' *American Psycho* outrages no contemporary taboos. Psychotic killers are everywhere. Hubert Selby's *The Room* and *The Demon* were early explorations of affectless violence. There was no twitching over Thomas Harris' creation of Hannibal 'The Cannibal' Lecter, a glamorous psychiatrist with unorthodox ideas of treatment until *The Silence of the Lambs* was released as a film. Derek Raymond was involved in the Strange Case of the Vomiting Editor over his *I was Dora Suarez*, one of a series of terrifying and moving books about the putrescent underbelly of contemporary London. Patricia Daniels Cornwell took a job in a morgue to get at 'the smell of death' for her serial killer novels. Peter Blauner's *Slow Motion Riot*, an account of crack gang killers, ignites the New York bonfire where Tom Wolfe failed.

The fact that some of these books, unlike Ellis', are genre novels (and thus widely read) attests to a touching faith in the power of serious literature. Downmarket, snuff-porn fans can glut themselves endlessly on splatter-punk and true crime; even a relatively serious psychiatric survey like Ronald Markham's *Alone with the Devil* can have you up-chucking into a dump-bin before you've even left the shop.

Helen Zahavi's book, with its endorsements from Julie Burchill and Andrea Dworkin, has been carefully targeted to play into the hands of feminists, who provide the only new twists in the censorship debate. The pro-censorship faction tends to be shamelessly inconsistent and self-serving. Imprecations against male writers and attempts to ban pornography other than lesbian erotica describe a war-torn territory where being right-on is an increasingly precarious highwire act. Fortunately there are women novelists who are able to broaden the debate beyond any simplistic feminist imperatives. Jane Delynn's book *Don Juan in the Village* is a stunningly cold, predatory account of lesbian conquest, wherein the narrator, as in Zahavi's book, usurps the role unthinkingly ascribed to men. Mary Gaitskill's extraordinary *Two Girls, Fat and Thin*, describes the acne and the ecstasy of American adolescence in an attempt to explore the roots of cruelty, dominance and submission in our society. She sets the debate around an Ayn Rand figure and the book adds considerable weight to the current discussion of sadomasochistic practices in feminist circles.

Constant readers familiar with, say, the Amok Press publications which give space to paedophiles, neo-Nazis, satanists and practising werewolves are honestly baffled by the controversy over Ellis and Zahavi. Equally so is anyone familiar with the more serious list of writers in Serpent's Tail's books of 'transgressive texts', 'High Risk' (Burroughs, Cookie Mueller, Karen Finley, John Preston, Pat Califia). Do the literati only read Anita Brookner – or Martin Amis if they feel daring? The inescapable, if somewhat dull conclusion is of course that *American Psycho* and *Dirty Weekend* have been adroitly marketed to attract media froth. However, attempts to up the ante on censorship in a country which already lags behind America and Europe are mischievous and irresponsible. But, as Jean Rhys wrote of the English: 'They ask to be shocked and they long to be shocked, but when you shock them – how shocked they are!'

Dora Carrington – in fact and film

Tom Cruise as the vampire Lestat, Cliff Richards as Heathcliff, Demi Moore or Sharon Stone as anything, Emma Thompson as Dora Carrington – groan, misery, nausea. Why do such cast lists – particularly when it's a film involving a familiar story or biographical portraits – depress us so? Because those being cast are stars and with stars you almost always know what you are going to get. Stars do not act. They present their – highly bankable – personae to the audience. As Paul Newman has said: 'Filmgoers . . . get something they hook on to and they like and *that's* what they want to see.'

William Goldman in his memoirs of working as a Hollywood screenwriter, *Adventures in the Screen Trade*, puts the matter succinctly: 'Stars will not play weak and they won't play blemished . . . Sure, Brando and Pacino will portray Mafia chieftains in *The Godfather*. But those are cute Mafia chieftains . . . they're only trying to hold the family business together. Try asking a major star to play a real Mafia head, a man who makes his living off whores and child pornography, heroin and blood; sorry folks, those parts go to the character actors and the has-beens. Or actors on the come who haven't yet achieved star status . . . Of course De Niro will play a psychopath in *Taxi Driver*. Some psychopath – he risks his life trying to save the virtue of your everyday, ordinary-looking child prostitute, Jodie Foster.' Goldman concludes that writing such 'Perfect Parts for Perfect People' ultimately destroys the soul. Publishing in 1983 (and predating Dennis Hopper who does perfect star villains), Goldman predicted that this trend led inexorably to the production of what he called 'comic book' movies – 'The comic book movie doesn't have a great deal to do with life as it exists, as we know it to be. Rather it deals with life as we would prefer it to be.'

Carrington is certainly a comic book movie. Although British screen stars tend to emphasise acting ability rather than starriness, this means that they are even more likely than their American counterparts to try and play against type. All stars do this occasionally (Stallone, Schwarzenegger, Streisand). The movies often fail but the actors are assured that they can still act and are still wonderful. They call such roles 'a challenge'.

Emma Thompson is indubitably a star; her name appears above the title. She has had a somewhat rougher time than many stars. Her skills and charisma are shot through, notoriously, with aspects that instead of making people melt, make them puke. She emanates an awful wholesomeness. She evokes the Chalet School. Thus, since becoming a star – and in that a star's own personality is part of their persona – she has had to work hard to highlight her most tolerable aspects. These include an evident decency and high-minded intelligence, qualities best served by films like *Howard's End* or *The Remains of the Day*.

Thompson was drawn to the role of Dora Carrington, in part because Carrington lacked such characteristics. Thompson describes the role as 'a journey into the unknown' and yes, she says 'One of the reasons it was such a challenge was that she's really not like me at all – her nature is totally different to mine.' This is obvious to anyone with any knowledge of Carrington. What actors find challenging makes a sane person weep. Why distort yourself to impersonate – badly – someone with whom you have nothing whatsoever in common?

Dora Carrington has been fascinating only to a small minority and even then, usually as an adjunct to Lytton Strachey and the rest of the Bloomsbury group. She escaped a stifling, suburban background to become a gifted art student at the Slade. Very distinctive with hair shorn into a golden bell-like bob, she was irresistible to arty men. Uneducated, possibly dyslexic, she was a strange, vacillating and secretive character who tormented her lovers and doubted her own talents. She fell violently in love with homosexual author Lytton Strachey. They lived together, had separate love affairs and she killed herself when he died in 1932.

The easiest thing to do with complex characters is to simplify them. Carrington was portrayed in fiction by Wyndham Lewis, D.H. Lawrence and Aldous Huxley all of whom concentrated on her sexuality. Similarly, the film *Carrington* focuses on one aspect of her life, her relationship with Strachey. This is presented as a great and unusual love affair, which it was. However, it leaves Thompson with only one thing to do throughout. She yearns. At the difficult moments when she is not yearning, she substitutes wry intelligence for emotion. Carrington's complexities escape her.

Jonathan Pryce does a good impression of the eccentric Strachey; a bearded, stick insect with gold pince-nez. (Naturally, Strachey's less appealing characteristics are excised.) In fact the costumes and accessories are so lovingly re-created that they could perform on their own, forget the actors.

Although often subtle – the script ignores Carrington's bisexuality, presumably to avoid the reasoning that only lesbianism explains her attraction to an old queen like Strachey – the film remains unbearable to anyone seriously acquainted with Carrington's life. And this is not solely a result of Thompson's emotional unsuitability for the role.

The only living member of the Bloomsbury group, Frances Partridge (who married Carrington's ex-husband Ralph Partridge) has already objected to the film. Films have a poor history of portraying artists – remember the ones about Jack Kerouac, William Burroughs, Henry Miller and Anaïs Nin, Dorothy Parker? *Carrington* too flattens the characters into caricature. Also it panders to the worst excesses of the Forster-Merchant-Ivory 'Endless Summer' films. *Carrington* is insanely bosky. Greensward, woods, downs; rustic boskiness rules. Blond men splash naked in forest pools; meals are al fresco. Why do the British think that bohemianism means eating outdoors? There are scenes of Carrington sailing the ocean deep with her final lover, 'Beakus' Penrose, that would shame the naffest advertisements. Carrington was a highly original person. Couldn't this have been expressed less conventionally than in this pre-WW2 summer idyll, coinage so debased (other than to Americans) that it has become an insult?

Additionally, Carrington's sex life is puzzlingly fudged. She is seen bored out of her mind during coitus with Gertler and Partridge. Suddenly, inexplicably, she is sexually rampant with Brenan and Penrose when she is on record as saying that Partridge was 'a most excellent bedfellow'. We also lose most of her personality – her whimsy, her humour, her ailurophilia, her cartoons and correspondence.

The Blooomsbury group prided itself on its lack of inhibition in sexual matters. This was often expressed – sometimes rather self-consciously – in talking dirty. Scatology was certainly a great bond between Strachey and Carrington to the point where Carrington's friend, Dorothy Brett, commented: 'She pandered to his sex obscenities, I saw her . . .' Nothing of this is seen in the film which takes the odd view that people – in private – do not mingle intellectual discussion with extreme crudity. ('They won't play blemished.') There is an attempt to grapple with the shades of procurement that hung over the relationship – when the hetero-sexual Partridge, the object of Strachey's affections, threatened to leave and destroy the ménage Carrington married him. But the film lacks any understanding of the fag hag psyche and what actu-ally comprises such a near-platonic relationship between man and woman. All is idealised, rare-ified and very respectable. Inevitably too, the film has all the pedestrian features of a period-piece – this means, in effect, leaving things out. There is no mention of the servant problem which ruled all middle-class lives; no indication of the appalling difficulties of rural life at the time – the freezing cold, the lack of amenities, the endless work. No sign either of the persistent obsession with health in pre-antibiotic days.

None of that. Just endless vignettes of self-absorption and sun-dappled days. The occasional thunderstorm and an incredibly pushy musical score tell us when to emote.

Traditionally, British films have retained some autonomy. But in the race for finance and the battle for commercial appeal, British subtlety and imagination are lost. Goldman's dire predic-tion was absolutely correct. The public want stupid. They want easily identifiable cartoon characters. They want comic book. They want stars, not human beings.

Films have vanished into a black hole between star egotism and public idiocy. Yet considering the appalling ignorance of Bloomsbury shown by the comments after a press screening – comments by people who are presumably paid for their cultural knowledge – it is not altogether the public's fault. Lions led by donkeys?

Christopher Wood: An English Painter
by Richard Ingleby

(Allison & Busby)

There used to be a scent available called 'Le Train Bleu'. Haunting, evocative, it was named for the twenties express which rushed hedonists from Paris to the Côte d'Azur. Jean Cocteau evoked those epicurean days in his ballet for Diaghilev, 'Le Train Bleu', with decor by Picasso and costumes by Coco Chanel. English artist Christopher Wood could be said to have riddden this blue train of cosmopolitan artistry and excess to the very end of the line.

Until now, 'Kit' Wood has been one of the most enigmatic figures in British painting. Born into a comfortable middle-class family near Liverpool in 1901, his brief painting career spanned the twenties and he committed suicide in 1930.

In Elaine Dundy's memorable phrase, Wood seems to have been one of 'Destiny's Tots' – those with a precocious sense of their own worth and talents and a desperaté need to have them prematurely acknowledged. For a provincial boy, Wood was extraordinarily responsive to the ways in which social and artistic success are intertwined. He knew intuitively that he must exploit his youth and good looks for all they were worth. 'The great thing is to do it young,' he writes to his mother. And again, later: 'The Duchess of Sutherland . . . Lady Cunard . . . Don't you think it is important to cultivate these people at my present stage?'

The London post-war art scene was eerily stagnant and Wood accepted an invitation to Paris from a wealthy homosexual, Alphonse Kahn. Soon, he was living with Antonio de Gandarillas, a witty, bisexual 'social ornament' who supported Wood for many years. At this point it becomes hard to repress memories of Cedric Hampton, the queeny dilettante in Nancy Mitford's *Love In A Cold Climate* who was so delightfully vague about his funds in Paris – 'It is not necessary to have jobs in Paris, one's friends are so very very kind . . .' Mitford knew Wood – and presumably many others like him. Anthony Powell has commented acidly on Wood's 'convenient bisexuality' and Ingleby himself writes: 'With his good looks and uncomplicated nature he was welcomed with open arms into a world dominated by men who were wealthy, influential and homosexual.'

Ingleby's book depends on the vast cache of letters Wood wrote to his mother and which he regarded as a sort of journal. In retrospect they do not serve him well. He frequently sounds colder, more arrogant and self-serving than the sweet, naive youth so lovingly recalled by friends. But then, who would wish to be judged by letters to a parent, in which one has to exaggerate success and suppress sin? One line from Ingleby can be applied to them all: 'He did not mention the drugs, the drink, or his friend . . .'

Gandarillas was a known drug-user (reputed to have snorted up the ashes of a friend's wife in the belief they were cocaine) and it seems certain that he introduced Wood to smoking opium. Wood concealed much from his mother but was naturally proud of his intimacy with Cocteau – cemented by a mutual interest in drugs and art – and a social circle comprised of the inevitable luminaries: Diaghilev, Picasso, Christian Berard, Luisa Casati, Tristan Tzara. Sometimes, there is a frustrating sense of secrets, undercurrents and stories untold, as when Wood becomes involved with the gamine Jeanne Bourgoint, the model for Elisabeth in Cocteau's *Les Enfants Terribles*, who killed herself after the novel came out.

Despite dazzling diversions, Wood pursued his artistic career with laudable dedication. Much of his early work is the necessary trawl through Post-Impressionist influences, from which he retained only Picasso and Van Gogh. From 1926 onwards Wood formed his second important alliance, with Ben and Winifred Nicholson, although their Christian Science household, child-centred and vegetarian, contrasts oddly with the *boîtes* of Paris. Wood yearned for an emotional and artistic partnership of his own, such as he idealised in the Nicholsons' marriage, but proved unable to realise this with either of the women he claimed to love, Frosca Munster and Meraud Guinness. (The latter married painter 'Chili' Guevara who was eventually to commit suicide so spectacularly, painting the walls furiously with his slashed wrists, chainsmoking all the while so that a huge mound of cigarette butts was found beside the body.) Ingleby notes of Wood's relationships: 'Deep down Wood was not capable of giving himself to another person . . . his principal motivation was a selfish one.' And despite long periods painting with the Nicholsons, he always returned to Paris and his opium.

Wood's finest paintings were produced in a six-week frenzy shortly before his death, as the colour plates show. These churning seascapes seem, like Wood himself, to combine animation and simplicity with a dark and ominous aspect.

Ingleby attributes his suicide to paranoia brought on by smoking opium dross when he could no longer afford the drug. But dross – the scrapings – is weaker than the original and Wood was an experienced opiomane. Might he not have been tragically aware that youth was fading, that he could not support himself, that the Wall Street Crash had ruined his patrons? He was unable to achieve marriage, or to live without drugs. The faceless figures in Wood's later work may be the self-portraits of someone who no longer knew who he was.

In life Wood's chameleon charisma concealed the commonplace. Ingleby meticulously reveals his importance, not as a personality but as an artist. Wood transfused something of European modernism into a moribund Britain and died just as his work was moving far beyond the early promise of a pretty, talented boy.

Wood threw himself under a train at Salisbury. It was the Atlantic Coast Express; the last blue train to the sea.

Lights Out for the Territory by Iain Sinclair

(Granta Books)
The Independent, 1997

Iain Sinclair's London has slowly mutated into literary territory as instantly recognisable as Graham Greene's 'Greeneland'. Open this book at random and there it is: 'There is a decayed Unitarian chapel at 49, Ball's Pond Road . . .'

All such mythical landscapes are the product of obsesssion and intellectual solipsism, retracing repeatedly the point at which the unseen eyebeam of the author crossed and identified further resonant imagery. Such territory is infinitely refracted and hallucinatory. Thus is Sinclair a bit player in the Cockney clichés of the Kray brothers melodrama or have the twin hounds of Vallance Road been finally brought to heel as permanent exhibits in the major arcana of the Sinclair epic?

It was Sinclair in his awesome 1993 essay for the *LRB*, 'The Look', who was able to divine the entire toppling of an empire from Tony Lambrianou's terrifying description of spotting Ron Kray, the Colonel, *without a tie*. 'This was a signal,' wrote Sinclair, 'a flag of surrender to the inevitable.' The bell was tolling, he concluded, for that precious sixties triad: 'Villainy, business, image'. If Sinclair can read all that into one open-necked shirt, imagine what he can do for the rest of London?

Since the publication of his last novel *Radon Daughters*, Sinclair has been dragged from the half-light of small press obscurity and hailed as one of the few major literary talents of his generation. His long, visionary apprenticeship in the shadows and his manifest intellectual integrity mark him as more than just a standard-bearer for alternative writing and artistic dissidence. Sinclair's view of London may be contagious but it testifies to a personal, idiosyncratic struggle with literary heritage and tradition, during which he has excised sentiment from the Beat sensibility, returned Allen Ginsberg's inspiration to its origins in Blake's London and created a parallel, mythopoeic universe of his own. It is ironic that Sinclair's earlier work – prose poems such as *Bladud*, *Suicide Bridge* and *Lud Heat* (the last being the *in utero* version of Peter Ackroyd's *Hawksmoor*) – was considered too obscure for easy publication while his later novels, far more difficult to negotiate, met with widespread praise. The early combination of documentary/reportage, autobiographical intersections with various texts and psycho-tronic archaeology allowed Sinclair to present clearly his multi-faceted view of time and history. This 'non-fiction' is such a convulsively mythical concoction in itself that the novels could only float further out in a trance state of linguistic hypnotics.

Either way, Sinclair's preoccupations remained insistently

consistent – ur-London, personal psycho-geography, the White-chapel murders; churches, cemeteries, graffiti, texts; chance configurations animated by authorial consciousness which allow an endless present, mingling fact and fiction, to bleed back through the ruins. These issues, plus tales of his all-too-real co-conspirators – deranged book-dealers, maddened poets – seep deliberately into his fictions while his own fictional creations stalk his essays.

As the compass needle shudders seismically when it points true, so these nine prose pieces – in which Sinclair, like Huck Finn, lights out for his Territory – form an animated, powerful psychic distillation of all that is best, most potent and accessible in the energy-field of Sinclair's work. Here is a mind at the height of its powers, someone who can quote Homer or Carl Hiaasen with equal facility, someone who sees the living streets of London as a crucible wherein Bill Sykes and Beckett's Murphy, William Blake, Wren, the Angry Brigade and a sludge of politicians, whirl forever, each illuminating the dreams and depredations of the others.

Of these nine essays, some – including the memorable account of Ronnie Kray's funeral, a guided tour of Rachel Whiteread's 'House' and a dismemberment of P.D. James' Cadaver Club – were originally comissioned as shorter pieces. Others are structured around the lengthy walks Sinclair took with long-suffering photographer Marc Atkins, in which 'drifting purposefully' they stalked, noted and decoded a fusillade of fragments.

Blake, Dickens and T.S. Eliot hover purposefully in the hinterlands. Otherwise, the view is a charged, post-William Burroughs smog of trace memories, synchronicity, psychic voodoo, urban paranoia, filmic metaphor, and morphic resonance. Simultaneously, Sinclair weaves a homespun, neo-occult web from the vast hoard that includes Dr Dee, Rosicrucians, Grail legends, the Invisible College, ley-lines, maps and conspiracies – an entire car boot sale of the alchemical and hermetic. These forces together, whether focused on pit bulldogs or Jeffrey Archer's residence at Alembic House, spark a spidery trail of correspondences threaded through history, and create a dense, invisible collage of essences and entities.

There is nothing faddishly New Age about this. Conversely, the mood is mordant, dark, ironic with the occult providing structures which – as with the tarot in *The Waste Land* – stretch like Jacob's ladder, 'pitched between Heaven and Charing Cross'.

Sinclair aligns himself with an angelic crew of London low-life chroniclers, including Alexander Baron, Gerald Kersh, Bernard Kops, Patrick Hamilton and Arthur Machen. He provides notable pen portraits of those he has known personally, including avant-bard art guerrilla Stewart Home, the late, much lamented Robin Cook, and poet Aidan Dunn. Other 'deregulated shamans, equal opportunity visionaries' also appear, including Brian Catling, Gavin Jones and cineaste Chris Petit.

The cornerstones of Sinclair's gnomic vision appear to be, firstly his self-definition as 'someone congenitally incapable of accepting the notion of "accident"'. Secondly, he is 'cursed with the obsession . . . books as icons, books as a form of race memory' and lastly he believes that the city can divulge an encoded, sub-terranean text. His foundation stone itself is text; signs, however they appear, can be read.

So, as when Sinclair describes the pit bulldog thrown from a balcony and granted a 'brief, privileged view of Hackney', so his readers too are launched and granted their brief, privileged view of a festering London, its pathologies lanced and exposed by a fine intelligence.

5

Short monographs

Whenever Sherlock Holmes came upon a subject that intrigued him and that he felt would benefit from thorough analysis and scrutiny – for example, the deductions possible from familiarity with the Fifty-Seven brand of tobacco currently in use – he would murmur to Dr Watson that he had either written, or intended to write 'a short monograph on the subject'.

I have never forgotten this recurring phrase of Sherlock Holmes, as I had an early and intense relationship with the works of Arthur Conan Doyle.

Thus I have always thought of my other prose writings (apart from fiction) as being Short Monographs. These are written primarily for my own amusement and are not really intended for publication. Naturally, they tend to reflect my own obsessions – literature, art, bibliophilia, crime, rock lyrics and the bizarre. Otherwise they serve as an adjunct to my diary in documenting personal experience. I suppose typical subjects would be: the Literary Deconstruction of Criminals' Prose (letters, ransom notes), Marie Laveau and New Orleans, the most important writings of Rudyard Kipling and J. M. Barrie, the rise of artist Austin Osman Spare (deceased), why I hate Woody Allen films, the meaning of Poetic Licence with particular reference to Andrea 'Dachau Brought into the Bedroom' Dworkin and Martin 'Experience' Amis, great popular fiction – *Gone With The Wind*, *The Valley of the Dolls* and *Peyton Place*; the eroticisation of our culture and its ensuing sexlessness, why World Travel is doomed and so on and so forth. Many of these pieces deal with my own library and book collecting (although I have written one about a haunted library in the Caribbean). I've collected one-letter book titles (from Andy Warhol's *A* to Louis Zukofsky's *Z*), novels that deal realistically with death (I found four), novels in which male writers get make-up all wrong (numberless), and self-published books of incredible craziness and obsession – there is one by a guy living in Ireland who became convinced that his near neighbour, a local factory worker, was the Yorkshire Ripper, with the author going to awesome lengths to make his theory fit the known facts.

I never met any bibliophiles (outside my family) before I moved to London and was surprised at how odd they are.

I won't weary the reader with more than two short monographs.

The first, 'Death Takes a Stroll Down Ladbroke Grove' is short and personal. The second – an examination of Thomas Harris' 'Dr Lecter Trilogy' – is longer, and mercifully not personal at all.

Death takes a stroll down Ladbroke Grove

I have seen a number of inexplicable things in my life. It may be an inherited trait, perhaps from Scottish tinker blood; who knows? My grandfather, a lifelong teetotaller, Elder of the Free Presbyterian Church, was a man notable for his extreme rectitude and integrity, yet even he managed to see our local village ghost or spirit – something I never did. She was a harbinger of bad times called the Kyle a' Lochan. She lived on a dead island where nothing grew, in the middle of a black, dead loch. Even the grass around the loch would die as soon as it appeared. The lady herself was only ever seen at dusk on the country road adjoining the loch, which is exactly where my pious grandfather met her. It would have been unthinkable for him to have invented this. Although profoundly shaken, once he got over the shock his primary emotion seemed to be embarrassment. He never forgot the encounter but mentioned it very rarely.

When anything similar happened to me, I quickly learnt to keep quiet about it. It was too easy for people to say I was crazy or over-imaginative, particularly in the light of my psychiatric history. But one, just ONCE, I had a witness, again a Scottish person of considerable integrity.

It happened some years ago, in summer. My friend – journalist and critic Jenny Turner – and I were planning to attend a book launch in the old Michelin Building on the Fulham Road. Jenny came round to our flat to collect me. As it happened I had just that day finished reading the fourth of some recent books about epidemiology, documenting all the recent, post-war viruses – filoviruses like Marburg and Ebola, arenaviruses like Lassa Fever and so on. I don't recall whether I mentioned this reading or not.

Anyway, we left the flat, went downstairs to the main front door and started descending the stone steps to Ladbroke Grove. As we did so I became aware of a tall figure approaching us on the pavement from the left. It was someone dressed in the black robes of a medieval Death figure, so heavily hooded and cowled that there was just a tiny slit for the eyes. It lacked a scythe but was wearing men's shoes. It stopped and stared at me. Jenny saw it too and managed to hail a taxi on the other side of the street. I was somewhat upset but she was able to get me over the road and into the cab. I looked out the back window of the cab and saw that the figure was again proceeding along the pavement, but still staring after me. Jenny said something about care in the community.

Many people have since tried, similarly, to rationalise the incident. It was an Islamic transsexual? (No. Wrong clothes for one thing.) It was someone so late for a dramatic performance that they put their costume on first? (Hardly – why were they going so very slowly if they were late?). I still think that we saw – well, let's call it the coming Plague; the Andromeda Strain virus that may one day pose a threat to human life. Actually, apart from not having a nose cone filled with useless herbs, the figure most resembled one of London's doctors during the Black Death.

Still, it can't have distressed me that much. We went to the launch and Jenny can barely recall the incident now . . .

The rehabilitation of Dr Hannibal Lecter

With reference to the three novels in which he appears – *Red Dragon, The Silence of the Lambs* and *Hannibal*

When the third novel starring Dr Lecter – *Hannibal* – was published in 1999 readers drew much innocent enjoyment from the fact that Thomas Harris had apparently tried to write the book in a manner sufficiently offensive to prevent Jodie Foster and Anthony Hopkins from repeating their roles as Clarice Starling and Hannibal Lecter in any film of the new book.

Harris' attitude was simultaneously admirable and ambiguous. Novelists invariably detest – as they should – any Hollywood adaptation of their work. The two mediums, the novel and the film, are actually incompatible, even with the best of intentions. However, without the quite startling success of the filmed version of Harris' *The Silence of the Lambs*, he would certainly not have commanded such a vast audience of avid fans. He would have remained an extremely competent writer of thrillers and that is genre and consequently of no serious account.

After the huge success of the film *The Silence of the Lambs*, Hannibal Lecter proved to be such a strong and memorable character that he remained imprinted on the consciousness of viewers and Lecter became yet another cultural icon in the colossal lucky bag of trivia that the west dragged along to the end of the twentieth century.

But Thomas Harris was essentially correct in his apparently negative opinion of the film's main characters. Jodie Foster as FBI trainee, Clarice Starling, was actually less infuriating than usual; Starling's character was moulded around the humourless earnestness and self-righteousness that Foster invariably, and naturally, emanates. But Anthony Hopkins as Dr Lecter was another matter entirely, and to my mind woefully miscast. (Welsh actors often seem to incline heavily towards melodrama and the audible slicing of ham.) Harris, like any good thriller writer, is committed to action, via plot, and he very rarely provides more than the briefest of physical descriptions. We only know of Starling's great beauty through a few comments, invariably made by her enemies. (The awful Dr Frederick Chilton, administrator of the Baltimore Hospital for the Criminally Insane where Lecter is kept in a cage calls Starling 'Remote and glorious. A winter sunset of a girl . . .'; the serial killer in *The Silence of the Lambs* (hereafter referred to as *Lambs*) Jame Gumb, after being shot by Starling, dies, his 'ghastly voice' choking out his last words 'How . . . does . . . it . . . feel . . . to be . . . so beautiful?')

In the case of Lecter, however, Harris provides numerous physical descriptions. He is 'imperially slim', small, sleek, dark and lithe, like an otter, or Starling thinks 'a cemetery mink. He lives down in a ribcage in the dry leaves of of the heart.' Lecter's eyes are mentioned repeatedly – 'Lecter's eyes are maroon and they reflect the light in pinpoints of red'; 'Behind his eyes was endless night'; 'The sparks in his eyes flew into his darkness like fireflies down a cave.' His voice is cultured 'with a slight metallic rasp'. He has six fingers on his left hand, the middle one being replicated – 'the rarest form of polydactyly'. In effect, Harris' increasing emphasis upon Lecter's physical appearance, coupled with Lecter's vast, inhuman intelligence and enigmatic personality means that Lecter is slowly transformed into a recognisable archetype – the dark and brooding Romantic Hero, in the Heathcliff mould. To create such a character convincingly is very difficult – the Gothic and Romance genres are awash with failed attempts. Maintaining the psychic tension between malevolence and tenderness towards the designated romantic heroine is notoriously arduous in fiction and it is my contention that Harris did not embark consciously on the task, it evolved.

In brief, then, it is obvious that Anthony Hopkins, whatever his acting ability, did not correspond at all, particularly physically, to the image Harris (or this reader) had of Dr Lecter. Harris did not emphasise Lecter's physical attributes to no purpose – even if it was partly unconscious, the incessant dwelling upon his seductive physical qualities was done for a reason. Hopkins could at least have worn maroon contact lenses – although the director Jonathan Demme and the producers obviously felt that Hopkins was A Great Actor and need not concern himself with physical minutiae. (Laurence Olivier was never too cavalier and self-assured to ignore physical detail.) To anyone who had read *Lambs* properly first, Hopkins was doomed. It was impossible to accept that he and Starling were incipiently physically attracted to each other, although the clues are there quite clearly in the text of *Lambs*.

The intesting question is, of course, to what extent Harris was operating knowingly.

It seems to me that Dr Lecter is an excellent example of something that happens quite frequently in fiction – that is, a character starts to grow and function independently of the author's original intentions. An author's unconscious mind plays a very large part in any fictional prose, and when a character breaks his appointed bonds and starts demanding centre stage, the signals are emanating directly from the artistic unconscious and bypassing the rational mind, until, as it were, the writer learns to ride and guide this runaway steed.

This process is common enough in fiction; an author will frequently remark that a character 'just took over'. However, the fictional development of Dr Lecter seems to be to provide a classic example of this process.

The three novels which feature Dr Lecter are all structured around the idea of change, or tranformation. In *Red Dragon* the serial killer Francis Dolarhyde refers to his killings as 'my Work. My Becoming, my Art . . .' In *Lambs*, killer Jame Gumb (a rough composite of Ted Bundy and Ed Gein) even breeds rare moths. In Dr Lecter's words: 'He wants a vest with tits on it' – in order to assist his transformation from ugly chrysalis into beautiful imago. In *Hannibal*, however, the tranformation is centred on Starling herself, and is in consequence, more subtle. In a sense she deserts law and order, to fraternise, to become one, with the enemy; the villains, murderer and monsters of whom Lecter is one. Or is he – in the metaphysical sense? Harris firmly destroys a fundamental part of Starling's character: her Protestant dualism, her previously infallible sense of right and wrong in the interests of endorsing Lecter's view that reality is infinitely more ambiguous and elusive than it has been in Starling's 'little low-ceiling life'. 'Life's too slippery for books,' says Lecter.

It should be acknowledged that Lecter is a completely ludicrous character. Cannibalism is extremely rare in western society. In the context of murder (say, in the case of Jeffrey Dahmer) it is invariably a sexual paraphilia. No-one kills for the *cuisine*, except Lecter, a famous gourmet. In addition, there has never been a serial killer so cultured, so learned and so successful in the real world. (Gilles de Rais, long ago, is the only possible parallel.) It says much for Harris' skill that we can suspend disbelief sufficiently to accept the total improbability of a Dr Lecter.

In *Red Dragon* Lecter appears in a wholly negative and destructive light. He is in the Maryland asylum throughout, after escaping nine murder charges on the grounds of insanity. Will Graham, a near-psychic agent is hunting Francis Dolarhyde at the behest of Jack Crawford (a man with 'an intelligence as cold as an

X-ray table') from the FBI's Behavioural Sciences at Quantico. Graham agrees that it has proved hard to diagnose Lecter – 'They say he's a sociopath because they don't know what else to call him . . . He has no remorse or guilt at all. And he had the first and worst sign – sadism to animals as a child.' Well, we never hear of that again.

'He's not insensitive,' says Graham who caught Lecter and was viciously wounded by Lecter's linoleum knife in the process. Dolarhyde is an 'Avid Fan' of Dr Lecter. They communicate through coded messages in a tabloid and Lecter provides Dolarhyde with Graham's address. Ultimately Dolarhyde carves up Graham's face, leaving him so scarred that he becomes withdrawn and alcoholic and vanishes from the trilogy.

Crawford hates Lecter and constantly reminds agents that 'Lecter looks only for the fun'. Never forget fun'. Lecter's 'fun' is the pain and suffering of other people. Up to a point Crawford is correct. But there is much, much more to Lecter. Barney, his male nurse at the Maryland asylum, tries to explain in the third book: 'Dr Lecter had perfect manners, not stiff but easy and elegant . . . he told me once that whenever it was "feasible" he preferred to eat the rude. "Free-range rude" he called them.'

The Silence of the Lambs is complex and action-packed, as they say. Will Graham's substitute is Clarice Starling, an FBI trainee and a protégée of Jack Crawford. Having a woman as heroine means that Crawford's position as alpha male in the novel is made clearer. Already, however, his power is beginning to erode. His wife, Bella, dies and he himself is getting old. He sends Starling to try to get Lecter to answer a questionaire. ('A census taker tried to quantify me once,' says Lecter. 'I ate his liver with some fava beans and a big Amarone.') Indirectly, Crawford hopes that Lecter might help with their search for the gruesome killer Jame Gumb, who has already killed and skinned six girls. Lecter knows from his former psychiatric practice exactly who the killer is but he is not about to surrender such powerful knowledge unless he gains significant advantages.

Later, Starling comes to regard this meeting with Lecter as 'the most remarkable encounter of her life . . . she had been startled, shocked, surprised'. Lecter has never previously responded to interviews although he corresponds with psychiatrists and contributes to professional journals. Expertly he dissects Starling as being white trash with a lot of ambition and a little taste. She endures his painful analysis. As she is leaving, the inmate from another cell, Miggs, throws semen on her. Note semen – not blood, urine or faeces. Lecter become agitated, calls her back and gives her an invaluable clue to the Jame Gumb case. That night he persuades Miggs to swallow his own tongue and die.

Starling meets with Lecter on several more occasions. Later, Barney summarises them thus: 'They exchanged information . . . inside a kind of formal structure. Dr Lecter gave her insight on the serial killer she was hunting and she paid for it with personal information . . . He said once that she was cursed with taste . . . he could see what she was becoming, she was charming the way a cub is charming, a small cub that will grow up to be – like one of the big cats. One you can't play with later. She had the cub-like earnestness, he said. She had all the weapons, in miniature and growing, and all she knew so far was how to wrestle with other cubs. That amused him.'

At the first meeting Lecter attacks the behavioural sciences concept of defining serial muderers. '*Organised* and *disorganised*. A real bottom-feeder though of that . . .' When Starling haltingly tries to define evil as being destructive, he snaps 'Evil's just destructive? Then storms are evil . . . and hail . . .' When she suggests he turn his intelligence on himself and finds out what happened to him, he is equally dismissive. 'Nothing happened to me. *I* happened. You can't reduce me to a set of influences. You've given up good and evil for behaviourism. You've got everyone in moral dignity pants – nothing is ever anybody's fault.'

In *Hannibal* we learn the reason for Lecter's endless cynicism. Aged six, at the end of the last war, he was stranded with some other children on his late parents' vast and blighted estate in Europe. A motley crew of deserters were driven to eating some of the children, including Lecter's little sister, Mischa. Some days later he sees her milk teeth in the 'reeking stool pit'. Since then he 'had not been bothered by any considerations of deity, other than to recognise how his own modest depredations played beside those of God who is in irony matchless and in wanton malice beyond measure.' (The Russian serial killer Andrei Chikatilo mentioned a somewhat similar experience of having observed cannibalism as a child.) Lecter now believes only in chaos and wishes desperately that Stephen Hawking's (now-repudiated) theory that the universe would stop expanding and start shrinking again and entropy reverse itself were accurate. If this were to happen, Mischa 'eaten, would be whole again'.

It is hard to decode the feelings between Starling and Lecter in *Lambs* as the book is so heavily plot-driven. Starling is obviously intrigued by Lecter and impressed by his intelligence and culture. He uses Starling's face as a model for Jesus on a grotesque cruxifixion watch he has designed, where the crucified arms tell the time and the second hand is in the halo. She keeps an origami chicken that pecks which Lecter made while being questioned about Miggs' death. The bird theme continues. She also keeps a dinky weather-bird toy belonging to FBI gunnery instructor John Brigham, after he has been killed.

Lecter is also very funny at times. When he describes how he killed one of his patients, flautist Benjamin Raspail, to serve his sweetbreads at a Philarmonic Orchestra dinner, Lecter says: 'Frankly, I got sick and tired of his whining . . . Therapy wasn't going anywhere . . .' He comments, ironically, as he and Starling meet more often during his captivity: 'People will say we're in love' and readers take this as a light and wholly improbable remark. The two touch only once, on the last meeting, when he hands a file back to Starling. 'For an instant, the tip of her forefinger touched Dr Lecter's. The touch crackled in his eyes.' Clumsily expressed, but unmistakable. Shortly afterwards he escapes (killing five people) and later writes to Starling, ending 'Some of our stars are the same, Clarice.'

She does not hear from him again until seven years have passed. The FBI is floundering, due to budget constraints, and so is Starling's career. Her huge triumph in catching Jame Gumb has made her powerful enemies, in particular her 'nemesis', Deputy Assistant Inspector General Paul Krendler of the Justice Department, whom she sexually rejected. Starling has a blunt manner of speech and no gift for career politics. Krendler's poison and the still-rampant sexism of the FBI have hampered her. She shares a house with her former African-American room-mate, Ardelia Mapp, a potentially very interesting character, more so than Starling really.

The book opens with a botched drug-raid in which Starling's friend John Brigham is killed and she herself is pilloried, most unfairly, in the media. This elicits a letter of support from Lecter, in which he reiterates: 'You can be as strong as you wish to be. You are a warrior, Clarice.' Although Lecter has previously mocked Starling's reverence for her late father, a night marshal shot to death on duty, and her mother who had to become a chamber-maid before Starling ended up in a Lutheran orphanage, Lecter here praises their values.

Jack Crawford can no longer protect Starling. Both his influence and his health are failing so the book lacks an alpha male until Lecter can be groomed sufficiently to step into this domi-nant role.

The plot of *Hannibal* revolves around the private bounty on Lecter's life and the corruption it engenders. One of Lecter's two surviving victims is Mason Verger, heir to a meat-packing fortune but bed-bound on a respirator in Maryland. Long ago Lecter made Mason feed his own face to some dogs that Mason had been starving. Even now, Mason Verger is a repulsive person; he has children from institutions brought to his home at Muskrat Farm, where he torments them and drinks Martinis made with their tears. (Dr Lecter only hurts Nasty People.) Mason wants to see Lecter eaten alive by wild boar that have been bred especially for the task.

Dr Lecter, being half-Italian, is living in his beloved Florence. He is adept at using different identities, moving money around and disguising himself. He has had his extra finger removed. (Although Lecter calls psychoanalysis 'a dead religion' there may be some significance in the loss of the extra digit. Erect, rigid, its removal suggests some flexibility, some softening.)

Lecter is living under the name Dr Fell – the name is taken from Thomas Browne's seventeenth-century translation of Martial – 'I do not love thee Doctor Fell/ The reason why I can-not tell/ But this alone I know full well/ I do not love thee, Doctor Fell.' Very funny. Lecter is convinced that the younger generation do not read. Having murdered the previous incumbent, Lecter works (for love of scholarship) as curator at the ancient Palazzo Capponi. (Incidentally, the great – and very real – painter Balthus is cited as Lecter's cousin. I wonder if he [Balthus] minds?)

Anyway, Lecter is happy. He does 'not require conventional rein-
forcement. His ego, like his intelligence quota, and the degree of
his rationality, is not measurable by conventional means.' He
delivers two wonderful lectures to the Florentine scholars. The
first is on Dante's sonnet at the start of 'La Vita Nuova' where he
describes his dream about Beatrice Portinari and contains the line
'She ate that burning heart out of his hand.' Cavalcanti was drawn
to the sonnet. Harris presumably knows Cavalcanti through his
love of T. S. Eliot and by implication, his awareness of Ezra
Pound. The second lecture, either from prescience or foreknowl-
edge, is on medieval depictions of avarice and hanging. A police
inspector, Rinaldo Pazzi, has recognised Lecter and has agreed to
take Mason's millions in order to hand him over to Sardinian kidnappers, rather than the police.

Lecter escapes by eviscerating and hanging Pazzi.

Note how important names have become in the trilogy. From
the start Harris has made some names significant. The word 'lec-
tor' means reader. Murderer Francis Dolarhyde translates as
'Dolour' and 'Hide'. Jame Gumb works for a company called Mr
Hide. Rinaldo Pazzi becomes 'a patsy' . . . A 'verger' is a church
caretaker and attendant, present at funerals. The psychiatrist
called in by the Vergers has a theory about Lecter and Starling. He
is called Dr Doemling. Yes, quite. Harris goes to some lengths to
discredit psychiatrists, with the exception of his own fictional Alan
Bloom. The name 'Lecter' also echoes T. S. Eliot's lines in *The
Waste Land* – 'Hypocrite lecteur, mon semblable, mon frère'.

As if responding automatically, Lecter moves back to the
States, to Maryland, where he continues to indulge his taste for
exquisite wine and food, for theatre and opera. Before he left
Florence he sent Starling a crate of incomparable unguents from
the *farmacía* of Santa Maria Novella. His note said: 'Do you ever
think, Clarice, why the philistines don't understand you? It's
because you are the answer to Samson's riddle: you are the honey
in the lion.' Lecter spies on Clarice. He seems to be preparing
himself for a meeting. He retrieves the bones of her father and
steals a great many narcotics and other psycho-active drugs from
a hospital. He also kills a horrible lout who shoots a deer out of
season. (Dr Lecter only kills Nasty People.)

Crawford sets Starling to tracking Lecter. 'He assumed she

had always wanted to chase Lecter. The truth was more complicated than that.' At this point Lecter thought of Starling as
'Engaging and toothsome. Tedious in her earnestness and absurd
in her principles. Quick in her mother wit.'

Paul Krendler has been bought by Mason Verger. He can't let
Starling contnue to hunt Lecter through his exotic purchases.
'Left alone, following the threads with the picky, petty homemak-
ing skills of a woman, Clarice Starling would find Hannibal
Lecter.' Starling knows that Lecter will be captured, as before,
because of his love of whimsy. But Starling is set up, like a bowl-
ing pin, and relieved of her duties.

The Sardinian kidnappers and the man-eating hogs have been
imported to Maryland. Lecter is captured when he tries to leave a
$1,200 bottle of Chateau Yquem, dated the year of Starling's
birth, inside her car on her birthday – 'Carrying a gift in an act of
utter whimsy'. Starling pursues and rescues him from a forklift
truck, minutes away from being eaten alive. She shoots a corrupt
policeman, amongst others, at the time. She is hit by tranquiliser
darts and Lecter carries her through the pigs – ' . . . they smelled
no fear' – to the car.

He nurses her tenderly, unravelling her psyche through hypno-
tism and drugs at the same time. Her dead father visits her –
although I know of no drug that could expedite this. Otherwise, I
assume he is using scopolamine. Lecter confides his hopes that
time will reverse and bring Mischa back. He feels that a prime
place in the world must be made for her. Starling's perhaps? She
parries such delusions quickly and kindly. 'Perhaps he felt a vague
concern that he had built better than he knew.'

Their relationship is finally consummated after a magnificant
dinner during which Lecter performs a pre-frontal lobotomy (and
then more) on the brain of their 'guest' Paul Krendler. ('All we ask
is that you keep an open mind,' jokes Lecter, in somewhat vulgar
fashion.) In eating Krendler's brains, Starling symbolically
absorbs the Justice Department and its corruption, also the FBI
and the ways in which it has failed her. She has become truly free,
a warrior. Has she? Or is she Lecter's puppet? Lecter's world view
has come to dominate the book and it appears that the author is
in agreement with many of Lecter's judgements.

So we have these two people, each with a good reason for

killing the other. This might be aphrodisiacal, I don't know. For a time, previously Starling was aware that ' . . . she was weary of something. Maybe it was tackiness, worse than tackiness, style-lessness maybe. An indifference to things that please the eye. Maybe she was hungry for some style.' Additionally, she was weary of technique. 'Having come to doubt the religion of tech-nique, where could Starling turn?' Her days have 'a gnawing sameness'. None of this is persuasive. One can find taste and style without becoming the mistress of a serial killer. Starling worried about 'Who the hell was she? Who had ever recognised her?' Her answer is 'Hannibal Lecter'.

Three years later, at the millennium in Buenos Aires, they are still together. Barney sees them at the opera and Harris gives us a glimpse of their private life. Harris says, with some opacity: 'Sex is a splendid structure they build on every day.' Clarice has also learnt Italian and adopted Lecter's mnemonic system of building a memory palace. Lecter's memory palace allowed him to endure captivity. He had 'extensive internal resources and can entertain himself for years at a time. His thoughts were no more bound by fear or kindness than Milton's were by physics.'

Harris describes their union thus: 'Their relationship has a great deal to do with the penetration of Clarice Starling, which she avidly welcomes and encourages. It has much to do with the envelopment of Hannibal Lecter, far beyond the bounds of his experience.' Harris does not mean this sexually. Starling was not a virgin. Much of Lecter's attraction to her must lie in the fact that she was capable of 'frightening him' and in his own mentor role – 'The monster was lost in self-congratulation at his own exquisite taste and cunning.' The possibility of sudden death must heighten their passion, or at least enhance their life together. On the night of the Krendler dinner, after he had finally killed their 'guest', Lecter says to her: 'That particular frequency of the crossbow string, should you ever hear it again in any context, means only your complete freedom and peace and self-sufficiency.'

Lecter is probably the only glamorous person of taste and cul-ture whom Starling had ever met. The same is not true of Lecter. He has had stylish lady-friends before. And left them alive.

It is harder to understand what draws Lecter to Clarice. We know he admires her courage and discipline. She is also very beautiful, with the speck of gunpowder from the Jame Gumb case high on her cheek, like a beauty spot, the one the French say stands for courage. Clarice is thirty-three when they consummate their long, teasing involvement. With endless money, jewels, designer clothes and so forth she can retain her beauty for some time. Nor does she feel – at least at the start – that she has compromised her ethics. She would easily have handed Lecter to the police but could not bear the thought of him being being tortured to death.

Really, however, she has little in common with Lecter. She is not a reader – in *Lambs* she did not know who Truman Capote was. She seems almost entirely humourless – throughout *The Silence of the Lambs* she says but ONE amusing thing. (When asked not to mention proton decay to someone, she answers: 'I'll try to talk around it.') Still, she is certainly a quick study and hungry for culture. The mentor relationship, particularly gendered along Pygmalion lines, can be strong and enduring.

Psychologically, Starling is not interesting. In fact, she is positively dull. On two occasions Lecter admits to being bored by her – once in *Lambs* when she is talking to him, he comments: 'I'm rather bored myself.' In *Hannibal* while he is exploring her psyche he thinks: *'These schoolgirl recollections were becoming tedious.'*

One of the problems is that although Harris apparently likes and sympathises with women, he has little empathy with them. Thus he finds it difficult to sustain his creation of a female character. Compared to Lecter, Starling is a blank.

So, finally, we are being asked to accept Dr Lecter as a romantic hero, a cultured, sexy, fascinating man who only ever killed Nasty People in the interests of gourmet cuisine, or out of necessity, as when he escaped. 'Haven't you ever had people coming over and no time to shop? You have to make do . . .' he says to Starling in *Lambs* when talking about his murder of 'Raspail of the gluey flute'. At the time we read Lecter's comments about having people to dinner and nothing in the fridge as an ironic, black joke, which it was. Now however, we are being asked to take him seriously. It is not possible. Cannibalism for *haute cuisine* is unknown in real life. Serial murder has always been linked to sex or avarice. Even the Japanese student who killed and ate his girlfriend in Paris, did so for reasons that were primarily sexual. I have only ever known *two* short stories on the subject of cannibalism in cooking. One is Graham Masterton's 'The Secret Shih Tan'. The other I read long, long ago in one of the original *Pan Book of Horror Stories*. I cannot recall the title, but it ended with a line like 'The chef put his hand on Laffler's meaty shoulder as he led him into the kitchen.'

Ultimately, the only thing Lecter and Starling *really* have in common is Technique. They have an avidity for detail, for how things work and how things are run. This obsessive quality dominated Starling's career and has enabled Dr Lecter to escape and evade capture. It is however, a slender threat of communion. Will it sustain their 'splendid structure'? Who knows?

Is Lecter capable of love? He has no lack of affect as Starling noted long ago. He loved his sister Mischa. I would like to believe that this is one of the rare romances when someone meets the only other person in the world who is their perfect partner. I do believe that this can happen, but in this particular case I am unsure. There are too many imponderables. In conjoining the couple, Harris has simultaneously bowed to the inevitable and presented us with the impossible. And that is a high-wire act posssible only in fiction . . .

Unfortunately, I believe Anthony Hopkins is to play Lecter again in the film of *Hannibal*. What a pity. What a very great pity.

AND, I hear that they have changed the ending. It will be much less 'amoral'. I see.

Fussing around with books like this. That's my idea of fun . . .

Epilogue

When I first handed in this manuscript last year it numbered, rather eerily, exactly 666 pages of A4 paper. The intervening months have been spent cutting and editing all that into a more appropriate sort of Satan's Neighbour at about 333 manuscript pages.

Even during this brief period I have observed considerable changes regarding books. Most of these seemed to be positive. The vast rise in Internet trading and the sucess of Amazon and their counterparts have meant there is now a worldwide market for books, many of them previously little known or disregarded. Many volumes long out of print are being reprinted – for example A. K. Dewdney's *The Planiverse* and James Thurber's *The Thirteen Clocks/The Wonderful 'O'*.

I will never feel entirely comfortable with books online until I can browse – and even then browser. com lacks the holy quality of handling real books. At the moment it is all too reminiscent of the British Library where you have to request the specific volumes you want. I had given up on Amazon US after initially ordering every American book I coveted. They provided a good few and then stopped. However, yesterday, after a gap of two years, they contacted me saying they had located the other volumes I had requested. About time.

Otherwise, the rampant growth of technology disturbs me. I can manage word processing but that's it. Yet all the time there are more and more computers (increasingly inclined to built-in obsolescence, I see, even Macs). Technology is doing all this serious stuff – flying planes, surgery – and very often their operators do not entirely understand what is happening or why and when a machine will crash. I can see that in a few years I will become even less capable of functioning in the world than I have been. Fortune will favour the techies. Already I feel anomalous – even if the Japanese make a squashy, foldable, pocket-size computer, just like a paperback on which one could theoretically download ANY text – I still feel that we are seeing the very end of Romanticism and that imagination and bibliophilia are no longer relevant qualities to possess.

Do you remember those little squirmy strips of paper for children? You put them in your hand and they move around. Books are really like that. They need to be warmed with flesh and blood before they will respond.

I feel sad about all the contemporary writers who are very good but neglected: Elizabeth Russell Taylor, Donald Rawley, Anne Redmon, Jo-Ann Goodwin and many, many more. Their plight is ever less likely to improve as we witness the end of any serious book reviewing in the broadsheets. You cannot review a book properly when it is being offered for sale at a discount at the end of the piece.

Otherwise, my most overwhelming recent experience has been of illness. I imagined chronic illness in a hopelessly literary way – say like Camille, or Mimi in *La Bohème* – all pearl-pale hands and haunted eyes and nightgowns with lace and frills at the wrists. I never seem to completely internalise the fact that fiction and life are two very, very different things. I got the lacy gowns, but the wrist frills were grey in a day. Serious illness is squalid and tiresome and isolating and upsetting. And really I should be ultra-thankful that I'm not a Victorian invalid – they didn't have laptops, or modems or e-mail, so obviously I am a whole lot better off, even when I'm complaining about the technology.

'So long as there is imgination there is hope,' wrote author Christopher Fowler. How much imagination *is* there now? It is rarely a prized attribute, but was it ever? I cannot think of anything wise or deep to say, here at the end, so I will just stop.